D0122146

CRAIG CLAIBORNE'S

A Feast Made for Laughter

For David Mowday.
Blessings

CRAIG CLAIBORNE'S

A Feast Made for Laughter

DOUBLEDAY & COMPANY, INC.
Garden City, New York
1982

Grateful acknowledgment is made for permission to use the following photographs and drawings:

p. 137 Drawing by Donald Reilly, © 1970 The New Yorker Magazine, Inc.; p. 143 *The New York Times;* p. 149 Drawing by Modell, © 1974 The New Yorker Magazine, Inc.; p. 155 Drawing by Opie, © 1971 The New Yorker Magazine, Inc.; p. 163 *The New York Times;* p. 166 Charles Baum; p. 169 *Life* photo by Arthur Schatz; pp. 170, 171 Evelyn Floret, *People Weekly,* © 1979 Time Inc.; p. 177 *Life* photo by Mark Kauffman; p. 180 Hans Namuth; p. 197 Irving Newman; p. 204 Lou Manna; p. 209 Drawing by Whitney Darrow, Jr., © 1976 The New Yorker Magazine, Inc.; p. 211 *The New York Times;* p. 213 *The New York Times.*

Grateful acknowledgment is made for permission to quote from the following:

The Poems of Emily Dickinson, edited by Thomas H. Johnson, Cambridge, Mass., The Belknap Press of Harvard University, reprinted by permission of the publishers and the Trustees of Amherst College.
The Chinese Cookbook by Craig Claiborne and Virginia Lee, Harper & Row Publishers, Inc., 1976.
"Three Stars, No Waiting" by Alden Whitman, The New York Times Company, 1976. Recipes copyright © by The New York Times Company. Reprinted by permission.

DESIGNED BY LAURENCE ALEXANDER

Library of Congress Cataloging in Publication Data
Claiborne, Craig.
A feast made for laughter.

Includes index.
1. Claiborne, Craig. 2. Cooks—United States—
Biography. 3. Cookery. 4. Cookery—Bibliography.
I. Title.
TX649.C55A33   641.5'092'4
ISBN: 0-385-15700-2   AACR2
Library of Congress Catalog Card Number 81-43437
Copyright © 1982 by Craig Claiborne

*For David Sanders who taught me to share his love of words;
for Willie Morris who believed this life would be worth recording;
and for my father who valued honesty above all and who encouraged
me to tell the truth.*

Acknowledgments

My feelings of indebtedness and gratitude to Joan Whitman for giving cohesiveness and intelligibility to the various, rather hodgepodge elements of this autobiography are beyond measure.

Joan has, over the years played an enormous role in my life, both as personal friend and deeply sympathetic, professional counselor. Among other things she is a neighbor who lives in Southampton.

After I left *The New York Times* in 1972 (the two events are not related) Joan became editor of the page—once referred to as the "women's page"—which features "food news." It was largely due to her entreaties and persuasions that I was encouraged to return to the newspaper as food editor in 1974.

She left *The New York Times* in 1977 and over the years she has edited several of my books. She and her husband Alden, once the obituary writer of *The Times,* have been for many years a source of comfort, inspiration, and enthusiasm on some occasions when I have felt decidedly discouraged about certain aspects of my life.

I am also much obliged to *The New York Times* for giving me permission to reprint certain copyright material, material that has appeared under my by-line and which I consider "pertinent and highly personal." And the generosity of *The Times* also extends to permission to reprint 100 recipes which I consider the choicest of those that have appeared in my column over the past quarter of a century.

I must acknowledge my debt to Victor Jacobs, my lawyer, confidant, and friend of many years standing; Cornelius John Smits III, my skipper on the U.S.S. *Naifeh,* a destroyer escort during the Korean conflict, and Anthony Joseph Reno, a fellow-yeoman during my enlisted days of World War II who served with me aboard the cruiser U.S.S. *Augusta,* both of whom helped reaffirm some of the facts that I have mentioned in this book relative to my military career; to Ruth P. Casa-Emellos, a brilliant cook who directed the *New York Times* test kitchen during my first years there; Stewart (Sandy) Richardson, for many years with Doubleday, who asked me to write this manuscript; Gloria Jones, a fine neighbor in the Hamptons and good friend, who directed Sandy's attention to my life; Estelle Laurence who labored over my manuscript and contributed inestimably to its readability and clarity; and Carolyn Blakemore, my editor at Doubleday, who offered me immense encouragement, and Jim Moser, her dedicated assistant.

Last but surely not least, mention must be made of my secretary at *The Times* for nearly two decades, Velma Cannon. She has been a good and loyal friend, perhaps the only person I know who could have endured rendering the hieroglyphics that come from my typewriter (since my Navy days I honestly can't type) comprehensible.

Contents

A feast is made for laughter, and wine
maketh merry; but money answereth all things.

Ecclesiastes; or, The Preacher
Chapter 10, 19th Verse

A man hath no better thing under the
sun, than to eat, and to drink and to be merry.

Ecclesiastes; or, The Preacher
Chapter 8, 15th Verse

A Feast Made for Laughter

My memories of the small town and house in which I was born seem vital to the person I became, but the memories are as distinct as they are sketchy.

Town is really not the word for Sunflower, Mississippi. With a population then of fewer than five hundred souls, it was a small village. Our home was fairly handsome and solidly built with a front porch and a sleeping porch and polished floors, which I believe were walnut or oak. There was a fireplace in almost all the bedrooms, of which there were several, but the fireplace I remember most was the one in the living room.

Although it snowed on certain years in that Delta region of Mississippi, the climate was for the most part temperate. I do not have any memories of a Christmas spent in that home of my birth, but I do vividly recall one day after my last Christmas in that house.

It was a bright, fairly warm, sunlit day and the Christmas tree and the stockings that hung at the mantelpiece had been removed.

The living room floor was being varnished by a black servant named Albert, a handsome, mahogany-colored man with a strong physique and hair the color of white ash cotton, whom I idolized. I had found in my Christmas stocking a set of sparklers and at some point before noon on that day after Christmas I ignited one of them. As it flickered away in the clear light of that room, for reasons that were not motivated by mischief I stuck the sparkler into a pail of varnish at the edge of the fireplace. It burst into flame and I can only recall my panic as I fled, petrified, but in great wonder as to what had caused such a conflagration. A fire brigade arrived, but I have no further memory of the incident except I know that the fire was extinguished without great harm to my home.

Next to setting my living room afire, the memory that reappears most frequently in those days in Mississippi was of one special sunlit morning. I do not remember at what hour I normally arose on weekday mornings to go to kindergarten, but on this particular occasion I presumably awakened at an uncommonly late hour and found not another soul in the house. I cried out and got no answer. It occurred to me in panic and a state of self-punishment that I was late for school. I felt deserted and experienced a sense of wild-eyed anxiety. I hurried into my clothes, gathered my satchel with its collection of crayons and books, and raced out of the house. I was out of breath, on the verge of tears, and halfway to the schoolhouse when an old man stopped me and asked where I was rushing to.

The Claiborne home in Sunflower, Mississippi, built in 1909–10. I was born in the front bedroom with the double windows.

"I'm late," I yelled. "School!"
He grabbed me and held me close.
"But, sonny, today's Saturday."

I don't know why that memory is so graven on my mind. But in most matters I have been a model of punctuality ever since. When I first found my career at a hotel school in Switzerland, I made high final marks because they put a high premium on that single virtue.

I remember another fragmentary thing about kindergarten. We staged a play based on a bit of folklore titled "The Musicians of Bremen," a tale for children that involves a conspiracy of fine barnyard animals who scare away thieves. I played the role of a cat who sat atop a host of other animals and screamed and yelled to make the noise that frightened the evil beings and sent them packing.

And speaking of fragments in memory I'm able to visualize in photographic detail the bed in which I was born and the name of the doctor who delivered me. It was Dr. W. R. Sugg. And the date was September 4, 1920.

It was a double bed and painted in ivory enamel. The headboard boasted a design of molded cherubs and angels and various garlands to link them together. There was a center ivory-colored wicker pattern on that headboard. Opposite the bed there was a matching wardrobe with double doors, and at some point I had written the name "Craig" on it in a childish scrawl. To this day, when I give a gift to someone close and about whom I feel sentimental, I sign the card that goes with it with an imitation of that early signature.

I remember that my father bought a new Atwater Kent radio, perhaps the first radio in our community. More than the sound that emanated from the apparatus, I recall that a long wire extended from the roof into the yard as an antenna for the proper reception.

In the middle of our living room were two musical instruments, an old Victrola (His Master's Voice) that had to be wound up with a hand crank on the side. My mother owned dozens if not scores of thick phonograph records by Enrico Caruso, John McCormack, Schumann-Heink, and Galli-Curci. The music I recall is the voice of McCormack singing "The Rose of Tralee" and the voice of, I believe, Galli-Curci singing "'Tis the Last Rose of Summer."

The walls of our home were hung with reproductions, paintings of horses by Rosa Bonheur and one by Jean François Millet titled "The Gleaners." We had rosewood bookshelves that were lined with the works of Dickens, Shakespeare, something called the Five Foot Shelf of Books, Kipling, Robert Louis Stevenson, Robert Burns, and the Bible.

Off to one side of the living room and occupying a prominent position was a baby grand piano by Steinway. My mother considered herself quite a musician.

It was long after my father's death that I took serious note of his land holdings in Mississippi, but I do recall that our house was situated on fairly good-sized acreage, the extent of which at the time it would never have occurred to me to wonder about. I do remember certain aspects of the property. There were walnut trees and at least two well-kept wooden shacks or shanties that were referred to as "nigger cabins." These were the homes of my Aunt Catherine and Albert, neither of whose last names I knew or to my knowledge ever heard. I believe that each cabin consisted of a small living and sleeping area with one or two beds. In the main room there was a fireplace that was kept in almost constant use because, in addition to heating, it was used for some small cooking purposes. The cabins always smelled nicely of smoke.

Although the climate in Mississippi was generally temperate, those shacks were inevitably a bit drafty. For that or whatever reason, the walls were covered with full-sized pages of the Sunday rotogravure sections of the Memphis *Commercial Appeal.* In those days color photography in newspapers was unheard of and rotogravure sections—rotogravure is a process whereby pages and images are printed in a shade of brown and white by an intaglio copper cylinder—were fairly common in the weekend sections of metropolitan dailies.

Portulaca grew in front and around the cabins inhabited by my black friends. We did not call it portulaca. It was referred to as "moss rose" or just plain "moss." The small plots were dry and ungrassy and the moss opened prettily when the sun shone. There were various kinds of chickens, including bantam hens and roosters, which my father raised for amusement, and I can remember them scratching in that poor soil.

Situated at some distance from those cabins was my father's smokehouse, where he cured his own ham and bacon. The smell of a smokehouse to this day vividly brings back my childhood home.

The cabins were without bathrooms but there was running water from a hydrant "out back" and portable basins were used for personal washing. There were outhouses, but I presume that most of the blacks used the white folks' indoor facilities either by consent or in secret. They also chewed tobacco or sniffed snuff as did a few of the poor whites. My Aunt Catherine did both.

Aunt Catherine was my black nurse and, although I do not have any memory of my first view of her, to me she always looked ancient. I adored her above all creatures, including my mother. I adored my mother on isolated occasions; Aunt Catherine was ever present, watching over me, holding me close, tending my fevers and shielding me from harm of any sort night and day. It was she who tucked me into bed at night and told me stories without end. She was wholly unschooled and the saying was that she'd had a dozen common law marriages; the names of most of her "husbands" she could no longer recall. It was not until my adult years that I wondered about her last name. She was simply Aunt Catherine and that sufficed.

Although Aunt Catherine fed me three times a day with my sterling silver baby spoon, I have no recollection whatsoever of her ever cooking a single dish. What she did do, and what is forever engraved on my soul, is churn clabber, a thickened sour milk, which she made on the back porch with butter and buttermilk. Her utensil was the traditional churn of the day, then available on that few-block main street town, a somewhat tall, wooden spherical container with a removable central top that had a hole in the middle. The top was inserted over a round wooden pole, at the end of which were two paddles, shaped like a cross.

When the clabber was added you simply maneuvered the pole up and down, producing a great mass of thick, smooth-textured buttermilk with golden flecks floating throughout, suspended in that snow-white liquid. These flecks were, of course, random bits of butter, only

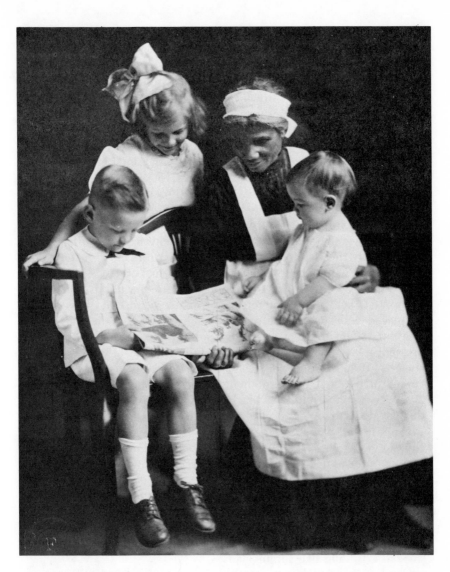

A family portrait. Me, sitting on the lap of my Aunt Catherine, with my brother, Lewis Edmond ("Luke") Jr., and my sister, Augusta Craig.

a fraction as large as bird shot, which made the buttermilk country— and special.

There were other uses to which that clabber was put. When undisturbed, it looked like a pristine-white batch of almond blancmange, but it would "separate" or "break" when a spoon or other utensil was inserted into it. Sometimes it was spooned into bowls for my childish pleasure. Sugar would be sprinkled on and very cold, heavy cream or rich milk would be poured over all and it would be eaten slowly like summer manna. Generally, I ate it sitting in Aunt Catherine's lap, rocked back and forth in her solid brown rocker on the porch that adjoined the rear of our house. She would rock away, telling me stories, as both of us watched the bantam chickens and guinea hens that clucked away in the back yard.

Other times she'd line a large round earthenware bowl with cheesecloth, empty the clabber into it, and bring up the ends of the cloth. She'd tie the gathered-up ends with string to make a bag for hanging. This would be suspended in a cool place on the porch, the string anchored to some of the gingerbread trim overhead, and a bowl would be placed beneath. It would sit through the cool night and in the morning, when the bag was lifted down from its nail, it would be opened up and there within, another delight for the table, cottage cheese. My father had a special passion for cottage cheese and he embellished it in, to my mind then, an odd manner. He would sprinkle it with an ample grinding of black pepper and pour cream on top. To this day, it is a combination of flavors that gives me pleasure.

In these and many things, my Aunt Catherine was the rock of my childhood. When I was in pain with an aching tooth, a bruise on the leg, a bloodied kneecap, I ran to her. If scolded by my mother, teased by my brother, or scorned by a playmate, I would bury my face in the skirt of that floor-length calico dress. Once I felt her touch, knew that warm good smell of the cloth that clothed her, it was trouble's end. I remember that smell to this day. She washed her clothes with lye soap prepared in the back yard and would hang them out to dry until they smelled crisp and like summer air.

One horrible day, I was brought in and told the dreadful news. We were moving, not only away from my house but away from my home town. And away from Aunt Catherine. We were going to Indianola, eleven miles away, the county seat of Sunflower County. And, of course, the reason for the move was financial. My father had nothing. Years later my mother repeated over and over that on the day we moved, his total financial worth was fifty cents.

And therein lies another memory, which—I was told later—I was too young to remember. It is something I never repeated even to my brother or sister until I was graduated from college.

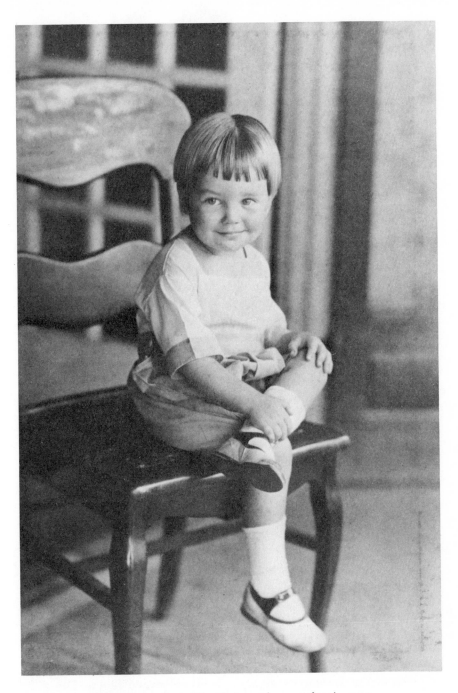

Himself, age three. The photograph was taken in 1923.

One summer afternoon I was playing behind a large, upholstered sofa when my parents came into the living room. There was distress in my mother's voice, a sound of despair or desperation. My father, as usual, was quiet, with only a word here or there to indicate that he was even present. I suspect, indeed I know, that he must have been choked with grief.

The conversation was brief but I learned, without coming out of hiding or in any way letting it be known that I was listening, that my father had that day been faced with one more unbearable upset. I did not know how; I do not know to this day what precipitated that one discussion. They sat on the sofa and my mother said, "But there is no choice. I simply have to sell the wedding ring." My father said, "Kathleen," and that's all I remember of that moment and of that day.

On the day we moved, the furniture was piled into trucks and into the back of our fifteen-year-old automobile—an Overland—and I suspect the only emotion I felt was the lost feeling of leaving Aunt Catherine behind. She was to remain with her oldest daughter, named Beulah. I was inconsolable, although there had been assurances night and day for two weeks that it was not as though I were saying good-by forever. We'd meet once a week if not more often, they promised. I could come visit or Aunt Catherine could come visit me.

Somehow, inevitably, I endured and my grief lessened as days and months passed by. And sure enough she came on visits and we hugged and she'd whirl me around in her warm embrace whenever she arrived.

"Honey chile," she'd exclaim, "you grown so!"

But within a year's time, those visits became less and less frequent until they were no more. And I accommodated myself to her absence.

My next recollection of Aunt Catherine occurred when I was ten or eleven years old. I came home one day from school and my mother was weeping. She dabbed at her eyes, red and swollen, and her speech was choked with sobs. It is funny that in this moment I remember that a dainty linen handkerchief, embroidered with roses, was one of her trademarks.

"Aunt Catherine is dead." She grabbed me close and held me and this was my first encounter with death.

I did not know nor in my innocence did I ask about the plans for her funeral.

But two days later, when I came home from play, I wandered into an anteroom off the kitchen and there, resting on a pair of unpainted wooden horses that my father had used for sawing wood, was a solidly made, simply designed wooden casket with the body of Aunt Catherine. My mother was there weaving by hand a blanket of blue and purple cornflowers. And I cried.

CRAIG CLAIBORNE

My mother was to know grief in some of its barest and vilest forms before the end of her days, and she knew it in the demise of Aunt Catherine. It was a just and pure grief. After all, that good and beautiful black woman had been a surrogate mother to all my mother's children. A long time after her death I learned that she had suckled my brother when he was a newborn.

§ § §

Postscript: Some years ago, when I had been at *The New York Times* for about a decade (I was then forty-seven years old), I was stopped in the corridor of the Times Building by Nash Burger for a brief chat. Nash was a writer whose by-line had appeared for many years in *The New York Times Book Review*.

"When you were a child, did you have a nurse called Aunt Catherine?" he asked.

"Good God, Nash, how could you have known that?"

Nash had a domestic working for his family in Connecticut. She was Aunt Catherine's daughter and had heard my name in the course of a casual conversation.

§ § §

On a summer day in 1981 I returned to the town and home of my birth. My pulse quickened and I was filled with nostalgia. I had not seen the house in which I was born for more than fifty-seven years, having departed from it with my parents in 1924 when I was four years old. It was, I discovered, splendidly maintained. I recalled the structure in total depth, the front room in which I had been born, the living room with the fireplace where I had plunged that lighted Christmas sparkler into the bucket of shellac. The sleeping porch was still there and I remembered the night sounds, when the family slept out on the cool screened verandah. Each bed had been equipped with a chamber pot on the floor beneath it.

In the course of that visit I was in the company of my sister and we recounted the days of our childhood. She recalled that there had been an old man in our youth and infancy named Telfair. It was Mr. Telfair's custom on Saturday nights to become roaring drunk on Bourbon and, as midnight approached, he would mount his horse and ride through the darkness, his rifle blazing. My father would make us scud beneath the beds to hide ourselves.

My mother's coterie of friends in those days when my father was a man of considerable means and land holdings included a Mrs. Diggs and a Mrs. Lancaster, and each of them competed to set the best table in town. They entertained often and in style. The serving pieces were sterling, the tableware of the finest imported china and crystal, and the napery pure linen. There were bread and butter plates—very fancy for a small hamlet of 500 souls—and, when appropriate, finger bowls in the center of which rose petals floated.

In the dining room during the time of our visit, two major changes had occurred. Many years before there had been a ledge that rimmed the entire room about two feet beneath the ceiling. And on that ledge were fancy porcelain plates that had come from around the world. The present owner of the house assured us on that visit that a small round hole in the floor still existed, the repository of an electric buzzer, which had been activated by my mother's foot as she sat at the head of the table and summoned one servant or another.

To the right of the house there still remains a barren field, the acreage on which my father and the servants had dug long three-foot-deep pits for the barbecues for which he was famous. The pits would be fired throughout the course of a day and covered with chicken wire. Chickens, whole hogs, and sheep would be placed on the wire or spit-roasted, sometimes throughout the night in preparation for an afternoon event.

There was a "colored" man, my sister recalled, named Mal Skinner, who tended the fires and barbecued the meats. He was an expert at slaughtering animals and cutting them into roasts, fillets, or whatever, a prized member of the kitchen staff. One day, after many years with my family, Skinner decided to make a hasty departure. My father learned of his decision shortly after Mal had hopped a train heading north. My father grabbed another train and went in hot pursuit, getting as far as the neighboring town of Clarksdale before he caught up with him. No amount of imploring could persuade Skinner to return. The family learned later that he had obtained employment with Swift and Company in St. Louis. He never returned.

There was, during that recent brief stay in Sunflower, something unsettling that was difficult to pinpoint in my mind. Most of the houses of my youth were still intact and in remarkably good repair. A lot of new houses had been built. But I had this feeling of some sort of disorder, of something out of kilter. And in my sleep that evening I recalled vividly what had changed. The streets of that town had been paved and there were concrete sidewalks. When I was a child there had been gravel roads all over town and concrete sidewalks only occurred here and there. Most often sidewalks were dirt and there were long, wide wooden planks to cover rough patches. Even the bridges in town that spanned the Indian bayou and the Sunflower River were constructed top to bottom of wooden planks.

CRAIG CLAIBORNE

And when I awakened I reflected for a brief while that it is a long haul from those gravel roads and dirt sidewalks to the shiny bright lights of Times Square.

§ § §

My mother was, undeniably, the most powerful and positive influence on my life. There were times when I felt her to be a veritable saint and over the years there were many who have shared that impression.

In my youth she performed what seemed to be sisyphean tasks to keep her family intact. One of my most cherished possessions is, curiously and unsentimentally, perhaps, a silver spoon monogrammed with her initials that was given to her as a wedding gift. Mother stirred all her sauces with this spoon, so much so that the lip, once a perfect oval, is worn down by an inch or so. It is, more than any other object, a symbol of the labor that she spent in providing bread and clothing in those awful days when my father had lost every cent that he owned along with a good deal of pride. It is important that I knew oddly little about the circumstances of my father and his relationship with my mother until I had passed my half-century mark, but more of that later.

When my father found himself totally without funds, without borrowing capacities, and almost without hope, the decision was made for my mother to take in boarders. This was a logical move because a rooming and boardinghouse was one of the few paths a properly brought up and aristocratic young southern woman could follow while holding her chin and prestige up.

My mother was a beautiful creature, with fair complexion, stately carriage, and magnificent eyes. She had been born in Marion, Alabama, to parents who adored her. Her father had been a well-to-do figure in the coal industry of the state and he had provided her with a solid liberal arts education at Judson College in Marion. I am told that when Judson College celebrated its twenty-fifth anniversary in the mid-eighteen hundreds my grandmother was the oldest living graduate. My mother doted on the fact that her family name was Craig and that she was "a Craig." She named me Raymond Craig and my sister Augusta Craig. (My mother's nephew, Raymond Craig, married my father's niece, Fredibel Claiborne, and they named their second-born son Claiborne Craig. There was some confusion when any of us was summoned at family gatherings.)

My mother had met my father through his association with her brother, Augustus, who had come to the Mississippi Delta to seek his fortune in the late 1800s. Augustus had purchased a construction company that owned the territory that later became Sunflower, the place of my birth. He also had considerable land holdings in that rich,

My mother, Mary Kathleen Craig, in her bridal gown. She married my father on October 21, 1907.

fertile territory. When my father and uncle went into partnership that firm was called Craig and Claiborne.

My mother had studied Latin and Greek and music. She was intensely well read and a brilliant conversationalist. She could sew a fine seam, play the piano, and was a splendid and inspired cook. She had learned to cook from her family and friends and from a 1912 edition of the *Fannie Farmer Cook Book.* That book was her culinary bible.

My mother was not only an excellent cook, she was a dedicated and, according to her friends at table, a highly skilled bridge player. It was bridge, I believe, more than anything else, that gave her solace and comfort when she was burdened with the running of a boardinghouse, which occupied her day by day for many years. She went through many diversions including knitting, at which she excelled, and oil painting. She did not paint murals or portraits, but flowers on wood, the oil paint applied in thick smears on wooden objects such as a fireplace screen, which I recall in particular.

But most of her afternoons were spent at the bridge table with friends whose names were Ida Mae Heathman, Julia Stubblefield, and Lillian Cox. One of the joys of my youth was to sit watching their game. They all told marvelous anecdotes tinged with gossip, but none I felt was more droll than my own mother. She would relate sometimes humorous, sometimes tender recollections of her childhood, or tales about servants of today and years gone by, and they were both affectionate and humorous in the telling.

Among other things, I was fascinated by my mother's speech. She was a born linguist, but she did color her speech with phrases that were distinctly southern. Her favorite flowers were magnolias and gardenias, which she invariably referred to as Cape jasmine. I always associated her Southernisms with these flowers. At times these phrases were used humorously, at other times merely as a standard part of her speech pattern. Many of her sayings were spiritual in nature. "My heavens above," she would say, and "I swear to the Lord," and "You exasperate my soul."

Occasionally she would resort to "Lawsy Muhssee," which, when properly interpreted, means Lord Have Mercy. There was one food for which she had a particular passion and these were "roassun ears." I was an adult before I realized that these were roasting ears of corn.

If she was slightly exasperated she would ask, "Why in the name of love," this or that had to happen. That, or "Why in heaven's name." Things frequently drove her "to the point of exasperation," and she would explain that "You're starting to try my patience." Either that or, "You're worrying the soul out of me." Or perhaps, "You're driving me out of my skin." If she feigned ignorance, willingly or not, it was "My life o' love, I don't know what you're talking about." Or, "To save my soul I don't know."

If I seemed to demand too much of her time or energy, she would exclaim, "Good Lord, you'd think that my only reason for living was to listen to you and do your bidding."

I was fascinated to think that in her book one could properly invoke the name of the Lord but not the name of God.

You could say "Good Lord-a-mighty" without qualms. But "Good God-a-mighty," a far more vigorous way of expressing exasperation, was definitely cruder speech.

Mother had special words of demeanment that she used for those gentlemen of whom she had small regard. "He's got as much gumption as a jackrabbit," she would observe. Or, "He's such a fiddledegibbet, he makes me nervous." Of others she would note that, "He would tell lies from here till kingdom come."

One of the most amusing Southernisms that came from my mother's mouth occurred on an afternoon when she addressed two friends who were about to enter an automobile. "If all of y'all can fit in the car, we'll leave." I had been away for several years and I had a vision of these two, all of them—hands, necks, arms, and so on—fitting in the car and not hanging out the windows or doors.

She also used one Southern expression that I have heard from other lips and the origin of which to this day mystifies me. That is "pure O. D." This or that, she would say, "is pure O. D. nonsense!"

She quoted the Bible often and her favorite admonition to me, which she pronounced in the most solemn, gentle dulcet tones conceivable, was "A soft answer turneth away wrath."

When I was a child it never occurred to me that my parents would age with the years. They were simply there. Eternally. One of the most profoundly moving moments of my childhood occurred one winter's night when there was a roaring fire in the fireplace. My mother had her back to the fireplace in a characteristic stance. She was holding her skirts up discreetly to the rear with the backs of both hands and suddenly something moved her to a quick sob. She was in her mid-forties. Tears flowed down her face and she sobbed gently, "I don't want to grow old."

Only once in my life did I explicitly express my devotion to my mother. One Mother's Day when I was in the Navy I wrote a letter explaining precisely why I loved her. It ended, "Because you're my mother, the most beautiful woman in the world. And most of all because you chose your husband to be my father."

§ § §

My father, Lewis Edmond Claiborne, at the time of his marriage.

My father was forty-five years old when I was born, fifteen years older than my mother, and there was a sadness about him in my early childhood that I believe transmitted itself to me. Throughout my lifetime, I considered him the most godlike, God-fearing creature I had ever known. Only once in my presence did he utter a curse word; he never willingly touched a drop of hard liquor; and he was a devoted churchgoer. My father was named Lewis Edmond Claiborne but was familiarly known to his family and friends as Luke. Because of certain financial reverses that he had suffered at approximately the same time as my birth, he was markedly taciturn about his own youth and adult-hood. It was long after his death that I learned many vital things about his standing in the community and the region of my birth.

There is a recently published book titled *Fevers, Floods and Faith* by Marie Hemphill that details the complete history of Sunflower County and Sunflower, Mississippi, the town where I was born. It was not until I read this book that I learned that my father had reached a fairly advanced state of maturity when he married my mother in 1907. He was thirty-two years old and a partner with his brother-in-law in a mercantile and construction establishment that owned many land holdings and "other business ventures." In 1905, fifteen years before I was born, "they built a gin with a grist mill as a sideline." My father was a founder of the banking industry in my town, namely the State Bank of Sunflower, of which he became president the year before I was born.

I am told that shortly after my birth there was a depression in that area of the world and that my father lost all of his land holdings plus a fortune in other business interests. He was, in short, destitute. And relatively broken in spirit. And that is when my mother opened her boardinghouse, assuming the reins of the family.

Until I was thirteen years old, my father, who was born in 1875, did not make a great mark on my life. I adored him but the two of us did not indulge in the usual forms of father-son camaraderie such as ball-playing, hunting, and fishing. My first impressions of him are of an older man dressed in rather somber clothing, either driving a pick-up truck, going to work as an accountant, or going to church. That, it seemed to me, is what he did mostly. He belonged to the Methodist church in Sunflower and to the Presbyterian (my mother was upwardly mobile and thought that the Presbyterians had more class than Metho-dists) when we moved to Indianola.

He faithfully went to church on Sunday mornings and evenings and to prayer meetings on Wednesday evenings. He often read the Bible between times. He said his prayers while kneeling at his bedside before he retired each evening and, on the rare occasions when my family dined alone (generally at Thanksgiving and Christmas), he said grace before meals. I once rode with him in his pick-up truck and in a minor emergency when he slammed on the brakes to avoid hitting another car he said "damn." I was a bit terrified. He often used expressions of exasperation, "Dadblameit," "Dadgumnit," and "Dadblastit." I'm cer-tain it never entered his consciousness that dadgumnit was simply a substitution of syllables for goddamnit.

His sole diversion as nearly as I could determine was playing soli-taire. He played it after the evening meal but he would not play on Sunday, considering that a breach of Sabbath. One Sunday afternoon, however, a guest entered his bedroom without knocking and found my father playing solitaire. He was never allowed to forget it as the story of the incident was repeated.

One Christmas, there was a family gathering on the porch of my home and my brother-in-law asked if anyone would like a drink. My father, naturally, declined, but my brother-in-law offered him a lemonade. Instead, he made a tom collins with gin and handed it to my father. My father, in total innocence, drank it all. When dinner was served, he stood and pitched forward, falling. He cried out with the anguish of Christ on the Cross, "Oh, son, what have you done to me?"

He had one expression that haunts me to this day and although I have searched I have never found the origin. "This world and one more and then the fireworks." It is a mystifying and potentially prophetic warning. He was also fond of saying to me, "Son, this is an imperfect world."

In moments of affection, my father addressed my mother as Trina, a diminutive for Katerina, which was presumably synonymous with Kathleen. In return, she invariably referred to him as Mr. Claiborne. Even in their most intimate moments in bed, I doubt that she called him anything else.

After I was born, the youngest of three children, I believe that my father was celibate. Although many of the men in our community and boardinghouse often had affairs, and frequently with black women who lived "across the tracks," I am convinced that my father did not cohabit with other women. But I do know that he harbored in one specific instance a feeling of lust for a woman. I can only intuit that there must have been other, unfulfilled wanton periods in his mind.

When I was very young, and throughout my adolescence, my favorite relative by far was a full-blown, sensuous, splendidly proportioned first cousin named Mary Alyce Claiborne, my father's niece. Alyce was one of six children and came to live with us when she was about twelve. She was like a member of the family and I looked on her as a highly amusing sister. She loved to tell lusty jokes that she would never repeat in the presence of adults. One of her favorite ditties concerned "The tattooed lady, tattooed from head to knee as far as you could see . . ." Alyce was remarkably well rounded, both physically and mentally. And she adored my father, whom she called Uncle Luke.

One evening I slept in the same darkened bedroom with my father. Alyce was in the bathroom with the door slightly ajar standing in the tub lathering herself. My father raised his head slightly, little aware that I was observing him and fascinated with his covert, stealthy, disguised lust as he gazed at her naked body. I shivered slightly with stirrings in my own body as I contemplated his absorption with her nude and delectable maiden form.

Since the age of reason, I have always believed that it was the early financial recession or depression in the area of the South where I was born that shaped my sexual and other emotional development.

Because of our financial status, it was necessary that every available bed in our home be filled, mostly with paying guests. I do not know when or how the decision was made that I would occupy the same bed as my father. I slept next to him, spoon-fashion, my slender upper arm securely holding him around his chest. That happened at the time when I had just achieved the capacity of seminal flow.

It was my father's custom to retire shortly after supper each evening, pausing first to take a hot tub bath before entering the bed which I shared. In the beginning, my going to bed with him was a casual, unplanned affair. Until one winter evening when I put my arm around him and onto his left arm. I followed that arm onto the hand and discovered his fingers enfolded around the throttle of his lust, the object that best reflects the strength and status of a man's desire.

In the years that followed I was to relive—in my cultivated daydreams—the enormity of that experience in my mind and I tried many times to describe the ecstasy of it, to come to grips with it by putting it into understanding. I have compared it to an electric shock applied with thundering haste to all of my existence. There was an all-engulfing gushing of adrenalin, the likes of which I have never known before or since. It was as though all of my being were inundated with warm waves of ecstasy, the sensation of drowning and awakening shaken but on a safe but hitherto unexplored island.

To say that it altered my approach and outlook on life, particularly where sex is concerned, is to put it mildly.

On that particular evening, no word was spoken between us, nor was a word ever uttered on the subject of his arousal and my emotion. But he did not banish me from his bed that evening or ever. I continued to lie with him that night and for countless nights that ensued. And when I would hear the breathing that indicated sleep on his part, I would begin an exploration of his body. The affair was never consummated and he never once acknowledged his awareness of my encroachments.

I do not wish to pursue this on the grounds that it would sound prurient or salacious or smack of sensationalism. Or a pronouncement of an excessive feeling of guilt. The incident did lead me into psychotherapy and I was told that my father was by no means unaware of those nocturnal happenings, that he merely feigned the sounds of sleeping. I also have been told that my father was guilty of child abuse, but I do not believe this.

I believe that he and I were both victims of our financial condition, that we became involved in a situation from which neither of us could extract ourselves. I do not believe that my father was a homosexual, although by writing that I do not wish to absolve him of all guilt. And if he were alive today, I would not beg his forgiveness.

I do believe that he was unutterably disturbed and confused by our relationship. Just as I know that one moonlit night, as we sat on the steps that led from our house in Indianola to the walk, there was a particularly anguished look on his face.

He reached for my arms and pulled me close. With the most earnest tone he said, "Son, I'm not worthwhile."

The next moment he asked me if he should take his own life.

I was chilled and speechless. I grabbed him in my arms and felt the comforting warmth of his head on my shoulder.

"Daddy!"

On reflection I believe that at that moment I was the one object he loved most in life and there was nobody, no living soul other than myself to whom he could have appealed in such despair.

§   §   §

If there had been any doubt in the minds of my mother and father about the success of the boardinghouse in Indianola—if success is to be measured by popularity—their fears were to be quickly assuaged. Within a week after the family had set up "housekeeping," "Miss Kathleen's" boardinghouse was filled with boarders and roomers. And for good reason. It doubtless was the most "genteel" boardinghouse in the Mississippi Delta, a land-rich territory whose northern and southern boundaries were once immortalized by David Cohn in his book *God Shakes Creation.* He stated that the Mississippi Delta extended from the lobby of the Peabody Hotel in Memphis (at one time one of the South's most prestigious and now recently refurbished hotels) to Catfish Row in Vicksburg. I have heard those limits repeated a thousand times in my lifetime.

In the dining room of my mother's boardinghouse, there was an oval walnut table large enough to seat twelve guests in total comfort; more if special occasions demanded. My mother was determined that her guests would be treated in all respects as though they were members of the family.

And thus the table was invariably set with her wedding silver, monogrammed MKC for Mary Kathleen Claiborne, a good deal of which I own. There was a silver water goblet, also monogrammed, at each place setting. And water or iced tea was poured from a silver pitcher, also monogrammed. In the beginning she used her monogrammed heavy linen napkins, but these quickly wore out through use. The replacements, however, were always of linen.

Although that boardinghouse was an immediate success as far as number of guests was concerned, we were, as always, plagued with debt. As a consequence, we lived in any given house for about one year. And almost one year to the day, we would move to another house. I never questioned why. Primarily, it was for nonpayment of rent, although there were other factors. Frequently, the owner of the house, oftentimes a widow down on her funds, would continue to live in the house while we occupied it. The comings and goings of the roomers and boarders must have taken their toll on the owner.

My brother, Luke, made light of the circumstances of our annual peregrinations.

"If anyone," he claimed, "ever saw a wagonload of furniture moving up or down the street in Indianola, the other inhabitants of the town would yell, 'Lock the door, for heaven's sake. Here come the Claibornes.' "

It is doubtless due to the differences in our ages that this is one of the few recollections I have of my brother or sister, during my early childhood. Augusta Craig, my sister, was born five years after my parents' marriage, and Lewis Edmond, Jr., familiarly known as Luke, Jr., was born four years later. I was born four years after that.

I had dual feelings about Luke. I considered him sort of god-like as a big brother, although he was far from a protective shield against the bullies whom I encountered and of whom there were many in that small town. On the other hand, in one sense I admired his masculine pose, which would be described today as "macho." He was equally sensitive and insensitive. Although Luke was only four years my senior, he seemed infinitely older and wiser than I. And remote.

He was, to my childish mind, a brilliant draftsman and two sketches come quickly to mind. My aunt Elizabeth had brought back from China, where she had been a missionary, a Ming vase in black and white. I recall the extraordinary, perfect detail in which Luke reproduced the image of that vase on paper. I remember with equal clarity opening up his book on algebra that he used in high school. On the rear, virginal pages, he had sketched the most incredible, perfectly shaped phallus I had ever seen, though there had not been many. It had a stunning impact on my eleven- or twelve-year-old mind.

Luke was also possessed of an exceptional mind, a mind in its own way diametrically opposed to my own. He was an excellent mathematician and he reveled in, as much as I was appalled by, anything mechanical or electrical.

One thing that I remember most distinctly about Luke was an evening sitting at the supper table. Like most Southerners in those days, we ate *dinner* at high noon. The evening meal was invariably referred to as *supper.*

I asked Luke to pass me a basket of Parker House rolls, for which my mother and the cooks in the boardinghouse were famous; they were the staple bread at the evening meal just as corn breads of one form or another (corn bread, corn sticks, hush puppies, and so on) were standard fare for the midday meal.

He picked up the bread basket and held it toward me. I carelessly reached for a roll at which point Luke let the basket fall onto the floor.

"Why'd you do that?" I asked in a tone that implied that he had lost his marbles.

"When anyone passes you a basket of bread, you take the basket. Or at least you touch it as a gesture of thoughtfulness." To this day I am disposed to drop a bread basket if I offer it to someone and he or she lets me hold it as the bread is taken.

On another occasion Luke scoffed at me for biting into a piece of whole toast rather than breaking off a small piece, which is, of course, in any gentleman's book, more civilized.

I find such reflections of my brother a bit ironic for, truth to tell, even at that early age I was a bit of a snob and I considered him a bit of an oaf. I could not comprehend why he took to the football field with such enthusiasm. The abuse and bruisings of body against body in the process of tackling, the smell of sweat, and the challenge of trying to outdo someone else while running for one goal or another put the appeal of football beyond my comprehension and reason.

In the course of playing football for the local high school, Luke lost two of his front teeth, which were immediately restored to his bleeding mouth and which, to the best of my knowledge, he was buried with. They darkened as time went on. I took the news of his injury in stride, characteristically thinking how dumb could he be?

When my brother went to Mississippi State University to major in civil engineering, he told me he was housed in a dormitory where he shared quarters with one roommate called Peter (Wood) and another Paul (Banks). When a fourth roommate appeared, my brother, paying attention to his biblical background, dubbed him "Mary," much to the newcomer's discomfort.

On graduation, my brother was invited back as an instructor in engineering and he was, I am told, the youngest person ever to have been invited to join the professorial staff on his graduation.

One of the last times that I saw my brother was on an island in the Pacific during World War II. He was stationed in the Ryukyu Islands on Ii Shima, Okinawa, best known as the outpost where the celebrated war correspondent Ernie Pyle was killed. I had flown in a military aircraft to visit him from Okinawa, where I was then stationed. I arrived at dusk and within an hour we were sitting around an officers' club drinking when the air raid alarm sounded. The island was suddenly in total darkness. Luke flew out of the club, dived into a foxhole, and I was left in that Stygian blackness, not knowing one direction from another.

I found my way out the door and heard Luke's voice from somewhere yelling at me to hurry. I took one dive and fell directly on his head.

Years after the war my brother died in American Samoa from causes unknown to me. He was buried with military honors in his colonel's uniform in Honolulu, Hawaii.

If my memories of my brother are paltry, my earliest childhood recollections of my sister are equally slight and for similar reasons. In the first place, she was eight years older than I and seemed "grown" by the time I reached puberty. In addition, I was totally in awe of her because of her physical style. To me she was the absolute reigning beauty of my childhood. In those years, on my rare visits to a movie house, I saw films with Ann Harding and Miriam Hopkins and they were my idols. To my mind my sister was a replica of one or the other, depending on which film I had seen last.

I presume that both my sister and brother in those lean years suffered as much hurt and anxiety as I, perhaps even more because they had been old enough to be absolute witness to my father's fall from power—financial, political, and otherwise. In retrospect, however, they both seemed to have been in emotional control, unfazed and undaunted by the Depression.

All of my impressions of my sister during my childhood are storybook images: a brown and white cotton gingham floor-length ballgown that fitted tight around her small waist and tucked into the belt of the gown a neat bouquet of blue cornflowers. Christmas, more than any other holiday, played a tremendous part in her life. She reveled in the season. Once, when I was less than four years old, there was no money in the house for stocking gifts for me. She collected an assortment of miniature dolls that she had displayed over the mantel in her bedroom. These I had coveted without saying a word. Her room I considered her sanctum sanctorum, her inviolate, private place. I rarely entered there, but I had noticed those dolls from the corners of my eye. On Christmas morning, even as a very young child, I was dismayed to find the toys in my Christmas stocking. It was the betrayal of a good belief and made me know for the first time that there was no Santa Claus. I was confused and disturbed, but I think even then I tried as bravely as I could not to show my puzzlement.

Not long after that my sister left home to attend two music schools, the Nashville Conservatory of Music and the music school of the University of Colorado in Colorado Springs. Shortly after her return she was married to Robert Woodward Barnwell, Jr., the scion of an old Mississippi family and at the time of their marriage a highly successful cotton factor trading in cotton futures on the Memphis stock exchange. They were married in the living room of my family home in Indianola, Mississippi, and the thing that I remember most profoundly is a baritone, a friend of the family, singing "Because," which must have been the most famous wedding tune of that day. When they got to the line "Because God made thee mine," I broke out in hushed tears, trying my best to stifle my cries. It all seemed so dramatic and horribly final, as if she was being whisked away from the bosom of the family by a vagabond.

My sister and her husband lived in Greenwood, Mississippi, and became the parents of three children.

§ § §

Although my mother was a fantastic and "born" cook, she was not alone in her efforts. Over the years she had a sizable roster of black servants, almost all of whom were estimable cooks and seemingly as devoted to my mother as she was to them. This was an age long before the time of the black revolution in this country, and my mother was, in a relative sense, kind, generous, and sympathetic to the problems and anxieties of the blacks. She was quite definitely a part of a culture that had its origins in the time of the slaves and though she was far from being a revolutionary, her relations with the blacks were as civil as custom would permit. She never "demanded" obedience. Words of abuse directed at a servant would have been unthinkable. If she was patronizing, if she treated her servants like children, it was simply her nature to treat many people, white and black alike, with kindly tolerance.

Curiously, I have almost no recollection of settling into my first home in Indianola. One of my first memories of that house takes the form of a young black woman whom I shall call Dora. Dora was, in many ways, unforgettable. She was delicate of build with fair, coffee-colored skin and an infectious laugh. Her mother and father were field hands, which is to say they hoed the cotton and, when the season was ready, they picked cotton and corn. She was born on a farm a couple of counties away. In her early youth she had been "given" to a well-to-do white family to "raise."

In that atmosphere she had been taught to read and write and to maintain a house. To her great credit, no one ever acted less like a menial than Dora. She was always turned out in a plain, neatly starched dress, her hair fastidiously combed and plaited. She was enormously quick-witted and with—deliberately, I thought—the mannerisms of a child. She could go against my mother's grain at which point my mother would exclaim, "Dora, nobody on earth can provoke me like you!" And inevitably Mother's reaction would turn into laughter.

She had come into our house as a cook, telling my mother in elaborate detail how she had made all the cakes and main dishes for her former employer or, more like it, patron.

The first time she tried to cook a meal it was a disaster. She couldn't even make biscuits and, in a southern kitchen, that was emboldened stupidity. "Dora, you don't know beans from bullfoot about biscuits," Mother said.

"No, Miz Claiborne, I don't," Dora admitted, and smiled.

In retrospect, I suspect that Dora enjoyed herself, trifling with my mother's easily flustered patience. In any event, Mother directed her out of the kitchen and made her a sort of nurse for me and a sort of lady-in-waiting for her. Without being too demonstrative, my mother adored her.

Little did Mother know that Dora decided to take it on herself to teach me certain facts of life that Mother would have felt highly unseemly for a child of my age to know. I had not yet reached the charming age of puberty.

"Huh," Dora would snort. "You don't rilly believe babies come from storks?"

She would invite little girls over for "sessions," which I suppose she considered highly enlightening. She would propose that the invited show me "hers" if I would show her "mine." I found the whole comedy more than a little painful and embarrassing and after a time or two I suppose Dora gave me up as hopeless.

In any event, we became great friends. If I wanted to skip school, Dora would put on an elaborate act about my not feeling well. She would go into the bathroom, flush the toilet, and tell Mother that I had vomited. Mother would call the doctor. The doctor would come in, feel my forehead, determine that I had a mild attack of "acidosis," and prescribe a glass of Coca-Cola with ice. I would miss school the rest of the day, all the while letting Dora get on with her act.

She loved to sing the songs sung by Ethel Waters. Her favorite song was "Am I Blue," which she sang and hummed for an hour or longer, paraphrasing this sometimes to ask "Am I black, I'm telling you." This, in its own way, prefaced in my mind the thought that black is beautiful.

Eventually, Dora fell in love with a tall, muscular, lean, tight-skinned black named John Stagg. John, too, had an uncommon intelligence. I have no idea where he came from but Mother put John to waiting tables, the knack of which he mastered in an hour or less. He would set the table, pour the ice water or iced tea, and pass the biscuits and fried chicken or whatever with considerable aplomb. Shortly it was rumored in the white world that John, in his world, was a heavy gambler.

John found a room in that tract across the railroad track that was called in my family "Colored Town." In the mouths of a good many others it was just plain "Nigger Town." Dora lived in a house behind ours.

And then one day it was announced that John and Dora were getting married. Dora told my mother first and, afterward, that girl-child was utterly transformed. Dora wore a perpetual grin. If the wedding was ever mentioned, John would look shy and embarrassed.

When they married, John gave her a wedding ring, a simple, unadorned metal band. After the wedding, whenever Dora and I were alone she would hold out her wedding-ring finger, displaying the circle surrounding it.

"I'm Mrs. John F. Stagg," she would declare and, grabbing me, dance around in a kind of delirium.

There was, and perhaps is to this day, a peculiar type of Southerner, born into what is called "a good family," hopelessly blind to human sensitivity. For them, blacks are blacks and consequently deaf and dumb. At table, they comment on black happenings in the presence of a black waiter, a maid, and so on, with total ruthlessness.

I recall well the evening a newcomer to that boardinghouse (I took pleasure in thinking that he came from the hills and not from the Delta) was talking in a very loud tone as John passed another helping of gravy or whatever.

"Never saw a nigger in my life who could tell you the time a day. All they wanna do is sleep and gamble. Take John here. John, how much money you dropped in that crap game last Sadduhday night?"

I glanced uneasily at John and I couldn't tell if there was murder or hurt in his eyes. He didn't speak but went about his duties.

My mother took the boarder aside and, for the first time in my life, I saw her enraged. She had sat silently through the meal but she told the man, patiently, "There is one thing I will not permit in this household and that is the abuse of the people who work here. You must never talk like that again." The boarder, flushed in the face and speechless, picked up his hat and left and, to my relief, never came back again.

Sorrow and weeping seemed almost like an affliction in that household. One day there was no sign of Dora or John and Mother walked to Dora's house.

She knocked and went in. Dora looked dazed, perhaps a little bit crazed. "John's gone," and then, "Oh, Miss Kathleen!" She buried her face in my mother's bosom and was held close.

No one ever explained why John left. Perhaps it was the gentleman from the hills. Perhaps he was in trouble because of gambling debts. He and Dora had been married a year when he left and there was talk to the effect that he'd left because Dora couldn't bear him a child. Anyway, he was gone, no one speculated where.

And not long after, Dora announced that she was leaving, too, but only for a week or so. She had a sick sister in Tennessee (a sister had never been mentioned before). And she wasn't heard from for a year or longer.

One day she telephoned my mother from California and insisted on speaking to all the children. She said she was happy, had a large house, and was making lots of money in a factory. Every now and then during the next fifteen years, without prior notice, she'd step off a Greyhound bus and come to see my mother. They'd spend hours in the kitchen, reminiscing.

And years later, when I was estranged from my mother, Dora telephoned me, this time from Chicago. She wanted to know why I never wrote my mother, "She loves you so." I had to explain, as patiently as possible, that you can't legislate love.

During the period of my childhood I remember best—and this was a time before, during, and after my own puberty—there were many other black servants.

§   §   §

Joe was a buffoon. A short man with close-cropped hair, there was something about him that looked just a bit oriental. A magnificent cook, he made the best lemon meringue and custard pies in the world. (In my mother's manuscript cookbook, which I often refer to, there is an entry for Joe's custard pie.)

Joe was, generally speaking, highly noncommunicative. But he was the first person to translate one of my juvenile culinary inspirations into an actual thing that could be served on toast. All my life I have liked the odd parts of animals—liver, brains (one of my father's favorite foods was scrambled eggs with brains), sweetbreads, tongue, and so on. When I was about eleven years old I somehow got the notion that creamed chicken livers would be a mighty tasty dish. Joe prepared half a pound or so of chicken livers in a cream sauce, well seasoned with black pepper, and I thought it must be one of the best things I'd ever eaten.

In the town where I lived, it was expected that all young boys would participate in the local school's athletic program. You played football, baseball, or basketball and, preferably, all three. In this respect I was a pariah and, as a consequence, there were very few white children I wanted to associate with or, perhaps, more to the point, who wanted to associate with me.

So Blanche's kitchen became my playground. Blanche was the chief cook and therefore it was *her* kitchen. She was tall, amply shaped, dark-skinned, and her straight black hair was pulled back into a bun. On those rare occasions when she would sit on the kitchen stool, she would grab me in her arms. Her bosom was a marvelous thing to lean against. Sally, her sister, also worked in the kitchen. She was much younger, light-skinned, skinny, and with curly and prematurely gray hair. She was friendly but aloof. I was underfoot, as they told me, morning, noon, and night. They would let me sample sauces; sometimes I was allowed to stir a sauce or baste a roast.

Occasionally, when we were alone, Blanche would pass the time waiting for a cake to finish baking going through picture books with me. She made a spectacular icing and, always on my birthdays, she would prepare my favorite foods—a butter-rich coconut cake, the coconut frosting over and around and between the layers of the cake like thickly tufted snow-white chenille. That plus ambrosia. Ambrosia, too, had coconut (plus orange sections in a simple syrup) and the combination might seem like heresy but to my young palate the combination was food for the gods.

When Blanche fried chicken, I always got a piece of crisply cooked gizzard or a chicken wing to stay my appetite until supper. And chicken we had—in pot pie, in stews, in soup, and mixed with other meats in main courses—and all for one simple reason. My father raised chickens in the backyard. Even when his brood was in short supply, we could always buy the chickens for pennies from one local farmer or another. They were depression food and if, throughout my career, I have printed more recipes for chicken than any other meat it is because it is the most versatile of viands. Although I dined on chicken at least once and oftentimes twice a day during my early years, my appetite for it has never faltered.

And that was my world, which, one bright morning, casually and without forethought shattered. My first, most incisive, and heartbreaking lesson in human relations.

It was shortly before noon. The weather was warm and the sky had a piercing brilliance, the sun's rays flooding the living room in my home. I must have been thirteen or fourteen years old and it was either a Saturday or one of the first days of summer vacation at the local high school.

I was seated, more accurately reclining, slumped in a chair, one leg over the chair's arm.

Hugh, one of the servants, was running the vacuum cleaner around the living room. He was a handsome, curly-haired mulatto. Sophisticated, a bit pudgy, and a touch effeminate. He was extremely fastidious, immaculately combed, and although he acted as errand boy and handyman, his fingernails were spotlessly filed and clean.

When Hugh came close to where I was sitting he said, without grinning or smiling, concentrating on the task at hand, "Craig, lift your foot."

I frowned and paused in my reading. I stood, book in hand, and walked to the other side of the room, staring out the opposite window. I felt the old stirrings of a crude southern maleness in my blood. I stared out the window and finally turned to Hugh, looking him straight in the eye.

"Hugh," I said, "as long as you live, don't ever call me Craig again. I'm Mr. Claiborne." Hugh looked at me a moment, went to the base plug, and pulled the cord of the vacuum. He wound it neatly and in silence, the loudness of which I'd never heard before and walked from the room.

I was petrified, stunned at my behavior. There seemed no place to turn and no place to hide.

An hour must have passed before I summoned the courage to push open the door of that kitchen. When I did enter, it was precisely as I had feared. Hugh was not there. Blanche was at the sink, her back to the room. Sally was wiping a kitchen counter. Neither of them spoke. I walked through the kitchen and out the back door.

Blanche never held me again. And ever after I was Mr. Claiborne. *Persona non grata* in the world of my childhood, the place where I once had been hugged and loved. Even, perhaps, needed.

§   §   §

There is one aroma that, more than any other, rekindles concrete thoughts of my mother in the kitchen. This is the smell of chopped onions, chopped celery, chopped green pepper, and a generous amount of finely minced garlic. This was the basis for, it seems to me in recollection, at least half of the hundreds of dishes that she prepared, and it is a distinctly southern smell. (A great southern chef, Paul Prudhomme of New Orleans, once told me that in Cajun and creole kitchens, chopped onions, celery, and green peppers are referred to as the Holy Trinity.)

And there is one dish, her own creation, and using this base, that I recall most vividly. This was chicken spaghetti, which she almost invariably made for special occasions—birthdays, holidays, Sundays. The boarders and her own family loved it and it has remained throughout my many years in the world of food a special favorite.

There were two holidays each year—Christmas and Thanksgiving—when my mother stipulated that meals would not be served to boarders, all of whom went to visit relatives or friends anyway.

I remember one nonturkey Thanksgiving that came about because the three children in the family announced that they were bored with a daily diet of poultry. A vote was taken. Almost in unison we asked for Mother's baked spaghetti. On that day we had it fresh from the oven for the midday Thanksgiving dinner; reheated for supper.

When the vegetables were cooked (they always remained al dente) a little ground beef was added and a tomato sauce containing cream, Worcestershire sauce, and Tabasco sauce. Worcestershire sauce and Tabasco sauce were primary ingredients in my mother's kitchen. Once the meat and tomato sauce were finished, the time came for the assembly of the dish. A layer of sauce was topped with a layer of cooked spaghetti or vermicelli, a layer of shredded chicken, and a layer of grated Cheddar cheese. The layers were repeated to the brim of an enormous roasting pan, ending with a layer of cheese. The pan was placed in the oven and baked until it was bubbling throughout and golden brown on top. The spaghetti was served in soup bowls with grated Parmesan cheese and two curious, but oddly complimentary side dishes—sliced garlic pickles and potato chips.

In my childhood, it would never have occurred to anyone to analyze or categorize the kind of food we dined on from my mother's kitchen. It was simply "southern cooking." In retrospect, it fell into three categories—soul food, which is a blend of African and American Indian; creole cookery, which is a marriage of innocent Spanish and bastardized French; and pure French, desserts mostly, from the first edition of *The Boston Cooking-School Cook Book.* To my mind that book was, in its original concept, the first great cookbook in America. For years it had no peer (Mrs. Rorer's works notwithstanding) and it was my mother's kitchen bible.

My mother had an incredible aptitude in her ability to "divine" the ingredients of one dish or another. She could dine in New Orleans and come back to reproduce on her own table the likes of oysters Rockefeller, oysters Bienville, the creole version (so different from the original French) of rémoulade sauce with shrimp.

There was another advantage to the old-fashioned southern kitchen: the talent and palate of the American Negro. I am convinced that given the proper training in the kitchen of a great French restaurant, any American black with cooking in his or her soul, would be outstanding.

With rare exceptions, all the servants in our kitchen arrived with a full knowledge of soul cooking, which is broad in scope. Essentially, it encompasses the use of all parts of the pig, more often than not boiled, plain, or with other ingredients. Pig's feet, pig's tails, hog jowl, and that most soul of all foods, chitterlings, the small intestines of pigs. It has always amused me, since I first encountered the regional cooking of France, to know that one of that nation's most prized and delectable of sausages—called andouille or andouillettes—is nothing more than chitterlings blended with various spices, onions or shallots, white wine, and so on, and stuffed into casings. For what it's worth, a New Year's party without grilled andouillettes in my house is as unthinkable as an absence of at least a couple of bottles of champagne. Once a year in my childhood home, Mother had a chitterling supper. Chitterlings, cooked and served with vinegar and hot pepper are, to some noses, a bit odoriferous. Therefore, the boarders were advised that they were invited to the chitterling supper, but if they found the aromas less than fastidious, they were cordially invited to find another place to dine.

The standard items of soul food that appeared almost daily at my mother's table were one form of greens or another, always cooked with pieces of pork, the feet, hocks, belly, and so on, sometimes salted, sometimes smoked. The greens were of a common garden variety, such as mustard greens, collard greens, and turnip greens. These would be put on to boil with a great quantity of water and salt and allowed to cook for hours. Once cooked, the liquid is much treasured by southern palates. It is called "pot likker" and you sip it like soup with corn bread. If you want to be fancy, you can always make corn meal dumplings to float on top of the greens. Black eye peas are also a regional treasure, some people think the finest of all staples. These, too, are cooked for a long while (preferably from a fresh state; if not, frozen; if not frozen, dried; and if none of these, canned).

One of the most distinguished roomers and boarders in my mother's house was a scholarly gentleman, well known in academic circles, the late Dr. John Dollard, a highly praised Yale psychologist and social scientist. Dr. Dollard had come to Indianola to do research on a book called *Caste and Class in a Southern Town* and with what might have been an uncanny sense of direction or perception, had chosen my house as his base of operation.

Dr. Dollard, a patient, kindly, amiable man was, of course, a Yankee and thus had a "funny accent." The other boarders did not take kindly to him for no other reason than that he was an "outsider." In the beginning he criticized the cooking of the greens, complaining that there was not a vitamin left in the lot. And as a result of his well-intentioned explanations and at the base encouragement of the other boarders, my mother willingly committed one of the most wicked acts

CRAIG CLAIBORNE

of her life. Dr. Dollard was placed at a bridge table, covered, of course, with linen and set with sterling, and he was served a mess of raw greens that he ate with considerable and admirable composure and lack of resentment. Always the detached and critical observer, I found my mother's role in this little game almost intolerable, although I said nothing.

§   §   §

Odd coincidences have occurred often in my life. One day, a decade or so ago, I wandered into the photographic studio where portraits bearing the title *New York Times Studio* were taken. I glanced at an assignment sheet and saw the name John Dollard, Yale.

As I walked out, John walked in.

"John," I said, "I'm Craig Claiborne."

"How's your mother?" he asked. "She's a great woman."

§   §   §

With one possible exception, the dishes prepared by my mother that I liked best were the creole foods. As I have noted, to this day, like the madeleines of Proust's childhood, I can smell chopped onions, celery, and green peppers, cooking together in butter or oil. This, to my mind, is the creole base, and it is a combination that often perfumes my own kitchen.

My mother would purchase one of Mr. Colotta's (Mr. Colotta was the only fish dealer for miles around) finest red snappers from the Gulf Coast brought in that morning, encased in ice, and weighing almost twenty pounds. A fish that size would barely fit in the oven. It would be baked and basted with oil and the creole base and it was as succulent and tender as anything I've ever tasted here or abroad. Her shrimp creole with the same base was robust and glorious.

It would be easy to recite the entire roster of her creole and other southern specialties. A remarkable Brunswick stew, an incredibly good barbecue sauce with tomato ketchup, Worcestershire sauce, and vinegar as a base. She made a delectable assortment of gumbos—crab, oyster, and plain okra. (The word gumbo, I was to learn in later life, derived from the Bantu word for okra.) Her deviled crab was spicy, rich, and irresistible.

There were two specialties of my home kitchen for which my mother made only the final preparation. In my earliest years, my father cured his own hams and sausages in the smokehouse out back and these she prepared with expert hands. On occasion she made country sausages, fiery hot and spiced with red pepper flakes before smoking, but more often than not she bought these from a neighbor. These sausages, for which I have developed a formula as closely paralleling the original as possible, I prepare today in a small portable smoker. Southern to the core, my mother frequently prepared beaten biscuits, one of the most curious of southern kitchen or back porch rituals.

Beaten biscuits are a blend of flour, lard, and butter that is worked together by hand. You then add enough milk to make a stiff dough, which is rolled out and literally beaten with any handy sturdy instrument. It might be a rolling pin, a shortened broom handle, even a hatchet or ax. You beat the dough, folding it over as you work, for the better part of an hour until it blisters. The dough is then rolled out, cut into small round biscuits, and pricked in the center with a fork. There are beaten biscuit cutters that cut and prick at the same time. And there are, or used to be, special beaten biscuit machines with rollers through which you roll the dough until it blisters, not unlike the old-fashioned clothes wringer.

There are dozens of dishes that come to my mind when I think of my mother's kitchen—fantastic caramels, divinity fudge, a luscious coconut cake with meringue and fresh coconut topping, the best, richest pecan pie in the world, incredible fried chicken, great shrimp rémoulade, chicken turnovers in an awesomely rich pastry served with a cream sauce—but two of the dishes that she made for very "party" occasions had a curious appeal for my childhood palate. Sunday dinner, which was served at twelve-thirty in the afternoon, was always paramount among our weekly meals and if she wished to offer the boarders an uncommon treat she would serve them as a first course toast points topped with canned, drained white asparagus spears, over which was spooned a hot tangy Cheddar cheese sauce. This dish was generally garnished with strips of pimiento.

Another for which she was renowned was a three-layered salad composed of a bottom layer of lime gelatin chilled until set, a middle layer of well-seasoned cream cheese blended with gelatin and chilled until set, and a top layer of delicately firm tomato aspic. The salad was cut into cubes, garnished with greens, and topped with a dab of mayonnaise.

Years later, when I was working for the American Broadcasting Company in public relations, I knew a reporter for the old, once thriving monthly called *Liberty* magazine. Her name was Beulah Karney and she was food editor of that journal. She once asked me casually if I could name the best cook in the South and I specified my mother. Beulah traveled to Mississippi and interviewed "Miss Kathleen." In the May 1948 issue there appeared an article entitled "The Best Cook in Town" and it described my mother's boardinghouse. Pursuant to a good deal of recent research, I found that issue in the New York Public Library.

One sentence stated "the six paying guests, all bachelors, said there wasn't much point in getting married when Miss Kathleen's food was so good." Four recipes were printed, including one for Miss Kathleen's Party Salad, that three-layered affair.

After World War II when I had settled in Chicago, my mother wrote in a school child's composition book a collection of her favorite recipes. They are in her own handwriting. There are recipes for Karo Caramels (The Candy You All Liked and All the Others So Much), Galatoire's Trout Marguery, Oysters Rockefeller, Mrs. Robert Johnson's Rice Pudding (Do You Remember The Lovely Meal We Had With Them In Chicago), Great Grandmother Craig's Grated Potato Pudding, Italian Ravioli, Grand Hot Cakes, Sister's Sausage, Charlotte Russe, and a Craig Wedding Punch, the recipe for which was more than two hundred years old.

To say that in my childhood I considered my mother to be a "blessed damozel," does not mean that in my early youth I was unaware of a few peccadilloes in her make-up. She was vain and I was aware of her vanity. She taught me—as she taught my brother and sister—that we were of noble blood and to the manor born.

"Never forget," she would admonish me almost daily, "that you are a Craig." Oddly perhaps, she never said, "Never forget you're a Claiborne." She practiced *noblesse oblige* with her servants but with her peers she was arrogant and imperious.

Because of the blue blood that I was assured coursed through my veins, there was a certain dichotomy in my ego and self-esteem. And I was subjected to countless humiliations, which I suffered meekly, because of my ennobled vision of my mother.

My greatest humiliation—and it occurred daily—was to be sent to the grocery store for provisions, a pound of butter, five pounds of sugar, a sack of flour, or whatever. In my mind I *knew* that we perennially owed the grocery store hundreds and hundreds of dollars. And the fact that the owners of the store, a couple of bachelors, lived in my mother's rooming house and admired her did not lessen my lacerations as I entered their business domain.

I was not a robust child. I had an extremely delicate nature and I was often on the verge of tears as I made that trek over the bridge to the store. As my mother acted out her role as a grande dame, I suffered in silence in my family's poverty.

Her friends and their children rode in automobiles and we had none. Taking a ride in an automobile was what one did to while away the hours in that small town. Some of the inhabitants would get in their cars and drive for only a block to visit a neighbor or drive two blocks to get to church. An automobile was the ultimate status symbol in that town.

I was aware that for the most part I had a gloomy, downtrodden look about me. My mother, misinterpreting this for boredom, would further humiliate me by calling up a neighbor and asking if he or she would not like to take me for a ride.

There is a condition that is known as childhood amnesia that stems from feelings of desolation, loneliness, and deprivation in the formative years of life and, although I have a fairly keen and vivid memory of the situations that caused these things in my own person, I am confused as to the precise dates of certain acts that caused uneradicable scars on my spirit and well-being.

Since I first learned to read I have had a phenomenal ability to spell. It was partly this ability, I believe, that motivated my earliest teachers and my mother to let me "skip" a grade, namely the first. I went from kindergarten directly into the second grade, a decision that I came to regret in my later years of schooling.

When I was probably seven or eight years old, I was chosen to compete in a county-wide spelling bee to be held in a small college in a neighboring town, Moorhead, Mississippi. I was not terribly ambitious or impressed that I had been chosen for that competition, but I was keenly anxious to win for the simple pleasure that it would give my family and friends.

As it happened, I placed second and I was not dismayed at my standing.

When I returned home that afternoon, my mother was in the living room with acquaintances and my sister, Augusta.

"How did you place?" someone asked.

"Second," I answered.

"You should be ashamed," my mother told me, and I was chilled with a distinct feeling of alienation.

Had she slapped me in the face, it could not have disturbed me more. Gradually and guardedly I started to cry. My sister put her arms around me and led me from the room while my mother picked up the thread of her conversation with her guests. I brooded on this for a good long while.

Quite early in my childhood I had been taken to Greenville to see the family doctor, Hugh Gamble, whom my mother idolized. It often occurred to me that had she been given the choice, Dr. Gamble would have made a fine husband for her. On one of my many visits to him, he diagnosed one of my small illnesses as a slight heart murmur and advised my mother that I should avoid strenuous exercise.

From that moment on she started to treat me with excessive concern, reminding me relentlessly that I was "fragile." Whenever I left her presence she would admonish me, "Don't hurt yourself." She often referred to me as "delicate" and took uncommon pride in advising friends and neighbors of my condition, not as though I were ailing but as though I had been given a major award.

It is true that I was never an athletic child and when I ran only a short distance I was afflicted with a stitch, a very real and stabbing sensation in my right side. At times, I was bent over double because of it, but I was loathe to discuss this with my family or anyone else because of a fear that it might be serious. I did not want to become a burden.

In Indianola, it was taken for granted that if you were male, you would quite naturally become a member of the football, baseball, and basketball teams, but I was not of that persuasion. I was convinced that I was "fragile," that I was incapable of developing muscles, and, besides, there was that pain in my side. It came on with any mode of roughhousing.

I was engulfed with childhood feelings of self-doubt and inadequacy. I felt that if my fellow townspeople were kind to me, it was out of sympathy. It was customary for most of the other children in school to be driven back and forth from their homes to the school building in the morning, at lunch, and in the afternoon. I walked for want of a family conveyance. I dreaded the moments when somebody would stop and ask, "Would you like a ride?" I'd turn my head and shake my head sheepishly. I loathed their magnanimity.

On the first morning of one fine school term, I do not remember the grade in junior high school in which I was enrolled, but I was seated in an arithmetic class that was taught by a supposedly grown man named Joe Green. Joe was the school athletic coach.

On that first morning, he passed out sheets of paper and asked us to write down the name of the sport in which we would participate. I returned mine with my name on it but with no indication of a sport.

On the second day, I returned to the class and, when it was called to order, the instructor had roll call.

When he got to my name he smirked.

"I see," he said, "we've got a sissy in the class."

To this day, in all my life, I have rarely known a more stunning and vivid pain. I have never known a moment more devastating or emasculating. The blood ran from my face and I was frozen with a kind of panic. It created a scar from which I never recovered and to this day I cannot add, multiply, divide, or subtract with anything remotely resembling facility. My life was colored from that moment on. I have never in all my life seen, start to finish, a football, baseball, or basketball game either in person or on television.

From that day on in junior high and high school I felt like a leper and I became the victim of a bunch of childish thugs who took delight in tormenting me, in pinning my shoulders to the ground while shoving their hands in my face.

One of my favorite lines in contemporary literature occurred some years ago in an essay by Woody Allen. He noted that as a child he was a nonphysical, vulnerable youth whose mother appended a note onto the back of his shirt whenever he walked out of the house. It read, "Do not fold, spindle or otherwise mutilate."

In my childhood I was very much a victim of my playmates' wrath and torture. The perfect target because I simply refused to fight back. Even had I felt myself physically able to resist the barbaric taunts of my assailants, I seriously doubt that I would have done so. In my adulthood, I have developed my own weapons of revenge, and these weapons consist almost exclusively of silence in the face of hostility and personal outrage. Mine enemies lose nothing more serious than my respect and friendship. That is why I consider my favorite and most consoling poem that of Emily Dickinson. I might even consider it the most fitting for my tombstone if it were not my wish to be cremated and have my ashes scattered to the wind; or, preferably perhaps, thrown into the sea, the better yet to feed the mouths of the progeny of all those fish and sea creatures that nourished me in my days on earth.

> It dropped so low—in my Regard—
> I heard it hit the ground—
> And go to pieces on the Stones
> At bottom of my Mind—
> Yet blamed the Fate that flung it—less
> Than I denounced Myself,
> For entertaining Plated Wares
> Upon my Silver Shelf—.

§ § §

But I had two friends, one an athlete, the other, like myself, a nonathlete. The nonathlete was David Sanders, who was quite literary and my mentor. David did not participate in sports, but he was the model of cool, calm self-assurance. He deemed sports to be contemptible and he was of such erudite nature, I believe the sports coach chose to ignore him for the simple reason that he could not comprehend such a droll figure. David was undoubtedly his superior when it came to brains.

But my best friend was a youngster named Gordon Lyon, Jr. It is not excessive to say that I worshiped him and he treated me with the greatest kindness and civility.

Gordon was the son of the mayor and his family was very well off. Indeed, they were conceivably the wealthiest family in town. Gordon's mother, Beatrice, was a great favorite and I loved her, too. She had a wicked sense of humor, told ribald stories, and took no part in the social order of my home town. She played golf when very few other women in town participated. She smoked cigarettes, which was then a far-out thing for a woman to do. She wore well-tailored clothes and minimum of jewelry and very much belonged to her own special world. She seemed to like my mother well enough but in a sort of detached way.

My mother liked Beät but not on intimate terms. Beät seemed to her a rather oddball, comic, worldly dame who was amusing enough but not someone you'd want to sit across a bridge table from on a continuous basis. Poker, perhaps, but not bridge. Not, of course, that my mother played poker. My feeling was that my mother considered Beät and her brood (she had a younger son named Rupert) a bit common, a good deal beneath her.

In any event, I had an intense boyhood crush on Gordon and I also liked my brief, if impersonal, encounters with his father, Gordon, Sr. There was nothing in the latter's make-up that prefigured his becoming one of the founders of the ignominious White Citizens Council. Although his name was not mentioned, a report in the Sunday *Magazine* section of *The New York Times,* dated November 12, 1961, stated that ". . . the first Council was formed seven years ago by a group of community leaders in the Delta town of Indianola . . . to retain control of resistance to desegregation in the hands of the 'better people.' Then, it was a semi-secret society." Mr. Gordon, I was told, was a principal instrument in its founding.

To my mind, Gordon, Jr., was one of the cleanest-living, handsomest, most stouthearted and bravest young men I had ever met. My great joy was spending weekends in his home, innocently sharing his bed.

He was a great golfer and played in professional matches when he was in grade school. I recall once his pride when he played in the same match with Cary Middlecoff.

Actually, we had very little in common. He liked girls and comic books, and his favorite radio program, which he listened to devotedly, was "The Lone Ranger." One thing that we shared was a liking for popular music and he could never get enough pleasure in hearing "Night and Day."

Every year his family bought a new Chrysler automobile and we would ride in Gordon's car literally for hours on weekends, driving with no goal in mind, simply circling the blocks in that small town or taking occasional jaunts into the countryside.

On Saturday nights, we would sometimes go to nearby roadhouses with a couple of girls and dance to a jukebox. One of the great popular music hits of the day was a recording of Ella Fitzgerald singing "A-Tisket, A-Tasket," and one weekend, lo and behold, Ella Fitzgerald, with a band headed by a leader named Chick Webb, came to play in a roadhouse near Leland, Mississippi. I couldn't believe it, for I worshiped Ella's voice. I also could not believe when we arrived at the roadhouse that Ella and the orchestra were cordoned off, presumably to segregate the black musicians from the white dancers.

Gordon was a year ahead of me in high school and I was desolate on his graduation for at the end of the summer I knew that our friendship would be in peril. Worse was the knowledge that he would be attending the University of Mississippi, whereas I was destined to go on my graduation the following year to Mississippi State College.

Our friendship continued throughout the summer vacations, and while still at the university, Gordon became a pilot in the Air Force. When I left college in 1942, I joined the U. S. Navy. Gordon was sent overseas and I never heard from him again. My mother knew of my devotion to him and would occasionally send me news that she had picked up from Beät.

I was in North Africa for a long period with the amphibious forces and I was a trifle perplexed to realize that several letters received from my mother had no mention of Gordon. I did not query her about the lack of news, considering it to be simply a matter of oversight and having a firm faith in Gordon's invincibility.

In early 1944 I was sent to the United States for schooling at the University of Notre Dame in its officer training program, from which I would graduate as an ensign.

I stopped briefly in Indianola to see my parents and my first inquiry was about Gordon. I learned, six months after the fact, that his plane had been shot down in Bougainville in the Solomon Islands. He was missing in action and presumed dead. My mother communicated this to me, stating that she had not divulged his death to me earlier, *for fear that I would be upset.*

My grief was grand. Not so grand, however, as my sense of betrayal.

I suffered in silence, brooding not only over the loss of my most cherished friend, but the feeling that once more my mother had gravely undermined my dignity; my privilege of adult emotion.

My mother, who was graduated from Judson College in Marion, Alabama, was not by any means a highly educated musician but she had a passion for music. She had a pleasant speaking voice but a miserable singing voice; she played the piano routinely, but well. Whenever she sat down at the keyboard she would quickly dash off a phrase of music from a slight work titled, I believe, "The Fountain."

My brother was tone deaf, but she was insistent that my sister and I have musical training of one sort or another. When my sister graduated from high school we were, to use a cliché, as poor as church mice, but my mother found the means to dispatch her to two music schools, one in Tennessee, the other in Colorado. The latter was run by Giuseppe de Luca, who had been a well-known baritone on the Metropolitan Opera stage. My mother considered this the proper thing for a young southern girl with cultural aspirations, although my sister's voice was not one whit better than mine, which was dreadful. My sister was under no illusions either about her voice and I think she was embarrassed and not a little bored by her stay at those schools.

I know that I was embarrassed once a month because I saw the bills arriving, some of them with stern notes that if the bills, which mounted unpaid month after month, weren't paid they were packing my sister back home. Somehow she managed to sustain her training for a couple of years.

I remember that during that period my sister returned home for a summer vacation when the ladies of the town decided to stage a festival celebrating the founding of Indianola, Mississippi. In the pageant would be depicted the naming of the place after an Indian maiden named Ola. (Got it? Indianola.) The pageant was held on the steps of what passed for a fancy mansion in town, and my sister was enlisted to sing "By the Waters of Minnetonka." She was garbed in a loose-fitting but proper floor-length skirt, with a circle of Indian beads around her head and a feather stuck in it standing up to the rear. There was a piano accompaniment. Oh God, it was a tonal disaster.

There was not much to do in that small town and so special events of that order, while not frequent enough to be called routine, were not to be ignored. When I was about five or six another of my black nurses, named Corrie Flagg, a sassy, good-natured, and humorous busybody, learned that there was to be a beauty and talent contest for children in the small local park. She made it her business to enter me in the contest and, in that the entrants were scheduled to be dressed for show in a swimming suit and I did not own one, she borrowed one from my brother, sewed it to size, leaving a bulge around the center. I was marched on stage where I proceeded to sing "Baby Face," having been properly coached by Corrie. Through some miracle I won.

During my childhood my mother's ambitions for me were that I would learn to play the piano and sing. My voice is a cross between a creaking door and a rooster crow, but I was put under the vocal tutelage of the wealthy widow of a lawyer in town, who apparently had little else to do with her time and regarded me as a charity case. The good lady coached and rehearsed me for weeks on end and to my mind there was no noticeable improvement in any pear-shaped tone.

Since both my mother and my voice teacher belonged to the Presbyterian church, it was decided that I would sing before the regular congregation during the course of one Sunday morning service. The song was to be "The Holy City," the range of which demands a hefty chest and God knows what inner assurance. I had neither. I sang and eventually reached the conclusion of the song, "Hosanna, Hosanna in the HIIIIGHEST, Hosanna forev-ERRRRRRRR-more." There was a dead silence in the auditorium and after the services were over one old man named Mr. Adams, who was deaf as a post, came over and shook my hand and said he admired my effort. That was, fortunately, the end of my career as a vocalist.

I fared better at piano practice, but I did not enjoy practicing. It bored me and I could never get it through my brain precisely why there were so-many-beats-to-a-bar and so-many-beats-to-another-bar. In that year's graduation exercises, no one could have been more astounded than I to learn that I had been given a year's subscription to *Etude* magazine as the most promising piano student in my class. I do not know why I was not encouraged to continue with piano lessons. It probably had to do with money.

My mother continued to play the piano and her music appreciation could be summed up in numerous popular standard "concert" songs of those days, at least songs that were sung on the concert stage in the South. These included many sentimental songs and many songs related to the black experience. She adored "Mighty Lak' a Rose," "Water Boy," "Short'nin' Bread" (to this day I can't believe the lyrics to that song), "The Rosary," "The Hills of Home," "On the Road to Mandalay," and, most of all, perhaps because of the lachrymose southern aspect of its lyrics, "Goin' Home," which had been set to music to the largo of Anton Dvořák's *New World* Symphony.

There were three composers and/or lyricists who were above all others represented on the music rack of her Steinway baby grand: Carrie Jacobs Bond, who wrote endless numbers that were popular in that day and age including "I Love You Truly" and "A Perfect Day"; Reginald De Koven and Clement Scott who were represented primarily by "Oh, Promise Me"; and Amy Woodforde-Finden and Laurence Hope, whose "Four Indian Love Lyrics" I recall with particular fondness, especially the Kashmiri Song: "Pale hands I loved beside the Shalimar . . ."

§ § §

My childhood was not totally without merriment. There was dancing in private homes to phonograph records, ten inches in diameter and played on a hand-wound machine. A few boys and girls would go from school to one or another's home and dance to Tommy Dorsey or Benny Goodman and listen, mournfully, to the young Frank Sinatra. We danced to music like "You," and "You and the Night and the Music," and, best of all, to "Night and Day."

In my earliest years I was not in any sense well read. Although I did read a little Bible, relished a little Shakespeare, memorized a little Chaucer ("When that Aprille with his shoures sote/the droghte of Marche hath perced to the rote.").

If I have any facility for cadence in language it is due not to the classics but to composers like Jerome Kern and George Gershwin; lyricists like Richard Rodgers' inimitable partner Larry Hart, Cole Porter, and Noel Coward, among a few dozen others. The family finances wouldn't permit more than an occasional visit to a motion picture. There was no television. So I bided my time (as the song goes) learning, without effort, the lyrics of all the worthwhile current music. And it was the greatest popular music ever created. Or will be. I knew the introductions and choruses as well . . . "You're the top" . . . "You'd be so easy to love" . . . "I have eyes for you to give you dirty looks" . . . "From all visitors and inquisitors we'll keep our apartment" . . . "Tokay" . . . "She had the looks and how she could deliver, the lorelei . . ."

I can, any old day (to use another Tin Pan Alley phrase) deliver a philippic against most education in America. As far as education and scholarly encouragement was concerned, I grew up "lost, and by the wind grieved." That's Thomas Wolfe. What I learned, I learned—in a sense—at random and from the street. That is to say, by association with passers-by. Not from educators. Not from respected and admired teachers. Nor from adults who cared about the mind. But from kids who, thank God, were possessed of a certain genius and, for one reason or another, had faith in me.

Chief among them was my friend David Sanders, that tall, gangly, brilliant scholar, who was, as I recall, one year my senior. There was, I believe, a greater disparity between David and his father than that between my father and me. David's father was a quiet, self-absorbed man, married to a somewhat sober-faced and somber woman and neither of them communicated much with the outside world.

They reminded me of the lines from Emily Dickinson, "The soul selects her own society, then shuts the door . . ." I never knew in detail what Mr. Sanders did professionally. I remember being told once (at my age at that time, who and what parents did—other than one's own —wasn't really all that important) that he had formerly been a school teacher. I presume it was true because his children, David in particular, possessed an incredible and awesome capacity for learning. And sensitivity. He was also the most cynical young man I had ever known. It was said that his father was a "skeptic" and "agnostic," although the words did not mean much to me then. I do recall that Mrs. Sanders used to make "home brew" in the kitchen or bathroom. As I remember it, the Sanderses had a special license to brew the mash because it was "good for Mr. Sanders' heart."

My first reasoned remembrance of David was that he was a reactionary. As I have noted, he was the only other kid in my high school who also did not care for athletics. He was above it. And for some reason, the faculty didn't care. Perhaps the football staff didn't think he was worth sneering at. I wish to God they'd shown me the same discourtesy and not singled me out as a target.

David was no sport and he made no bones about it. He knew, he said, that one horse could outrun another. And who needed his brains addled in a boxing ring? Or his teeth kicked out in football. He was a gratifying influence in my life.

But not only because of that splendid, cool, calculated estimate of the sporting life. He read the Bible (not as a religious tract) and Shakespeare and Emily Dickinson and Robinson Jeffers and Edgar Lee Masters and Thomas Wolfe and T. S. Eliot and Robert Frost. Not only that. He quoted them.

My earliest "literary" recollection of David has to do with Ecclesiastes. It is the verse beginning "And the doors shall be shut in the streets, when the sound of the grinding is low, and he shall rise up at the voice of the bird, and all the daughters of music shall be brought low . . .

"The almond tree shall flourish and the grasshopper shall be a burden, and desire shall fail . . ."

David had one great passion in life that, in retrospect, is to me endearing. He wanted to write the great American novel, to be titled *Desire Shall Fail.* I must confess it remains in my mind, sentimentally, to this day, one of the greatest titles ever contemplated for such a novel.

While the other children were out playing baseball, basketball, or whatever, David and I would walk for hours talking about poetry. I think that he would not have treasured my audience so much had I not been the only other boy in town who cared more about words than a playing field. In any case, I was there and he was there and thank God. Even though he seemed so much older and more mature than I. When I was thirteen he must have been all of fourteen!

We'd walk across cotton fields and kick at the dust and he was decidedly the mentor. I believe he loved his scholarly, older brother role.

On summer days David and I would wander into the green and leafy woods that bordered the neighborhood, occasionally taking a sandwich of some of my mother's leftover roast chicken. On even more rare occasions David would bring along a pilfered or purloined bottle of his father's home brew and we'd become mildly, wickedly intoxicated as he read or recited from memory such lines as Frost's "The woods are lovely, dark and deep"; or Dickinson's "There's a certain slant of light, on winter afternoons, that oppresses, like the Heft of cathedral tunes," and "Much madness is divinest sense," and the Songs of Solomon. David, with a built-in tristesse that was hard to define, a somewhat sallow look, and a sadness about the down-turned corners of his smile, loved irony.

A. E. Housman, too, was a much recited favorite: "Malt does more than Milton can to justify God's ways to man," he would speak as he swilled another swill of homemade beer. And, also Housman, "The cow, the old cow, she is dead."

During that period I had an intense desire to make David respect me as a being capable of profound thought and understanding. To this end I wrote poetry and short stories. I wrote one maudlin bathos-bathed number called "So Big," apologies to Edna Ferber, about a young boy sacrificing his life for an older brother. My poetry consisted, instead of thought, of assorted, unrelated phrases hung together without imagery or meaning. David, patient, absorbed, and unsmiling, was the soul of indulgence.

Other than David Sanders, there was one other individual who went to some length to nourish my interests in literature. Her name was Thelma Moody, a big-boned, big-bosomed, stately spinster with black hair streaked with gray, pulled tightly back on her head and tied in a bun. She gave the appearance of being a bit stern but I had a feeling that she understood and felt compassion, perhaps even a kind of love and tenderness. She was one of the few teachers I knew in those days with whom I could experience a sense of communication.

She taught high school English and literature, loved the works of Shakespeare, and tried to "impose" his plays on her students. I could understand *Romeo and Juliet,* but when it came to the complexities of *A Midsummer Night's Dream,* she might as well have been speaking Greek or Latin.

Several of the ladies who taught at Indianola High School either roomed or boarded at my mother's place and Miss Moody was among them. At meals I frequently sat next to one or another of the teachers, including Miss Moody.

It is not said in a sense of inordinate pride or immodesty, but since my days in the cradle I have felt a strong, ironbound sense of honesty and ethics. It undoubtedly came about with my father's inflexible religious streak as the holy example.

Nonetheless, at the end of one school semester, the time came for the final examinations in Miss Moody's literature class and I had stayed up half the night, not making head or tail of a diagram to be committed to memory, a series of interconnected circles showing the intricate relationships of the various characters—Titania, Bottom, Oberon, Puck, and all the rest.

Studying in solitude, I became frightened. And did the unthinkable. I sketched those interconnected circles on the back of my left shirt cuff and donned my sweater, which covered the evidence rather neatly. Shortly thereafter, burdened with guilt and self-hatred, I walked downstairs to the dining room for breakfast and, as luck would have it, there was but one seat left at the dining table. It was to the immediate right of Miss Moody, who was in the middle of her fried egg and grits.

I seated myself and after the usual morning pleasantries were exchanged—slept well, nice day, and so on—I started this insane drivel directed at Miss Moody.

"Someone said that high school students cheat on their examinations and I don't know why they'd try. They're bound to be . . ."

At that moment I saw her staring at my shirt cuff and there, my sweater sleeve halfway up my arm, was the horrible, incriminating evidence. I quickly ducked my arm under the table, lowered the sweater sleeve, and excused myself. I ran upstairs, changed shirts, afraid and more guilt-ridden.

In class the examination began, Miss Moody at the blackboard. We were asked to repeat the diagram on the clean sheets of paper before us. As we worked in silence, Miss Moody came and circled my desk to be sure my cuffs were clean. They were.

My marks came high.

And, I've never cheated again.

Except when pitting my wits against a bunch of thieves and scoundrels. Or someone who would betray my trust and friendship.

§   §   §

Show me a man who claims to be wholly without prejudice and I will show you a saint or a liar. Of course, I came from Mississippi. And in my youth it was rank in many ways. There were chain gangs at work on the levee. There were cells of the Ku Klux Klan throughout the state. Lynchings happened. The town where I grew up, Indianola, like several thousand other Mississippi towns, was divided by a railroad track. On one side was the respectable middle-class white sector. Across the tracks was "Nigger Town."

But I profess that I survived that childhood with an astonishingly small amount of prejudice.

Over the years, some of my New York friends, Jews, have chided me (affectionately) with, "Whaddaya mean, some of your best friends in Mississippi were Jews. In Mississippi they never heard of Jews."

Ironically, some of my mother's best friends were and that takes a bit of explanation.

My mother was a dreadful snob and she considered most gentiles "tacky." She thought the Jews she knew, particularly the women, had class and they had things in common, including pleasure in conversation and tale-telling.

Of the numerous friends I had who were Jews, the one I idolized was Anita Wolf. Anita had a great face, a shapely body, a tremendous wit, and, besides, she played the piano. She dressed well and she had style, a fairly rare commodity in my home town. Her favorite compositions when seated at the pianoforte were Fritz Kreisler's "Caprice Viennois" and Louis Alter's "Manhattan Serenade."

Among many things that endeared the Wolfs to me was their holiday foods. It was in Sadie Wolf's kitchen that I was initiated into the joys of matzoh balls, gefillte fish, matzoh brie, and so on.

An unforgettable memory of Anita occurred one Passover when, obviously, she had been fed a surfeit of holiday dishes in homes of various relatives and friends scattered in the region.

One morning I walked across the street (the Wolf home was, for a brief period, directly across from ours) and heard Anita's voice raised in protest.

I walked into her bedroom and she was jumping around in the bed, dressed but barefoot, yelling, "If somebody feeds me one more matzoh ball I'm going to kill them."

Similarly, if to a lesser degree, I had several friends who were Italian. Not only that, they were exotic. They were Catholic. The Italians in my community (there were only 3,500 people then) ran restaurants and one dealt in fish. There were, among others, the Renaldos, the Colottas, the Polizzis, and the Labellas. Here, too, I think of them now mostly in terms of food (except for Tony Renaldo, whom I remember as a tall, athletic, gentle, and sensitive friend), particularly Charlie Labella's hamburgers.

Charlie Labella had a "place" on the highway leading to Leland. Labella's was a hangout for young and old alike and perhaps the only restaurant of any distinction in town. It may sound odd but Labella's wasn't thought of as a restaurant at all. Labella's was, simply, Labella's. It was an institution and, although they undoubtedly served other foods (I believe you could order spaghetti with meatballs), their one great and undeniable specialty was hamburgers. They were, as far as I know, Charlie's own creation and, therefore, unavailable outside the town limits of Indianola. I loved them and presumed in my childhood that they were some mystic creation, unreproduceable outside that one kitchen.

I was an adult, living in New York, when it occurred to me that if I could tune my tastebuds into that long-vanished past (the original Labella's, I am told, folded a few years back), perhaps I could re-create those wonders. My memory and taste served me well. I recalled that a chili-with-meat sauce was ladled onto the top of the burger before the top of the sandwich was added. With a little experimenting I added a bit of finely chopped garlic to the meat before grilling and that, in essence, is the Labella burger. Of course, the quality of the meat is important and so is the flavor of the chili-with-meat sauce.

As I have noted, the Italian fish dealer brought in fish and seafood —red snapper, oysters, clams, shrimp, pompano—from the Gulf Coast once a week, each Friday, and you had to place your order a week in advance. My mouth still salivates when I think about the giant-size red snappers, which, when my mother purchased them, she baked, basting often for an hour and longer, with her creole sauce. The fish she cooked was large enough to serve ample portions to the dozen or more boarders (sometimes small tables were hastily installed close to the large oval "family" table where the boarders dined) and the children and servants as well.

The only two other "aliens" who lived in Indianola during that period were a Mexican and a Yankee family of four. The Mexican didn't speak English, the Yankees didn't speak Southern, so they were considered more or less on the same social level.

The Mexican walked the streets of the town with a pushcart that cradled some of the most tempting, mouth-watering hot tamales you could hope to sample. They consisted of incredibly well-seasoned shredded meat encased in a finely ground and sumptuously rich casing, the whole wrapped in dried corn shucks and steamed. You could eat six or a dozen and more and still be hungry.

I felt horribly deprived and hoodwinked the day he disappeared as suddenly as he had arrived. The rumor was that the "authorities" had found a hundred and more cat skeletons under his makeshift cabin, these the source of his meat filling. He was banished from the town and never seen again.

As to the Yankee family, they were gentiles and Catholic, to boot. It was said that the mother in the case was as penurious as she was un-Southern, and that, although they weren't all that poor, she used to add tea to the toilet water so that if you simply urinated in the bowl, you needn't flush. This to save water and money.

I have often noted that you have to suspend disbelief at times if you are to accept my confessions of ignorance about certain—to some people, obvious—facts of life. The following is a case in point.

Until I was a junior in college, I honestly believed the Catholic church to be a wholly Italian institution. I mean I did not realize, with the exception of that one Yankee family, perfectly decent, white, gentile, non-Italians belonged to that particular religious "sect." I was living in a fraternity house at the University of Missouri when I suddenly discovered that it was a hotbed of German-Americans. All of them were Catholic.

When I was very young and standing not more than four feet high, we indulged in three supernatural pleasures. We told ghost stories, we tiptoed through the cemetery after dark, and we would surreptitiously peek into the windows of the Roman Catholic church. Someone would lift me onto his shoulders and I would squint into that room with the bleeding figure of Christ and sculptures of a weeping Mary. Suddenly I would be dropped from that perch beneath those stained glass windows and all of us would run like hell, titillating and trembling vaguely from that childish and "unearthly" experience.

By far the most "exotic" influence in my life was not a bizarre or eccentric personality at all, but a rather shy, soft-spoken, and brilliant woman who stood barely five feet tall. Her name was Elizabeth and she was my father's sister. Like him, she had been born in Brownsville, Tennessee, shortly after the Civil War.

I first met Elizabeth when I was seven years old. She arrived in my home, having spent more than thirty years as a respected Methodist missionary in China. She had been educated at a Bible school in Kansas City, Missouri.

I was enchanted with her and she loved me. She was an incredibly neat, fastidious woman who dressed mostly in black cotton dresses with subdued, starched lace blouses. Shortly after her arrival there appeared numerous boxes, all marked with Chinese calligraphy and containing a host of fine gifts that had been given to her by children whom she had taught as well as their fathers and mothers. There were magnificent porcelain bowls and statues, the one that impressed me most being an ivory carving of a very old, bearded gentleman bearing a staff in one hand and a peach in the other. I was told that she had taught the three daughters of Charles Jones Soong and that their names were Ai-ling, Ching-ling, and Mei-ling, but the import of this was totally lost on my young mind. How could I have known that one of these, Ching-ling, became the wife of Sun Yat-sen and another, Mei-ling, would be the wife of Chiang Kai-shek. Of the three she adored most Mei-ling, whom she once described to me as a fragile-sensitive child who loved to be held in my aunt's arms. In China my aunt first taught in the science department of McTyeire School in Shanghai. She spoke and read Chinese, studied at the Tsing-haw college in Peking, and became deeply interested in botany as a profession. She worked closely with fellow scientists in the scientific classification of Chinese flora.

In 1925 she was appointed head of the Nge Kar Ang School in Soochow and that year what came to be known as the Peking riots spread to central China. The massacre of missionaries in Nan-King drove all American citizens to Shanghai. She came home on furlough in 1927 and never returned.

My aunt held me utterly fascinated with her tales of adventure as a missionary. Although in Soochow she had worked closely with the children of "less fortunate families," there is no doubt in my mind that she much enjoyed her relationship with the wealthy, elitist members of Chinese society.

She once told me that one of the richer Chinese Christians of Shanghai had expressed a great desire to leave some sort of monument to himself and asked for suggestions. She informed him that what she missed most from her childhood home were pecans and that she had never seen a pecan in China. Whereupon he ordered several thousand pecan seedlings from a nursery in Tennessee. Together, or so her story went, they got in a boat and traveled up and down the Yangtze Kiang planting seedlings every thousand yards or so. Shortly before her death she told me she had seen an article in *National Geographic* with photographs of pecan trees growing on the banks of the Yangtze River and this was a considerable triumph and consolation in her mind.

It was through Elizabeth's influence that I first discovered the niceties and delights of using chopsticks. She taught me how to manipulate them when I was a child, and to this day I prefer to use chopsticks to knives and forks.

I much admired Elizabeth's philosophy of life and to my knowledge she was never moved to lure me into a hardbound Christian mold. In fact, although she was devout in her faith, we rarely discussed religion. During her later years I spent a good deal of time with her when it became necessary to place her in a nursing home in Nashville, Tennessee.

I have one fond recollection of her that had to do with eating. I had been with *The New York Times* for about ten years and felt prosperous enough to send her an airplane ticket from her home in Nashville to New York. The month was October and she was at the time in her mid-eighties.

Pierre Franey and I met her at Kennedy airport (then known as Idlewild) and drove her to my home in East Hampton. We stopped en route to buy a pint of scallops, which were in season. We decided to make a menu of scallops in a cream sauce with buttered fine noodles.

As we worked it occurred to me that the sauce we had in mind was made with chopped shallots and a reduction of dry white wine. I whispered to Pierre not to let my aunt know that wine was one of the ingredients. I also decided to pour myself a scotch and soda, as deviously and covertly as possible. As I unscrewed the bottle of scotch I realized that she was standing at my side.

"Elizabeth," I said sheepishly, "I was trying to hide from you the fact that I enjoy a drink or two before dinner."

"Craig," she said gently, "wouldn't it be a dreadful place if I tried to re-create all the world in my own image?"

Although Elizabeth had opened her own enterprise and prospered as a landscape architect in Nashville after returning from missionary work, she had fallen on hard times, having spent a fortune for cancer treatments for her apartment mate of many years, Ina Davis Fulton, another former missionary. All the prized possessions that she had brought from China mostly vanished as gifts to friends and family and it fell to my lot to go to her home and pack her belongings for her move into a nursing home.

When I arrived in her apartment, where she lived alone, she told me that she had saved a special treasure for me, one that she had earmarked in my behalf for several decades. It was a table that had been hauled, she related, over the mountains of China by Genghis Kahn and once rested in a Peking museum. She unwrapped a six-sided wooden table top of elaborate filigree design that fitted neatly onto a base of six hinged wooden panels also of filigree that could be folded compactly into one neat package.

She implored me to take this marvel to the Metropolitan Museum in New York to have it carbon dated.

On my return to Manhattan I unveiled this treasure to an acquaintance, a skilled interior designer, Clorinda Whitcomb, who, on hearing my tale, laughed uncontrollably.

"Genghis Khan," she scoffed. "Are you honestly naïve enough to think they were using metal hinges in the twelfth century!"

She stored my table in the attic of my New York apartment and there it rests today, too fragile for practical everyday use.

There is a sequel to that story.

A few years later, perhaps four, I was invited by Alfred Knopf, the publisher, to join him in a flight to New Mexico for a barbecue.

In order to get there we had to drive from Santa Fe to a small farm near the northern border of the state. We had a fine feast of barbecued mutton with beans and chile, beer and wine, and after the meal it was necessary for me to return to Santa Fe to catch my plane.

I was offered a lift by another guest who was taking the same route and as we neared the city he asked me into his home for a drink, which I willingly accepted. As I sipped a scotch and soda, my eyes shifted to a corner of the living room where I spotted to my vast amusement what amounted to an actual if smaller reproduction of my aunt's six-sided table. I smiled and turned to my host.

"Did you," I asked, "ever have an aunt who was a missionary in China?"

He frowned incredulously. "How on earth did you know that?" he asked.

I have often wondered since then how many thousands of filigree tables those inscrutable Chinese used to turn out each year as they said good-bye to their missionary friends.

§ § §

One of the earliest and, to my mind, most curious conflicts in my home had to do with genealogy. I say curious because both my father and his sister Elizabeth were among the least vain people I've ever known. They were defensive in most things that dealt with the sin of pride and they declared themselves plain human beings in the sight of the Lord; but they both seemed to take comfort in their ancestry.

My mother held as often as not that her children and she were descended from royal ancestors, and as far as I can recall she once invoked the name of Mary Queen of Scots. I wasn't impressed. Such lineage did not compensate for grocery bills left unpaid and the humiliation that accompanied that knowledge.

Once, in his more prosperous years and I believe before my birth, my father had indulged his interest in his own ancestry to have a family tree drawn up, an elaborate, handsomely constructed affair that occupied the better part of one wall of our house in Sunflower.

From the moment that mural was installed, I sensed that there was trouble in the house. The feud was dignified and quiet but I was aware of hurt feelings, and at some point, the "tree" in a symbolic sense, got the ax. My father had it removed and transferred to my aunt, whom my mother did not hold in high esteem, on my aunt's return from China.

I have only a fleeting memory of the family tree and the feuding that resulted from it, but it is also true that I was not particularly fascinated by my heritage until I began this autobiography. Truth to tell, I suspect that at least part of my recent and present interest in my ancestry has more to do with reckoning scores than an interest in tracing my genes generations back, a sort of petty and perverse desire to prove that the Claibornes were "better" than the Craigs. But if one is to give heed to the words and thoughts of Daniel Webster, "The man who feels no sentiment of veneration for the memory of his forefathers, who has no natural regard for his ancestors or his kindred, is himself unworthy of kindred regard of remembrance."

There is an association near Brownsville, Tennessee, where my father was born, called the "Tabernacle Historical Committee." Tabernacle was the name of "a little church in the forest." Each year a hundred or so members of the Taylor family of Tennessee gather at a camp meeting as they have for more than a hundred and thirty years. A 630-page book, privately printed in 1957 and titled *The Taylors of Tabernacle,* came into my hands quite by accident when I began this autobiography.

It traces the origins of the Taylor family back to well beyond the first joining together of the Claibornes and Taylors, which occurred in 1834 when Elizabeth Ann Taylor married Alexander Claiborne. I learned from the family tree that appears in the book, my father and I are descended on the Taylor side from Edward I, the King of England who died in 1307. He was married to Princess Eleanor of Castile. Numerous lords and ladies came from that royal mating.

During a recent brief visit to the New York Public Library I found a book published by the Virginia Historical Society, Volume I, and could determine that "The ancient family from which the patentee [my ancestor, William Claiborne] descended derived its name from the Manor of Cleburne, or Cliborne, in Westmoreland, near the river Eden. The Manor is named in Doomsday Book (A.D. 1086), and the family was for many generations lords of this place, and of Bampton, Candale, and Kyne. . . ."

I know that the patentee referred to, William Claiborne, arrived in Virginia in the early 1600s, with three servants. I even learned the names of the servants: William Harris, William Morris, and Jon Pipps. Passage for the servants was paid on June 3, 1624.

William Claiborne was "borne" about 1587 and he was engaged by the Virginia Company of England to go to Virginia as a surveyor "with a salary of 30 pounds a year and a house." On April 6, 1642, the King appointed him Treasurer of Virginia for life—how long he held the office does not appear.

It may seem a minor point, but William was descended from Elizabeth and John de Cliborne of Westmoreland, England. Elizabeth descended from Malcolm II, King of Scotland.

William, according to an article in *The New York Times* (April 25, 1981), is credited with being the first settler of the state of Maryland in 1613. The gentleman "sailed out the bay to the southern tip of Kent Island, built a fort and trading post." The Archbishop of Canterbury came to "Kent Island to take part in a service commemorating the 350th anniversary of Claiborne's establishment of a church . . ." in the new colony.

The occasion, I was happy to note, was celebrated with a feast of crabs, for which the region has been famous for a few centuries.

I am equally pleased to note that one of William's grandchildren, notably William Charles Cole Claiborne, and I have a common ancestor. He happened to be the first governor of Louisiana and was formerly governor of the Mississippi Territory. He died in New Orleans in 1817.

That is why, when you race through New Orleans on your way to plates of gumbo and jambalaya, oysters Bienville, dirty rice, or a poboy sandwich, you'll be hard put to get there without traveling on or crossing a street named Claiborne. To my mind, that's enough for this man's family tree.

P.S. I am not descended directly from William Charles Cole Claiborne as was sometimes rumored in my family when I was a child. William had one son named Nathaniel and another named Burnell. William Charles Cole was descended from Nathaniel. For what it's worth, I was descended from Burnell.

The Claibornes accounted for, if there is one part of the heritage of the Craig family of which I am proud, it has to do oddly enough with finnan haddie.

Since I first encountered finnan haddie on a breakfast menu at the Connaught Hotel in London more than twenty-five years ago, it has been my long-held notion that this smoked-fish delicacy is one of the consummate breakfast foods of the world. Give me a platter of choice finnan haddie, freshly cooked in its bath of water and milk, add melted butter, a slice or two of hot toast, a pot of steaming Darjeeling tea, and you may tell the butler to dispense with the caviar, truffles, and nightingales' tongues.

Some years ago on a trip to Spain, I was enchanted to learn of a possibility—however remote—that one of my ancestors "invented" finnan haddie (the name derives from haddock smoked on the seaside banks of Findon, Scotland), and, in my books, that is something to celebrate. My mother always maintained that she was descended from Scottish nobility. I forget which king or queen it was. I was not impressed. But, ah! to think that the sweet smell of smoke under haddocks is part of my ancestry; that is something else.

Crossing a street in Barcelona, I stepped off the curb and broke two small bones in my foot. A young man, a merchant captain named James Buckett, saw my body crumple to the ground and rushed to my side. He helped me back to the hotel, fed me aspirins, and, as I awaited a doctor's decision, we talked.

The talk, of course, veered to food, and I told him of my great fondness for finnan haddie. Jim told me that he was from Aberdeen, Scotland, only six miles from Findon. He laughed.

"Did you know it is entirely possible that finnan haddie was first 'created' a long, long time ago by one of your ancestors on your mother's side of the family?"

I told him, no, of course not.

"Like you," he said, "my mother was a Craig. All the Craigs have been fishing people and lived up and down the Scottish coast around Aberdeen.

"The 'discovery' of finnan haddie was accidental and had to do with a house fire. I can't fill you in on the details, but I have an uncle named James Lees in Aberdeen who can. Drop him a note. He's the family historian. As for me, I must run now. My plane leaves in an hour and I've a boat to catch." He gave me Mr. Lees's address and departed.

When I returned to New York, I wrote James Lees and explained the circumstances of my writing. A few weeks later I received the following:

"My grandmother, Helen Wood, was born in 1812 in a small fishing village called Findon, known locally as Finnan, situated about seven miles south of Aberdeen.

"Helen grew up in this village whose livelihood depended on the menfolk going to sea in small boats called yawls. In those boats they pitted their wits, skills and energy against the sea to reap its harvest.

"These yawls were without decks, compass or engine and were propelled by sail or oar, but the fishermen, nevertheless, ventured 38 or 40 miles off shore to cast or 'shed' their fishing lines.

"It isn't surprising that disaster was forever close at hand, and personal tragedies—lost limbs and frequently death—were something the community lived with.

"The women had an important role to play because, in addition to caring for large families, they also assumed the arduous tasks of baiting the lines with mussels, gutting and cleaning the fish, then processing the fish by tying the tails of a few fish firmly together with dry grass and eventually hanging these bunches over rods known as tinters.

"These tinters hung overnight in the fish sheds or 'hoosies.' The following day the fish were packed into vast wicker baskets called creels. In the absence of an available market, the fisherwomen strung the creels around their necks and shoulders with ropes and off they went to 'hawk' or sell their fish at farms, crofts and villages 10 or 15 miles inland.

"In 1835, my grandmother married her true love, a fisherman called James Craig, and in time brought up her family, baited the lines, cleaned, prepared and hawked the fish.

"Everything seemed to go according to predestined plan until one summer morning some 128 years ago, when my grandmother woke to discover wisps of smoke seeping from the fish shed. It appeared that sawdust strewn on the floor to absorb the moisture dripping from the fish had caught fire.

"The family speculated later that the fire was started by the refraction of light from the sun as it passed through the primitive hand-crafted glass of the windowpanes. A spark of heat had ignited a fragment of sawdust in the afternoon and that had gone unnoticed when the hoosie was closed shortly before dusk."

Whatever the cause, Mrs. Craig discovered "to her great mortification, that half the precious catch of fish had been 'damaged' by smoke and they were now golden yellow in color.

"She decided they were still edible, however, and as she set out on her journey, her creel was filled with fresh white fish. But on her arm she carried a basketful of the smoke-damaged haddocks. As she walked along the country roads, she offered each of her customers a gift of the smoked fish. In those days of hardship, there were few to refuse such bounty.

"To her astonishment, when she returned to these customers a few days later, she was repeatedly beseeched for fresh supplies of the 'smoked yellow haddocks.'

"In that brief period, according to family records, finnan haddie came about. From that day on, the sawdust in the 'hoosie' was deliberately set alight and allowed to smolder. The fish drying houses became kilns, and another cottage industry was born.

"You come to Scotland and I can assure you of, one, a warm welcome and, two, a plate of 'yellow smoked haddock' poached in milk or fried with bacon and eggs, and you will come to understand that Northeast folks over here know what's good for them."

The proper way to poach finnan haddie for breakfast or brunch is to place it (defrosted if frozen) in a skillet with water barely to cover. Add about half a cup of milk and, if desired, one bay leaf, two cloves, and two slices of onion. Bring to the boil but do not boil. Let the haddock gently simmer about two minutes or until the fish is piping hot. Do not cook long or it will toughen and become fibrous. Drain the fish, spoon it onto hot plates, and pour hot melted butter over it. Serve immediately with lemon halves on the side and a pepper mill for those who wish it. After a first course of freshly squeezed orange juice, serve the fish with buttered, boiled potatoes, buttered toast, marmalade, and tea or champagne. Breakfast coffee is not a suitable drink with smoked fish.

§ § §

If I were to name the single most invidious, burdensome learning that best exemplifies the perfidious nature of my education from kindergarten through college it would be the following:

"The square of the hypotenuse is equal to the sum of the squares of the other two sides."

I was told to learn that in junior high school and to this day I do not know why. I had it drilled into me. I was queried about it on several final examinations. Over the years I have lain awake nights thinking and brooding about it.

Who cares about a hypotenuse? Who cares what it is equal to? Why was my brain burdened with such nonsense?

I am angry. I am angry because I was hounded by various teachers to learn the difference between a transitive and intransitive verb. I had to learn to parse sentences. Or at least to pretend that I knew how to parse sentences. And to this day, I don't know how to pass muster when it comes to parsing. I was taught at some point to use a slide rule. And on and on and on they attempted to cram my so-called brain with nonsense that has been totally useless to me for these three score and more years.

Why was there nobody in that vast school system out there to lead me by the hand? Educate. From the Latin *educare* and *educere.* To lead. To bring out. I doubt that a handful of the teachers and professors whom I met over the years had the slightest notion of the origins of the word educate. They did not lead me. They dragged me and jerked me about and, for the most part, it seemed to me, in the wrong direction.

No one bothered to discover that my natural bent was toward literature and the humanities.

If there are certain lapses in my memory because of childhood amnesia, there are even more stunning lapses in my memory with regard to my schooling beyond high school. I have pitifully small and unpleasant recollections of my days in college.

In the beginning I was encouraged by my mother, God knows why, to become a doctor. And thus I enrolled in premedical work at the age of eighteen at Mississippi State College in Starkville, Mississippi. My curriculum included such (for me) imponderables as calculus and chemistry, science and geometry.

There, I was as much disturbed by my daily life as I was by the subjects that were part of my daily "training." In that my brother—a professor of engineering at the college—belonged to a fraternity and in that he lorded it over me, it was unthinkable that I not join his fraternity. I suspect that there was some form of sibling rivalry between us, but I forget what occasioned it. In the first place, he "played sports," and I considered him a bit of a lame-brain because of it.

Nonetheless, I duly joined Pi Kappa Alpha, and what I remember most about those "fraternal" years is having to "assume the position," which is to say bend over "to have your butt paddled" or "your ass spanked." I endured all this in silence. I also, at the behest without appeal of my fellow "brothers" and upperclassmen, trotted their dirty clothes to the laundry. And, ah those early smokers. All the young men sat around smoking cigars that perfumed the air with such a stench that to this day I hold cigars in vilest esteem.

Even more memorable were the initiation rites, the evenings when in the semi-darkness they would approach the quaking freshmen with a sizable number of large, heavy volumes tied into a bundle with a trailing string. The freshman was "encouraged" to mount a ladder or chair and to stand there naked as the abbreviated trailing cord was tied around his testicles. He was then blindfolded. He was handed the heavy compact load of books and instructed in harsh tones to drop them.

Oh, God! Before the books were dropped, of course, the cord had been severed with a knife.

I was mired in educational quicksand. Good Lord, I detested my "learning." I got the vapors at the scent of formaldehyde, fainted at the sight of blood, and at the midpoint of my sophomore year, I did not, to my recollection, have a passing mark in any of my studies.

While in high school I had done some writing, terrible poems and an essay or two, and it was decided that I had some talent for it. I don't know who decided that and am not sure that I was instrumental in the decision. I believe I was. I think that David Sanders' faith in my ability to spell and run two sentences together with some flair helped, and the University of Missouri was decided on. That, I believe, was my decision. I had heard that Eugene Field had once attended school there and I had a childhood passion for the writings of Field.

Could it be that I was tantalized at a very early age by his poem:

When I demanded of my friend what viands he preferred, He quoth: "A large cold bottle, and a small hot bird!"

And I could quote "Wynken, Blynken, and Nod" from the time of the cradle.

The university also boasted that its journalism school was the oldest in the world.

I most certainly did not distinguish myself at the University of Missouri. I lived at the fraternity house, was treated there with some respect, and had a few limited friends in the house. I actually came to look on some of them as "brothers" in the loosest use of that word.

But I was poor and miserable and brooded over the cost of this "education" to my family.

There are great gaps of memory relating to my stay at the university. The memories that I do have are a bit bizarre by some standards.

I remember a formal dance to which I was invited. I had a girl friend whom I liked a lot, Ida Mack Keith. The dance was for the entire student body and I did not have formal clothing. Not even a black tie.

My mother had a nephew by marriage, a well-to-do in-law whom she considered the absolute end of masculine refinement, who lived in Knoxville, Tennessee. His name was Ernest Dooley and he had been born into money. And he, obviously, although advancing in years, undoubtedly had formal attire. After my mother's imploring, Ernest delved into the family cedar closet in the attic and came forth with a pair of formal trousers and a striped, swallow-tailed coat, which he proceeded to ship to me.

When this splendid bit of haberdashery arrived, I tried it on and it fit perfectly. I admired my image as a swain. I sent the clothes to the cleaner and they came back deftly wrapped in white tissue paper.

On the evening of the dance, moments before I was to fetch Ida Mack, I donned these refinements and put on my well-worn second-hand shoes, inherited some months earlier from my brother. As I bent over to tie the laces, there was a loud and sudden rip and the rear trousers were hopelessly in tatters. Instant amnesia. I have no further memories of that evening including whether I fetched Ida Mack and whether we went to the dance or not. Chances are I got drunk.

It would seem that throughout half my life, my memory had been a collector of embarrassing incidents in which my mother played a role.

I look back with some awe and uncomprehension at the fact that at the University of Missouri I wrote a musical comedy. This is nothing that was ever recorded in the annals of the school.

It was a dreadful little effort called *Much Ado About Mary.*

The reason for my writing the show in the first place was an annual stage event at the university called, in those days, the "Savitar Frolics." This was a now-defunct University of Missouri version of Harvard's Hasty Pudding Show and the University of Pennsylvania's Mask and Wig Show.

The plot of my less than riotous comedy concerned a lady of loose morals named Mary O'Toole, who had become pregnant by an unknown lover. This unsavory bit of baggage was in love with a splendid, handsome football hero named Peter, a campus idol.

The villain of the piece, Dirty Dan McGee, was a licentious quarterback who detested Peter's sterling character and who hit upon a scheme to undermine Peter's good reputation. Dan spread the base rumor that Mary had been impregnated by Peter, all this to encourage the school authorities to dismiss him.

The conclusion came when all the members of the football team rallied around Peter, each of them declaring that he had impregnated Mary and each insisting that he was the father of the child. Curtain with rousing chorus.

Curiously enough, I also wrote the words and music for this ill-conceived vehicle. I cannot write a score, but I composed the lyrics to fit melodies that I hummed over and over to myself. One of these songs was a sentimental ballad called "God Gave Me a Heart."

"God gave me a heart,
Gave me a soul, that I might love you more each day.

God answered my prayer,
Made my only dream of love come true,

And most of all God gave me you."

A second was a spirited fox trot titled, "Out of My Mind."

"Out of my mind,
I loved you out of my mind,
Just like a contract drawn up and signed . . .

Out of my soul,
I loved you out of my soul,
And that's one thing I con't control

And some day you will be sweetly,
And so indiscreetly,
Out of my mind, out of my mind." Oh God!

I was rather proud of my juvenile efforts and made the grievous error of writing some of the details of my composition to my mother. To my supreme embarrassment, and typically, she called a senator from Mississippi and tried to have him use his influence to have the Savitar Committee select *Much Ado About Mary,* as the production of the year.

I cringed in humiliation and felt a curious, sublimated loathing for my own mother.

Other than that the days that I spent at the University of Missouri seem highly forgettable and insignificant.

Like most Americans of a thinking age in that era, I do recall in depth the events of the afternoon of December 7, 1941, and the announcement of the dropping of the bombs on Pearl Harbor. I was sitting at my typewriter writing a letter to my friend Gordon Lyon, who was an air force cadet at the University of Mississippi, and simultaneously listening to the NBC Symphony under Toscanini.

And war was declared and I was interviewed by the U. S. Navy in the form of a chief petty officer who had come to the Missouri campus to select those who would be qualified for officer training. I was rejected for the rather peculiar reason that I had a malocclusion of the upper and lower teeth, but I wanted to go into the Navy and was told by one petty officer that if I knew how to type I could enter the service as a yeoman, third class. In that I didn't know a petty officer from an admiral I agreed enthusiastically to take typing lessons, which I did, a six-week crash course. On the ninth day of June in the year of our Lord one thousand nine hundred and forty-two I received a sheepskin diploma, declaring me a bachelor of journalism. Within a month I had donned my navy blue uniform and become a yeoman, which was, in those days, a male secretary in uniform. Officially I was known as a yeoman, third class. I stress "officially" for I would dislike to be known as a third-class anything, including idiot.

My naval uniform was issued at the Great Lakes Training Center outside Chicago. I was a gangling, acne-faced youth from Mississippi, weight 120 pounds, height 5 feet 11 inches, and totally mystified about the ways of the world. I had drunk lots of beer in college (I also recall drinking scotch with Coca-Cola over ice in those days) but I had never sampled a glass of wine and the most sophisticated, exotic food that I had sampled was jellied consommé madrilène, and that I remember well. I had eaten it for lunch during the Chicago World's Fair, where I had gone with Ruth Davis, a grownup from my home town in Mississippi. Ruth and I had dined that day on arrival in Chicago at Central Station and the taste of that soup, onto which I had sprinkled lemon juice from the wedge perched on the edge of my saucer (the soup was served in a coffee cup), was like chilled but heavenly manna. On reflection I know that it was inevitably out of a can.

My first assignment in the Navy was in the intelligence division located in the Board of Trade Building in Chicago. I was bored with my duties, which largely involved typing form letters, sorting mail, and stuffing envelopes.

So when a cable came through from the naval headquarters in Puerto Rico asking for additional communications personnel, I volunteered for the simple reason that most of my friends and acquaintances from high school and college days were serving overseas and I thought that duty in Chicago, or in America for that matter, didn't sound very patriotic. The Board of Trade Building was certainly not an adventurous place to be. And as far as I knew they were waging battles in Puerto Rico.

I was shipped out, as they say, but not to Puerto Rico. I was sent to Norfolk, Virginia, one of the chief and most important naval ports during the war.

But I *thought* I was en route to Puerto Rico and we were under strict command for security reasons not to divulge our official orders, destinations, or arrival. Mother love, however, superseded government regulations and I felt that I could not leave America without informing my mother. I telephoned her from a private phone booth, deploring the fact that the call might be intercepted. I did not tell her my destination, but that I was leaving the country and it wasn't Europe. For some reason, my orders were altered and I found myself going to Norfolk on a ferry boat in the month of July 1942.

I was going about my yeomanry duties with more enthusiasm than in Chicago because of the movement of ships, large and small, out of that port. There was also a great deal of secrecy of an increasingly hushed nature along about October. I was still typing letters, sorting mail, and stuffing envelopes. But toward the end of the month I was typing mimeograph forms for something called Operation Torch.

Around the end of October a curious thing happened. I had heard from a fellow yeoman that large things were afoot that were not to be discussed. And on that evening, I had a telephone call from someone in the Navy Department, whose identity I did not know and do not know to this day. He informed me that I was to be given orders to go overseas. But the mysterious revelation came next. He asked if I *wanted* to go on a very dangerous mission. I told him yes. It occurred to me later that my mother was somehow involved in that telephone call. I have to this day a sincere feeling that I was about to be ordered to the invasion of North Africa and somehow she had got to Senator Eastland of Mississippi and demanded that I not be sent overseas. The Navy had opted to give me a choice in the matter.

I was shortly ordered to duty aboard the U.S.S. *Augusta,* a heavy cruiser. I was given a steamy bunk below decks and had to march down several ladders to get to my quarters, which were inhabited by several hundred other gobs or swabbies as we were sometimes referred to. I was on duty each day in the radio and communications "shack," and I was simply told that we were on routine naval training maneuvers.

My principal duties seemed to me then to be childish and absurd. I was given a list of several hundred names and told to simply write nouns, words that didn't relate and were pertinent to nothing in particular. Just random nouns.

We were halfway across the Atlantic when a shipmate whispered to me in the most confidential manner that we were approaching Casablanca for the North African invasion. During that first week in November, there was a lot of military talk over the loudspeakers, talk relating to the invasion, and suddenly I heard familiar words coming out of the air. They were my nouns. I had been sitting for hours on end on previous days unknowingly making up code names for the invasion, known as Operation Torch.

Although I participated in the invasion of Morocco (my boat actually anchored at Fedala near Casablanca during the fighting) and I was witness to an awful lot of bombardment and more than a little carnage,

I was not devastated by the sight. I do not say it as a mark of an odd kind of innocent courage but I was not afraid. The entire show was beyond my comprehension and seemed more like a celluloid spectacle, something called "The March of Time" I might have viewed on a movie screen. I watched ships sink, bodies fall overboard, and the gunfire was deafening.

My ship anchored on the morning of November 8, 1942. Shortly thereafter I experienced one of the most exalting, joyous, goose-bump-making moments of my life. I was standing aboard the front deck of the U.S.S. *Augusta* when a voice boomed over the loudspeaker that the enemy had surrendered and that the beaches belonged to the Allies. The news itself was not nearly as devastating to me emotionally as what followed. Somewhere aboard that ship, someone had put on a recording of Albert Schweitzer playing Bach's "Toccata and Fugue in D Minor," an absolutely ear-splitting, breathtaking, all-engulfing sound, as if trumpets from heaven were blaring from that loudspeaker. Tears welled in my eyes and I was not ashamed. I was unbearably proud of the feeling. Glory to God in the Highest.

As far as the Navy was concerned, I was not scheduled to remain in North Africa. In the normal course of events, I was to return to America on that cruiser. But a day or so later my boat moved closer inshore at Casablanca and I borrowed a pair of binoculars. And in that moment I got my first glimpse of that splendid city with its spires and domes and camels and natives in their burnooses and robes, and I ached to be a part of that landscape. It was a desire too outlandish to contemplate seriously.

The admiral aboard the *Augusta* was one of the most brilliant, warm, and handsome men I had ever encountered, John Leslie Hall, a Virginian. Admiral Hall, as it turned out, played a sizable role in my life. Although I had never met him, I had admired his seemingly indomitable figure from a distance and I was awed by his presence.

During the crossing on the cruiser and while I was concocting those code words, my immediate superior had been a lieutenant from Michigan named Donald McQueen, with whom, although I was a mere enlisted man and he an officer of some rank, I had got along admirably. We had had many friendly conversations, some of which had gone beyond the ordinary course of an officer-enlisted man relationship.

On the morning that I had my first glimpse of Casablanca, I saw McQueen strolling on the deck and mentioned that I had a great, highly unrealistic, and romantic desire to go ashore.

"Why not?" he asked, half mockingly.

"If only," I said.

"Why not ask Admiral Hall to let you join us?"

"What do you mean?" I asked.

"Hall," he said, "is getting off the ship to go ashore as Commander in Chief of U. S. Naval Forces, Northwest African Waters. He'll be stationed in Casablanca and I'm to join him as flag lieutenant." That is to say that McQueen would be a personal military aide to the commander.

I don't know what on earth gave me the temerity or audacity to do what I did. But one of my mother's most frequent biblical quotations kept hammering in my brain. "Ask, and it shall be given you; knock, and it shall be opened unto you." I walked up to the bridge where Admiral Hall was standing and introduced myself. A genuine greenhorn before a towering giant.

"Admiral Hall," I began. "You're going ashore and I wonder if you don't need a secretary to join you. I'm a pretty good typist."

He smiled, the kindest, most benevolent smile I've ever seen. Who knows? Perhaps he liked my southern accent. Or perhaps he felt he just might need a "good secretary."

"Can you shoot a gun?" he asked me.

"I could learn," I said.

"Well, get yourself a gun and speak to Lieutenant McQueen. We'll go ashore tomorrow."

To say that I was ecstatic would be putting it mildly. I could have kissed that deck with happiness!

We did go ashore and I checked into a vast warehouse sort of place with a dirt floor and animal dung from one end of the building to the other. There were hastily rigged folding beds spaced about one foot apart. The quarters had been, I soon learned, an old camel barn. I couldn't have cared less. In my state of bliss, the aroma could have rivaled the best perfumes of Araby.

World War II was, of course, the last of the holy wars. To die in it for the cause of humanity and justice was to elevate your soul to God and I would have willingly given my life, although at that point I had never loved life more. Simply being involved in uniform was a supreme moment, the ultimate time in hundreds of thousands of lives of soldiers and sailors all over the world. And never again would they live in such a state of exaltation.

I have of that war thousands of trivial recollections. The city of Casablanca was largely left unharmed by bombing and I succumbed to the mysteries of the place. We would furtively walk around the small, winding, labyrinthine streets of the Casbah. I was fascinated by the many soldiers and sailors who would come out of those half-dark doorways, some still buttoning their trouser fronts. Prophylactic stations were to be found on many streets nearby. With my sense of hygiene and smothered propriety I would never have dared enter one of those doorways, even if that had been my inclination. But I was intrigued by the wicked will of my counterparts who did.

I remember getting in a jeep and traveling around the Moroccan countryside with McQueen. We would stop in villages at noon and find some place to dine. The menu was invariably roast chicken, sautéed potatoes, with luck a simple salad, and a bottle or two of red Moroccan wine.

The most memorable feast, however, and one that I swear to this day gave me my initial, unquenchable interest in food and food preparation, was in the home of a native Moroccan. I do not recall his name nor do I recall the precise reason why we had been invited into his neat, modest, but colorful home in Casablanca.

The invitation came to me from Lieutenant McQueen and we drove together to the home from whose kitchen came some of the most elegant and, to my uneducated nose, exotic aromas I had ever known. There was the blended scent of spices that I would later come to know in depth—cumin, coriander, cinnamon, saffron, and ginger. We sat down to dine after consuming a bottle or two of Moroccan red (the wine was offered, I suspect, as a gesture of hospitality to American guests; in Moroccan homes the ordinary drink with couscous is a very sweet, mint-flavored tea).

We were seated, as is the Moroccan custom, on the floor, which was lined with bright, multi-colored pillows. For the first time in my life I ate with my fingers, no knives and forks, as is customary in that country. We were served magnificent lamb couscous with sweet dried fruits and that best of all hot sauces, harissa, a fiery blend of chilies and coriander. For dessert there were sections of some of the sweetest oranges I have ever eaten. Minted tea was served with the dessert.

I also had my first taste of genuine French cooking in Casablanca. Food in those lean years was hard to come by and in one of my long walks through the city I discovered a restaurant called La Comédie. Oddly, because of protocol, I never invited Lieutenant McQueen to join me. Although we traveled together on weekends, it would not have been proper, I believe, for him to have been seen dining with an enlisted man in a public and well-frequented spot.

La Comédie was charming and like a well-run French bistro. I have, oddly enough, no great memories of the menu and am fairly certain that it contained mostly simple grilled chicken and egg dishes. I made the acquaintance of a Monsieur and Madame Dupont and spent a good deal of time in their company, referring to them as Maman and Papa. On my days off I was often in their home where, once more, we dined on roast chicken or an omelet.

It was also in the town that I first discovered French pastries. There were a few patisseries in the heart of town and I would walk past, occasionally stopping in to buy a small barquette or tartlet, and in these I first sampled pastry cream, or *crème pâtissière,* topped with various fruits such as plums, apple slices, or cherries. My absolute favorite was a small tart with a pastry cream filling topped with cooked, seedless tangerine sections, and glazed with a tangerine jelly.

Admiral Hall remained in Casablanca for about eight months, and then his command was transferred to Oran. The core of our administrative staff was small and to negotiate the move from Casablanca, each of us was assigned a staff vehicle. We drove in convoy (Admiral Hall had flown to Oran in a military plane), me at the helm of a four-wheel-drive jeep, and it was, to tell the truth, a great moment in my life. Sitting at that steering wheel and crossing the Atlas mountains and plains through Meknes and Fez, I felt for the first time a sweet surge of masculinity I had never known before. I was the Alexander Selkirk all my childhood dreamed of being. ("I am monarch of all I survey, My right there is none to dispute.")

I have one outrageous memory of that trip. One early morning with the sun crashing down on the rough road bed, we stopped at an American army encampment to ask for a breakfast ration. It was a primitive setup with tents, a special tent for the kitchen "mess" with stoves, latrines, and so on. The latrine was a slit trench with powdered lime to be used for sanitation purposes.

We ate in the mess. The breakfast menu consisted of canned fruit juice, scrambled eggs that had been prepared from a powdered state, reconstituted milk, and fried Spam. Plus coffee and a fairly decent if somewhat stale bread that apparently had been brought in from some local bakery. In my hunger, I downed this banquet with some enthusiasm and before resuming our dusty journey on that hot highway went, for the first time in my life, to an army latrine. I had barely put my foot in the area when I smelled the natural odors of human elimination and lime. I quickly ran to one side and vomited, retching uncontrollably. It occurred to me in that moment that there was a wider gulf between me and my brother than I had ever imagined. If that was the infantry, in which he rose to be a colonel, he was more than welcome to it. While outdoor latrines, K-rations, and the barracks life might suit him to a T, they were not for me. The Navy, to my innocent mind, meant hot meals, a comfortable bed, flushing toilets, and, most important, afloat or ashore, a shower with hot and cold running water. Curiously enough, throughout my various stints in the Navy, I was privileged through fate to have those things.

It is trivial, of course, but one of my favorite memories of Navy life concerns a Sunday afternoon when my ship was moored in one of the Southern ports in the mouth of an English river, Portsmouth, I believe.

I had gone ashore with my best friend, another sailor named Anthony Joseph Reno, and we had taken a train to Torquay, one of the most appealing of English costal towns.

I had heard of something called "high tea," and was encouraged to ask Tony to join me for an hour or so in an English tea room that I had spotted some days before.

We walked from the train station to the restaurant and there, posted at the entrance was a sign that declared, "No prams allowed."

We hesitated and walked away. We didn't know if we were prams or not.

My stay in Oran was largely uneventful. I was still the admiral's secretary and remember little else except walks around the harbor and one expedition to Algiers, where I saw Franz Lehár's *The Land of Smiles,* with a cast (at least to me) of unknowns. But a momentous thing happened in Oran, an incident that involved a case of slight deception and about which I still feel a tinge of guilt and personal chagrin.

I was devoted to Admiral Hall. And he trusted me like a son. He had such implicit faith in himself and the infallibility of my shorthand and typing that he never perused a letter that he had dictated.

In September of 1943, a directive was issued throughout the Navy by the Bureau of Naval Personnel asking superior officers to recommend enlisted men for training in what was officially designated Class V-7, and unofficially referred to as training for "90-day Wonders." That is, officer training at any of various colleges and schools around America, from which one would graduate as an ensign.

When the directive passed my desk for delivery to Admiral Hall, I took immediate note of it. And sat down to type a letter of recommendation directed to the Bureau of Naval Personnel in Washington that I be sent back to America for Class V-7 training. I sent this through Admiral Hall, adding in my own words his recommendation of approval: "During this period he has performed his duties capably and efficiently." I still have the papers in my naval files at home.

Admiral Hall, when I covertly composed his endorsement, was in Algiers for a brief visit. Before he returned I inserted this letter of endorsement amid a good deal of correspondence awaiting his signature. When he returned to his desk, he asked me to usher in a visitor. And as he talked to the visitor he signed his correspondence.

I do not know to this day if Admiral Hall read the recommendation before signing. But sign it he did and it was duly in the mail within minutes.

Because of his signed endorsement there was small doubt in my mind that I would shortly be on my way back to the United States. And I had one great source of regret. I knew in confidence that we were planning the invasion of the Continent via France and I longed to be a part of it. I counted a commission more valuable, however, for the end of the war was a long way off.

Meantime, Admiral Hall and his staff, including myself, boarded a communications vessel known as the *Ancon, AGC-4*. It would be simple to say that I merely bided my time until the letter from the Bureau of Naval Personnel arrived. But a nasty bit of fate intervened.

The *Ancon* was berthed one winter's day in late 1943 in the coastal city of Portsmouth in southeast England. I had gone ashore that afternoon on "liberty," and about five o'clock stopped by a local pub. I ordered one scotch, then another and another. I had not drunk more than I was accustomed to, nor enough to shove me into oblivion. But I shortly arrived at that state and how it happened I will never know. There is a remote possibility that I had been drugged but it seems unlikely.

What I do know is that liberty expired at nine o'clock, the time when all good sailors in the harbor were supposed to catch the liberty boats back to their respective vessels. At that hour, I was passed out beyond recall and came to in bed at the local YMCA at four o'clock in the morning, seven hours late. I was in an understandable state of agitation. Not only was I late but my pea coat, which would shield me from the bitter cold of that British morning, was missing. And worse, perhaps, where navy discipline was concerned, my white sailor's cap was nowhere to be found.

In those days it was essential that you wear that cap at all times when not under cover, which is to say in an unsheltered, unroofed place. And in the navy tradition, you had to have that cap on when you saluted. I made the only hasty decision that conformed to logic. I would return to the dock and grab the first work boat that would return to the *Ancon* with the day's provisions. I walked for several miles to the dock and explained my dilemma to the crew, all of them enlisted men and sympathetic. They agreed to let me go up the ship's ladder laden with one provision or another, a sack of potatoes, a crate of milk, or whatever.

At 7 A.M. when the work boat arrived at the *Ancon,* the crew stood up, myself alongside them, and each of us hoisted a load of food to our shoulders. One by one we marched up the ship's ladder and, as each of us got to the gangplank on the boat deck, we saluted the officer of the day standing watch. When my turn came, I saluted, hatless. As I walked on, the ensign in charge stared at me in disbelief, mentally scratching his head in wonder. I took two steps more and started to turn a corner when he yelled "SAILOR!"

I went back and, true to regulation, he pulled out a slip and fountain pen. He asked my name, informed me that I was several hours over leave, and put me on report, which is to say that I would have to stand by to be "tried" at the captain's mast, whenever it was held. He signed the report slip Ensign William Hill.

I was in a state of anguish and torture. If I were convicted for failing to return to the boat on time, I would be punished and this would go on my record, which would, without question, prevent my return to the States for officer training.

I was still on Admiral Hall's staff and my chief petty officer, my immediate superior, was a nice, kindly fellow named John House. John and I were not close friends, but we did enjoy each other's company and occasionally, when ashore, would share a beer together.

John was well aware that I was waiting for that magic missive from the Navy that would eventually get me a commission and, in friendship, he spoke to the Master at Arms of the *Ancon* and explained my predicament. The Master at Arms, a sort of sheriff where discipline aboard the vessel was concerned, riffled through the report slips and withdrew the one with my name on it. He did not destroy it. He simply slid it aside. If no one made a stink, it would eventually be ignored, in which case it would be tossed into the trash or the sea.

I lived in a private hell. Once a day, Chief House would come to me and say that Ensign Hill was questioning the Master at Arms as to the slip on the sailor who had come aboard after liberty had expired. The Master at Arms would stall him with one excuse or another.

About a week later, the blessed letter arrived from the Bureau of Naval Personnel ordering me to go to Notre Dame in South Bend, Indiana, for officer training. A day or so later, my affairs in order but the report incident still unfinished, I wrapped my belongings in my white sleeping bag, which I neatly tied with lines, naval fashion, and filled my "ditty" bag with incidentals.

I carried the possessions topside, making ready to go down that ladder for the last time. Who do you suppose had the duty at the gangplank? Ensign Billy Hill! I prayed for death. Mine or his.

He looked at me without a gleam to indicate that he recognized in me a culprit or lawbreaker.

He smiled and asked, "Where ya going, sailor?" I thought surely the jig was up. I expected to be commanded to go back to my quarters.

I told him that I was going back to the States for officer training. He grinned from ear to ear, his white teeth showing. He grabbed my packed sleeping bag, hoisted it over his right shoulder, and preceded me down the ladder. As I stepped into the liberty launch I turned and looked at him. He saluted.

I returned the salute, fighting back tears.

That was in January 1944, and I enrolled at Notre Dame the following month. I graduated without honors but with the rank of ensign and subsequently was sent back to England as executive officer of a submarine chaser, notably *SC 1330.*

As I have noted, I had one major regret about going back to America. Admiral Hall and his staff were involved in the invasion of northern France at Cherbourg and I missed it.

Too much talk of one's military career is like a surfeit of popcorn or having one too many Cognacs in the course of a long evening. For what it's worth, I was, during my career, involved and present not only at the invasion of North Africa but of Italy and Sicily as well.

After I became an ensign and served in the English Channel as executive officer of one submarine chaser, I was transferred to the Pacific for the mopping-up operations there. I served once more aboard a submarine chaser, this one the *SC 1036,* and participated to whatever small degree in the invasion of Okinawa and was present in Japanese waters at the time of surrender. I was witness to several direct attacks of kamikaze aircraft flying into the sides of aircraft carriers at Okinawa but, like my earliest adventure in the Navy during the invasion of North Africa, it looked like something theatrical and somehow removed from my very own uniformed existence. Aboard that last sub chaser we spent most of our time, however, in Okinawa, running from one typhoon anchorage to another. At one point the ship was outfitted with German mine-sweeping gear and we were *supposed* to sweep mines. We had the distinction of being the first American vessel to enter the East China Sea after the defeat of Japan, and there were mines everywhere. But we survived. Every time we launched our mine-sweeping gear, it sank.

I was aboard that boat when the war ended around the world and there was a mass exodus of naval personnel, both officers and enlisted men, from bases ashore and all the ships at sea. And the skipper of my vessel declared that his time was up and that I was wholly competent to take command. It was a curious, bizarre, and stupefying situation. Here was the commanding officer giving me a command to assume command and what could I say? In all of navy history there has probably never been a more incompetent navigator or communications expert than I. It was not only that in my assuming command I would be endangering the operation of one naval vessel. There was the crew of one officer and twenty enlisted men. The quartermaster—an enlisted man of enormous talent—who had done all the navigating aboard had gone home, leaving only an eager but not too skillful junior to replace him. And other key personnel had returned to the States, leaving the boat horribly understaffed.

Besides which, the boat itself was in terrible circumstances. As I have noted, we spent most of our time not fighting an enemy, but hurrying from one typhoon anchorage to another to avoid hurricanes, which were all too frequent in Okinawan waters. We would tie up at close quarters, generally sandwiched between two other submarine chasers, and we all had wooden hulls. My boat's hull had sprung leaks in several places but these had gone unreported by my predecessors and colleagues just in case the war ended and, who knows, maybe the boat would sink.

Nonetheless, I became skipper. I was called into the office of the port director at Naha, Okinawa, and told that my ship was to be returned to America with me at the helm.

I begged his pardon, but, I stated, I would not accept the responsibility of taking that boat anywhere without a navigational escort. I told him the sorry truth about the *SC 1036*. The radar did not function. Therefore, navigation had to be done with an automatic compass that had not been calibrated in several years. The other important piece of navigational equipment was a brass sextant that was corroded. And lastly, we had a radio setup in which we could receive messages but could not transmit.

He agreed to let us sail the next day with a tanker soon en route to Hawaii and, once there, we could have all necessary repairs made.

We sailed on schedule with the tanker and got to Guam, where we refueled. Our capacity for fuel was extremely limited.

About halfway between Guam and Hawaii, with several hundred miles still to go, a message came to us in the middle of the night from the skipper of the tanker that his vessel had broken down and to proceed independently. "Flags," as the signalman was known, was a youngster of about twenty who ran down into my cabin with the transmission.

He wakened me in the middle of the night.

"Skipper, skipper, we're supposed to sail alone."

"Are you nuts?" I asked him. "Go send a signal and tell him we are staying. We'll circle him until help comes."

The signalman left and, within seconds, the entire crew crawled hurriedly down the ladder into my cabin. "But, skipper, let's go! We can make it. Our wives and sweethearts are waiting for us."

I personally couldn't navigate a small boat across the pond in Central Park with any hope of getting to the other side. But, foolishly, I succumbed and at dawn we got underway.

We did a lot of what is called dead reckoning. Somebody tried to polish up the sextant to make it reasonably, but only reasonably, accurate. Someone got out a pencil to determine how much we would have to compensate to make the numbers on the compass halfway accurate. Someone volunteered that it was off twenty-five degrees.

And by the light of the sun and the stars and the grace of God, two or three days later, without mishap, we sailed directly into Honolulu Harbor. No one was sure, of course, that that was where we were but as someone else said, "This must be the place."

When I stepped ashore, as my luck would have it, the first person I met was an old college roommate who was in charge of personnel at the shipyard. He became convinced of my total incompetence and, through his friendship and good offices, I was fortunately relieved of my command. I sailed back to the United States on an aircraft carrier and the voyage is a complete blank in my memory. On the fourth of February, 1946, I was officially released from military duties.

I have medals and papers to prove most of the facts in this account. But I only bring them out for Hallowe'en parties.

§ § §

Relatively speaking, but only relatively, I had had a glorious war. I had seen and fallen in love with Casablanca, I had sampled my first taste of "foreign" food in the form of couscous, I had tasted family-style French cooking—roast chicken and omelets and salads with *sauce vinaigrette* and tarts filled with pastry cream. Drunk my first wine. I had traveled around England and Scotland, sailed the waters of the Clyde and Forth Rivers, visited Robert Burns's birthplace in Ayrshire, and learned to my great delight, and thanks to a navigational chart on my small craft, the origin of the name Craig. It is, among other things, steep rock rising out of Scottish waters that is used as a navigational aid. When recently in Scotland I was told the name most frequently refers to "a rough, rocky cliff. Craggy." Craig is also, more appropriately perhaps in my case, defined in The Oxford English Dictionary as the neck or throat. It cites as one Scottish usage "Pit that ower yer craig." Translated, it means "swallow that." "It's all away down Craig's close," means that it has been swallowed.

§ § §

When I left the Navy, my future was as open as it was opaque. My options were devastating and overwhelming because I was not accustomed to making decisions, at least not of a serious sort. Chicago? New York?

I knew better where I didn't want to go than the direction in which to travel. I didn't want to go home to the cares of cotton and boarding-house living and live burial in a family bosom. I had tasted enough personal freedom in the service. An important factor as well, I felt that my sexual needs would be poorly served in a small town in the Mississippi Delta.

New York was, to my mind, far too glamorous and sophisticated. The people there were all rich and carried on nifty repartee as they sipped their cocktails for two in some secluded rendezvous each afternoon at five before heading for 21 or the Stork Club and later to Harlem to dance the night away. Broadway babies don't sleep tight until the dawwwwn . . . or so the songwriter said. No, no. New York was an upper and I was a downer.

For some reason, mostly because I had met a couple of nice guys from there, Chicago sounded quiet, comfortable, a town large enough to get "lost" in. They didn't have Broadway. They didn't have Times Square. As far as I knew, they didn't even have an opera house or a fine arts museum.

There are a few curious things about my separation from the navy.

I do not recall the place of my separation.

I do not recall when or where I shed my naval uniform.

I have no recollection of the greeting I received on my return home. Nor do I recall going there.

I do not recall seeing my father and mother for the first time.

Between the time of that separation from the military and my "civilian" life, there is a mental gulf that extends over a period not only of weeks but of months.

I went to Chicago to live in late spring or the early summer of 1946. I moved into a small apartment on LaSalle Street and the thing that impressed me most was that it was necessary to use a communal toilet in the hallway. It was a circumstance that I tolerated for thirty days (I had given the landlord a month's pay in advance). I picked up my belongings and moved into an apartment hotel with all comforts one block south of Evanston, and the following December I went home for the Christmas holidays. I know that I went home because of an inscription in the first cookbook I ever owned, a gift from my sister.

The book was the 1943 edition of *The Joy of Cooking* by Irma S. Rombauer. The inscription in my sister's handwriting is "Always remember to wash the fowl . . . The merriest Christmas of all, 1946. Sister."

The book, to which I still refer for sentimental reasons, gained much use in the small apartment which I occupied. Silent testimony to that fact is that there is no longer a spine on the volume and the pages are well stained with the juices of one roast, one sauce, or another.

The "fowl" to which my sister referred was one of my first ventures in cooking as a bachelor. In that period of my life, I seriously believe I was demented.

When I was a child, most if not all the chickens cooked in my home were slaughtered in my family's back yard and cooked the same day or the day after. The first chicken I cooked in Chicago had been bought in a supermarket and contained the neck, liver, gizzard, and so on, wrapped in paper and stuffed inside. When I brought the chicken back to my small kitchen, I simply salted and peppered it on the outside and shoved it in the oven. I had not bothered to remove the paper-wrapped giblets and the chicken, when taken from the oven, possessed a stench that appalled the nose.

To this date, nearly forty years later, I find that whole incident unthinkable, but it must have happened. My sister had laughed with delight and thus the inscription.

In addition to *The Joy of Cooking,* that Christmas my sister had also given me a chafing dish and two freshly killed pheasants.

I had taken the train from Memphis to Chicago and arrived in the midst of a blinding snowstorm. Taxis on that December evening were at a standstill when the train pulled into Central Station at 10 P.M. or thereabouts and I had to walk at least a dozen blocks, the snow ankle-deep, clutching that chafing dish, which had been compactly packaged, under one arm. I reached a subway stop and went to my small apartment.

I had read somewhere—*Gourmet* magazine, perhaps—that game should be "hung" before cooking.

My father was an occasional hunter and often came home in late fall with a sack full of partridge and quail, which were always eaten the next day. And the weather in the Mississippi Delta would not have been conducive to hanging game in the first place. It was too mild.

In any event, I arrived in my Chicago "digs" and unpacked *Joy,* the chafing dish, and the game birds, which I proceeded to hang. I found a piece of string which I tied around each bird's neck. I then looped the string around the faucet of the kitchen sink.

There is no need to dramatize this further except to say that if this was Thursday, I had invited guests to dine on pheasant the following Saturday evening. Along about Friday night, the stench was unbearable and I tossed the birds out the window and into a foot or more of snow. I have no earthly recollection of what I fed my guests that weekend.

One of the chief pleasures of those weekends, though, occurred on those rare occasions when there were enough funds to splurge, to have Sunday brunch at Jacques Restaurant on Michigan Avenue. In those far-off and naïve days, it seemed to me like the grandest restaurant in the world.

It has rarely been mentioned, but my first job in Chicago was as a not-terribly-creative employee in the advertising department of the Chicago *Daily News.* Although I had graduated from the University of Missouri with a degree in Journalism, to which was added "in advertis-

CRAIG CLAIBORNE

ing," I loathed all aspects of it. To me the whole field of advertising is Cloud-Cuckoo-Land.

An acquaintance of mine from navy days was working directly across the Chicago River, onto which my office faced. He was in the publicity department of the American Broadcasting Company and he offered me a job. I think I left the *News* the same afternoon (years later the paper folded but the two events are not related) and found myself "handling," among many other things, publicity for Don McNeill's "Breakfast Club," which went off the air about thirteen years ago. At the time it was a breakfast staple in American homes, a not bad show with pleasant music, college humor, and enough corn to fill the nation's silos. At the height of its popularity, it had millions and maybe zillions of Americans marching around the breakfast tables to the tune of something like "Good morning, breakfast clubbers, how do you do you, we woke up bright and early just to howdedo you."

The work was pleasant enough but essentially boring. It required writing publicity releases for numerous shows for which I had little respect, "planting" items that were basically contrived in various gossip columns, drinking endlessly at the bar of the Wrigley Building, as well as at the bar of the Civic Opera House where the broadcasting studios were located.

After three years in Chicago I found the town closing in on me. In the sense, that is, that when I walked up or down Michigan Avenue or LaSalle Street, I would recognize and be obliged to greet with a smile what seemed like half the city's inhabitants. Radio bored me and I loathed getting out of bed at what passes for dawn to make my daily visit to the set of "The Breakfast Club"—too much cheer and early morning goodwill. Those were the swaddling days of television and my duties had expanded to publicize programs like "Super Circus" and a group of juvenile quiz shows which mercifully died in their cradle, although it must be said that the quiz shows which currently infest all the major networks are not one whit more sophisticated. To compound matters, my private life had become tedious and complicated, those fires of a first passion cooled to the point of extinction and no amount of heavy breathing could rekindle them.

It was Cecil Beaton who observed that "the world's second worst crime is boredom; the first is being a bore." To act a bore in the eyes of others I may not easily avoid. But boredom, given the powers of perambulation, I can.

In late 1949, my great romance having petered out and faced with total ennui where my professional work was concerned, I applied for a passport. For the first time in my life I had amassed $1,000 and had this in a bank account. I was also eligible for schooling under what was known as the G.I. Bill of Rights.

There is no accounting for the fact that I have been a francophile since the cradle and perhaps years before in another incarnation. If I could have named my one major dream in life since I learned to reason, it was to visit and live in France. It is not to exaggerate to say that all my life I had felt an alien in America. I was not comfortable in Mississippi; Chicago seemed spiritually removed to me even as I worked and ate and loved there.

And thus in late fall I boarded an American student vessel, the name of which is lost to me. There was nothing memorable about the voyage to France, certainly not the food. We arrived in Cherbourg and took the boat train to Paris. I felt like a small mouse when I got into the cab at Gare St. Lazare. A small mouse just loosed in a warehouse full of cheese.

It is a bit mawkish, I know, but the moment the taxi turned the corner on the Champs Élysées, driving toward l'Étoile, I was possessed with the most extraordinary feeling of coming home after years and perhaps centuries of absence and I started to cry, muffling the sounds so that the driver couldn't hear.

Alas. I could not have known how brief my honeymoon would be with the City of Light. I was, as it turned out, a damned callow fool, an unmitigated innocent. And I paid dearly for my naïveté!

I had planned to remain at least a year in Paris and in a financial sense this was wholly feasible. The city was—compared to Chicago, my chief frame of reference—a bargain. That is not to say that I was financially equipped to dine in what might even remotely be called style. I had to watch my francs and centimes with unaccustomed care and, in one sense, this was the greatest blessing of my stay. So necessarily cautious was I in my expenditures, it never occurred to me to take a taxi anywhere. And thus I walked everywhere, morning, noon, and night. I rarely rode the metro or subway. I came to know the *plan* of Paris by heart. Had I been led blindfold to any section of the city, I could have, blindfold removed, told you precisely the arrondissement I was in.

Tickets to concerts were to be had for centimes and I listened to marvelous music in the Salle Pleyel, the Salle Wagram, and—the hall that I cherish most to this day—the Salle Gaveau. I heard Andrés Segovia, Darius Milhaud, Wilhelm Backhaus, Alexander Brailowsky; saw a performance of *Auberge du Cheval Blanc (The White Horse Inn)* at the Châtelet, and, I hesitate to confess, I saw my first opera, *La Bohème*, one of the most inundating experiences of my life, at the Palais du Chaillot. Totally involved, never before or since have I undergone such strong emotions as I listened to a line that is imbedded forever in my brain: An elderly man turned to me and said in English: *"La Bohème* is all there is or ever will be of youth."

I was living in a five-story walk-up on the Rue de la Victoire. My *chambre* was a drafty place, small, with a fireplace which, in the cold winter months of 1949, had to be kept fueled. Else one had to go to bed and sleep under the devil's own contrivance, that overstuffed comforter called a duvet so much admired in French homes. It is a great puffy coverlet of eiderdown stuffed inside two large pieces of cloth. It is a French government edict that the cloth must be as slick and shiny as possible to ensure that the duvet, which can't be tucked in, will slide first to the right side, then to the left, always off the bed throughout the course of a cold night. That is one reason that for several weeks I spent so much time at concerts. It was cheaper than wood for the fireplace and the concert halls were heated.

My landlady was a Madame Roncaret, an aging woman with a face that was literally a mask of white powder punctuated with red lip rouge and purple eye shadow. Her hair was dyed a peculiar shade of orange and she wore a great deal of perfume. She resembled, in short, a Toulouse-Lautrec creation. She taught piano and all day long I could hear études by Czerny and Chopin. She was a dreadful snob and a worse cook.

Once, trying to exercise my French on her, I brought up the subject of music, about which my fund of knowledge was miserable. The only French composer who came to mind was Gounod so I told her, purely in the interest of conversation, that "Guess what music I prefer? Gounod's 'Berçeuse' from *Jocelyn.*" She went into a fifteen-minute tirade about liking music that the hurdy-gurdy man in the Parc Monceau would hold beneath his contempt.

I dreaded Friday lunch in Madame Roncaret's *salle à manger.* It was invariably grilled sardines which, to my certain knowledge, had been pawned off on her when, at the end of a third or fourth day of unrefrigeration the fish monger could not otherwise dispose of them. In short, they possessed a most unlikely perfume that deadened the appetite. Other days we dined on white sausages that contained more cereal than meat. These were alternated with *viande haché,* generally grilled and undercooked and a bit gristly. That is why to this day if someone asks me if I have ever dined on horse meat, I give them a tentative, "I'm not sure."

After lunch I would walk back to the Left Bank, always choosing a different route, a different bridge to cross, and generally indulged in my one great extravagance. I would stop at a pastry shop, spending minutes surveying the pastries—great cakes with butter-cream frosting, puff pastry fantasies like Napoleons with pastry cream fillings, and *palmiers,* which are given the dreadful name in English, pigs' ears. I would generally settle for one small fruit tart, a barquette perhaps, the cherries, gooseberries, or plums symmetrically posed atop a small cushion of pastry cream flavored with an *eau-de-vie.* Those were joyous days, many of them spent at Les Invalides, the Louvre, and twice I indulged myself in tours, once to Versailles, another to Malmaison. I was drunk with love for Paris; the smell of Gauloise cigarettes; the taste of *café noir* with croissants each morning, the odor of anisette at nearby tables. In those days I did not care for the taste of Pernod but it sure smelled like Paris as much as Marseilles, and that smelled good.

Today I look back ruefully and with a certain consternation to think that I did not allow myself to visit more than a meager handful of restaurants. But then I remember that I literally thought twice and I counted my sous before taking the metro. On the rare occasions that I did go to restaurants it was generally a *steak-pommes frites* establishment. It was in my first fortnight in Paris that I tasted what was, I presume, my first sampling of French cuisine, the food of North Africa notwithstanding. One late afternoon I walked along the banks of the Seine alone, feeling like generations of young Americans before me— like the original *flâneur.* I crossed Pont Sully and found myself in front of a small restaurant called Le Bossu, which, sadly, no longer exists.

I studied the menu posted in front and my eyes rested on the least expensive dish, *les oeufs brouillés à l'estragon.* I entered the restaurant and sat down. I ordered that dish and a glass of white wine. The dish was, of course, scrambled eggs with tarragon. I was consummately happy. I had never tasted such heavenly food. Since that couscous in Casablanca, I know full well that it was my first encounter with tarragon. I walked out of the place with a great desire to kiss the good lady who had welcomed me in the first place.

During that stay in Paris I was once taken to Brasserie Lipp, where I ate my first *choucroute à l'alsacienne* and again ached with the glory of knowing for the first time the grand heights to which sauerkraut could be elevated.

I also dined once at a small Arab restaurant and, for sentiment's sake, ordered couscous, which wasn't as good as I had remembered it in Morocco. I nonetheless reveled in it as I always have and always will.

And one Sunday that is indelible in my memory, I took the train to the suburb of St. Germain-en-Laye and dined at the Pavillon Henry IV. On this occasion I really splurged. I ate tournedos Henri IV, the grilled slice of beef fillet with its garnish of béarnaise, plus soufflé potatoes and a watercress salad. I went into my usual and ecstatic trancelike state at that first sampling of béarnaise sauce (again with tarragon flavor). That *plus* an initial biting-into of crisp, puffed soufflé potatoes were almost more joy than one body could contain.

There soon came, regrettably, an end to these frugal but magnificent pleasures, a far less elevating side to the nights and days as I passed them in Paris.

There is an old canard that if you sit long enough at the Café de Paris, Place de l'Opéra, sooner or later everyone you have ever known will pass by. The same could be said of the Alliance Française on the Boulevard Raspail on the Left Bank. If Paris is where all good Americans go when they die, the Alliance Française was, it seemed to me in those days, where they went while they were alive. That is, if they wanted to speak French. And that is where I enrolled on arrival in Paris.

During my years in Chicago, I had been much taken by a tall, well-educated, and fascinating brunette who worked in the Midwest bureau of Time-Life. Her name was Zelda, to select a name at random. She was the daughter of a nationally known politician and my association with her had been polite and purely professional.

Along about the second month of schooling at the Alliance Française, I wandered in error into a room where a class was in session. I was suddenly startled to see a redhead who, on seeing me, stood up and rushed over to greet me. It was Zelda, who had given herself a cardinal rinse.

That meeting would, as the weeks passed, spell disaster. The total catastrophe. For Zelda and I became chums, a friendship held together by a great bond of drinking. I could not afford to indulge myself in fine or even mediocre restaurants. But the cost of rum and Cognac was suited to my purse and drink we did, many's the night, into oblivion.

Because of that void, which lasted several weeks, there isn't a great deal more to be said about my stay in Paris except how and why it ended.

For a bizarre reason, Zelda, who was Jewish, and I, who do not profess to any form of organized religion, decided to go to Rome in late December. The reason was that 1950 was to be the Holy Year in the Roman Catholic Church. We also thought that a visit to St. Mark's in Venice on Christmas Eve would be romantic fun, God knows why. Oh, beautiful for pilgrim feet!

To compound this midwinter insanity, I decided on a madder scheme. I must have had about seven hundred and fifty dollars left from my initial thousand that I had saved in Chicago and with which I was funding this sojourn in Paris. In addition to that, I had two checks, each totaling sixty-five dollars, issued by the U. S. Government, my monthly stipend for education under the G.I. Bill of Rights.

I decided that I would play the black market, a quite respectable thing to do in those days. But at that point in time, playing the black market was sheer folly. Immediately after the war, you could make quite a little profit by selling hard currency in the form of U.S. dollars. But at the time that *I* decided to wheel and deal, the profit to be made by the sale of a few dollars illegally as opposed to what you could get legally from the bank could be counted in pennies. But this was the situation. In 1949 you could not take a fifty-dollar bill, to choose an arbitrary amount, or a government-issued check to a bank and receive dollars in change. You would have to accept francs.

The black market was played thusly: You took your hard currency or government check to a bank in Switzerland and they would give you American cash. You returned to France, found someone willing to pay you a higher-than-the-bank price for this hard currency, and the difference in exchange was your profit.

And so Zelda and I boarded the train for Lausanne. We stayed there one night to give me ample time to convert every bit of exchange that I owned into American dollars. The next morning we boarded the train for Milan en route to Venice.

In Milan we took a stroll. We spotted a group of men huddled around a black table on which they were playing a shell game, the sordid mechanics of which are, even at this late date, too painful and embarrassing to recount. Zelda and I were ripped off for one hundred dollars each within the space of five minutes.

Next stop, Venice.

In Venice on Christmas Eve, as midnight approached, we walked to the Basilica San Marco only to discover that it was bolted shut.

The next day or the day after, we returned to St. Marks and on the way we met a man, a slender, dapper, handsome type, all grace and charm, who gave the impression of suddenly being much taken with Zelda. I shall call him Carlo. We joined him for coffee on the Piazza San Marco and within the space of an hour he had given us his *curriculum vitae*. It would seem indeed that within those sixty minutes there was little about himself that he had not revealed. In perfect English, he stated that he was divorced. His wife had run off with a professor from Princeton. He had a child, he explained, as he extracted a portrait of a young tyke who looked like something by Botticelli. He taught language and he would like, on the following day, to show us Titian's workshop, a landmark that very few tourists were fortunate enough to be shown. He lived on the Lido, ventured back and forth across the lagoon by rented boat, and so on.

The three of us took a stroll and met a young lady, a tourist alone from Brooklyn.

The four of us agreed to have dinner. With all those dollar bills from Swiss banks crammed into my vest pocket, I was feeling outrageously flush. I said that I would be the host.

It must be said that in the closing years of the 1940s, Italy had still not recovered economically from the ravages of the last war. The black market still flourished there. *La dolce vita* was in the distance.

Our Venetian friend noted that Zelda had the makings of a cold coming on and so he stepped briefly inside a shop where he purchased black market Kleenex for her. And her favorite brand of American cigarettes, which she was wont to chain smoke. Also black market. A few steps further, our friend stopped and bought a bottle of Italian brandy. It was then proposed that we go back to our *albergo* to have a drink in my room.

The four of us sat around a small table, a glass at hand. In retrospect, I recall that Carlo was inordinately generous in pouring three of us helpings of brandy. He poured himself small portions, watered down, protesting that his tolerance for alcohol was minuscule.

At seven o'clock Zelda was beyond maneuvering and was put to bed in her room across the hall. The remaining three of us continued our carousing into the night and into Taverna la Fenice, at the time one of Venice's most celebrated.

I have no recollection of that dinner. Memory came back to me fleetingly and I remember removing my wallet from my breast pocket and paying the bill, which seemed staggeringly high.

It was bitter cold when we deposited Miss Brooklyn at her hotel and walked to mine. Carlo protested that it was too late to take the boat back to the Lido and, therefore, he would check into my *albergo*. He was assigned a room adjoining mine.

I stumbled or otherwise got my body into bed and unconsciousness. There was a knock at my door and I presumed it was Zelda in need of a match or other light for a cigarette.

I yelled, "Come in," and it was Carlo who quietly entered and just as quietly shut the door, turning the key in the lock with his left hand behind his back.

"Where's your money?"

"I don't have much."

I was cold and terrified as well.

An uncharacteristic thing had happened when I had gone to bed. I am meticulous, fastidious to the point of a slight neurosis. A wayward ash, a dog's hair, a stray needle or hairpin can disturb and distract and unsettle me until it is removed from sight.

On this evening, I had taken off my jacket and hung it carelessly on the knob of a chair in the room.

Carlo started for it.

I am no hero but I was petrified at the thought of that money loss. I, naked, tossed the covers off my body and stood, hoping somehow to thwart his advance toward my wallet.

He lunged, pushed me back onto the bed, my back against the wall and a blade of solid steel pointed at my heart.

"Mind yourself," he said, backing toward the jacket. Out of my breast pocket he withdrew my wallet and passport. He lifted every bill from the wallet, tossed the wallet and passport on the bed. He backed to the door, unlocked and opened it, and stole out into the hallway, closing the door behind him.

I hurriedly dressed, terrified. I had not one cent and only a few lira to my name, in Italy or elsewhere. There was no one in my family, no friend in Chicago to whom I could appeal for aid. In all the world, only Zelda.

I made my way across to her door, passing meanwhile Carlo's room. His door was fully ajar, the bed lamp was lit, and he was reclining against the pillow, reading. On the night stand was Zelda's Kleenex.

I awakened Zelda and asked her to keep an eye on Carlo. I would go to the police.

There were no taxis and I walked in the freezing darkness to the police station, only to discover that no one spoke *inglese*. I would have to wait for the morning guard.

To make it brief, the police went to the hotel and searched Carlo's room behind closed doors. An hour later they emerged to tell me that there was no sign of my money.

Over the years, as you may have noted, in times of stress, my memory pulls a disappearing act, and it did here.

I can reconstruct the past in bits and pieces.

But for the record, if you examine the pages of Venice's leading newspaper of the last week in December 1949, you will note a black headline buried somewhere within that says, *"Giornalista Americano Rapinato en Albergo."* *Rapinato,* I hasten to add, is not a cognate meaning what you might be wondering. It means robbed.

I do know that Zelda (she did not then nor did she ever want for money) agreed to loan me the entire sum of money that I had lost. Provided I would continue with her on the Italian *viaggio* as far as Florence, that splendid town, which had been part of our original itinerary. Indeed, Zelda threatened to turn me loose without a lira if I did not continue to keep her company.

To be truthful, I wanted nothing so much as immediate passage back to America.

We took the train to Bologna for the express purpose of dining at Papagallo, which we understood to be one of the finest restaurants in all of Italy. We dined on tagliatelle and even in my state of grave and continuing anxiety, it was a transcendental experience. Never had I eaten such noodles, golden, thin to the point of near translucence, and bathed in heavy cream and freshly grated Parmesan cheese. We also had a superb encounter with *filetti di tacchino* or thinly sliced breast of turkey with prosciutto and Gruyère cheese. I might add that, as of a few months ago, I paid a sentimental visit to Bologna and Papagallo's and I think it was one of the worst meals of my life. The food was a disaster and the service was worse. The interior of the restaurant was equally seedy and depressing.

Not to belabor the travesties and trials of that trip with Zelda, the next day we were to take the train for Florence. We arrived at the train station well in advance of our scheduled departure and stopped at a small trattoria for a pre-prandial apéritif (I had only recently been initiated into the joys of Italian vermouths).

There was a single stipulation in my financial arrangement with Zelda; I was not to be trusted with money. She would dispense such funds as were necessary for food, drink, and repose. Around her neck and over her shoulders was strapped an uncommonly capacious and heavy leather bag, inside which she carried a small, oily, and supple purse, the most interesting aspect of which was that it was stuffed bulging with international currency. That in itself would not have seemed unusual but the fact was that an expert in forensic chemistry could easily have traced each piece of currency to which bar Zelda had dined in throughout her stay in Europe.

Zelda adored finger food of any sort. Thus you would find paper drachmas not too daintily stained with olives and lakerda that had given her pleasure in the plaka in Athens; pesetas that smacked of angulas in oil or other tapas that she had tasted at her favorite tascos in Barcelona; francs that had been briefly anointed with the oil of anchovies or other dainty tidbits she'd nibbled while standing at small counter bars in Marseilles.

Shortly before the train pulled into the station, Zelda indicated that she must make a hurried trip to the *lavabo* and to hasten things she handed me her purse, so redolent of good times. I took it, walked to the cashier, and paid for the apéritifs. Zelda returned and I returned the purse.

We boarded the train, which was crowded with Holy Year pilgrims, me burdened with my small suitcase and several of her numerous pieces of luggage. We took our seats at the only places we could find in separate compartments. Just before the train got underway, she stuck her face in the door of my compartment.

"Do you have my purse?" she demanded eagerly.

"No," I yelled, and as the wheels of that vehicle started slowly turning, we jumped off the train. I was frightened. My God, I thought. The ultimate dilemma.

"Zelda," I started, "what'll we do now! We're broke."

"Oh, piddle," she said, "it's not the money. My passport was in that purse. And so were some prescriptions for drugs that I can't live without."

Back to the Italian police, once more with feeling.

The rest of that trip was mostly anticlimactic.

The next day, with a cable from home in her hand, she was issued another passport by the American consul. And money was not the grave concern I had imagined it would be. When she opened her

---

suitcases at the hotel where we spent the night, I noted that tucked here and there was a comfortable assortment of packages containing traveler's checks in denominations to nourish the spirit.

After a few days in Florence, I returned to Paris by train and it was almost a classic finale to that misbegotten expedition. The train was packed and in my third-class compartment I sat facing a toothless, unshaven old man whose breath reeked of garlic, gorgonzola, and a wine that was referred to in my childhood as dago red.

I waited in Paris for a week to accommodate myself to the French Line's boat schedule. The francs and centimes that I owned (through Zelda's generosity) seemed more precious than ever.

As it turned out, I was not to leave Europe that year without fate giving me one final thumbing of the nose.

On the night before I was to catch the boat train, I had rejoined Zelda at our favorite bar that dispensed cheap Cognac and rum. We had called it a night at three or four o'clock in the morning. I had slept through the sound of the alarm clock at 6 A.M., and awakened with an hour to go before the departure of the train for Cherbourg.

I hastily shaved, showered, shoved clothes into a bag, and ran into the cold morning streets of Paris to hail a cab. No small feat at that hour and in the section of Paris where I lived. At eight-forty I found a taxi and hurried into the back seat, alarmed.

I realized that seconds were important in making that nine o'clock departure.

In my very best, lamentable French, I told the driver of my dilemma. I then reckoned how much the fare would be to the station. In my anxiety I decided that I would make ready twice the amount and add a handsome tip as well.

My memory is faulty after all these years as to the exact sum, but I believe that I had agreed to give the driver six hundred francs, which would have been exceedingly generous.

I fished in my pockets and discovered that all I had was a thousand-franc note.

"Driver," I said (or tried to say), "I want to give you six hundred francs to get me to the train station as fast as possible. I only have a thousand francs. I will give you that and you give me four hundred francs. There will be no time to lose at the Gare St. Lazare."

He was a charming old man. While driving at utmost speed, he reached into his wallet and handed me four hundred francs.

We arrived at the station at two minutes to nine.

I bolted from the cab, coattail flying. And so had the cab driver, yelling his lungs out.

A second later a group of bystanders grabbed me and held me stock-still.

CRAIG CLAIBORNE

"Let me go," I yelled. "You're crazy."

"But, monsieur," one of them who spoke English informed me, "the cab driver says he gave you four hundred francs and you gave him nothing."

It was true. In my haste, I had not forked over the thousand-franc bill.

When I got to the ticket-taker, I was told that the boat train had departed on time five minutes ago. I wanted to cry. I hadn't even said good-by to my landlord and landlady. I simply couldn't go back and say I needed my room back, I missed the train.

And then the ticket-taker said, smiling, "Don't bother. You missed that tourist-class boat train. The first-class train leaves at ten."

And in this time of trial and travail there was one factor to give me spiritual uplift.

I had booked passage on that legend known as the *Île de France* and it was sailing from Cherbourg to Manhattan.

Although I had dined on scrambled eggs with tarragon at Le Bossu and *choucroute à l'alsacienne* at Brasserie Lipp, I was to taste my first sample of *classic* French cooking aboard that ship.

To be sure, I was traveling tourist class. But on that first night out, what was placed before me was a dish of such stunning magnificence I felt—without hyperbole—what amounted to a spiritual revelation. It was as though a key had been turned, a door opened, and suddenly I was offered the essence and extract of some sublime, supernal elixir that was all I'd ever hoped for without knowing what I had hoped for.

The dish was listed on the menu as *turbotin à l'infante*. To this day, I believe that my career in food can be dated from that one meal. It was a heady experience the like of which has never been equaled, although closely approximated on occasions that I can count on the fingers of one hand. Never again has anything tasted so audaciously good as that young turbot with white wine sauce.

At the end of the meal I requested the recipe and the next day I found it under the door of my cabin. This is the recipe, neatly typed as I received it in French:

Recette De Turbotin A L'Infante

Mettre le turbotin assaisonné intérieurement et extérieurement dans un plat beurré avec un oignon moyen émincé et un bouquet garni. Mouiller de quelques cuillerées de vin blanc, ou de fumet de poisson au vin blanc. Cuire à couvert à chaleur douce.

Égoutter le turbotin; le dresser sur un plat de service.

Le napper de sauce vin blanc préparée ainsi composée: Réduire des deux tiers un décilitre et demi de fumet de poisson au vin blanc. Laisser tiédire et ajouter 2 jaunes d'oeufs-monter au fouet à chaleur

---

douce. Dés que les jaunes ont pris un peu de consistance ajouter peu à peu 150 grammes de beurre fondu en fouettant toujours.

Assaisonner. Ajouter quelques gouttes de citron. Passer à l'étamine. Napper le turbotin. Ainsi nappé, le faire vivement glacer au four brûlant.

COMPAGNIE GÉNÉRALE
TRANSATLANTIQUE
French Line

That recipe translates into English as follows:

Recipe for young turbot infante

Place the young turbot, which has been seasoned inside and out, on a buttered baking dish with a chopped, medium-size onion and a bouquet garni. Sprinkle with several spoonfuls of white wine or of fish stock plus white wine. Cook in a slow oven.
Drain the fish. Transfer it to a serving dish.
Spoon over the fish a white wine sauce prepared as follows:
Cook down by two thirds, a deciliter and a half of fish stock made with white wine. Let it cool to lukewarm and add two egg yolks beaten over low heat with a wire whisk until they become frothy and lemon-colored. When they have reached the proper consistency, gradually beat in 150 grams of melted butter. Beat briskly as the butter is added. Season the sauce. Add a few drops of lemon juice. Put it through a fine sieve. Spoon this over the fish. Place briefly in a very hot oven until nicely glazed.

Where my impressions of that meal and that moment are concerned there was one other important and indelible in my mind addition to that dish. Each serving was garnished with a puff pastry crescent. It was my first taste of that gossamer confection. I have never eaten another bite of puff pastry anywhere and in any form that tasted quite so flaky and incredibly airy. It was insubstantial enough to defy the laws of gravity.

Somewhere, I told myself. Somewhere out there, and I don't know where, there are secrets to be learned. Who knows? The Lord works in wondrous ways . . .

And thus I returned to Chicago, a bit chastened and wiser and hoist on my own petard. My escape route had come full swing to a dead end.

The reason why I returned to Chicago was simple. I was not only broke but in debt. And I realized that, thanks to the kindness of my former roommate in Chicago, I would have a warm place to bed down and hot meals to sustain me until I could find my new direction.

Alas, my new direction was parallel to my old one. Back to the perfunctory greeting, the boring press releases that are the heart and soul of a public relations office. And the organization that I joined was a massive building called the Merchandise Mart, then known as the world's largest office building.

Now, as I have noted on numerous occasions throughout this work, my naïveté, my lack of sophistication in some areas is almost total.

The Merchandise Mart was and, presumably, still is owned by what is known as the Kennedy Family. I must confess that when I joined "the Mart" in early 1950, I had never heard of the Kennedy Family. I probably had read that there was a congressman from Massachusetts called John F. Kennedy but this had never settled into my consciousness as an interesting, much less salient, fact. Politics bore me.

And I soon realized that a lot of other things bored me, not the least of which was Chicago, second time around.

But a few things of personal great moment happened during my second stay in the Second City. Not things you're apt to broadcast nationwide. But important things. One of these involved Sargent Shriver, a handsome, urbane man who later married Eunice Kennedy. Sargent was second in command at the Mart (it was said that as Joe Kennedy's future son-in-law he was the éminence grise of the edifice).

I much admired Sargent. He was exceedingly cordial and courteous in his relations with me. He had an ingratiating nature, a warm handshake, and a way of smiling that made you feel good. Eventually, of course, he became the American ambassador to France.

As deputy director, or whatever title he bore, the public relations division of the building was to be found in his chain of command. He was my ultimate "boss."

The *raison d'être* of a public relations department of the Mart was, naturally, to impress the public favorably with the imposing nature of that august building. The better the public image that existed, the more tenants that would apply for leases.

It fell my lot one day to call the food editor of the Chicago *Tribune* about a potential article involving the building. There was on the ground floor of the Mart an organization called the Merchants and Manufacturers' Club and the Friday special of the club's chef was bouillabaisse. I had tasted it and, to my far from educated palate, it was superb.

I called the *Trib* and asked for Ruth Ellen Church, a pretty, enthusiastic lady who wrote a widely read food column under the name Mary Meade. I told her about the chef's bouillabaisse and she agreed to have lunch with me.

A couple of weeks later she wrote an article accompanied by step photographs showing how incredibly simple and fast it is to prepare a bouillabaisse, even in Chicago. We became friends, a fact that was, a couple of years later, to make a mark on my subsequent career.

In the summer of 1950, I was suffering once more from a severe case of restlessness and galloping stir fever. I wanted out. And fast.

Unfortunately, it had taken me months to repay that "fortune" I owed to my friend Zelda. I no longer had the freedom and mobility that comes from having a thousand dollars in the bank.

My release came from the oddest source. The White House. Harry Truman had the nation become involved in what came to be known as "the Korean conflict." I volunteered for duty in the Navy.

For the first time in my life, I had kept my own counsel in this matter. I had not disclosed to one solitary soul that I had written to the Navy asking them to call back this sinner. It is still a bit burdensome on my conscience that I blatantly stated in my letter that "this act is for patriotic reasons."

And one fine night I returned to my apartment in Chicago to find a large envelope, the likes of which, having spent four years filing such envelopes, I was all too familiar with.

I found that I had become a master of deception.

When I arrived in my apartment I was greeted by my roommate.

"My God," I said, "an envelope from the Navy. You don't suppose that after all these years they're calling me back?" The fact is, such a "greeting" from the Navy would not have been all that unbelievable. Since the end of World War II I had been a member of the U. S. Naval Reserve, not for patriotic reasons but rather to augment my small salary during both my stays in Chicago.

Pretending it was a joking matter, I said I would have several martinis before I opened that manila envelope, which, I hoped, would contain my salvation. An hour or so and about ten martinis later, I did open the envelope and read:

"You will report to the U.S.S. *Alfred Naifeh (DE 352)* wherever she might be . . ." I could have kissed the ground and yelped for joy. Instead, I put on my most morose mask and told my roommate in mournful, if not to say funereal tones, that I was in a state of shock.

A moment or so later, I was to be placed in a state of shock that bordered on the catatonic.

I telephoned my *immediate* superior at the Mart, Robert B. Johnson, and informed him (same mournful tone) that I had been recalled into the Navy.

Without so much as a pause, he said, "Don't worry. Sarge will get you out of this. He'll call John Kennedy tomorrow and arrange something."

At that, I did in truth become morose. A fine kettle of bouillabaisse that would be. Shriver calls Kennedy, Kennedy calls the Bureau of Naval Personnel, the bureau looks in its files and finds my patriotic plea, and I wind up, hooted, ridiculed, and jeered at on LaSalle Street.

The next morning I was ushered into Shriver's office. Some remark was made about my age, that there were plenty of younger men, and yes, perhaps he might call John F. Kennedy.

I quickly jumped into the breach. I protested that even if my orders were canceled, it looked like a long "war" and that I had spent a number of years in the Naval Reserve. Sooner or later my number would come up again. Besides, I droned on and on, I needed a new wardrobe, I couldn't afford to buy new suits with the threat of naval induction hanging over me, and on and on and on.

"She," meaning the vessel to which I had been assigned (the vessel on which I was inflicted would be more accurate), was in dry dock in Hawaii. I was to be the operations officer. And believe me, as my skipper was all too soon to discover, I could not read a navigation chart with any degree of accuracy. To this day I would be hard put to describe what an operations officer was, except it had to do vaguely with communicating from one vessel to another, plotting maneuvers, and so on and so on to the point of total ennui.

I felt sorry for my skipper. Real sorry. Captain John Cornelius Smits. Nice guy. He'd seen my record and looked forward to my coming aboard as though I were John Paul Jones. Brilliant career. College graduate. Four years World War II. Decorations for the invasions of Italy, Sicily, and North Africa. Total years of naval duty, including Naval Reserve, eight.

I would be hard put to sort out which of my derelictions brought him closer to cardiac arrest.

Well, there was one night while sailing along the shore line around North Korea.

I had the deck. That is to say, I was in charge of the ship while the skipper slept or otherwise relaxed off duty. I was topside looking at the stars and gossiping with "Flags," the signalman, who used the Morse Code when he sat down to play or flags when he wanted to contact another ship in visible distance.

Many times over the years I had heard the expression, "Request permission to blow the tubes."

I hadn't the foggiest notion of what they were talking about or why they asked. I presumed that "tubes" were things that trailed along the after part of a boat and you blew something out that might clog them up.

The tubes, in actuality, mean the smokestack. And the smokestack is something that I occasionally leaned against when I was topside. You blow the tubes to get rid of excess soot.

And the man who presses a switch to blow the tubes always asks the deck officer for permission to blow them as a guarantee that the ship is underway and there is a wind of sufficient intensity to waft away soot and other irritants.

The man below called up to me, "Request permission to blow the tubes."

"Permission granted."

At that precise moment we just happened to be totally becalmed in the waters off Wŏnsan. The soot went up in some vast, dense, all-embracing monolithic gust and came right down again.

It might not have required Lewis Carroll's "seven maids with seven mops swept it for half a year," but it sure took the better part of the next day to get rid of the lampblack that enveloped that generally sleek and shiny vessel of which my friend the skipper was so proud.

Or the time not long after his anger had finally become, not expunged but temporarily arrested, when I had the deck again. This time in broad daylight.

I cannot, as I have explained, add, multiply, or subtract. I count with my fingers. Until a considerably advanced age, I did not know left from right and at times would resort to feeling my heartbeat to make certain which side was left. I have lived in New York for more than twenty-five years and I still, particularly when late for the theater, will exit from a restaurant and walk east when the theater—as most of them are—is west. When I take a subway, I more often than not get on a train that takes me to Harlem when I want to get to Greenwich Village.

On this sun-bright day, along about noon, the skipper was having lunch in the wardroom. I was topside "navigating." The shore line was in full view and I used all my navigational aids—parallel rulers, charts with their compass roses, et cetera—to get us out to sea where I had been told to go.

I carefully plotted the course and reckoned that it should be forty-five degrees to the right.

I told the helmsman to come right forty-five degrees.

Slowly the boat maneuvered.

And as I glanced straight ahead I noted that we were heading directly for shore.

The quartermaster looked straight ahead, a querulous glint in his eye. He shook his head a moment and looked at me.

"Lieutenant," he said quietly and tentatively, "I think this may be the wrong course."

"Not according to this chart," I said. Then I stared straight ahead again and it occurred to me that something *was* wrong.

I yelled to the helmsman, "Full right rudder."

With that, the ship veered right with speed and emphasis. It coincided with a sudden ground swell that caused an upheaval grand enough to slide the skipper's luncheon special off the table and onto the deck in the dining room.

In about ten strides he bounded up the ladder and was yelling like a tormented, betrayed gorilla at whom too many stones have been cast. I have never understood great anger when life is short at best.

Another time we were sailing into Tokyo harbor one bright, clear, sunny morning when a British man-of-war, a massive, terribly imposing cruiser, came into view and started to pass us.

The skipper stood smartly on the upper deck; I was below. He yelled down, "Render honors." Now I don't know about you, but as far as I was concerned, he might as well have been yelling Greek.

I yelled back, "Do what?"

I looked up. He was grabbing his hat either to throw it at me or keep his brains from erupting and spilling out all over the rail and onto the lower deck.

"RENDER HONORS," he screamed.

There is an old navy saying, "When in danger or in doubt, run in circles, scream, and shout." To me it didn't seem appropriate, so I did the next best thing. I grasped the nearest noisemaker, which, in this case, happened to be the rope of the iron bell generally used to sound the hour. I pulled it back and forth with such resounding enthusiasm and vigor they could hear it plainly from top of the mast to the bilges and when I looked up the skipper had a look of such horror and disbelief I felt ashamed. Oh God, I thought, I've hurt his feelings.

There are some elements about my life that are not easily comprehended and I think the reason why is that long ago I discovered that this whole thing of existence is a great cosmic joke.

In any event, there is such a thing in this world as a gooney bird. That is slang for an albatross and the scientific name for the winged creature is *Diomedea Albatross.*

I discovered my first gooney bird on the island of Midway, the island much celebrated for its triumphs and disasters in World War II.

The charm of a gooney bird is that they have very large, snow-white breasts and a curious inability to fly. Their wing span is considerable but there is something inefficient in their muscular make-up that permits them to ascend into the air for a brief period, only to come crashing down again—formidably—on their breasts. Something heroic in their soul makes them persist, endlessly, through daylight hours, to make that one splendid soar into the skies. But they never, never get more than a few feet off the ground before they come plummeting earthward.

It may not seem rational but the first time I saw a gooney bird I was totally entranced with the valor of its lot. Perhaps I could identify gooney birds with my own soul.

During those navy years of the Korean conflict (not Korean War, mind you; that would have been too dirty), I had once more accumulated my "thousand dollars" and I banked it as freedom money. There were long periods of idleness on board that destroyer escort. There was much time for self-appraisal and personal decisions.

"Look," I told myself. "You're more than thirty years old. What do you want to do when you grow up?"

"I like to write," I answered myself. "And I like to cook."

And suddenly the ideas melded.

"I want to write about food." With that, I ended the conversation.

In those days, the most talked about and written about cooking school in the world was the Cordon Bleu in Paris. Then located on the Faubourg St. Honoré, it was *the* ultimate place to have "studied." It had been started by Henri-Paul Pellaprat and at the height of its excellence it must have been a formidable place with which to be or have been associated.

I decided to go there. I realized that with my navy savings plus the G.I. Bill of Rights, I could probably afford it.

It was at this point that my mother had one of the few most positive influences on my life, for which I give her total credit.

I outlined to her my plans for Paris training.

She wrote to tell me that only the night before she had met the banquet manager of the Peabody Hotel in Memphis, Tennessee. He had, she added, spoken in enthusiastic terms of a hotel school in Switzerland.

He had jotted down the name of the school, L'École Hôtelière, L'École Professionnelle de la Société Suisse des Hôteliers. Or, in English, the Professional School of the Swiss Hotel Keepers Association.

I had been notified that my two-year stint with the Navy was officially coming to an end within three months.

I wrote the hotel school and applied for admission.

With admirable timing, I had a note from the school's director telling me that they would accept me. But that, at present, their rolls were filled for at least twelve months. If I could wait . . .

I could wait. But not aboard a destroyer escort on which I was about as useful as a broken gyroscope.

I dispatched a cable to the Navy Department stating my desire to "ship over" in the Navy for an extra year. Provided, I added, I be sent to Midway. In that, I was motivated, purely and simply, by my desire to live next to my gooney bird soul-mates.

Within a matter of hours my offer was accepted and the official communiqué stated that I was to be transferred to Midway as "Communications Officer." At that late date, communications from Midway (which had long since ceased to be an important military base) to anywhere would have been no more significant than extending birth-day wishes or Valentine greetings.

For reasons I have never known, a subsequent counter-check cable arrived. In this one, I was ordered to an atoll in the Pacific—namely Kwajalein—to serve as assistant port director.

Small matter that I wouldn't know "port directing" from how to use a pair of parallel rulers or how to adjust with panache a pair of fine-tubed binoculars.

Between these assignments—a tour of duty aboard the destroyer escort and the projected atoll—I found myself briefly in San Francisco, which proved (eventually) to be a glorious salvation against the tedium of too much paradise, incomparable sand beaches, and endless sun. I bought a machine for long-playing records—in those years they were still a novelty of sorts—albums and single recordings of music, mostly operatic and mostly the works of Puccini and Verdi; a copy of the Bible; and the complete works of Shakespeare. In making those purchases I had acted with incredible foresight.

For the fact was that a *chief* port director alone would have been an incredible case of overstaffing. I doubt that ten ships a year put into that magnificent harbor. An *assistant* in that office was as ludicrous and farcical as importing seagulls to increase the bird population.

When I stepped ashore, it was obvious to the commanding officer that somebody had goofed. And the C.O., in his wisdom, after looking at my record, had the acuity to put me in a position of total inconse-quence, of negligible responsibility, where I couldn't endanger lives.

I was made "billeting officer," which is to say the person in charge of assigning quarters to both officers and enlisted men. The enlisted men went into the local barracks; the officers into the Bachelor Officers Quarters.

And thus, my first official act was to assign myself to what must have been the choicest billet on the local map. I gave myself a room with a terrace opening immediately onto the beach and ocean. What's more, it was outfitted with new Philippine teak and bamboo chairs and sofas and desks, upholstered in a fabric that might have seemed a little dazzling back home.

There was a refrigerator on the terrace and a small stove, which turned out to be a merciful blessing. The food dished out to the personnel on Kwajalein was the standard G.I. fare of that era, which is to say it was guaranteed not to be poisoned but not much more appetizing than Spam.

My repertoire did not include fish *meunière* or a fine bouillabaisse, but I had mastered enough technique to turn out a decent platter of sautéed local fish and a few things in cream sauce. I could produce a creditable breakfast of poached eggs Mornay with ham. And beverages were certainly not lacking. My billet was next door to the "stores," where one could buy wines and spirits and beer for pennies. I recall very well that a fifth of gin in those days cost sixty-five cents.

Each day that followed another on Kwajalein was as much like the day just past as the waves that lapped the shore outside my billet. I remember singing Christmas carols in a warm, pouring rain, driving with friends around the island to carol to whomever would listen; I remember being present when the commanding officer's red cocker spaniel was run over by a jeep and going to the dog's "funeral" when he was given a decent burial beneath a lone pine tree by the side of the sea; and I remember a nurse, black-haired and sensual, who, when I told her I was going to a "cooking school" in Switzerland, advised me to take the money and go to an analyst instead.

And eventually my time was up. I had my driftwood, giant clam shells, and spherical Japanese fishing floats packed. I returned briefly to Chicago en route to Switzerland.

During that layover in Chicago I telephoned my old acquaintance Ruth Ellen Church of the Chicago *Tribune* to ask if I sent her articles on cooking, would she consider them. She gave me a tentative yes. And less than a week later, on April 15, 1953, I had found my destiny, although I did not know it at the time. I was issued a *"livret pour étrangers,"* a residence permit for foreigners by the Swiss police. It was valid for eighteen months.

The Swiss hotel school had made it clear in their brochures and announcements that it was not an establishment dedicated to turning out waiters, cooks, and chefs. Its stated purpose was quite clear. The institution existed to perpetuate the highest standards of Swiss hostelry. The aim of the school was to turn out men and women who would, in time, become the managers of hotels. The sons and daughters of Swiss hotelkeepers were, I'm quite certain, and properly so, given primary consideration in their applications for admission.

In those years, the school was in its original quarters—an L-shaped, solidly built, large, unhandsome but functional structure with a towering fir tree in the center court of the "L." The tree was twice as high as the tallest roof, of which there were five, each representing, I have always presumed, marks of expansion. It was then located on the Avenue de Cour in Ouchy on the banks of Lac Léman or, in English, Lake Geneva.

On entering the doors of that establishment, I had, indeed, as they say in Christian hymnals, planted my feet on firmer ground. I felt, somehow, a quiet exaltation and exhilaration. That is not to say that I was transmogrified, suddenly shorn of my usual burdens, including a sense of insecurity, both emotional and financial. Those feelings were as much a part of me as my teeth and my appendix.

The École Hôtelière de la Societé Suisse des Hôteliers as it existed on the Avenue du Cour during my period of training in 1953–54. The school was later demolished and reopened at Chalet-à-Gobet just outside Lausanne in 1976.

In retrospect, I think I had discovered for the first time a sense of discipline. And this contributed a sense of well-being.

By discipline I do not mean the sort of discipline to be found in the military or a discipline induced by a threat of corporal punishment. I mean a personal discipline exercised for the sheer beauty of it, a discipline I have noted a thousand times in professional chefs who work in a kitchen. You move in one direction and time your moves to avoid physical conflict with those who work around and beside you. You anticipate such moves reflexively and a timing, co-ordination, and precision are achieved equal to that of a fine Swiss watch movement. If you are casual in your motions as a chef or cook or maître d'hôtel or waiter, you're going to wind up with an awful lot of soup on the floor.

The courses at the hotel school were three. One for cuisine, one for table and banquet service, and a third for *comptabilité,* or accounting. I had no interest whatsoever in accounting and, therefore, eschewed it.

If, in those days, I had been asked to state my goal in attending that

---

school, I could have given only a vague reply. As a matter of fact, it seems to me that once more I had gone to that school solely by instinct with nothing other than a vague pattern in mind. I had applied for admission, motivated by a desire to improve the quality of my life with little serious thought that it would lead to a solid career.

God knows, I had no thought of becoming a chef, much less a headwaiter. I was free. I had no family to support or account to. I wanted to learn about French cuisine and European wines. The fact that I had an opportunity to study table service was simply a bonus. It had not been a part of my plans when I had applied for admission. But I found myself equally at home wearing a waiter's uniform as I did wearing a cook's apron. I was inordinately proud, incredibly gratified in my role as waiter. In either role, I found myself in a mild state of euphoria as I made new and grand discoveries each day, whether about transforming a basic hollandaise sauce into a maltaise sauce (by adding grated orange rind and a little orange juice and whipped cream) or in learning that personal hygiene is as important as how to ladle soup from a tureen, whether to serve from right or left, and the techniques for removing dishes during the course of a meal.

I remember dozens of seemingly insignificant details.

One of the most impressive characters on the staff of the school was a veritable balloon of a man, a M. Michel, who breathed with difficulty as he toddled up and down the stairs, admonishing students if their fingernails were not immaculately clean; castigating them if they were so much as one minute late for one of his classes; and giving a baleful look to anyone who was guilty of a trivial infringement. He held contempt for most Americans, for many of them a few years earlier had chosen the hotel school as a way of staying in Europe after the end of World War II. Like me, they had been eligible for study under the G.I. Bill of Rights. They treated the poor old man scandalously, a favorite trick being to hold a swinging door open until he approached, only to let it swing shut onto his belly.

On one occasion, a delegation of hotel men were scheduled to visit the school and certain students were designated to create table decorations for the ten dining tables to be used for the occasion. My concept was to create a wine table, on which I placed vines with dead leaves that I had found on one of my walks around the banks of Lake Geneva. I designed menus with grapes on the cover and was uncommonly pleased with my inventiveness.

When M. Michel came into the dining room, he thundered at me that flowers were suitable for a white tablecloth but not dead vines, and on and on and on. Fortunately for my ego, a conference was called with his colleague, Conrad Tuor, and it was decided that it was too late to change the décor and it would remain.

Of all the faculty of that school, it was M. Tuor whom I admired to the point of idolatry. A kind, handsome, well-tailored man of athletic build (he was an excellent skier), he seemed the very model of what that school stood for. He was civil, sympathetic, and yet aloof. He possessed a marvelous *sang-froid* and my single aim, it seems in retrospect, was to gain his approval. To have him look me in the eye and see the beginning of a smile tracing his lips because he admired how quickly I had mastered carrying a dozen wine goblets in one hand; or how well I could navigate between tables while holding a dining room tray full of dishes. Or how expertly I could carry four bowls of soup (three on the left hand, wrist, and forearm and one in the right hand).

I remember the first class under his instruction. It had to do with how to hold or carry a waiter's napkin.

He asked me how I would carry it. I had never thought about it before, had no inkling that there was a special technique for something so obvious. I took the napkin he handed me in my right hand, lifted my left arm slightly, and, with military precision, directed it under my left armpit. He tugged at the napkin and extracted it, explaining that a napkin under the armpit was highly unhygienic and therefore not acceptable. Thereafter I sported that napkin smartly draped over my left forearm.

A photograph of the "table-service" (as opposed to cooking training) class of 1953. I am in the second row, third from the left.

When one took the *cours de service,* the students "on duty" waited tables each day in the main dining room where the other students ate. We were dressed in traditional black trousers, white shirts, black bow ties, and white or black waiters' jackets. The "crew" at each service station in the dining room would stand in line awaiting the bowls of soup to be served, or the main courses, or desserts. Other students would man each serving station, ladling out the soup, carving the meats, spooning out the vegetables, and so on.

One day as I manned the serving of the various foods, something happened that colored my restaurant criticism for more than a decade.

The main course for that day was *escalopes de veau viennoise*—breaded, sautéed veal scallops garnished with anchovy fillets, lemon, capers, and chopped hard-cooked eggs. Plus a purée of potatoes. I managed to negotiate the veal scallops with suitable panache onto the plate that another student extended to me. And then I ladled on the purée. Not just a modest spoonful, but enough to cover half the plate.

"M. Claiborne," M. Tuor said, color rushing into his face, *"rien n'est plus vulgaire,"* or, "Nothing is more vulgar than an excess of food on a plate!"

I wonder how often I have used that line in fact or by implication in restaurant criticisms around the world.

Tuor, who only recently retired, took an almost paternal interest in students who showed special consideration and enthusiasm in his instructions.

It was customary for the students at the school to serve at various times—holidays, weekends, after hours, and so on—at a *stage,* pronounced stahj. You then became a *stagiaire.* Actually, a *stage* was simply on-the-job training. The students at the hotel school were much in demand in restaurants and hotels around the country. And it worked to everyone's advantage. The hotels and restaurants got reasonably well-trained waiters at a minimum cost; the students received experience and a small amount of money for their labors.

Over the months, I worked as a waiter in ski lodges as well as at grand luxe establishments such as the Lausanne Palace and the Beau Rivage on the banks of Lake Geneva.

Although all the students at the school were required to take courses in the French language, my mastery of that language through the years had proceeded at an *escargot*'s pace. I was by no means fluent when M. Tuor told me (he did not speak English, or if he did he would not admit it) that (as I got the message in my garbled fashion) a group of international "pole-stairs" was assembling at the Beau Rivage and there would be several tables of Americans, among them "a Meestair Gahlue." His eyes opened wide at the mention of the name as though it should throw me into a state of equally wide-eyed excitement. It didn't register. But I got the message; someone very important would be at a banquet at the Beau Rivage and I was to serve the head table.

When the evening arrived, I learned that the meeting was for an international committee of pollsters and the gentleman in question was George Gallup.

The banquet began and all went well until the lamb was served and the moment arrived to pour the red wine. I poured the red wine into the white wine glass, instantly petrified that M. Tuor, then roaming the room, had noticed my gaffe. Very little, when he was in a dining room, escaped his scrutiny and I was frightened.

I quickly leaned close to Mr. Gallup's ear and said, "Oh, my God, Mr. Gallup, I poured red wine into your white wine glass."

He looked up at me and smiled.

"You don't suppose," he said, "I could possibly have known the difference." He was aware of my discomfort, quickly picked up the menacing glass and drained it. I thanked him and proceeded to pour more of the liquid into the proper receptacle.

When summer came, the students were assigned to various hotels and restaurants around Europe—France, Germany, Austria, and so on —to perform their *stages*. Most of them, however, were assigned to hotels and restaurants in Switzerland. I was sent to a place called the Reinhard Hotel in a lake resort named Melchsee, a small mountain-climbing and ski area in the mountains that could only be arrived at by *téléférique*, or cable car.

It was a splendid summer, for the hotel looked out on magnificent mountains that were alive with edelweiss, and on a small, cobalt-blue lake that swarmed with salmon trout, which the chef cooked to perfection, poached and served with a hollandaise sauce. It was there, as a waiter, that I got my first taste of *Bündnerfleisch*, or *viande séchée*, one of the finest dried meats in the world. The customers, all of whom arrived on foot, must have consumed a ton of it in the course of my six-week stay there. It was sliced thin to the point of transparency, served on silver platters with garnishes of cornichons, sliced partway through at intervals and arranged to resemble small green fans.

As in many Swiss hotels, there was also a small basement room reserved to serve cheese fondues and that incredible dish called raclette, made with *Bagnes* cheese, half an enormous wheel of which is held close to a vertical charcoal fire, then scraped off onto small plates, to be eaten with boiled potatoes, pickled white onions, more cornichons (gherkins), and a generous grinding of black pepper for digestion. It was generally washed down with Swiss white wine or beer.

That summer was an idyll and one of the happiest of my life as of

Me in the summer of 1953, in front of Chez Max, a much frequented bar located directly across the street from the hotel school on Avenue du Cour in Lausanne.

that date. My relations with the Reinhard family became warm and close and I was invited back as a guest for the Christmas holidays, three months away.

And in early fall I began the course in cuisine, the actual reason I had come to Switzerland in the first place. Not that I had regretted the months I had spent in table service. I had, indeed, done well.

When I had arrived at Lausanne, my command of French was childish (I am still, regrettably, not thoroughly conversant in French). There were sixty students in the service class and I had graduated fifth. I have said repeatedly and only half jokingly that I was awarded that certificate of high standing, not because I was that proficient in the profession, but because I was always punctual in my attendance in class. The school put a high premium on *ponctualité.*

When my class in cuisine began, my euphoria and sense of well-being were heightened, if possible. What I felt at times bordered on ecstasy and for very good reasons. Basically I knew that I had found my niche, my place of comfort, and I was heartened by my success under Tuor's guidance. I could wield a fork and spoon with considerable grace and dexterity when serving the *pommes soufflé* or *crêpes* or asparagus or the various croquettes that came from the kitchen. I had learned to hurriedly replace, almost as if by legerdemain, a tablecloth suddenly wetted by an upturned glass of wine.

But more than that, I was starting to feel like an adult for the first time in my life. Reasonably secure. Even self-assured. And how little I could have foreseen my mother's shadow hovering in the pantry.

The wonders of the world that I learned to experience at that hotel school under the tutelage of my various cooking instructors are beyond measure. From the first mayonnaise and the first hollandaise; the easy mastering of the making of puff pastry (at one point I was making uncounted pounds of it five days a week with no more thought than when I make a pie pastry today); the shaping and baking of *bouchées,* tartelettes, barquettes; the making of ramequins and *rissoles* and pâtés; the preparation of *beignets,* soufflés, and quiches. Quiches, Lorraine or otherwise, were wholly unknown to Americans at that time. I discovered blanquettes and fricassées, fish cookery and roasts. I learned to braise and sauté and to clarify consommés. And how to prepare glorious dishes like those named *toulousaine,* made with a suprême sauce with chicken, sweetbreads, quenelles of veal or chicken.

I have never doted on most desserts but the course in patisserie under the guidance of Charles Ganguillet was more fun than a carnival. Under him I learned to make breads, brioches, croissants, kugelhopfs, savarins, babas, and the dozens of good things that can be fashioned from *pâte à choux,* or cream puff pastry. There were meringues and creams and, most of all perhaps, for that is where my fancy lay, gelatin desserts like Bavarian creams, *riz à l'impératrice,* and charlottes. There was *crème renversée* and *crème Beau Rivage,* sweet soufflés—both baked and frozen—and omelets. And sherbets and frozen bombes.

I felt blessed, I thrived emotionally and suddenly it was Christmas.

My lines of communication with the Reinhard family had not been broken and I took the train to Zurich and the *téléférique* to the hotel, the grounds of which were three feet under with snow. Several acquaintances, English students at the school, had come along as paying guests.

It was a spectacular holiday that ended in an emotional tragedy.

I had never had an athletic bone in my body but, at the suggestion of the Reinhard family, I took skiing instructions on the first three days of my visit. It was a heady, exhilarating experience, going down those small beginners' hills at what seemed like an intoxicating speed.

On the fourth day, the English students noted my enthusiasm on those small slopes and they taunted me to come along to the top of the hill. I took it both as a dare and as a possible adventure. And so, in their company, I traversed that snow-laden track to the ski lift.

I buckled myself in and we started to climb. At that point there was no turning back. And up we went. And up. And up. And up.

I unbuckled and piled out and glanced down at the bottom of that incline and reckoned it must be at least ten thousand feet away. And, God knows, there was no place, no way to hide and the only direction was down.

It took me three hours to get down. The English party would slide down about twenty feet and position themselves to catch me. It would not have gone faster had I had my feet encased in a gunny sack.

By the time we reached the bottom, the Englishmen were out of sorts and angry that I'd spoiled their day. So they left me with a few hundred feet to negotiate across the snow before attempting the climb up a small hill and the safety of the hotel. I was both tired and terrified to be alone. And just as I started to turn sideways to clinch my skis one at a time up the last climb, I coughed and the snow was splattered with blood. I don't know why I hemorrhaged.

I made it back to the hotel and quieted myself as best I could with a few straight shots of kirschwasser.

Two days later, after a night of crushing pains in my chest, I was taken on a tortured ride to a hospital in Lausanne where I was given massive doses of antibiotics to counteract an acute attack of pneumonia.

It was a severe illness, not only physically painful but psychologically. I felt cheated and endlessly grieved that I was missing weeks of my beloved instruction. Gradually I recovered and at the end of two and a half weeks, the doctor came to tell me that I could leave the hospital the next morning.

But a devastating thing happened.

That afternoon I had a call from Ernest Loewer, a *chef de cuisine* and one of my most respected instructors in the school. He was a tall man of serious mien, shy and not overly affable to the students. He very much kept his distance.

I was both surprised, if not startled, and pleased at his visit. Flattered is not too strong a word. And then he spoke.

"I had a telephone call from your mother, who asked me to visit you . . ."

I don't recall his reaction. I cringed. It was an insupportable humiliation. Here she was, her whole presence filling that room and smothering me, her infant son, her thirty-odd-year-old babe in the cradle.

I don't have any memory of M. Loewer leaving or saying good-by. I only know that an hour later the pains in my chest became so intense that my doctor was summoned to diagnose a total relapse of my condition. I also know that he looked baffled and totally bewildered as though he had come across a disease that had not yet been catalogued in medical journals.

I remained in the hospital for two additional weeks and was not permitted to return to my classes at the hotel school until the first of February. In my absence I had missed two periods of instruction that I had desperately wanted to participate in—ice sculpture and sugar-working, including the making of spun sugar. The pains in my chest were incessant and I was in constant agony but at least I could function. And apparently well. At the end of the term exercises it was announced that I had finished eighth in my class with a coveted *"mention très bien"* on my certificate of studies.

§ § §

By far the most turbulent, inundating, tormenting, and tumultuous incident of my adult life was my *final* and *total* estrangement from my mother. In any summation of my life as it had thus far been lived, it looms so large as to be impossible to ignore. Whether good or bad, for better or for worse, I am at peace with myself, the cause and effect of my separation from her.

Prior to that separation I lived in an atmosphere of total suffocation as—it seems to me—only a mother's love can suffocate. I felt emasculated in her presence. And even in the presence of her letters. I was inundated with her letters, which served as a giant-sized umbilical cord wrapped unceremoniously and noose-like around my neck.

Throughout my college days and my years in the U. S. Navy, I would receive at least once, and more often than not twice, each week, fat documents filled with gossip and remembrances, but more than that, declarations of love and admiration that make the exchanges between Robert Browning and Elizabeth Barrett seem adulterated and naïve.

"I love and miss you. Each evening in my nightgown, I kneel at my bed and pray that God will reunite us before I die. That He will lead you to know and understand and forgive your attitude towards me.

"I harbor but one single wish in this life, that you may know that there is no perfect love except that of a mother. Next to that of our Saviour, it is . . ."

It seemed to me that as time progressed during my years in the Navy, whether in the Atlantic or the Pacific, her letters became more obsessed.

"The love of a mother is the most god-like thing in the world. Only that of God alone and His Son . . ."

She scarcely mentioned my father. "Your father sends his love." My father rarely wrote.

There were times when I was at sea that her words leaped out tarantula-like at me and I had no defense. I could look wildly into the winds and toss those missives over the side of my destroyer escort (the time that stands out most clearly is during the Korean conflict), aching with despondent anger and bewilderment at this all-embracing, smothering love. There was no place to escape on that boat, no place to scurry to, no walls to crack my skull on without making a horribly unmilitary-like spectacle. No place to cry except into a pillow. And that I did. Silently. And in buried fury. No place to scream.

I wonder how many hundreds, no thousands of shredded pages of her words have fed fish from Guam to Japan.

I kept reminding myself, as she kept reminding me, that she was my mother. I would remember that in my infancy and early childhood I had idolized her. I could visualize her spectacularly beautiful face, that magnificent head of wavy hair, at one time or another almost floor-length. I recalled the laughter that we had shared together. I felt insane. The world at large, those who knew her, admired her for her good humor and enchanting tales of her life as it was or had been.

And then came the awful confrontation, the most powerful and poignant moment of my adulthood. It occurred in a room and in the corridors of the Waldorf-Astoria Hotel on Park Avenue.

Although I can relate the smallest details of our encounter that evening I cannot remember the exact year. I was in my mid-thirties.

On the evening in question we had quarreled. Quietly. I had been drinking moderately but in her presence at that moment I felt a power-ful need for a drink. We had just returned from the theater and I was depositing her at the hotel as all good southern sons and lovers must do, at her "doorstep."

On that evening I had felt her physical presence more closely than usual. She sat too close to me for filial comfort. It was an annoyance I could never have spelled out to her, nor hinted at.

In her hotel room before I kissed her good night, I was angry and somehow I must have expressed this.

"Sometimes," she said, "you really drive me to the point of exasper-ation." She placed her tiny, lace-edged, embroidered handkerchief onto her mouth and turned her head away from me. "I'm your mother and that's all I've ever wanted to be."

"But, Mother," I said, the word mother coming out as reflexively as breath or an inadvertent yell, "that's what I mean!"

I was quietly furious, emotionally embittered, and frustrated. It was not the frustration of the moment but an accumulation of emotions that had engulfed my body almost since birth. I had felt it when I was in that hospital room in Switzerland and had suffered a relapse of pneumonia; at the University of Missouri when she had tried to use a senator's influence to have a play produced; at etc., etc.

It seemed to me that in this episode, it was as though scores of years, lives, hopes, generations of sons and mothers were involved in this evening at the Waldorf, a curious place for Southerners of that genera-tion. But I would still beg for an accommodation with her.

"Mother, listen to me. Please. I can't always be your baby. Why can't you understand, why can't you realize?" I paused. "Why must you be so eternally, so God-horribly a mother!"

She turned to me, eyes reddened, inflamed. But she wasn't crying, the handkerchief dabbing at her nose.

"Mother, please. Can't you understand? Please." Pause. "Mother? Can't we be friends?"

"Your *friend?*" Her cold, unsentimental sarcasm was rising and frightening. She twisted her mouth right and left, up and down, and turned away.

"How can you *speak* to me like that?" she asked plaintively. "I know I haven't been much as a mother. But it wasn't easy to maintain my family. To make ends meet. I made every sacrifice and . . ."

The tears were beginning to well up in her eyes.

"I can never be anything except your mother; I don't know how to be." And now the tears were flowing freely.

"Mother," I said. "Good night," and walked out of the room, know-ing full well that the indomitable Miss Kathleen would survive with or without my presence.

I never saw her again.

Throughout my life, whenever my mother had wanted to reprimand me for a real or imagined slight or hurt, she would declare, "You're going to be punished for that." She did not imply that she was going to do it. Nor was my father. She meant the Lord was going to get my hide, either in heaven or here on earth.

It wasn't the Lord that got at me. She did. Even in death, through remembrance of things past.

Curiously enough, my mother, after that evening at the Waldorf, was instrumental in initiating an action that would end in a lifelong severance of our relationship. It had become desperately clear to me that her emotional hammer-lock hold on me was forever. A caged animal, I felt, wants to claw and resist and attack. Purring doesn't help if it doesn't open doors, unleash leashes. After our last meeting I had felt hopelessly impuissant; I had lost reasons to resist. Overwhelmed with what had been impudently, but accurately, called smother love, I retreated more than I was accustomed into the shadows of alcohol.

On her return to Mississippi I received a letter from her containing a check for a hundred dollars. It was a great deal of money for her to offer. It was a great deal of money to me at that moment. I didn't make much more than that in a week.

"My darling son," she wrote, "I think you are ill. I want you to take this money and go to a psychiatrist."

Of course, it was a ridiculous gesture, but I didn't think of it in that way. I think she was honestly concerned with my well-being. I might have been desperate, I might have felt caged, but I wasn't angry. In retrospect, I think I felt a surge of relief, that for the first time this represented some sort of compromise on her part. At the time, however, I could not verbalize my feelings on the subject.

What the hell. I certainly had nothing to lose. Besides, it might be interesting to see the inside of an analyst's office. Like peeking into the windows of a Catholic church as a small child. Might even see what an analyst's couch looked like. It would be at least worth the hundred bucks.

I was thirty-five years old and I was, in retrospect, courting disaster. I lived in a tawdry apartment in the section of New York known as Yorkville or Germantown, an interesting old neighborhood where German immigrants had congregated and settled when they migrated here a generation and more ago.

There were beer "gardens" and Konditoreis and Brauhauses and assorted other restaurants that specialized in dishes like sauerkraut and pork hocks and pickled pigs' knuckles and hogs' head cheese. It was there that I would of an evening, almost any evening, drink myself into a stupor, touring the streets, dangerously roaming in search of sexual gratification. Some of my uniformed objects of desire would have been capable of arresting me on the spot.

With that hundred dollars in my pocket, I steeled myself one fine morning and entered the offices of a doctor who practiced near my apartment. I was shown into the doctor's inner office.

"Sit down," he said. I sat.

"Is this your first visit to an analyst?"

"Yes," I replied, "and I'm here mostly for advice." I started to explain that I had a hundred dollars in my pocket for starters and a mass of problems. The doctor arranged his face in a compassionate manner coupled with a look of bemused exasperation and explained gently but distinctly that August was coming on, that he would shortly be going away on vacation, and that even if he weren't, his calendar was full and besides, he implied, charity was not his bag.

I stood, prepared to say good-bye.

He also stood and walked toward me, gazing more than a little probingly into my eyes.

"Listen," he said. "There's an out-patient clinic in town. It's known as the Payne Whitney Psychiatric Center at New York Hospital. They do take patients for treatment for a very small fee. It might be about twenty dollars a month."

That was, of course, more than twenty years ago. He jotted down the name and address.

"Tell them that I referred you. But don't hold out much hope. They've got a waiting list a couple of city blocks long. But perhaps they can take you in the fall. Talk to them now."

I felt an uncommon feeling of relief when I left his office. I grabbed a cab and shot over to the hospital.

I was shown into the office of a young doctor who conducted routine interviews.

"I must tell you," he said with some urgency, "there are absolutely no openings at the present time. You'd be lucky to get treatment within a year. But I'll go through a few routine questions anyway."

In approximately five minutes I had described my perilous present and my parlous past. I made uninhibited confessions about my childhood and my carryings on, night after endless night, since I had arrived in Manhattan. I stayed fifteen minutes or so, far longer, I surmised, than the period for which I was scheduled.

"Okay," he said, "come back Friday. We'll give you consultations twice a week and the cost will be five dollars a week. When you come back you will see Dr. Thomas Smith."

In my books there is today no conflict between psychiatry of a benevolent sort and religion. I don't mean a "born again" feverish type of religion or a God-of-our-fathers token-style religion. But I believe in God, a merciful, protective Being, somewhere out There, Everywhere and Nowhere, a Being who cares. Or perhaps I'm superstitious to the core. My *God* may be only my lucky stone, my healing worry beads, something to caress or appeal to in times of danger or distress. What I'm trying to say briefly is that in my mind some Being (my own father who was then in heaven), some caring Thing, led me to that clinic.

What if, I think of in horror today, I hadn't been directed there? The possibilities are too awful to contemplate.

For those who are unaware of such things, I might add that psychotherapy and psychoanalysis, while related, are two different things. To explain the difference in my own superficial manner, psychoanalysis digs much more deeply into the human psyche. Like digging out a deep-seated cancer. Psychotherapy is much less weighty. In discussions with your doctor, you simply talk out your problems, let them emerge to the point that you can face them. And as they emerge you explore the degree to which you and others have given them shape and size. You learn to evaluate blame. You learn that you may have been taught to place blame on yourself unreasonably and without question. And sometimes, with luck, you learn to forgive yourself for the "sins" that you have innocently allowed others to insinuate in your own soul.

Psychotherapy, in my own case at least, simply involved lengthy and detailed conversations, explorations in cold and sometimes painful details of every disturbance, major and minor, in my own life. Dr. Smith did not preach, he rarely admonished me to conduct my life in one way or another. He simply directed me to let my own feelings, thoughts, truths, and falsehoods come forth, out of those regions where I was most deeply disturbed. Through my own probing, through his persistent questioning to determine the "real" reason that certain events had occurred in my life, I was able to forgo, millimeter by millimeter, day by day, my self-detestation and therefore, self-destruction. My God, what forgotten truths and happenings the mind can dredge up, what horrors lie buried under layer after layer of fantasy and wishful and unwished-for hope and self-hatred.

Of pure psychiatry—as opposed to psychotherapy—I have little knowledge. I only know that it is more profound.

Nor could I explain in one brief chapter how I was able to stop writhing and to emerge from the straightjacket of my childhood; to loosen all those knots that my mother had so thoughtlessly, so innocently and diligently—with the best will in the world—tied.

Briefly, I simply explored my life from the crib to the present. I learned and somehow came to understand the devouring nature of the woman from whose womb I had emerged. I learned to shed ties, more often than not with hideous effect but without retreat or apology. I learned that my father might well have been, probably was aware, and with God knows what inner pain to his own being, of my sexual dreams, of my desire to possess him.

Did I learn to loathe my father? Of course not. How can you loathe someone who was not responsible for his actions, an unwitting victim of circumstance. My father was an innocent, to my mind a supernatural innocent with an unswerving belief in the goodness of man and life on earth and an eternal belief in the goodness of God.

Do I still hate my mother?

Of course not. She, too, was a victim of culture, of her time and place. The ultimate southern belle. An aristocrat living in her illusory spiritual (and at times actual) garden of magnolia and Cape jasmine. She was uniquely born into a southern world in which the family was not composed of individuals but the body entire, one bond, one blood.

Thus, in that mystic land, known as the South, as the mother's heart pumped blood through her own veins and arteries, thus it courses— or so she believed—through the body of her children, rhythmically and in time, heartbeat for heartbeat, even though those children had emerged from the womb days, months, years, even decades earlier.

And if any member of the family wandered away from the heart and hearth it was an amputation, pure and simple, the deprivation of a limb.

§ § §

My schooling finished, there was little doubt in my mind as to my next destination. In sum, it seemed that there was no place to go but Manhattan. Certainly not Chicago (which has subsequently become one of my favorite cities), and life on the West Coast seemed too superficial and idyllic.

When I arrived in New York, my life was as pitiable as it had ever been and, but for the good graces of my Staten Island cousins, I would have been destitute. I was at ends as loose as spaghetti boiling in a pot.

I desperately needed advice and direction. In search of that I visited various publications, including *McCall's,* then considered the best magazine for food articles, *Ladies' Home Journal,* and *Gourmet* to talk with food editors. Each of those with whom I spoke dropped one man's name. One of the editors agreed to arrange an interview with *him.*

The reigning man on the hotel scene in those days was a bifocaled gent named Claude Philippe, the grand panjandrum (he often signed his name Claudius) of the Waldorf-Astoria. I gained admission to his august presence and found him to be a thoroughly terrifying, unpleasant bully. Among other things, I was still suffering those residual chest pains following that bout of pneumonia and other complications in Switzerland.

When I walked into his office I found him as rude as I found him abrupt. He had a battery of four or more telephones on his desk, all of which seemed to be ringing in unison. He held one phone up to his left ear, another to his right ear, and he was talking into both. Secretaries and assorted male flunkies of the Waldorf's banquet department, of which he was the head, kept charging in for instructions or a daily dressing down, or porting him snippets of food and drink so as not to interrupt his labors.

I was inclined then, as I fear I still am today, to have an abiding faith and belief in the goodness and altruistic nature of mankind. If there was anything I did not want to be then or ever it was a hotel or restaurant man. I was in Philippe's presence as one in need of advice. I had heard from many quarters of this man's omnipotence and in my innocence presumed he might guide me down God knows what proper path simply by saying a word.

Instead, in the din of that room and the electric passion that seemed to invade that man's presence, I stood petrified and in a state of semi-shock.

He extended me a hand freed for a second from his telephone and scowled as he spoke. God frowning down from Olympus.

"Well, speak up," he commanded. "What are you here for? Charles," he said to an assistant, "call room service and tell them to deliver two dozen long-stemmed roses to the Duchess of Windsor's suite and tell them that Elsa Maxwell said that the magnum of champagne delivered to her room last night was lukewarm."

He interrupted himself and glared at me again.

"I don't know what I want. I simply wanted advice."

"I've no time for this nonsense. This is a banquet department and I'm not conducting a counseling service. I understand you graduated from some hotel school in Switzerland and you're looking for work. If you want to work in this department, the hours are from nine to midnight, seven days a week, and the salary is seventy-five dollars a week with meals."

My chest was killing me. And yet I was genuinely amused at this tawdry, Alice-in-Wonderland performance. The man's crazy, I thought, and if he's willing to employ me so precipitately, without so much as an inquiry as to whether I know the difference between a white wine and red wine glass, whether I know the difference between a hollandaise and béarnaise sauce, between a finger bowl and a soup bowl, this man who is banquet manager of what is generally touted to be the finest hotel in America, then by God, I'll sign on for a while.

Besides, I was dead broke and needed money. Even the pathetic sum that he'd mentioned. I was hired on the spot.

Needless to say, perhaps, my stay at that hostelry was brief.

My first assignment, which came directly from Philippe, was as preposterous as my sudden employment.

It was customary and doubtlessly still is in New York for representatives of the banquet departments of various hotels to cater to the well-to-do sponsors of various social and charity functions in the hope that they would stage some grand event—a ball, an enormous banquet, a wine and cheese tasting, and so on—in their particular hotel. It was big business. And if the society or organization was stylish enough, it was good publicity as well.

Newspapers had society columns and it followed that these various events were published as news of the day. "The April in Paris Ball will be held at the Waldorf next week," "The Grande Dames of Champagne will hold their annual festival at the Pierre," and so on.

Philippe approached me with a sheaf of newspaper clippings, all of which mentioned current social affairs to be held in one hotel or another. The various functions had been arranged. The hotels had been firmly chosen. And the newspaper accounts all listed the times and dates, and so on.

"Telephone each of these groups and ask them to change their plans. Tell them we'll welcome them to the Waldorf."

I accepted the clippings from him, struggled with a smile, and went into my private cubicle, closing the door after me.

I found pad and pencil and started my rounds of telephoning.

As each party answered the telephone, I explained that I was a member of the Waldorf's banquet department, that I understood that he or she had planned a function to be held at such and such a hotel on such and such a date, but how pleased I'd be if I might have the honor of discussing their affair for the following year. I simply wanted to know, I said, who to contact at some future date.

I noted the names of everyone I'd spoken to. I made a notation, a brief résumé, of every response and a day or so later I walked into Philippe's office to make my report.

"Well," he said, dark-rimmed glasses penetrating deep into the recesses of my mind. "Well," he bellowed, "what have you arranged? Has anyone shifted their function to the Waldorf?"

"Mr. Philippe," I began, humility dripping from each syllable. "I have spoken to the entire list and have plans to meet them for next year's . . ."

He interrupted me, anger burning at his temples, veins throbbing.

"YOU'RE A FAILURE!" he screamed, slamming his hand on the desk.

I, who all my life had feared scenes, who would rather be branded a coward than face an emotional conflict, had the most exquisite desire to laugh. I suddenly wasn't afraid of this bespectacled, unhandsome piece of pâpier-maché with vocal cords. I walked out of his office, said good-by to the few friends I'd made during my five-day tenure, and left the hotel as hurriedly as possible.

I'd rather sweep floors or drive a cab, I thought.

I could never have divined that the day would come when I would give that ill-mannered poseur his due when he became an owner of Le Pavillon restaurant.

I only knew that my chest pains were better. And that I was out of a job.

It was a Friday morning when I walked out of that famous address at Fiftieth Street and Park Avenue. I was feeling rather spry and, for me, I had an unaccustomed sense of self-confidence. I made my way on foot to the Plaza Hotel, that grandest of New York hostelries. I had not gone there for sentiment, however. I was there because the editorial offices of *Gourmet* magazine were located in the penthouse.

I took the elevator at the south side entrance and walked into one of the most palatial suites in all the city; oak-paneled walls, carpets, and so on.

I asked to see the editor and was ushered into the offices of Ann Seranne, a tall, bosomy, glorious-looking blonde who, I learned years later, was really named Margaret Smith, from Hamilton, Canada. Ann was on the food scene long before the world ever heard of Julia Child. And of all the people who have had no professional training in food, was, and still is, one of the greatest, most creative food personalities in America. She started out in her very young years as companion/housemistress for Crosby Gaige, a theatrical producer who was considered to be one of the few great gourmets in America in the first half of this century. Gaige signed his name to several cookbooks that were actually written by Ann.

I've always been amused by the story Ann tells about the time she declared her independence from Gaige, whom she loved.

It is her contention that Crosby Gaige taught her almost everything she knows about food (a fond exaggeration) and wine, which is considerable.

Gaige owned an estate in upstate New York called Watch Hill Farm. He was lord of the manor and dearly loved to indulge himself in hedonistic pleasures, particularly those that involved the table.

During Ann's years with him, he requested that each morning he be served an egg dish and it was his wish that he never be served the same egg dish twice. Ann prepared his breakfast each day and, sure enough, she never duplicated a dish made with eggs. There were eggs poached, cooked *mollet,* scrambled, turned into omelets, made into soufflés, shirred, and so on. She accumulated over a period of years sufficient recipes to prepare another book and she showed the manuscript to Crosby Gaige.

"I told him," she declared later, "that this book was too personal and that I couldn't have another name on it." She found a publisher, Doubleday, rightly affixed her own name to it, *The Art of Egg Cookery,* and its success was admirable.

Crosby, incidentally, married Cecelia, the housekeeper who succeeded Ann. The book is dedicated to Cecelia Gaige.

When on leaving Philippe's I walked into Ann's office, she stood and smiled with a warmth that could have roasted chestnuts. But she was pressed for time.

I told her that my one great goal in life was to write and, more than that, to write about food, for that was the only thing that I was morally equipped to write about.

Ann could scarcely have been more hospitable and patient, but she did on occasion glance at her wristwatch (this distraction was more noticeable with her than with most people because the watch itself was situated not on the back of her wrist but rather on the underside where the pulse is). After all, it was Friday afternoon. And she owned a house, a refuge on the dunes at Fire Island. And like many New Yorkers with weekend abodes, it was her habit to disappear from Manhattan as soon after the clock struck the noon hour as possible. Within the space of half an hour I related my experiences at the Lausanne hotel school and mentioned in passing that I had a degree in Journalism.

"Have you ever had anything published?" she asked.

"No," I said. "Nothing serious. I once sold two brief articles to the Chicago *Tribune.*" And that was the truth. Each of the articles, I told her, had measured less than six-column inches in the newspaper.

She stood and withdrew a lipstick from her purse. An obvious gesture to signal that I was about to be dispatched in only a moment.

"If you want to try your hand at an article for me, I could use one on the subject of tea. About three thousand words and with recipes!" She extended her hand, started for the door, and said good-bye.

My emotions raced between delirious joy and the agony of probable failure in the assignment. But there was one thing certain. I had no obligations other than to myself. And I was too poor to have any destination other than the five-cent ferry back to my cousins' home on Staten Island.

So I walked to the public library at Forty-second Street and Fifth Avenue and checked out every conceivable volume that might be related to tea. En route I had purchased a note pad. I must have, within the course of that Friday afternoon, painstakingly copied down a hundred pages of notes in longhand.

When I returned to my room on that other island, I borrowed a battered Underwood and transcribed all my notes into a more legible form.

I worked the following day and made a final draft—with recipes for a hot tea punch, a chilled tea beverage with orange and mint, spiced tea, tea with rum, and a frozen tea ice.

I dubbed this effort "Steeped in History" and on Monday morning, promptly at 9 A.M., walked into the offices of *Gourmet* magazine. I greeted Ann Seranne when she came in the door.

She paused and frowned and gave me a slightly puzzled look. "See here," I could imagine her saying, "you're becoming a downright pest." I handed her my manuscript.

"Come in," she said, and led me into her office. She read the manuscript hurriedly, shaking her head occasionally, glancing at me, reading, and with the trace of a smile on her lips.

"I like it," she said. "In fact, I'll buy it. We pay three hundred and fifty dollars an article."

I wanted to laugh or cry, but more to the point I was speechless.

"Well, I must confess I never thought I'd see you again." She paused. "Okay, how about doing an article on vodka?" That did it. I felt finally free to move my body and belongings to Manhattan. No more ferry boats; no more dining in the bosom of relations with whom relations were strained. I moved within two days to the West Side YMCA, which was and is located on Sixty-third Street, only a step or two from Central Park. My room wasn't much larger than a small cubicle but it had a comfortable bed and a bare table on which to place a rented typewriter. Less than a week later I had an article on vodka in Ann's hands. The article on tea appeared in *Gourmet* in the January 1955 issue, the article on vodka, "Blithe Spirits," two months later.

When Ann received the vodka article, she made an appointment to talk to me seriously about steady employment, which I desperately wanted.

"Unfortunately," she said, "our budget's a bit restricted and there aren't any openings. I certainly can't create a niche for you or anyone else." This conversation took place in late May or early June.

"The only thing I can offer you is a job as receptionist. And, as I told you, that position won't be open until October. Even if you could afford to wait until then, would you really want to have such a menial job—opening reader mail, answering telephone calls, greeting the hundreds of oddballs that come into this magazine every day?"

"Yes," I said. I might have added that I would have washed all the dishes in the test kitchen in addition to see my name in print.

"Okay," she said. "It's your funeral."

Precisely how I intended to pay my keep over the next five months did not immediately enter my mind. Although I had training both as a cook and as a waiter, I was still afflicted with that old ego problem. I would never have applied for work with a respectable restaurant and, besides, I presumed that all the waiters in Manhattan of necessity belonged to a waiters' union. What's more, I knew not one restaurant owner nor one member of any restaurant staff.

And thus I did what countless generations of unemployed New Yorkers have done before me. I consulted the employment pages of what was then known as the good gray *Times*. And wound up one Monday morning at a sleazy, small, ill-staffed employment office in the mid-forties on the West Side of town.

I was interviewed by a short, dumpy, coatless, thin-haired, red-faced pudge of a man who had an unlit cigar butt dangling from one side of his mouth.

"The only job I can offer you," he said without enthusiasm, "is in upstate New York. It's a summer joint located slightly north of Nyack. They need someone to double as waiter and bartender. You ever tended bar?"

"Yes," I said, which was not exactly a lie. They had taught "bar" at the hotel school. "And I've waited tables, too." I didn't lay all my cards on the table by telling him that I had waited tables at some of the fancier hotels in Switzerland. He couldn't have cared less and I knew it. I was an able body that could fill an available slot, which would mean a few, very few, bucks in his pocket by simply making a telephone call. He made the call and the next morning I was on my way to a town whose name I have comfortably chosen to forget and, more specifically, to a roadside restaurant or tavern known, to choose a name discreetly, as the Do-Drop-Inn. That is only a wee distortion of the actual name of the place.

That was to be, as it turned out, one of the most interesting and awful summers of my life.

It may or may not be pertinent that it has always been my contention that God in His heaven invariably awards me with answered prayers, my psychological built-in defense against the terrors of this world. If I have faith, He will protect me against mine enemies. If I will it, He will give it to me. Jesus loves me.

Once, years ago, I confided to a friend that there was one role in the world that I would love to play. I wanted to be a bartender for the simple reason that alcohol bares men's souls and allows them, nay, bids them, to remove their masks and disclose their confidences and frequently in a voice of sufficient timbre that these "innermost secrets" can be overheard by a bartender. I wanted to tune into the world's "innermost secrets." Little did I dream how boring and deadly those secrets could be. At the end of two days you pray for a hearing aid to tune them out. A bartender becomes confidant and psychiatrist to some of the most stupefyingly dull and repetitive people on earth.

I showed up at the Do-Drop about noon and met the man who was to be my patron for that endless summer at the foot of the Catskills. He turned out to be a good-looking, baby-faced, dishonest oaf whose name I recall too vividly to print for fear of retaliation, even at a date this far removed.

What I remember most about him is that his eyes never met yours head-on, even when he was romancing you rather than ordering you to get down on your hands and knees and scrub the floor of that bar with extra effort.

Mornings it reeked of stale beer and bad alcohol blended with last night's cigar smoke mingled with the odors of oft-used deep-fat frying that emanated from the unclean premises known as a kitchen.

The normal complement of the restaurant was four employees, although that number varied depending on the temper of the boss from fray to fray. The staff consisted of a cook, for whom the cares of the world had long ago driven him to drink; a slightly demented and woefully scented scullery lad, whom I knew to be a petty thief; and a second bartender-waiter named Paul, whom I happened to admire because he was so awesomely contented and without ambition.

Paul had a bottomless collection of filthy stories and he was a fine drinking companion, full of total insouciance and nose-thumbing. On the days when the boss, whom I shall call Josh, made his weekly trip to New York, Paul and I would try to outdo each other in drinking up the profits, more often than not buying drinks for any and all comers who happened to arrive half an hour before the bar closed.

Josh must have been aware of our indulgences but he would never have fired either Paul or me. He had never dreamed that he would have in his employ so much talent at his disposal to be paid such insignificant salaries. And that we would augment our salaries that summer by consuming our patrons' drinks I will not deny.

The summer was one of the hottest on record. Irremediably scorching. The employees were bunched together in what would have been an attic if such quarters could have been dignified by so lofty a term. We slept in single cots directly beneath a sullenly, unremittingly hot tin roof. On alternate days, Paul and I would go to the bar to swab the floor, toss the empties into the garbage, and clean the toilets when the scullery lad had—or willed—a day off. Because of the heat, sleep was almost unthinkable.

There would be an hour's break in the morning when I would walk the countryside; lunch would be scheduled from 11 A.M. until 2 P.M.; more bar cleaning; two hours off in the afternoon; and work at the bar or in the dining room until eleven or midnight, depending on the crowds. On weekends the bar was open until the last guest floated awkwardly, stumblingly, out into the darkness.

Tips from the motley clientele that frequented the place were not lavish but they were adequate—I was able to clear a hundred dollars a week. On my one day off each week, I would gather my dollar bills and my change and take a bus into Manhattan. The manager of the Roosevelt Hotel had attended the Lausanne school and, as a consequence, I got a room at a discount.

I would take the bus into the city in the morning, check into the Roosevelt, sleep until five, go to one bar or another for two hours, splurge on dinner, drink a few glasses of Cognac, and take the last bus back to the restaurant. When I took early leave from that establishment, I had approximately $250 in cash, the entire sum of my savings over a period of about three months.

I couldn't space that job through until October when I could become receptionist at *Gourmet* magazine. Not because of the throbbing heat; not because of the riveting hours; but because of a curiously old-fashioned sense of ethics.

One morning I was unable to sleep until the accustomed hour of seven o'clock. The heat was more intense than usual. I'd risen at dawn, showered, shaved, and ambled downstairs to clean the bar.

I spotted Josh behind the bar, seated. He was fiddling with bottles, which especially at that hour seemed strange and unaccustomed. He didn't drink. (I have always been suspicious of uninitiated thoroughgoing teetotalers.) He wasn't aware of my presence. In his left hand he held an empty bottle of Chivas Regal. There was a funnel in the neck of the bottle. In his right hand he held a bottle of bar scotch, an inexpensive, chemical-tasting blend. He was pouring it into the bottle labeled Chivas Regal. I quietly made my way back up the stairs. It would be dramatic to say that I was shocked. To my great regret, I wasn't. It was to my mind a hitherto unformulated pattern of his. The fact was simply too perverse, too believable to be shocking. I thought about it for a considerable time and shrugged my shoulders. After all, it was his life, his ethics, not mine. He was corrupt. I was not through professional association corrupted by his evil. We weren't "buddies," although he had fascinated me over the weeks and I accepted, had even liked him on his own distorted terms. But there was certainly no need for a sentimental confrontation nor for me to give him moral preachments. So be it. The event passed in silence.

During my days as a bartender, the legal "drinking age" for New Jersey and New York was different. In New York you could buy a drink across a bar when you were eighteen years old. In New Jersey the legal age to buy such a drink was twenty or twenty-one. As a consequence, there were a few hundred kids from New Jersey who came each Saturday night to the Do-Drop-Inn to fill their gullets, and I phrase that inelegantly but factually. Many of them generally drank gallons of beer in the course of the evening, which scarcely surprised me; I'd done the same thing in college. A lot of the young girls were curiously adventurous in their drinking and to this day I can't fathom why. They would order drinks that had been popular in the 1920s when their mothers and perhaps their grandmothers were "flappers," drinks such as a pink lady or a jack rose or a Singapore sling or a sloe gin fizz.

Needless to say, those various decoctions, blended in the stomach, inevitably led to nausea and the sounds of retching and, on Sunday mornings, the floor and toilets of the room marked "Ladies" were slick with vomit. It took gallons of detergents and spray and disinfectants to cleanse the surroundings, including the air.

The days passed and the nights and at long last September came. A month remained before I was to part with the tortures of that summer forever. I had twice spoken to Ann Seranne, who expressed pleasure that I intended to join the staff of *Gourmet.*

With the advent of Labor Day, the young crowds started to throng to the Do-Drop-Inn with greater thirst gusto than ever. On Friday night of that weekend there was standing room only. For some reason or another, a group of spirited young kids had arrived from Quebec and the place took on the sounds of Babel at its most boisterous.

Along about ten o'clock I took a break and walked out the back door for a breath of air.

Josh followed me.

"Want to make a few extra bucks this weekend? I don't mean few. Lots."

"How?"

"I tell you what you do. Not a kid in this room will leave here sober tonight. Simply add ten bucks to every check and we'll split."

I frowned. Silence. A mixed bag of emotions flooded my body. Tell him quietly to go copulate with himself? Spit? Jab him in the stomach? Yell?

"Thanks, Josh. I'm not that hungry."

"You won't do it?" he asked, for the first time glaring at me straight in the eye in that half darkness.

"Never. Peculiar I may seem to you, but I've never robbed and been nastily dishonest in my life."

The next morning I packed my bags and, without saying good-by, boarded the earliest bus back to town. I was depressed, filled with a curious sense of relief, but, most of all, prayerful that I had enough cash to see me through the next few weeks. I took the subway back to the West Side Y.

Gourmet magazine was, in those days, no worker's paradise and my jobs were multiple. I manned the telephone, directed incoming calls to the proper parties, and answered "reader correspondence" both by letter directly to the reader and in print, courtesy of a column called "You Asked For It."

Within a short period of time I relinquished my job as receptionist and was elevated to an untitled position working in the magazine's elegantly paneled library and sitting behind a massive oak desk. In that position I continued to make entries in the letters column. More importantly, I took over a column called "Along the Boulevards." I also edited the recipes that came in under the name Louis Diat. His monthly contribution, called "Menu Classique," was, in fact, written by his amanuensis, a lady named Helen Ridley. My labors also included writing and supplying recipes for major articles each month.

There were several issues during the months of 1955 when I contributed major articles with no accreditation, articles with titles like "Ugly Duckling of the Deep" (lobster), "Pariah Pigs and Hallowed Hams" (pork in general), and "Les Crèmes de Carême" (Bavarian creams). There is only one thing more lacerating than a whiplash to an author's ego; ergo, seeing written words for thoughts that he gave birth to without an acknowledgment of his name. Eventually, I did get credit for what I consider one of the best articles I ever wrote. I had been asked to write an article on hunt breakfasts. I explained that I had never been aboard a horse in my life, never seen a fox, and had no idea what those rich folk, whom Oscar Wilde termed "the unspeakable in full pursuit of the uneatable," ate at the end of the chase.

I stated that I should fly down to hunt country in Virginia and write about an actual hunt breakfast. I was informed that there was no money for such a whimsical, nonessential caprice. Where was my talent?

And so I contrived the piece quoting Samuel Johnson as well as Wilde: "It is very strange and very melancholy," Johnson had written, "that the paucity of human pleasures should persuade us ever to call hunting one of them." I concluded the article, a spoof on my own inability to ride, with serious recipes for dishes that included a double partridge pie, a grits soufflé, broiled tomatoes, veal kidney flamed with

Cognac, mushrooms in Burgundy wine, beaten biscuits, a pecan and Bourbon cake, and pocketbook rolls. The recipes for the biscuits and pocketbook rolls had come from my mother's manuscript cookbook.

During my days of employment *Gourmet* was in no sense known for its largess. Although my output then was prodigal, my income was staggeringly small. It was something along the lines of five thousand dollars a year. I could have made double the sum by selling them two articles an issue as a freelance writer. Ann Seranne had resigned, in part, at least, because her efforts to get me a raise of a few hundred dollars a year more in salary had failed. Her replacement was a pouter pigeon of a lady, a sarcastic, domineering martinet (or is it martinette?), for whom I had no respect.

Ann had, on her departure, opened a public relations firm and she asked me to join her. I accepted her offer with alacrity and fled.

Although I was overjoyed to leave *Gourmet* magazine, there was still that constant crick in my neck from looking back over my shoulders at imagined disasters. Here I was working for a small unknown public relations firm called Seranne and Gaden. The principals were Ann and Eileen Gaden, a photographer and stylist whose greatest claim to fame was that she had taken all the photographs for Volume I of *The Gourmet Cookbook,* one of the earliest all-time great money-makers among cooking tomes.

The reason for being of a public relations firm is, of course, to sell as subtly or as stridently as possible a manufacturer's product. Publicity differs from advertising in that a public relations firm is engaged to "plant" articles in the media, which is to say in newspapers, magazines, radio, and television. Advertising involves the spending of hard cash for media space or time.

The principal product to be "sold" by Seranne and Gaden was something called Fluffo, a golden shortening. There were a few other piddling nickel-and-dime accounts on the firm's roster but "golden shortening" paid the bills.

I have no desire to denigrate that product but the brain-washing techniques we employed to get it into the American kitchen were legal but where taste is concerned, questionable. Fluffo was a vegetable shortening much like Crisco. The difference was that it was prepared with a yellow dye to make it look like butter. Thus, in as subtle a manner as possible, we promoted the product to the American cook not only as a good frying and pastry making ingredient (which it was), but also as a butter substitute (which it was not). We even wrote a cookbook in which we recommended using the shortening not only in the batter for a wedding cake, but as the basis for a raw, butter-cream substitute for decorating the cake.

I was known as the contact man at Seranne and Gaden. That is to say, it was my job to act as swain to the food editors in New York in an effort to peddle them ideas involving one of our products or another. Mostly Fluffo.

In that era all the food editors in Manhattan were women. In all of America there was not a male food editor on a single metropolitan newspaper.

To pursue my job of wooing the ladies of the press, I was encouraged to open an account at the late Colony restaurant, which was in that epoch one of the six most prestigious restaurants in Manhattan. The reputation was in those years deserved, for it was under the stern, watchful, and caring eye of Gene Cavallero, Sr., who came from the grand tradition of restaurants.

But snobbery prevailed there as in all the best restaurants in town. You were treated well or poorly depending on the niche you occupied in life. If you were really rich and famous and, preferably, stylish, you were seated in one of three places. In a corner table at the bar, which resembled a tent room and had a blue and white awning, or at either of the red plush corner banquettes in the main dining room.

The first time I escorted one of my newspaper ladies to the Colony we were seated way to the rear at an obscure and, as I remember, miniature table that would have been ample only for someone who was dining alone. In retrospect, I certainly don't blame the captain or maître d'hôtel or whoever seated us. I was certainly not dressed in what might remotely be thought of as sartorial splendor. And, the ladies who graced my arm certainly did not look as though they had stepped out of the pages of *Vogue* or *Town and Country*. To tell the truth, they looked underpaid and dowdy.

But a funny thing happened on the wine steward's way to the Colony's cellar and suddenly I found myself with a certain amused status.

George Stritch, now deceased, was the wine steward, a tall, gaunt, well-tailored man with a hawklike face and deadly serious mien. He had a natural air of aloofness and disdain, a coolness, one publisher observed, sufficient to chill a case of white Burgundy.

He was decidedly unimpressed with my comings and goings at the Colony, presented the wine list, took the order, and opened my wines with a robotlike detachment.

Part of the curriculum at the Swiss hotel school had included some fairly concentrated instruction in wines, but my knowledge was almost wholly that of the textbook or the printed page. I had certainly not been to the vineyard born and, at this particular stage of my life, my sampling of the fine wines of Europe was rudimentary. I could distinguish between a red Burgundy and a red Bordeaux, not only by the shape of the bottle but by the characteristics of the wine itself, and that was just about it.

I had invited the food editor of the New York *Post,* the late Alice Petersen, to join me for lunch at the Colony. Alice was an amply endowed, cheery sort who laughed a lot at my most innocuous pleasantry, and shortly after our arrival we ordered from the menu and the wine list was presented.

I asked for a bottle of Puligny-Montrachet, a fine white Burgundy with which I had some conversance. It must also be said that my peripheral vision is commendable.

Shortly after taking my order, the steward returned with a bottle of white wine, neatly wrapped in an impeccably starched white napkin. He poured a drop of wine into my glass and out of the corner of my eye I spotted between the folds of the napkin the word Chassagne.

I lifted my glass to my lips, sniffed and tasted. I swirled the wine smugly and knowingly around in my mouth and swallowed.

I looked up at Stritch.

"This," I said, "is very odd. It tastes like Chassagne-Montrachet."

"But no, monsieur," the sommelier protested. "It is Puligny-Montrachet. The vineyards are very close together in Burgundy."

"Do you mind," I asked, "if I see the label?"

He unwrapped the napkin and almost fainted. The keeper of the wines below had, indeed, sent up the wrong bottle. A short while later, Stritch, full of apology and embarrassment, brought Gene Cavallero himself over to meet and shake hands with this *wunderkind* with the mythical palate. I must say that while I never made it to the corner table in the bar nor the left or right red banquette in the main dining room, I was never given a seat in obscurity again.

In those years, Jane Nickerson was food editor of *The New York Times* and she was, to my mind, the most inventive and diligent food writer in Manhattan. What she did not know she researched with great gravity and concern.

She had had no formal training in food, however, and we at Seranne and Gaden offered her the plums of our creation—a genuinely fine cake recipe plus photograph, exceptional cookie recipes, and so on— all made with yellow shortening.

I had met Jane Nickerson in 1954 and my introduction to her had not been wholly without guile. The month I returned from that Swiss hotel school my life was both physically and emotionally miserable. I was disturbed and perplexed and had as little sense of direction as on the day I graduated from college some twelve years and a couple of wars earlier. I felt a sense of desperation that evidenced itself in an acnelike condition on my face.

The sum of my professional experience as noted had been in public relations in Chicago and almost from the beginning I had come to regard that "profession" with contempt. I considered it sordid to barter my friendship, to bestow it on people whom I would never have invited in my home, except for the favors that they might dole out to me.

And yet in my meeting with Jane Nickerson, that P.R. background stood me in good stead. I had learned that editors are not all that unapproachable. Most newspaper writers are hungry for a new idea, a different point of view, something that can fill up so many column inches day after day after day. I telephoned Jane.

"Miss Nickerson," I began, "how would you like to interview a young American who knows all about French cooking and a lot about wine?"

"Yes," she answered. "Who is it?"

"It's I," I said.

She was amenable and I invited her to lunch the following day at a small, now defunct, and not-too-expensive Italian restaurant in the East Sixties.

When I met her, we shook hands and ordered extra-dry martinis.

"Miss Nickerson," I said, emboldened by the gin. "You have the one job in the world that I want." It was a pleasantry, something said in passing, a token remark to tell her in what grand esteem I held her position. She smiled wanly and the interview began. It appeared on May 10, 1954, and the column began, "Craig Claiborne, a fresh-faced young man who has just completed ten months of study in a hotel school in Switzerland, enthusiastically talked to us about French cooking the other day." She went on to describe the details of the final cooking examination when I had prepared *poisson au vin blanc*, my newly learned "secrets" of making mayonnaise and hollandaise sauces, and so on.

The article that she wrote resulted in an incident that was to be another of the most embarrassing times of my life.

During my navy days I had a fond acquaintance named George van Pelt and, on Kwajalein, he and I had spent hours complaining about navy food and listening to the recordings of Verdi and Puccini that I had in my possession.

George had read the article and telephoned me.

"A few friends and I," he said, "would be incredibly pleased if you'd prepare that same meal you prepared at your final exam. We don't care what it costs. Buy all the ingredients, including the best wines, and let's dine in style."

If I felt self-confident about nothing else, I did, at that point, feel secure in what I had learned at the hotel school.

And so, I agreed. We needed, I proposed, a dining room suitable for the occasion and he suggested the apartment of a friend who lived in Brooklyn.

A Feast Made for Laughter

On the day of the affair, I shopped all over Manhattan, the shopping bags that I carried from store to store, sometimes on foot and sometimes getting in and out of cabs, getting heavier and more bulky with each stop. One of my biggest problems then was (and for many people it is now) finding fresh fishbones with which to make an absolute essential for the fish in white wine sauce, the ultimate creation of the meal. Eventually, I found the bones, bought the cream, wines, various vegetables, meats for soup, fresh herbs, spices, salad greens, just-ripe cheeses (good cheese was hard to come by at that time), and various fruits and liqueurs to prepare a dessert.

I had been given a key to the apartment in which I was to get my act together. I was a stranger to the place, having never met the owner. When I walked into the kitchen I came close to panic. There were no saucepans, no wire whisk, no wooden spoons, and not much of anything else that would make for sane food preparation.

I decided to make do. I found a skillet with a handle that seemed a bit shaky. I found a colander. I found a salad bowl. At least there was running water and a stove that worked.

I went about the trimming and scraping and chopping of the vegetables and herbs for the fish broth, which I wanted to make first. One, because the hour was fast approaching when the guests or sponsors of this affair would arrive. And second, because a good fish broth is crucial to any *poisson au vin blanc.*

I put the fishbones into the skillet for want of a saucepan, added my aromatics and water, and brought the elixir gently to the boil. It was to simmer exactly twenty minutes, just as instructed at school. I finished washing salad greens, made salad dressing, cleaned berries, put them in a bowl, and added sugar and Grand Marnier.

The doorbell rang, I opened the door and said hello to whoever had arrived and returned to the kitchen. I placed a sieve in a bowl and lifted the skillet to strain the stock. The handle twisted and in that split second the floor of the kitchen was awash with broth and a mass of fishbones and vegetables. As I recall, I tried making that white wine sauce with white wine and water and it was another of the low marks of my life. I think the total amount of money that had been spent for that fiasco, including the wines, was just under a hundred dollars.

§   §   §

During the early months of 1957, Jane Nickerson had informed *The New York Times* that, for reasons of family, she was resigning as food editor. At that time she was married to Alex Steinberg, who had moved to Florida to make his fortune as an entrepreneur in the manufacture of yoghurt, which was not, twenty years or so ago, a staple dairy product in every home refrigerator. If anything, it was a product that seemed a trifle exotic to most Americans and the largest consumers were Europeans and health food addicts.

Jane and Alex were the parents of two young children and it was in their interests that she decided to make that move.

Since the time of my interview and first meeting with Jane we had become casual friends, the kind who meet at what is commonly referred to as "food gatherings," which is to say in the home of one or another food professional who presumed to be a good cook. We were certainly not intimate friends of a kind who would pick up the telephone to discuss personal cravings and destinies.

I knew nothing of Jane's decision until one morning, months later, when Eileen Gaden came into the office and announced to Ann and me that Jane Nickerson had told *The Times* that she "is leaving on the first of September, whether they have found a replacement or not . . ."

I was a bit startled at the news because of my respect for Jane as a journalist and also because I knew of her devotion to her job. She was a workaholic, a lady who often went into the office seven days a week to pursue her career. She was a diligent researcher with a thoroughgoing interest in learning more about the world of cuisine.

Although I had told Jane that she had the one job in the world that I wanted, it never occurred to me, with my beleaguered feeling of nothingness, to wonder, even remotely, if I might fill her chair.

A man as the food editor of a major metropolitan daily, especially the august *New York Times,* my fingers racing over her typewriter keyboard, would seem wholly bizarre.

And Eileen turned to me.

"Call '21,' " she demanded, "and ask for a table for four. Let's take Jane to lunch to say good-by."

With perfunctory gestures I telephoned "21," requesting a table for four for lunch at 1 P.M., not a filament of thought in my head or heart that it would be an arrangement for the meal that would alter my life irrevocably.

We met and Jane was in a state of semi-exasperation.

"I honestly think," she said, *"The Times* didn't believe me when I said I was leaving." People simply don't leave *The Times.* They stay there until they die or are dismissed. For her part, she indicated, it was the toughest decision she'd ever made. The waiter brought a bottle of Chassagne-Montrachet and I sampled it. We raised a glass to Jane.

"Oh, they've interviewed people," she continued. "Anybody who can type with one finger who has ever scrambled an egg has passed through those doors." She ticked off an impressive list of names, all of whom were known to me.

"But *The Times* is being strong-willed about it. And now I have no choice. I have to call their hand by walking out."

At that moment, it was like having a light turned on inside my brain. I swallowed another glass of wine and could scarcely wait for that meal to end. We finished the meal with coffee and Cognac and said good-by to Jane.

When we returned to the office I made straight for my cubicle and closed the door. I inserted a sheet of paper in the typewriter and wrote a letter full of guile and innocence. Since then, I have paraphrased that letter a thousand times in my brain.

"Dear Jane. This is not a letter of application. You said today at lunch that everybody in New York has applied for your job and, after a few glasses of wine, I have screwed up my courage to ask you for advice.

"Do you think that *The Times* might even remotely consider an application from me?

"You know as well as anyone my qualifications . . . and the esteem in which I hold *The New York Times.*"

I did not get a reply to that letter. And in mid-August I went with a long-time friend, Henry Creel, to a seedy but clean oceanside hotel at Ocean Bay Park, Fire Island, to spend a two-week holiday.

While there, I did something that was highly uncharacteristic.

I telephoned Jane. And I think I know why I did.

It seemed highly unlikely that Jane would not answer a letter from me. Perhaps she had not received my letter. Or, perhaps . . .

"Yes," she said, "I did receive your letter and submitted it to *The Times* as a letter of application. Don't get your hopes up. You mustn't, for I think the chances are very slim. A man as a food editor . . ." she said, her voice trailing off and leaving a few marks of insinuation of her own.

Of course, I didn't get my hopes up.

Two days later, however, the phone rang. It was Jane. Would I come into the office, she asked, for an interview with Elizabeth Penrose Howkins, who was then editor of what was known as the women's page. It was on that page that the food column appeared.

I rushed back to the city on the nearest available Long Island Railroad car, changed clothes in town, and bolted to the newspaper.

It was an interesting interview, conducted mostly, in, of all places, *The New York Times* cafeteria.

When I walked into Mrs. Howkins' office that day, she was simply, stylishly, elegantly dressed in a little black dress by Chanel. She wore a strand of pearls, a close-fitting black hat, and white gloves.

I later came to learn that Betty Howkins was one of the last of the great grande dames who acted as the editor of a women's page. Trim and pretty, soft-spoken but firm when occasion demanded, she had been editor for several years of *Glamour* magazine before joining *The Times*.

One of my favorite stories about her concerns an interview she had had numerous years ago, when a young woman named Geraldine Stutz applied to her for a job with *Glamour*.

Miss Stutz was fresh out of college when she met Mrs. Howkins.

"My dear," Mrs. Howkins told her, "you are too young and you do not have enough experience, but I shall hire you anyway because you have style, and that's the only thing we can't teach you." Mrs. Howkins came to be known as a woman who hired unseasoned but hungry writers who were to achieve notice on a wider scene. Miss Stutz later went on to become president of Henri Bendel.

Mrs. Howkins died in January 1972, and I think I did not know the depth of her feeling for me until I read her obituary the morning after her death.

"Perhaps," I read, "her proudest appointment was that of Craig Claiborne as food editor. In breaking tradition by choosing a man for what had been considered the powder puff side of journalism, Mrs. Howkins argued with conviction that the best chefs had always been men."

Moments after I had entered her office, she asked me to have a bite of lunch upstairs at the ninth-floor cafeteria.

Over tuna fish sandwiches and tea, I told her briefly about my past. I gave her copies of all the articles I had written that had appeared in *Gourmet* magazine; a hastily typed résumé of my "career;" a tear sheet of Jane Nickerson's interview with me. We chatted briefly—she had another appointment early in the afternoon—and after lunch went back to her office. She shook my hand.

"I like you," she said. "But you must meet Turner Catledge and Lester Markel. They will decide whether you join *The Times* or not. It's their ultimate decision."

Turner Catledge was the managing editor of the daily newspaper. Lester Markel was Sunday editor. Turner Catledge was a "good ole boy" from Mississippi, a slow-talking, genial, smiling man with a thousand southern anecdotes. I must say that it had taken me years to try to talk like a Yankee. But in the presence of Turner I slowed my speech and slurred it more than I normally do.

I had learned that Turner had attended Mississippi State College, as I had. One of the first questions he asked me was where I had gone to school.

"Missippi State," I said. Not Mississippi State. Missippi State. That was more like it.

"Where did you live, son?"

"Polecat Alley," I said, speaking the name of an old, run-down section of the Quadrangle, the dormitory where many students were housed.

"So did I," he said with enthusiasm, giving me a hearty smile.

I gave him a brief rundown of my "career" and we shook hands.

I was then dispatched to the eighth-floor offices of Lester Markel, about whom I had learned a good deal within the space of a day. Lester Markel was a lean, leathery, bespectacled man with a short shock of hair that always seemed to be standing up on the top of his head as though he had been suddenly startled.

He had an awesome, fearsome appearance to me, a total stranger. Stories about him were legendary and legion. They said he spat thumbtacks and had broken the spirit of more than one gentle soul who had worked on the Sunday Magazine. He rode herd and worked his ordinary mortals far beyond human endurance. A dressing-down by Markel was not likely to be forgotten in this or any other lifetime.

Jane Nickerson had mentioned to me that Markel had one woman in mind as a replacement for her. I knew the person in question and must say that she had a fair share of talent. Not exceptional. Just fair.

Markel greeted me without enthusiasm and I have no clear memories of that interview except for one exchange that is italicized in my brain.

I told him that one advantage I had over most food editors was that I spoke French.

Out of the blue, he asked me, "If you joined *The Times* would you consider the food column as a service column or a news column?"

I knew that he was a hard-core newspaperman. And, therefore, I knew the answer that would please him. A news column.

"A service column," I said. "There's very little news of food that is all that interesting. Recipes," I added, "are."

"I don't agree with you," he said.

I don't know why but a lyric I had recently learned from Leonard Bernstein's *Candide,* then a current Broadway show, came into my mind.

"I'm easily assimilated," I said. He smiled and I was escorted to the door.

I had been told to stop by Catledge's office once more after my meeting with Markel.

Catledge greeted me again and we both stood.

"I like you, son," he said. "I think you may work out fine."

"But, Mr. Catledge, I'm not sure that Mr. Markel does!"

When I left the building I was not all that encouraged. Sure, Catledge was the one to make the grand decision. And I sincerely believed that he liked me. On the other hand, Markel had terrified me and I felt that in a final confrontation he would be the tougher man in a two-man encounter.

CRAIG CLAIBORNE

I took the next train back to Fire Island and resumed my holiday. Two days passed and there was no word from New York.

On the third afternoon I had walked down the wooden boardwalk from the hotel to the beach and as I ambled along, my feet in the surf, I heard my name yelled a hundred feet away.

"Craig," Henry yelled. "It's *The New York Times!*"

I raced back, stumbling in my haste.

I grabbed the phone and it was Jane.

"You've got the job," she said, and I sat down.

I walked back to the beach alone and started to cry; those sobs could have been heard in heaven.

Just as I had earlier found my "place" in Lausanne, Switzerland, a few years earlier, I suddenly "belonged." I didn't know where. Just in this world.

When I calmed down I walked to the water's edge and started brooding.

Oh, God. What on earth would I write about?

I saw a fisherman hauling in a bluefish.

That's it, I told myself, I'll write about bluefish and how to cook them.

But then, I thought, what about the week after and the week after?

And so I sit here almost twenty-five years after and I have never yet missed a column that was due.

§ § §

One of the most curious facets of my life has been the ability to turn out what might be considered prodigious amounts of work that, in the long run, has produced a reasonable amount of success in my given field, while living—even today—with a feeling of blight and a lack of self-esteem and a feeling of general unworthiness. For years I have been haunted by the *New Yorker* cartoon in which a patient, discussing his condition with his psychoanalyst says, "Doctor, why do I feel so inferior to people I know I am superior to?"

It would not require an analyst's training to comprehend the meaning of the dreams that have been recurrent throughout most of my life. They could be catalogued under three names: the Jump, the Cobweb or Mire, and the Climb.

In the Jump, there are two arcs, like an arched bridge that has been severed in midsection and each arc removed to a distance. As I climb one of the arcs I am compelled by God knows who or why to glance into the space beneath and the character varies. At times it is a dark void, at times a bottomless pit, and at times a churning cluster of clouds or smoke. The problem is to jump and land safely on the second arc. I've never made it, my heart beating like that of a lamb pursued by hounds.

The Cobweb and the Mire are so similar in feeling that except for their physical nature, they are identical. When it is a cobweb, I try desperately to climb the web to escape some unknown pursuer and, as I climb, the webs sag and break and I continue a frantic, hopeless tugging until I expire from exhaustion. In the case of the mire, my body is sunk in a black, surging, mudlike mass trying to reach an impossible destination.

In the Climb, there is a scaffold with a crazy complex of beams and joints that must be climbed and both my body and mind are panicked and frustrated, for the upper reaches go on into infinity.

To call my knowledge and understanding of the occult and psychic phenomena slight is to understate the case. And yet, perhaps because I need to compensate for my feelings of failure and other shortcomings, I believe that there are and always have been mystic forces acting in my behalf. Supernal beings. Among other things, as I have stated, I do believe in God, although I do not belong to any organized religion. I envision God as some vague, bearded, robed, paternal figure out of a Michelangelo painting, something perhaps from the frescoes in the Sistine Chapel. And when I am in need (even for trivial, small, material things) I pray to Him quietly and, perhaps because of my belief, which makes me act positively when I might have otherwise acted negatively, I often find my prayers answered.

I also believe in palmistry and mind reading and extra-sensory perception.

In a related sense, when I attended the hotel school in Switzerland, I have vivid memories of long walks in solitude in which I would implore my God 1) to give me the ability to write and write well and 2) to give me financial security and 3) to give me peace of mind.

A curious thing happened in 1958 when I had been with *The New York Times* for approximately one year.

One of the most important and well-established figures in the world of food at that time was Helen McCully. Helen had been for many years the respected and talented food editor of *McCall's* magazine, which during her years there had considerable clout in what was then known as "shelter" publications. Let me say as an aside that when I first came to New York, desperately in search of work and advice, I applied for a job with Helen. I outlined my high-flying visions of what I considered the future of food—serious cooking and classic sauce preparations and so on—and she scoffed at the idea. As it turned out, I was at that early age something of a Nostradamus in predicting what is now called this country's gastronomic revolution.

Despite this clash of ideas, Helen and I became good friends and at the time of which I speak she had lost her position with *McCall's*. In addition to which she had invested a good deal of money in a fly-by-night food venture and had lost every cent. She may not have been destitute at the time but she could certainly classify as being "broke." And her condition bordered on desperation, although she hid it well.

She asked me one evening if I would invest with one or two other friends in an evening of having our palms read. The cost of that one-night session would be about fifty dollars, which she felt she couldn't afford alone. Helen would serve one of her cold buffets for which she was famous (come to think of it, famous or not, Helen's buffets generally turned out to be *vitello tonnato* served with cold rice tossed with parsley and, as often as not, a cold ham).

The evening arrived and along about eight-thirty an Amazon entered, a tall, stout woman dressed in a wrinkled floor-length floral print dress, her hair tied in a disheveled bun.

Each of us was escorted, one at a time, into the bedroom to have his or her palm read.

I must say that at that time, my name was as obscure as a minor constellation under cloudy skies. I had not become involved in restaurant criticism nor had I published or seriously dreamed of publishing a volume on cookery. I was, as I seemed always to be, in the best of times and worst of times, in debt.

And so the lady palmist took my right hand in hers. As she ran her fingers in the palm's crevices with the web pattern that bespeaks who we are and will be, she spoke in grave tones.

"I see water and travel." Ah, so, I thought. Someone had told her or she read somewhere that I had spent a great deal of time in the Navy.

"I see shelter and books. And good fortune."

I listened to her attentively but without a great deal of persuasion.

Within six months I had signed a contract to publish *The New York Times Cook Book*. Within a year I had traveled around the world on an eating expedition with James Beard; Lester Gruber, owner and host of the London Chop House in Detroit, and his wife; and the late Helen Evans Brown, the well-known West Coast cookbook author. Within four years I had purchased a plot of land in East Hampton on which I subsequently built my first "shelter."

By 1959 I had received a number of letters from various New York publishers of considerable stature inquiring whether I would consider publishing a cookbook bearing *The New York Times* logotype. My ego was, as usual, in delicate balance. I was flattered at their offers but not nourished by their encouragement. Couldn't be. Mustn't dwell on it, mustn't contemplate such sweet gratifications.

It must be said that I was aware in my mid years that *The New York*

Times was the ultimate job of my life. I was never unmindful of my great good fortune, the seemingly endless blessings that had been bestowed on me by having my name—me as the least of these—associated with that stately journal. It was, to me, the grandest newspaper in the world. I am not ashamed to say that there were times when no one knew, in solitude, I was literally moved to tears when I reflected on my association with the paper. As much as I could possibly be, I was gloriously happy. To walk inside that building on Forty-third Street, to enter it and read, engraved on the left wall, these words of Adolph Ochs's: "Each day a new beginning; every morn is the world made new," gave me a feeling of abstract completeness. It was a heady experience, like a first love affair.

It was with this feeling of rapture that one morning in March 1959, I wrote a memorandum to the publisher, Arthur Hays Sulzberger, with a proposal. In it I stated that I had had numerous inquiries as to the possibility of publishing a cookbook bearing *The New York Times'* logotype. I was wholly altruistic in this matter.

I told him that I felt that such a book would redound to the prestige of the paper. I added that I would be willing to produce such a book under any terms that he dictated. I said that I would edit the book for such commission as he deemed fit; for a share of the royalties; or for a flat fee.

Within a day or two I received in the interoffice mail a brief note from his deputy, Ivan Veit, dated March 27, 1959. I don't think I fully comprehended the scope of that letter. It gave me the rights to the title of a book to be called *The New York Times Cook Book* and that gift was, to borrow a phrase, too strong for fantasy. It was, in fact, in the first few days, hopeless for me to conceive of the implications.

I realized in later years that I would not have needed an agent to sell the book, but I did need a helmsman to steer me through those various offices, and so I engaged John Schaffner, who, at the time, was literary agent for James Beard.

With me in tow we visited approximately ten publishing houses, at each of which I was greeted by one menial editor or another. The only publishing firm where I was greeted in person by the president was Harper & Row. It was Cass Canfield, Sr., who came out personally to shake my hand. For that simple reason, I signed a contract with that organization.

It is not said with a sense of denigration or any lack of appreciation for the monumental nature of the gift that had been so suddenly delivered into my hands. But I don't believe for one moment that the management of the paper, meaning Mr. Sulzberger and Mr. Veit, were really aware of the magnitude of their gesture.

In the spring of 1959, food and cooking had not, as they eventually would, become the major topic of conversation at cocktail parties, even more than ball games. Fact of the matter is that if the males of those days had shown so much interest in food, they would have been put down as a little odd. I am amused, incidentally, to think that *The New York Times*, in hiring a male as food editor, went far in taking the onus off the male role in food preparation. It also helped in the years that followed my joining the paper that I interviewed scores of male cooks.

It was also an era in which there were "shelter" or "family" magazines, supposedly catering to adult minds, that would not print recipes that called for wine, on the theory that it might offend readers in the so-called Bible Belt.

It was in that climate that I was given the rights to use the title *The New York Times Cook Book*. And thus, I am convinced that in my early years with the paper, the management regarded the food page as so much trivia, an *amuse-bouche*, so to speak, that no one of serious mind would swallow.

And to put things in total perspective, I would have been inclined to agree with that notion. I suspected that there were a few thousand people out there who perused the columns and some few hundreds or dozens who cooked from those pages, but I could not possibly have foretold that some time *The New York Times Cook Book* would become a standard item in American kitchens. Five years after it was published, a junior executive in a major publishing firm (not Harper & Row) stopped me at a cocktail party in Manhattan.

"In time," he said, "you will realize that you have a classic book on your hands. It will find its place in cookbook literature with *The Joy of Cooking* and the *Better Homes and Gardens* cook books." I laughed at him, but for the first time I started to take a detached look at this gift of my great, good, and generous benefactor.

I will make this brief. When *The New York Times Cook Book* first came off the press, I greeted it with as much anxiety and depression as I did elation. Oh, God, I thought, there are probably a thousand errors in each chapter. Readers will be telephoning and screaming at me at all hours of the night and day. I had no confidence in the recipes, all of which had appeared in *The Times*'s food columns and all of which had been tested.

Here I will make a confession of a truth known only to those who have edited and published my books. I have *never* proofread a galley before a cookbook of mine was published. I am psychotically fearful of discovering errors in recipes, typographical or otherwise.

It was my honest belief when that book first came off the press, a belief that I maintained for several years, that *The New York Times Cook Book* would not sell more than thirty thousand copies. I firmly believed that at the end of five years it would disappear from book shelves and thus go into oblivion. I was not even comforted, not given a warm feeling of encouragement, when at the end of three years, Harper & Row saw fit to deliver me a gold-embossed edition of that book, bound in leather and with the inscription, elegantly printed, "Presented to Craig Claiborne in celebration of the sale of sixty-five thousand copies of *The New York Times Cook Book* from the publisher, Harper & Row."

A short while back there was an advertisement in *The New York Times* for the book. It stated, "More than a million copies sold."

There are not many people, even on the staff of *The New York Times,* who know that because of that book, the newspaper set up a special book division. Today it has become a reasonably important publishing house and it is called Times Books.

§ § §

There was one insane moment at this time in my life when I was on the brink of marriage and, to my bride-to-be's infinite good fortune, she was miraculously saved from having that knot tied, if ever so inadvertently, by Leonard Bernstein. Although that splendid, and much admired musician, whom I have briefly met only once or twice in my life, was unaware of his interference. The wedding banns, for that intended and ill-founded marriage, had been published in a house organ of *The New York Times* titled "Times Talk."

I had met a young woman whom I shall refer to as Owens Talley at a small buffet in New Jersey and among those present were numerous men discreetly involved in loves that, in that faraway era, "dare not speak its name." Owens was a good-looker, to use a phrase. Slender, strikingly proportioned, a fine head of hair, rosy-cheeked, and blessed with an appealing sense of humor. She moved effortlessly around the roomful of "mixed" psyches and sexual inclinations.

I was enchanted by her. Within the next few weeks, it was my great pleasure to escort her to the theater, to dinner parties where she blossomed as "a friend of *The New York Times* restaurant critic," and so on. The fact that she would not drink spiritous liquors, even wine, interested and somehow disturbed me. She did, in fact, tell me that she had parted from her last spouse because when she drank she tended to "blow up."

Our courtship continued over a matter of a few weeks and ended in bed. On a fairly regular basis, either her bed or mine. She informed me that she found me wholly compatible sexually and her demands were often impassioned. I was also interested and slightly bewildered that, although she enjoyed the theater, she had a particular loathing for opera in any form. I was disturbed by this because I have a thoroughgoing love for opera in almost any form. I say *almost.* I detest Gilbert and Sullivan.

Owens was aware of my sexual tendencies, which had been discussed between us at brief but agreeable lengths. I asked her to marry me and she accepted with what I considered alacrity. I promised to be as faithful as I could but added that my vows were chancy. She urged that we be married within days.

Curiously, considering the intimacy of our relationship, Owens seemed to make a point of not introducing me to her old friends and I knew that there were several to whom she referred at times directly or obliquely. I presumed that perhaps they were mutual friends and that association with them would awaken painful memories of her last husband, from whom she had only recently divorced after a long separation.

One day, however, she told me that there was one person, her closest friend, named Erika, whom she would enjoy inviting to dinner, a very special meal for only the three of us. The conversation at that meal was to be quite intimate.

I decided there and then to put my most elaborate and polished foot forward. Although my financial footing in those days was a bit rocky, I did have a decent but small collection of my mother's silver and had made what had seemed to me then a huge investment in Baccarat wine glasses. I must have had six costly crystal goblets, and these I treasured.

The meal that I'd planned was a Swedish smörgåsbord that included an assortment of herring dishes—curried, mustard, and so on—to be served with aquavit encased in an ice sculpture, plus boiled potatoes with dill. There would be a liver pâté and cocktail-size Swedish meatballs. And a main course of roast leg of lamb with tomatoes and mushrooms; salad with cheese; and, for dessert, an opera torte (which I had purchased at a bakery) with a cream filling and almond paste topping. I had also purchased a fair assortment of wines, one Burgundy and one Bordeaux, to be served with the main course and cheese. Anything to impress Owens and her friend.

Dinner was to be served in my apartment at eight. About an hour before Erika arrived, Owens, in her dressing gown (she maintained a small wardrobe at my place), came and asked if I minded if she had a glass of Bourbon. My bar, I must admit, was well stocked with all the spiritual products of Kentucky, Scotland, Russia, France, and beyond.

I was puzzled by her request.

"Owens," I said, turning on my most gentle, paternal manner, "as long as we're together, don't ever beg my permission to have a drink. Your freedom is my freedom."

And so she poured herself a shot glass of Bourbon, which she proceeded to belt down in the flicker of an eye. A brief moment later she belted down a second. And a third.

Shortly after Erika arrived we sat at table and as the herring was eaten with black bread, the aquavit started flowing into the small glasses. "Skål," we all said in unison, lifting our glasses and tossing the white, dazzling, caraway-flavored liquid into our open throats.

The meal had been in progress for minutes when Owens started to needle me. About anything. I told myself that she was jesting. About my fastidious nature. About my real or imagined snobbishness. About my scolding her for certain lapses in taste when we dined together in public. Her criticisms soon took on an edge that became more malevolent and frightening, God knows along what lines.

The embarrassment around that table swelled and Erika stood and felt for her handbag. I tried to quiet Owens and persuade Erika to stay but there was no balm to be had or used in the Gilead of that night.

Erika left. There was silence in the room and I refused to be drawn into the passion that soon subsided. I walked into the kitchen to clear up the dishes and put away the untouched leg of lamb and the opera torte. I rinsed the Baccarat and placed them on a rack to drain and dry. Owens, who had become contemplative, went into the bedroom and put on her dressing gown.

At this point I walked over to the phonograph and put on a recording of Leonard Bernstein's brilliant music for *Candide.* It is a spectacular score and includes an extraordinary spoof on the world of opera and all its foolish plots. It is called "Glitter and Be Gay," and contains a bagful of runs and trills and *tessitura* hijinks that are hilarious but might be mistaken as serious opera by the unaccustomed listener.

As I had gone to the phonograph Owens had walked into the kitchen to continue cleaning up and sorting out forks, knives, plates, and so on.

As the musical spoof from *Candide* continued there was a sudden crashing sound like the thunderous shattering of a window. Accompanied by the voice of Owens at high pitch.

"You son of a bitch," she screamed, "turn that opera off! This minute!" She came into the living room where I stood, fearful of going into the kitchen to view the broken shards of whatever would greet me.

"But, Owens," I said, "that isn't opera, it's parody. He's kidding the very thing you detest. . . ." It so happened I was standing in front of a sofa and she struck me in the chest with such force she knocked me down. Onto the sofa. And I remained in my knocked-down but upright position.

Owens, in her dressing gown, angrily paced into the bedroom, picked up her street clothes, and stormed into the bathroom, the door of which opened directly into my view.

She spent several minutes in the bathroom and when the door opened again, I noted that her wrist was bleeding. Oh, God, I thought, what a bore.

"*Hey, do you happen to know what Craig Claiborne looks like? There's a guy out there with a notebook making funny faces at the coquilles Saint-Jacques.*"

Cartoon.

"Where's my purse?" she demanded.

"It's on the chair at the entranceway. Don't forget to take it." Owens walked into the night, and as they used to say on Tin Pan Alley, "What can you do at the end of a love affair?"

§ § §

When I became food editor of *The New York Times,* on September 9, 1957, I had small acquaintance with the first-rate restaurants of New York, let alone those of Europe and elsewhere. The simple and obvious fact was that I had never possessed enough money to dine in the style to which I might have liked to become accustomed.

At that time, I could have pretty well summed up on one hand the "good" restaurants with which I had some conversance. They would have included Trader Vic's and the Blue Fox in San Francisco (I had eaten there during my navy days) and Jacques' restaurant and the Cape

Cod Room of the Drake Hotel in Chicago. I had dined but not often at the Colony, "21," and Voisin in New York.

But I knew that my professional credentials were beyond dispute. I had not waited banquets at Lausanne's Palace Hotel and the Beau Rivage—now remodeled and still one of the grandest hotels in Switzerland—for nothing. Because of my training at the hotel school there wasn't a poorly made sauce that could be pawned off on me. I was a till-the-death defender of the faith of classic French cooking. I knew the names of the *répertoire de la cuisine* from *américaine* and *andalouse* and *anglaise* through *viennoise* and *zingara* by heart and taste. My connoisseurship of wines might leave something to be desired, but I could not be traduced by an uppity waiter or captain or maître d'hôtel or a second-rate *chef de cuisine.*

After joining *The Times* I did not suddenly become what might be called an avid restaurant-goer. I did, however, dine routinely at some of the best-known restaurants in Manhattan and, inevitably, when a new restaurant would open, I would visit it twice or more to make a report of its quality. The two most important restaurants to be reviewed in my first years of serious restaurant criticism were La Caravelle in November 1960 and Lutèce in March 1961. Stars were not yet awarded.

The first restaurant column to run on a weekly basis appeared on May 24, 1963. It included capsule reviews, about one hundred words each, of Del Pezzo, Jimmy's Greek-American restaurant, the Black Angus, and La Petite Maison. None of these to my knowledge is still in existence.

It has long been my contention, and I can prove it by thumbing through vintage dining guides, some of them nearly half a century old, that New York was not, fifty years ago, a great city in which to dine. Most of the premier dining spots appear to have been the great hotels —the Ritz Carlton at Forty-ninth and Madison; the Brevoort at Fifth Avenue and Eighth; and the Lafayette at Ninth Street and University Place. Ryan James, in his guidebook, *Dining in New York* (John Day Company, 1934), reserves his most lavish praise for Henri Charpentier's Café at Rockefeller Center, for The Marguery at 270 Park Avenue, and, of all places, Barbetta's. I admire, in particular, the author's commentary on the maître d'hôtel: "Probably the most bored maître d'hôtel in all New York is Mario, the chief gloom at the otherwise delightful Barbetta's."

Lüchow's, the author adds, had lost most of its luster although the food was still the best German cooking in America. Jack and Charlies', which eventually became the "21" Club, is relegated to the back of the book and given three lines. The once celebrated Sherry's, he states, "is another name that has outlived its earlier elegance."

I will accept the testimony of my long-dead predecessors in food criticism that dining in New York at the turn of the century in the company of such people as Diamond Jim Brady and Lillian Russell was, in some small sense, comparable to dining in some fine European capital. But I will accept it with vast reservoirs of doubt.

Two great catastrophes had beset American restaurants within my lifetime. The first was Prohibition, a national disgrace that lasted thirteen years beginning in 1920, the year of my birth. It was a stunning blow to what, as far as I know, might have been an age of elegance where dining is concerned. Bars were closed and no wine was permitted. Wines and spirits have traditionally been the financial mainstays of the restaurant and hotel industries. Most of what were reputed to be the great dining establishments simply closed their doors and disappeared.

Prohibition was repealed in 1933 and, just as a fledgling restaurant industry was learning to fly, it was clobbered again eight years later with World War II.

That is why, when I came onto the restaurant scene, there were relatively few celebrated (I will not say great) restaurants in New York or in the United States, for that matter. In New York the list of highly touted restaurants included Le Voisin, the Colony, the Café Chambord, the "21" Club, the Brussels, the Quo Vadis, Maude Chez Elle, and Le Pavillon. Of those, only the Quo Vadis (now under a new management) and the "21" Club exist.

From my earliest days as a food editor and critic, I sensed something radically wrong with the New York restaurant scene. Within a few months I had visited virtually every well-known and numerous small restaurants in Manhattan. I had started to make random notes during each visit. I became a good friend of Gene Cavallero, Sr., who had founded the Colony and, although I didn't think he had the greatest kitchen on earth, it was credibly high on my list of nice places to dine. Generally speaking, however, the level of sophistication in both dining rooms and kitchens in those days would boggle the mind. The "21" Club was and still is one of the great places to visit in New York, but has anyone ever gone there for the sheer pleasure of dining on great cooking? I doubt it. It isn't a restaurant; it's a club, a place to see and be seen, and that is reason enough for its existence. New York would be a poorer place without it.

I was first taken to the now defunct Pavillon by the late, great wine authority, Frank Schoonmaker, for whom I had a tremendous admiration. In years to come I was to spend almost a month in his company touring the vineyards of Burgundy and Bordeaux and eating in the great restaurants of those regions. The menu at Le Pavillon on that visit included a rice pilaf with mussels—one of the world's ultimate dishes—followed by tournedos Rossini, followed by a salad with Brie cheese, and, finally, my favorite dessert, *oeufs à la neige,* or poached meringues in a custard sauce.

The food was for the gods and, with Frank's certain knowledge, so were the wines. A Montrachet with the fish; La Tâche with the fillet. There is one more thing about the meal that rests indelibly in my mind. I had read that Ludwig Bemelmans once said that Le Pavillon was unquestionably the finest French restaurant in Manhattan. And, he added, perhaps France as well.

When Frank and I were seated, Bemelmans occupied the banquette directly behind us. I was introduced, shook his hand, and glanced down at his plate. He was eating *viande haché,* a fancy name for hamburger. And undoubtedly the greatest hamburger to be found in a French restaurant in America. Or France.

Gradually, as I visited more and more restaurants of whatever genre, the awareness became entrenched in me that where dining well was concerned, in that era, New York was, in truth—awesomely—a "hick town."

The only much-read and much-quoted critic in town was Clementine Paddleford, a well-meaning soul, whose prose was so lush it could have been harvested like hay and baled. At this distance (Clem died in 1967), I don't think I could be charged as a jealous enemy of my colleague. She was hailed by many (her reputation was nationwide) and held in grand esteem by some of her readers even in Gotham. She was, of course, food editor and restaurant critic of the late, lamented New York *Herald Tribune.*

The truth of the matter was, however, that Clementine Paddleford would not have been able to distinguish skillfully scrambled eggs from a third-rate omelet. I am not at all sure that she ever cooked a serious meal in her life.

But she had a readership that was estimated at the time of her death as 12 million.

To quote from her obituary that appeared in *The New York Times,* to Clem, an ordinary radish was not just a radish but "a tiny radish of passionate scarlet, tipped modestly in white." Mushrooms were the "elf of plants," or "pixie umbrellas."

There is one anecdote about Clem that I find unforgettable.

Clem owned a cat, a drowsy female called Pussy Willow.

Pussy Willow slept on her desk in the food editor's "In" basket. When Pussy Willow was gathered to Abraham's bosom, Miss Paddleford was overcome with sentiment. She declared that the cat must receive a proper funeral and be buried in the "In" basket.

She and her friends took the cat's body to Clem's country home in Redding, Connecticut, and the cat was buried.

When the writer returned to New York she made a horrifying discovery.

"My God," she cried, "my book manuscript was hidden in that basket!"

Poor Pussy Willow. She was exhumed and the manuscript retrieved.

The other restaurant critics in town, such as they were, were equally inept.

It was gossiped that they would dine in any given restaurant and then have a long post-meal conversation with the chef to have him explain what they had eaten and were criticizing in the first place.

In that atmosphere, I took it upon myself to write a devastating attack on the restaurant situation in Manhattan. It was one of the most momentous decisions of my life. Because of it I met Pierre Franey.

I had finished the piece during the first week in April 1959. The editors liked it and asked me to furnish an illustration to accompany the article.

There was one restaurant in town for whose kitchen and dining room I had nothing but unreserved praise. And that was Le Pavillon under the expert guidance of Henri Soulé, a man whose influence over even the present, generally admirable state of dining in New York will never be reckoned. He was a short, robust, puffy-faced man who terrified certain members of his staff and not a few of his customers. He was king and his customers were his courtiers, who willingly danced to his tune, be it a jig or a waltz. The likes of Le Pavillon have not been equaled in Manhattan and I don't think there is a restaurant owner in town who would dispute that.

He was a man before whom men and women trembled. Including me, although in those days my personal acquaintanceship with him could have been measured in minutes. I knew him well by reputation, however, and this scared me.

Thus, I telephoned M. Soulé a bit timorously one morning and, rattling on as fast as possible so as not to lose my courage, I said, "M. Soulé, I am writing an article on the restaurant situation in Manhattan and in it I claim that Le Pavillon is the only great establishment in town. I need a photograph to illustrate that point and I would like to photograph the chef in your kitchen."

He invited me over to discuss it, at which time he gave his permission. He could scarcely have been kinder to me or more gentle in his tone.

With photographer in tow, I descended the stairs from dining room to kitchen and shook hands with the chef, who turned out to be Pierre. We spoke the same language. Even our origins were similar, born in St. Vinnemer, a tiny village in Burgundy, he grew up in a small town in soil-rich Burgundy called Tonnerre. Tonnerre in French means thunder. I was born in a hamlet in the soil-rich region of the Mississippi Delta called Sunflower. We were born on opposite sides of the Atlantic within four months of each other.

But more than that, we spoke the language of cuisine. I was capable of discussing with him a well-made court bouillon, the makings of a *glace de viande* or *fond brun;* the fine points of a *sauce Choron* or *sauce Maltaise,* a *sauce Bercy* or *Marchand de Vin* or *Bordelaise.* We both doted on the same types of food—charcuterie; grilled pigs' feet; *boudin noir* or blood sausage; *andouillettes* or tripe sausage; *confit d'oie* or preserved goose; thick peasant soups, and so on.

We took a photograph of Pierre (he was thirty-eight years old at the time and had a fresh, innocent, boyish face) wearing an immaculate, starched *toque blanche* and apron, standing, arms folded, before a boneless striped bass stuffed with a mousse of sole and a champagne sauce made with wine, shallots, mushrooms, butter, and cream. Pierre is, simply, the greatest fish cook in America.

The photography session took approximately forty-five minutes. We shook hands and said good-bye.

The article, bearing the headline "Elegance of Cuisine is on Wane in U.S.," appeared on the first page of the Sunday *New York Times* dated April 13. It won a publisher's award for that year.

That might have been the end of my acquaintanceship with Pierre except for a third, penultimate meeting, which involved him and Soulé, that one far less tranquil and, for both men, a bit traumatic.

Pierre had had for many years a curious relationship with Soulé. It was a father-son, love-hate entanglement that gave Pierre approximately equal amounts of pleasure and pain, depending on Soulé's whims, moods, humors, and caprices, which seemed to most people who knew him to be in a constant state of flux.

I had the greatest respect for Soulé as a restaurant owner and enjoyed his friendship. He was even responsible, as I will mention later, for my move to East Hampton, another of the greater happenings in my life. As a human being, however, his sterling nature was at times tarnished by petty, personal matters.

In all of Pierre's twenty-five years at Le Pavillon, he was asked—perhaps allowed is a better word—only once to come into the dining room while the customers were eating and drinking and enjoying themselves. That was when I dined there with friends and asked if I might speak to Pierre. This was only a month or so after that article about "Elegance on Wane" appeared.

The custom was, during Pierre's tenure as chef, as follows: He would meet with Soulé in the dining room each morning promptly at eleven-thirty. It was Soulé's pleasure at each noontime meal to lean slightly toward a customer whom he particularly favored and say in a discreet tone, "I have something very special that my chef has prepared for you today." It might be a roast boneless squab, lobster *américaine, poussin* or baby chicken *polonaise,* and so on. Each morning Pierre would dis-

Henri Soulé—in my view, the greatest and most influential restaurateur in America in this century—in the old Pavillon.

cuss these special items with Soulé and prepare only eight or ten portions. Pierre would then return to the kitchen.

They also conferred in the dining room each Friday afternoon at three, or after the last customer had cleared the premises, at which time they would discuss and outline the restaurant's menus for the following week.

The working staff of Le Pavillon's kitchen was—as were the staffs in all the city's other luxury French restaurants—notoriously underpaid, ranging from about $100 to $150 for a five-day week. By working overtime on Saturdays they could boost their salaries to $200 or $280 a week.

In those days, attendance at the luxury restaurants in Manhattan fell off during the hot summer months when *le beau monde* went to the country for weekend jaunts.

In early 1960, Soulé decreed that throughout the coming summer there would be no overtime. Pierre, enormously sensitive to the plight of his staff, was hurt and confused.

He tried to reason with Soulé. His workers, he maintained quietly, would be earning less than a living wage without overtime. The entire staff was essential to the quality of the kitchen on weekends, even though the number of customers dwindled.

Soulé was adamant. Discussions upstairs, sometimes downstairs, between the two turned into negotiations. Soulé would not go to the kitchen. Pierre refused to go to the dining room. They both became embittered and stopped speaking. Pierre walked out for the last time in mid-February of 1960. The restaurant closed temporarily on the last Saturday in February.

The curious thing, the closing had gone unnoticed by the press. It had even been ignored by the gossip columnists.

I learned about it through a casual telephone call; someone had requested me to make a reservation for him thinking, wrongly, that I had influence.

I went over to the restaurant and Soulé was there in those cavernous surroundings, so mausoleum-like without the roses and lights and crystal reflecting in those mirrored walls. Nothing can look more hauntingly desolate than a restaurant without illumination and people. Soulé was a solitary figure, wandering aimlessly around those premises.

He was cordial but reserved and we talked briefly. There wasn't much to say. Within the hour I walked over to the Vatel Club on West Fifty-seventh Street, the leading chefs' organization in America. Pierre was president.

He greeted me and, once more, the conversation was not lengthy.

I went back to *The Times* and wrote the article that bore the headline

"Restaurant Men Simmer and Menu Goes to Pot; Le Pavillon Shut in a Gallic Dispute." "A feud," I wrote, "that appears to be more than a tempest in a demitasse cup appears to have closed what many consider the finest French restaurant in the United States." I must say that my sympathies lay more with Pierre than Soulé and it showed. I dedicated a major part of the article to the injustices as outlined by the chef, and the article ended with the following: " 'From the beginning,' Monsieur Soulé reminisced, 'Pierre or Pierrot as I called him, was like my son.' And Monsieur Franey, for his part, acknowledged his filial feeling. Both are choked with emotion at times when discussing the other. Tears well up and the wrath begins." When the article appeared there was a photograph of Pierre to the left and a photograph of Soulé to the right. The next morning the gossip columns were filled with barbs directed at Pierre from Soulé.

And I believe to this day that this episode was the first planting of the seeds of the long-lasting friendship between Pierre and myself. He could not believe that he had been given equal space, even been sided with—by my simply reporting the truth of the affair—against his former *patron.*

A week or so later Pierre and his wife, Betty, came into my apartment in Manhattan where he and I joined forces in the kitchen for the first time. The three of us dined on quail *beauséjour* (with bay leaf and garlic cloves); a purée of celery root; watercress and endive salad; vanilla ice cream with strawberries sweetened and perfumed with kirsch. We drank toasts with a vintage Château Lascombes.

That was the beginning of a relationship without which my life would have been impoverished, a relationship that for twenty years and more has enriched the food pages of *The New York Times.* My debt to Pierre and the debt of the readers of my column to him are well beyond measure.

I have been asked and I have often asked myself, "What if our paths had not met? What if he had never crossed swords with Soulé?"

I would have remained as food editor of *The Times.* I would have continued to write what I hoped was a creditable column from the beginning, a year and a half before we met.

With two exceptions, *The New York Times Cook Book,* the manuscript for which was almost completed before we began our association, and *The Chinese Cookbook,* co-authored with Virginia Lee, every book that I have written is weighted with recipes that Pierre has offered me with a singular affection and unselfishness. After Pierre joined *The New York Times,* we shared in all cookbook royalties.

§ § §

Wars, economics, social change, and what is now known as "upward mobility" are the four factors that determine to the greatest extent the climate in which restaurants will come into being and flourish.

Since the end of World War II, the nation has been blessed with more than thirty-five years of relative peace. There was, of course, the Korean conflict in the early fifties, and the heartbreaking catastrophe of Vietnam in the mid-sixties and early seventies. But those were "limited" actions. There has been a vast social revolution where blacks, women, and morals are concerned and, although it was a revolution marked by acts of violence, it has been relatively quiet and stable. Miraculously, the nation survived Richard Nixon.

The climate has been, in short, favorable for restaurants. Hundreds and thousands of people who a dozen or twenty years ago had to think twice before going to some small French bistro for their *coq au vin* or beef *bourguignonne,* now find it financially feasible to visit restaurants that are relatively luxury-style to sup on the *nouvelle* and traditional cuisine.

And that is why New York has, indeed, become an incredible place in which to dine. If when I joined *The New York Times* I could count the number of fine French restaurants on one hand, today there are a score or more. And not only is the city blessed with excellent French cuisine but Italian and oriental as well. The number of good Japanese restaurants in Manhattan is staggering, whereas in 1955 there was but one of any stature, the Miyako at 20 West 56th Street.

In the late 1950s it was necessary to go to Chinatown to get a Chinese meal that was relatively sophisticated and beyond the chop suey-chow mein level. Today there are dozens of excellent Chinese restaurants that flourish on what might be called a grand luxe scale in midtown. And what has happened in Manhattan has happened to an only slightly lesser degree in San Francisco and Los Angeles and points in between.

§   §   §

I have often been asked how a young person could go about becoming a restaurant critic and the answer is not easy.

Basically, it involves two things, the ability to write and conversance with food. I have also been asked a related question: If you were to go back and reshape your professional life, how would you alter it?

In the first place I believe that the ability to write well and that "taste" as it applies to dining are instinctive. I think that you are born with a seed for making a sentence that reads well, as well as one for learning to be discriminating where food is concerned.

My interviews over the years have been conducted at times with a stenographic pad, but more often than not with an electric typewriter. Sometimes I have both at hand as in this interview with Bernard Clayton, Jr., the distinguished cookbook author. This was taken in his kitchen in Bloomington, Indiana.

Since I was an infant, I have been curious about the sound of words and their meaning. I have also felt instinctive about the taste and smell of things as they appeal to, or repel my nature. I have a kindred spirit in a friend who once told me that he believes in an earlier incarnation he must have been a hound dog, one that sniffs at everything and is apt to put anything into his mouth that appeals to his sense of taste and smell.

In my earliest youth I can recall eating clover leaves, some of which were deliciously sour like sorrel. I remember trying spears of dried grass that, I realized later, tasted like buffalo grass, which Russians put into vodka and call *zubrovka*. I sniffed a garden herb that, in more mature circumstances, I came to know was a member of the basil family even though I had not known basil until I was in my mid-thirties.

During my childhood, I loved to "pick" at foods that appealed to my sense of sight—crisp, browned bits of fried chicken that fell to the bottom of a serving dish; the crisp tail ends of fish that clung to the sides of a deep-fat fryer; the burnt edges of toast that were trimmed away; the remnants of pulp from squeezed lemons and oranges; the tines of a fork that had been used to beat mayonnaise; the burnt or partly burnt crusts of pies; the half-jellied fillings of fruit pies that had oozed out while baking; even random bits of ice that had been chipped away from a block. I've rarely seen a berry on a bush—ripe or half-ripe or green—that I didn't want to pick and pop into my mouth. In my early youth there were many nut trees on the property, walnuts and pecans, and I could not resist picking up and cracking open those that fell to the ground. The brownish, black, and green stains of the black walnuts were particularly interesting and the fruit of the unripe nut was sweet. I sampled unripe berries of all sorts, including mulberries, which grew in abundance, and the leaves and stems of evergreens. I had a cousin during my early years who considered himself quite a fancier of fine foods and he would bring odd, curious cheese into the home—limburger; the brown, caramel-sweet gjetost of Norway, goat; and it sometimes seemed the more monstrously perfumed the better. I would pull the stamens from flowers and the inner stems of new weeds and sample the nectar as though I were a bee. I know full well the taste of clover.

I have never considered myself a great writer of prose, poetry, or anything else. But I write because I have to write, not only as a source of income but because of some inexplicable physical and mental need.

But don't think I was "taught" to write. I write because of association. Childhood associations mostly. My mother was a fine writer although her writings were limited mostly to letters to family and friends. But her frames of reference were first rate. She had studied the Bible in depth. My home library when I was quite young included all volumes of the Encyclopedia Britannica, the complete works of Shakespeare and Charles Dickens, among others.

In junior high school and high school I was exposed to a great deal of popular poetry—Emily Dickinson, Robert Frost, Edward Arlington Robinson, Edgar Lee Masters—but my fondness came not from my adult teachers, but from a shared enthusiasm with that one friend, David Sanders.

But equally as valid in the learning process of how to write was a keen, rabid admiration for the well-made lyrics to popular music. As I have noted I could quote you the introduction and bridge to all the finest popular music of my day—that of Cole Porter, Rodgers and Hart, Jerome Kern and his collaborators, including Oscar Hammerstein II and P. G. Wodehouse, George and Ira Gershwin, and others.

"First let me introduce myself. I'm Craig Claiborne, and this is Julia Child."

Cartoon.

I graduated with a degree in Journalism from the University of Missouri but I did not *learn* to write at that school, nor was whatever small talent I had for writing nurtured at the school. I am simply of the opinion that you can't be taught to write. You have to spend a lifetime in love with words. The only two tools you need are the best encyclopedia and dictionary that your purse can afford. After that you're on your own.

It must be said that I did have a role-model in my writing through many years although he was unaware of it. His name is Berton Roueché and he later became a neighbor and friend in what are known as the Hamptons. I cannot analyze the writing of Berton nor can I say precisely what there has been over the years that has exerted an appeal to my mind that is undeniable. He writes with an incredible craftsmanship, so neatly tailored and disciplined that it is more like hearing a good and never boring story, seated before a roaring fire while sipping a fine snifter of Cognac. His writing is warm and conversational. And superb.

Berton has written many short stories and a couple of novels but his writings have mostly taken the form of countless essays for the *New Yorker* magazine, the best known of which appeared under the name "Annals of Medicine."

I have never considered myself a journalist in the genuinely basic and most romantic sense of that word. I have never chased an ambulance or covered a fire; I have never been to a police court; never ridden a paddy wagon; never interviewed a politician; or written about hurricanes, holocausts, or havoc in the streets, major or minor. My "beat" (with one hysterically funny assignment aside: I was asked to write about a men's fashion show at Macy's department store and I know less about men's fashion than a department store dummy) has simply been the world of restaurants and dining. In my more than twenty years of "reporting," I have rarely had a deadline of any sort. That is to say that most of the material that has borne my by-line could have appeared equally well at any month or day within a decade and it would not have been noticed as untimely.

Of course, you do write about shad and shad roe and asparagus in the spring; barbecues, picnics, lobsters, corn, and tomatoes during the summer months; scallops, pumpkins, turkey, and cod during the fall and winter months.

And, too, there were those interminable years as restaurant critic when I *did* write about the opening of The Four Seasons and Lutèce and La Caravelle and there were those endless visits to the restaurants of Europe, but there wasn't a great deal of panic about getting there first. Revolutions and heart-stopping moments in the world of food and restaurant criticism are hard to come by or feel breathless about.

Come to think of it, I can recall only one momentous, get-it-in-print-as-soon-as-possible moment. The day that Jacqueline Kennedy selected a Frenchman to be chef at the White House. Even that, today, sounds a little trivial and tame by journalistic standards.

Over the years I have had a hundred and more letters from would-be food journalists informing me that they have degrees in Journalism, that they had newspaper experience, and so on, but what foundation could they lay in order to qualify themselves as "food experts"?

The answer is experience and, ultimately, I would follow the path that I took nearly thirty years ago; i.e., to go to a professional cooking school in Europe, preferably one that teaches classic French cooking plus international cooking plus wine, table, and banquet service.

Failing that I would go to a professional cooking school in America, preferably one with the standing of the Culinary Institute of America in Hyde Park, New York.

In the interim, I would take cooking courses from as wide a variety of good teachers in Manhattan as I could find and afford. And read as wide a variety of magazines and newspaper columns as are devoted to food. You will inevitably wind up reading volumes of nonsense and trivia but there are several that speak with unmistakable authority.

It is true that within the past ten to twenty years America has become the most sophisticated country in the world where *communications* about food are concerned. There is an embarrassment of great literature that has been made available to the public in books and magazines that is without peer anywhere else on earth.

One of the most impressive collections on international cooking is contained in the Time-Life Foods of the World series, the first volume of which was published in 1968 and continued through twenty-six volumes.

The greatest volume on the food of France—and perhaps the finest analysis of one nation's cooking and eating habits ever written—is Waverly Root's *The Food of France*. Not only will this book give you an idea as to how one nation's food culture is structured, it will indicate how almost any nation's food use is structured if you analyze it properly.

Although an intimate *reading* knowledge of food and cooking is essential to the making of a good food critic and/or restaurant critic there is nothing to equal a direct acquaintanceship with the taste of food and wine. This is best achieved by *learning* the techniques of cooking and sampling the food under the guidance of a professional chef either in a restaurant kitchen or a professional cooking school.

A final glazing of one dish or another is done under the salamander in my kitchen in East Hampton.

The next best thing is an adventure in travel and eating. This, of course, demands money and more money of a sort that few ordinary aspirants to the world of food reporting can conjure up in the course of a lifetime, much less during the days of an aspiring apprenticeship. The apprenticeship of tasting, that is. Given the wherewithal, you should travel by boat, by train, and by air throughout the Orient and Europe and, depending on your aspirations, a few other spots over the globe as well. You should visit every first- and second-class restaurant, dine in small out-of-the-way eateries, sample all the "classic" and "regional" specialties of each country you visit, and taste all the notable and some not so reputable wines as well.

Finally, I would amass the greatest collection of fine books on food and cooking, starting with the French and branching off into international foods. These I would study in depth, using them not only as bedside material, but putting the recipes to practice in the privacy of my own or someone else's kitchen.

You will find elsewhere, a section on my personal preferences of the best books on food.

Another final touch.

§ § §

I have often been asked if, during my years as a restaurant critic, I was ever offered a bribe, and the answer is no. Only twice have I had a "problem" with gifts that might smack of bribery. One of these involved Henri Soulé, the other, one of the oldest established roast goose and bock beer, which is to say, German, restaurants in Manhattan. I must add that that restaurant, located somewhat south of Forty-second Street, has changed management once and perhaps twice since that long-gone era.

In late December of the year I joined *The Times,* I returned to my Yorkville apartment one cold, late afternoon and opened the door. There, in stacks of twos and threes, from one end of my living room to the other, were a galaxy of gaily wrapped packages. I had to step over them to make my way through. I opened one package—a case of Black Label Scotch; then another—a case of Cognac; and another—a wooden crate containing a magnum of vintage champagne; and so on. There were no cards, no name attached to any but one of that mind-and eye-boggling collection of wines and spirits.

Eventually I came to a package that contained a crystal decanter and there, glued on with Scotch tape, was a card that said simply, "Merry Christmas" and the signature of the owner of the famed Bierstube.

My naïveté knows absolutely no bounds. To say that I was puzzled and bewildered is to play loose and free with the language. The crystal decanter had come from a restaurant owner, but who in God's name was responsible for the other gifts?

Once more I carefully picked up all the scraps of Christmas wrap, searching for a card or some clue as to my generous benefactor. I did not have any friends who could begin to afford such largess.

I would waken nights, disturbed to think that I had somehow not found the card to identify my mysterious gift-giver, disturbed that I had not, could not, write a thank-you note.

A year later I had moved to a handsome, spacious ground-floor apartment on West Thirteenth Street in Greenwich Village, the kitchen of which had windows and good ventilation.

One bright Saturday morning shortly after the middle of December of that year, I was reading when there was a knock on the door. I opened it. Double-parked outside was a moving van. Standing facing me was a fresh-faced young man, smiling ear to ear. He carried on his shoulder a gaily wrapped package that might have been a case of wine or booze. Lined up behind him was a series of many other similar packages.

He walked past me, set down the package from his shoulder, went to the sidewalk, picked up another package, deposited it, walked past me, and at some point said, "Boy, you're a lucky guy."

I frowned. "Where," I asked, "did all this merchandise come from?"

He grinned and named the German restaurant.

Quite honestly, the blood rushed from my face. It suddenly occurred to me that I and numerous friends had consumed almost all of the wine and spirits that had been deposited in my apartment the Christmas before. I felt betrayed not only by the restaurant but by my former innocence.

I stopped the kid dead still.

"Look," I said, "I know you won't understand this, but will you please take all those packages and put them back aboard that van and tell whoever sent this stuff that I said thanks, but no thanks."

He stared at me openmouthed but eventually he got the message and back the merchandise went. For a flickering instant, I also hated myself for my damnable conscience.

With Soulé it was another matter.

In mid-December of 1964, a restaurant called Le Mistral opened in Manhattan. It was elegant, the food was excellent, and I gave it a long and favorable review (unfortunately, it was short-lived and closed about seven years later).

The owner was Jean Larriaga, who had worked under Soulé at La Côte Basque. It had occurred to me many times over the years that there are scores of restaurants in America, even today, the owners and personnel of which had at one time "trained," which is to say worked under Soulé. Among a few there was the still-celebrated La Grenouille, founded by the late Charles Masson, who had worked not only at Le Pavillon but under Soulé at Le Restaurant du Pavillon de France at the 1939 World's Fair. There were Robert Meyzen and Fred Decré, owners, and Roger Fessaguet, chef, of La Caravelle. There was Roger France, then chef at The Four Seasons and so on. His disciples could be found in fine restaurants throughout America.

At the time my review of the new Le Mistral was to appear, I decided to run in the same edition a "family tree" which would diagrammatically detail the restaurants and the names of the personnel who had worked under Soulé.

That appeared on a Friday.

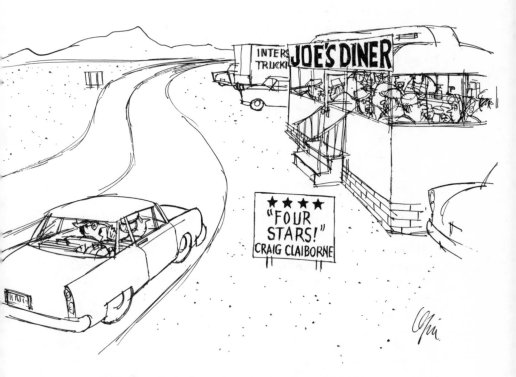

"*At the end of a long, hard day's drive, I daresay.*"

Cartoon.

The following week I had a telephone call from Soulé. He did not say "Thank you." He spoke to me somewhat sternly.

"I must see you," he said. I cringed.

"About what, M. Soulé?"

"I must see you," he repeated. "When can you come to Le Pavillon?"

I agreed to visit him the next morning at 10 A.M.

When I arrived he was walking around the tables in the main dining room, moving silver, holding glasses up to the light with a napkin in one hand. He was not wearing a jacket, which seemed a bit surrealistic.

He shook my hand and said, "Come with me."

He led me into his private office in the center of which was a desk cluttered with correspondence. He motioned to the swivel chair at the desk. The room smelled of cigar smoke. As I have already mentioned, I loathe cigar smoke.

He walked over to a heavy safe, twirled a dial, and opened it. He took from it a red leather box with the name Cartier engraved in gold.

He handed it to me.

I opened it and saw a magnificent gold watch.

I removed it from the case and engraved on the back was "To Craig Claiborne, In gratitude, H.S." I was enormously touched. I stood and kissed him on both cheeks.

In the taxi back to the office I brooded. I knew that I couldn't keep this watch even though I was fully aware it was given to me, not as a gesture of being "bought," but of genuine gratitude and affection.

Back at my desk I telephoned Clifton Daniel, then managing editor of *The Times*.

"Mr. Daniel," I began. "I've a beautiful problem."

"What is it?" he asked.

"I want to show it to you."

"Come down," he said.

I went down to the third floor, the nerve center of the newspaper, and walked into his office. I showed him the watch.

He paused, inspected it thoroughly, and said, "You are right. You do, indeed, have a beautiful problem."

After some thought, he said in somber tones, "I'll have to think about this."

His "thinking about," I surmised, would have to be discussed with the publisher.

He did not reply to me by Monday. Nor Tuesday. I was becoming more than a little uneasy. On Wednesday I telephoned him.

"Mr. Daniel," I said, "if I must give that watch back, I'll have to do it soon. Can I keep it or not?"

"No," he said. "I know it wasn't given to you for any awkward reason. But as a member of *The Times* staff you simply cannot accept a gift like this."

I breathed a sigh of relief. I had only had that watch on my arm once. It had weighed a ton.

I wrote Soulé and Clifton Daniel wrote Soulé, each of us explaining that we knew the goodness and innocence of his generosity, et cetera, et cetera, *but* et cetera, et cetera.

I earnestly wished that the entire episode had never happened. It was my fault that a gulf was created in our friendship. I was embarrassed that I could not accept the watch. I was also, foolishly as it happened, fearful of Soulé's response.

I didn't see him again—to tell the truth, I avoided seeing him—for months. And then one day a friend from out of town asked me if we might possibly visit La Côte Basque; he'd never been and its reputation was of the highest.

I called and made a reservation.

When we entered, I was greeted warmly by Soulé. He embraced me with a warm bear hug.

During the course of the lunch he took me aside.

"If you ever leave *The Times,* or when I die," he said, "that watch is waiting for you."

And when he died, the watch was returned to me!

§ § §

Henri Soulé died January 27, 1966, and I wrote in *The Times* that he was "the Michelangelo, the Mozart and the Leonardo da Vinci" of the French restaurants in America.

If his name looms large in this book it is because he was purely and simply the most unforgettable character I ever met. And in ways large and small he influenced my life.

He was a man of towering standards with cool disdain for the commonplace and the sham and a keen appreciation of those who dined in his company on such fare as vintage champagne—almost always Dom Perignon—mousse of sole *tout Paris;* pilaf of mussels; pheasant with truffled sauce, and the dessert that I admire most, *les oeufs à la neige.*

His influence on the restaurant scene, during his lifetime and even today, was vital and monumental.

For one reason or another I spent many hours in Soulé's company and, although his niche was beyond question, he was damnably hard to portray in words.

M. Soulé was born March 12, 1903, in Saubrigues, a small village near Bayonne in the southwestern corner of France. He began his career as a bus boy in the Continental Hotel at Biarritz. From there he went to the Mirabeau Hotel on Paris' Rue de la Paix and thence to the Claridge on the Champs Élysées. At the age of twenty-three he was said to be the youngest captain of waiters in Paris. One of the great influences of his life was the late Louis Barraya of the Café de Paris, under whom M. Soulé became manager and chief of staff.

In 1938 he was tapped by Jean Drouant, of a distinguished French restaurant family and brother-in-law of M. Barraya, to help run a restaurant at the World's Fair in New York. He arrived in this country in March 1939, with sixty kitchen workers and thirty-eight maîtres d'hôtel, captains, waiters, wine stewards, and the like. M. Soulé was designated general manager of Le Restaurant du Pavillon de France, most often referred to as the French Restaurant. It opened May 9, 1939.

As one chronicler of such matters has noted, the original menu reads "like a nostalgic memento of another century: suprême de barbue Mornay, $1.50; homard Monte Carlo, $1.75 . . . and crêpes suzette, $1.25."

In October 1941, a short while after the fair closed, he opened Le Pavillon at 5 East Fifty-fifth Street. From the beginning it became the haven for the *beau monde.* The restaurant moved to 111 East Fifty-seventh Street on October 10, 1957.

The restaurateur then opened La Côte Basque at the Fifty-fifth Street address. That was in October 1958. For several years M. Soulé also owned The Hedges, a summer restaurant in East Hampton. It was opened in 1954 for summer dining only.

During his lifetime there was a frequent temptation to say that he was a simple individual struck with the genius of running a restaurant. He was, in truth, not a man of probing, philosophical insights who could sit by the hour discussing nuances of taste. Neither was he a markedly sophisticated man except as his temperament was keenly attuned to the desires and status of his customers: a master of the delicate chess game that involved seating the sensitive and rich.

He was a man of so many contrarieties of temperament it often seemed he was at least half a dozen men. There was Soulé, the elegant and thoughtful host. Soulé, the nervous and fretting supervisor of napery and tableware. Soulé, the haughty and frigid feudist with former employees. Soulé, frequently an amusing conversationalist but just as frequently withdrawn. There was Soulé, the man with a perfect eye for food. Soulé, the imperious and disdainful eminence for those who think food is merely something to eat. And there was, most enigmatic of all, the third-person Soulé—Soulé by and of himself and a person apart from himself, not I or me, but with regal grandeur, Soulé.

§ § §

When European restaurateurs, such as Louis Vaudable of Maxim's and Claude Terrail of La Tour d'Argent, visited this country, it was rarely without paying their respects to Soulé.

One anecdote about Le Pavillon, told by M. Terrail, concerned a series of dinners offered him several years ago in a number of swanky homes in Manhattan.

"At the first of these dinners I was served a *quenelles de brochet*—a feather-like forcemeat of poached pike—and it was superb. I praised it without reservation. The second night in another home we were seated at table and suddenly I was served *quenelles de brochet* again. I frowned but said nothing and at the end of the meal I repeated my compliment.

"Well, on the third night I was taken to Le Pavillon for dinner and Martin, the maître d'hôtel, bent close to my ear and said, 'May I suggest the *quenelles de brochet*? I recommend it.'

"I turned to him and said, 'Martin, what is this with *quenelles de brochet* in America? Is it starting to replace the hamburger?'

"At that point, M. Soulé solved the mystery. Each of the hostesses had telephoned the restaurant and ordered a principal dish sent to their home. How was Soulé to know? They only specified it must be something exceptional."

§ § §

Soulé was an unabashed snob. One of his former maître d'hôtels once told me that Soulé deplored, above all, people who weren't well dressed or, in his mind, were physically unattractive.

"He used to order," my friend said, "twenty-four tall, standing roses to hide customers who in his eyes and mind were downright ugly."

§ § §

Two of the qualities that characterized Soulé were an intensely stubborn nature and an iron will. Once he had made a decision, no amount of cajoling or reasoning could talk him out of it, a fact that once became humorously apparent to Pierre Franey.

When Pierre was still chef at Le Pavillon, he and his wife were invited to dinner at Soulé's country home in Montauk. It was to be a simple evening of champagne and lobster *américaine,* the latter prepared by Pierre.

"If there was one point about which M. Soulé was absolutely single-minded," Pierre reminisced recently, "it was the use of hot plates for hot food. On that day the oven was set for about 400 degrees, and M. Soulé put the plates—Limoges, I believe they were—in the oven, eight or ten of them. There was more champagne and when we were about to sit down to dinner, the plates were hot as a blast furnace. M. Soulé took them out of the oven and put them in the sink to cool them slightly. He was about to turn on the water and I watched him, speechless. Finally, I said, 'M. Soulé, I don't think you ought to turn on the water; those plates are hot.' He said, 'I have a very good heating system and the water is very hot.' Well, he turned on the hot water and the bottom plate cracked and as the water level increased the second plate, then the third plate, and the fourth plate, and so on, all the way to the top. Not a plate was left intact."

§ § §

Soulé had the temperament of a man who could never indulge in physical violence or in fisticuffs except under extraordinary duress, and as far as anyone remembers he only came close to it once. That was when a bad character entered the restaurant and proceeded to the bar. No one, not even the bartender, realized that the man was intoxicated until he had finished a second martini and staggered over to the cold buffet with its lobster in aspic, pâtés in crust, and all the rest. Fred Decré, one of the owners of La Caravelle and then a captain at Le Pavillon, saw the man pick up a knife to slice the Paris ham and when Decré rushed over, the man directed the knife at him.

"Leave me alone," the man threatened, "or I'll use this."

Other members of the staff rushed to M. Decré's aid and they managed to guide the offender to the door but not before Soulé arrived at the fracas and offered one swift kick that missed by a mile.

"There," he said, dusting his hands, and throwing out his chest. "There, you see, that is how Soulé treats a man who is not a gentleman."

"Soulé never touched him," Robert Meyzen, another owner of La Caravelle and former employee of Le Pavillon, later recalled. "But he walked around like a peacock for a week."

§ § §

Because of the prominence of Le Pavillon, it is natural, too, that it had its share of the bizarre personalities who dined there or attempted to. One time a woman came through the revolving doors with hat slightly askew, a tawdry shawl around her neck, and the seams of her stockings in a spiral. When she demanded a table, the restaurant owner tried to use gentle persuasion to get her to leave the dining room. The more adamant she was, the more insistent he became, and eventually it was necessary to give the lady a gentle push. With this, she screamed into the room, "Don't you touch me, sir! Do you know who I am" she shouted. "The daughter of the Pope."

§   §   §

There were many reasons why Soulé dominated the field of the French restaurants in New York. First and foremost, the restaurant was as much a part of his life as anything could be. It was in a sense his passion, and he gave to it beyond the point of exhaustion. His attention to detail, his concern with the minutiae of a restaurant, were phenomenal in a city where many of his colleagues were merely businessmen and mercenaries, men with black ties and small backgrounds who turned to the restaurant field because of a supposed aura of glamour.

But, according to Soulé, the reason for his success was always his *équipe* or team. He said a thousand times, "The *équipe* is everything," and his *équipe* was, to the greatest degree possible, the Tiffany of the restaurant world. But behind the *équipe* there was a spirit that never would, never could settle for mediocrity. And the *équipe* was always aware of it. On the day of his death, a former employee and one of the finest chefs in the United States, called me and said quite briefly, "Our leader is dead," and I suspect he spoke for the most conscientious members of the restaurant industry, because there was not a French restaurant in Manhattan that was not the better for the standards imposed by Henri Soulé.

After his death, there was still an establishment known as Le Pavillon, and it was located at 111 East Fifty-seventh Street. But the subsequent management of the place allowed charity ladies to come in to solicit funds. At one point a color television was brought in to allow customers to watch, one forgets which auspicious event. Someone said that a religious service was performed there. And music was introduced. On one occasion one of the new owners, seated, actually waved good-by from his table. And who was this new management? None other than my old employer, Claude Philippe, and I gave him his due by simply telling the awful truth about the restaurant under his management.

The influence of Soulé on the American restaurant world will never be measured, but if one travels in restaurant circles there is a phrase that recurs like a timeless refrain: "You remember him; he worked under Soulé."

There is no such thing as an academy or school for complete French restauration in this country for either cuisine or table service. The closest thing to it was Le Pavillon.

Although I did not admire Henri Soulé for the *sang-froid* and hauteur that he had displayed in terminating his relationship with Pierre, I liked him. And he did have, as I have noted, an ineradicable, indelible, albeit inadvertent influence on my life.

That influence began in 1954, nearly five years before we were to finally meet. In the early and mid-1950s there still remained "social seasons" and they were more clearly defined than they are today. At this remove it is difficult to imagine a world in which air-conditioning was very much of a novelty. As one traveled from restaurant to restaurant or hotel to hotel, there was no total assurance that one room or another would be air-conditioned. I can remember as late as 1959 attending editorial meetings on what was then called the women's page when the question arose, "In this day and age, no matter where you travel—Europe, Tokyo, Mexico, and so on—you always walk into an air-conditioned room. Is it possible that no one need think any more about traveling in summer with two wardrobes, one for warmer climates, one for cooler?"

Thus, in 1954 when the rich and fashionable among us departed for the mountains and seashore, the luxury restaurants of Manhattan closed their doors from the Fourth of July to Labor Day.

The Hamptons of Long Island—Westhampton, Southampton, Bridgehampton, and East Hampton—were relatively unknown, more "tony," and far less touristy than they are today.

It was Soulé's thought to open a restaurant in the Hamptons that would become the summer watering place for his well-to-do clientele when Le Pavillon closed for the summer. He purchased a handsome, old, many-roomed mansion known as The Hedges, so called because it had belonged to a family named Hedges who first settled in East Hampton in 1725. He spent several thousands of dollars refurbishing the old house, inside and out, landscaping, installing a professional kitchen, building a wine cellar stocked with the finest Burgundies and Bordeaux, and so on. He also brought along the staff from the Pavillon, headed, of course, by Pierre Franey, whom I had not yet met.

Pierre rented a small cottage on Gardiners Bay where he installed his family for the summer. The following year he purchased another small cottage on the same body of water and he and his family were living there at the time that my friendship with him started to flourish.

When Pierre left Le Pavillon he became associated as a vice president with the late Howard Johnson, the founder of the ice cream and fast food empire. And thus, for the first time since his childhood, Pierre had weekends to relax and enjoy himself as he might choose.

I was several times invited to spend weekends with his family and they were memorable—clambakes on the beach, great kettles of Gardiners Bay bouillabaisse, seafood chowders, picnics on a small strip of

MENU

ROLLING DUNES PICNIC

AUGUST 20, 1966

Steamer Clams Louse Point
Cucumbers Pretty Pirate
Pickled Carrots Laughing Lady
Bennett Cookies

Roast Loin of Pork, Hog Creek
Black Beans Bonac

Cheese .... Fruit
Bread and Butter New York Times

Wine . 1952 Haut Brion

Picnics have figured prominently in the lives and activities of Pierre Franey and me during our residence in the Hamptons.

water-locked land called Cartwright Shoals, and cookouts that included boiling thirty-pound lobsters from Montauk.

Travel from New York to East Hampton was far more tortuous than it is today. The highways have been vastly improved and there are other amenities, including a fast jitney service to and from the city.

In 1962 I had received my first six-month royalty check from *The New York Times Cook Book* and, while it was not a vast sum (it was something like ten thousand dollars), it was more money than I had ever dreamed of having in a bank account.

Pierre encouraged me to buy property in the Hamptons. I scoffed at the thought.

"Never!" I said. "I'd no more travel three hours to get to this place than fly to the moon."

On December 8 of that year, one of the longest newspaper strikes on record hit *The New York Times*. It lasted nearly four months and I became despondent. In those days my passion and ardor for the paper were profound and, in that I belonged to the Newspaper Guild and could not cross the picket line, I grieved and felt totally displaced.

"If you built a house," Pierre cautioned, "it would take your mind off your troubles." And in the same year we were invited to dine on Shelter Island at the home of Marion Taylor, who was known to a few hundred thousands on her WOR radio program as Martha Deane.

Her home was built what seemed like a thousand feet directly over the bay, and at sunset, with small boats in the distance, calm waters, and gulls going home to nest, it was simultaneously pulse-quickening and sedative.

As we sat around a fire, eating a fine platter of roast chicken with tarragon, sipping a ten-year-old Médoc, and talking, mostly about the newspaper strike, I could scarcely have believed that within twenty-four hours I would contract verbally for a plot of land, and a house, to boot. But I have always been impetuous and do not regret the trait.

Someone had told Pierre of a piece of property located on Gardiners Bay—elevated about twenty feet above the water—that was about to go on the market. After a couple of glasses of Cognac we said good night to the Taylors and drove at midnight (there was a full moon) to the side of Gardiners Bay off a road named King's Point. It was a forested site, but we got out of the car and made our way through brambles and bush to the edge of the water. The view was more intoxicating than another glass of *fine champagne,* the name for the finest blend of Cognac.

The next morning I telephoned the owner of the lot and asked if it were for sale. She said yes and I agreed to purchase it. The same morning I made an agreement with an architect with equal celerity. And the following December, with a friend who is a decorator, I walked

CRAIG CLAIBORNE

through Bloomingdale's and within the space of two hours, every room in that soon-to-be-completed dwelling was basically furnished—bed, dining table and chairs, a few antique pieces, and all.

From the beginning, 271 King's Point Road was a place of Saturday night revels. There was in truth a golden age of gastronomy in my home that lasted until 1976, when Pierre joined the staff of *The Times* as my collaborator, as the "60-Minute Gourmet," and as equipment editor. After that date we worked more normal hours, cooking together during the week rather than only on weekends, or on Wednesday nights as we had done in my New York apartment, and entertaining only occasionally.

The revels in that kitchen often began as early as five in the afternoon with a scotch and soda or another not-too-innocent potable. Our young bodies seemed immune to the perils of alcohol and we imbibed to the fullest. A typical menu during those glorious fun-filled years would be an hors d'oeuvre followed by a soup followed by a fish course followed by a main course followed by salad with cheeses followed by dessert followed by coffee and Cognac or a stinger.

With the fish course there would generally be bottles of chilled white Burgundies; with the main course, a few great Bordeaux; and with the cheese course, a bottle or two of great red Burgundies. With the desserts, the finest champagnes.

I would often regale guests during the course of an evening's revelry with Duff Cooper's famed quotation from *Old Men Forget:*

"I can truthfully say that since I reached the age of discretion I have consistently drunk more than most people would say was good for me. Nor do I regret it. Wine has been to me a firm friend and a wise counsellor. Often wine has shown me matters in their true perspective and has, as though by the touch of a magic wand, reduced great disasters to small inconveniences.

"Wine has lit up for me the pages of literature, and revealed in life romance lurking in the commonplace.

"Wine has made me bold but not foolish; has induced me to say silly things but not to do them.

"Under its influence words have often come too easily which had better not have been spoken, and letters have been written which had better not have been sent.

"But if such small indiscretions standing in the debit column of wine's account were added up, they would amount to nothing in comparison with the vast accumulation on the credit side."

The more serious part of the Saturday night ritual was that as Pierre (and any visiting chefs) cooked, I stood at my typewriter and recorded exact ingredients and instructions for all the dishes we would dine on. These would subsequently appear in *The New York Times Magazine.*

A characteristic moment in my kitchen while working with Pierre Franey. He is at the cutting board and range creating new dishes; I am at the IBM, following him step by step at the keyboard.

I am indebted to a late accountant who admonished me to keep a record of the menus served in my home and the names of the guests who dined with me. Because of that advice, I have amassed ten volumes that I number among my most favored possessions. Oddly, I can open almost at any page and remember in detail the circumstances of one evening or another.

I note that on the seventeenth of December, 1979, we dined on a cream of wild mushrooms; a roast haunch of venison St. Hubert; purée of chestnuts; and endive *meunière*. There was salad with Brie, followed by orange sections marinated in Cointreau, and "les cookies de David Dugan." David Dugan was the son of the famed founder of the Dugan Bakery in Brooklyn and he had dispatched the cookies as a pre-holiday gesture.

On the fourth of May, 1976, with guests, the main courses included saddle of venison with *sauce poivrade* and a civet of rabbit plus noodles. There was salad and, for dessert, profiteroles filled with vanilla ice cream. The wines included Château Haut-Brion 1971, Château de la Chaize 1974, and a nonvintage Krug Champagne.

A noon-time oriental feast outside my kitchen and near the swimming pool of my first home in East Hampton. The foods included roast duck, spareribs, and assorted vegetable platters.

On the twenty-seventh of October, 1968, we dined on *coquilles St. Jacques au gratin;* rack of lamb *en couronne;* salad with assorted cheeses, and, for dessert, a mélange of fruits. The wines included a Puilly-Fuissé 1966; Château Brane-Cantenac 1959; Château Léoville Lascases 1959; Dom Perignon Champagne 1961; plus *"alcools et liqueurs."*

Some of the pleasantest of meals were those of midsummer when the food was served buffet-style. On the last day of August in 1969, we sampled *les crudités,* a cold cream of sorrel soup; a hot casserole of tripes *à la mode;* cold poached striped bass with a mustard mayonnaise; mussels *à la ravigote;* cold, baked country ham; cold ratatouille *niçoise; "le melon en surprise";* assorted cheeses; and fresh chilled pineapple with rum.

The wines included Beaujolais and Chablis, plus *"La bière* Rheingold."

That is not to say that all the meals served in my home were elaborate French banquets. Far from it. There are entries for Chinese chrysanthemum pot. For pizza and hamburgers and chile con carne. For a cheese-grits casserole. Cold grilled chicken with a simple salad of sliced, in-season tomatoes with Stilton cheese and watermelon for dessert. And there are menus for all the dishes that were cooked when Virginia Lee came into my home for almost two years when we were preparing *The Chinese Cookbook.*

One of the grandest accounts of life in those days appeared in *The New York Times* on March 28, 1976. It was written by Alden Whitman, for many years the distinguished obituary writer for *The Times.* He is the husband of Joan Whitman, once women's news editor of the paper, who was very much involved in my return to *The Times* after a two-year hiatus.

Alden's account was preceded by a mockup of a listing in the style of the *Guide Michelin.* The account appears in full below:

3 Stars, No Waiting
‡‡‡‡***Chez Claiborne (Craig Claiborne
et Pierre Franey) "bord du mer, parc
fleuri." East Hampton. — wc
Spec. Cuisine Variée.

The rubric above, adapted from the Michelin guide, that indispensable Koran of Frenchmen and those purse-free enough to visit France these days, means that Craig Claiborne, the food editor of The New York Times, and Pierre Franey, his associate and former chef of Le Pavillon in Manhattan, operate a splendidly appointed restaurant, one with a particularly fine ambience and, above all, one that serves the very best meals—repasts that are worth a special trip to savor.

There are several exceptions to be noted immediately. Mr. Claiborne's country cottage is open only on Saturday evenings and on special feast days such as New Year's Eve, and that admission is by invitation only.

In the opinion of those upon whom an invitation has been bestowed and who have eaten in many of the world's ranking restaurants, the Claiborne-Franey establishment richly merits a three-star rating (the most Michelin accords any restaurant). "Craig Claiborne is the proprietor of the only three-star restaurant, certainly on Long Island and perhaps in the United States," Paul Bocuse, himself a chef of renown in France, remarked last summer.

Apart from sociability and the pleasures of the table, Mr. Claiborne's Saturday evenings serve a practical purpose. It is then that he and Mr. Franey prepare and test the recipes that appear in Mr. Claiborne's articles and books. This has been going on since 1964, when Mr. Claiborne built a home on a bluff overlooking Gardiners Bay. A couple of years ago he remodeled the house to accommodate a full professional kitchen, with a Vulcan gas range along one wall and a collection

Having a ball with a batch of dough in the kitchen of my first home in The Springs, East Hampton, 1970 or thereabouts.

of equipment and gadgets that one would not ordinarily see outside of an outstanding kitchenware emporium.

Because Saturday evenings are a time for creation and testing, guests over the years have sampled dishes from all over the world, from Annamese fare to Zanzibarian delights. When Mr. Claiborne was writing his Chinese cookery book with Virginia Lee, the menus were invincibly Chinese. Guests never know what's in store for them, but few have been known to offer regrets. And one regret is sufficient to blackball a prospective guest almost forever.

Those who are asked are drawn either from among friends of Mr. Claiborne or Mr. Franey or from those whose palates Mr. Claiborne believes are likely to be impeccable. He draws the line at gourmets, a word and a concept he regards as insufferable. Epicures, yes, gourmets, never.

Some are fairly regular patrons. One is Henry Lewis Creel, an affable retired Shell Oil financial specialist, who minds the bar and whose margaritas have made his reputation. An amateur cook of talent, Mr. Creel is publishing this year "Cooking for One Is Fun," a collection

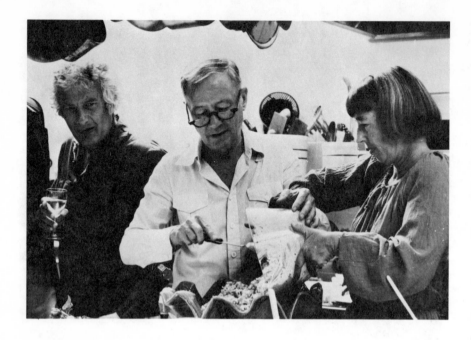

At a party in my home, author Joseph Heller sips wine while watching the food being dished out by me with the aid of my good friend, neighbor, and editor, Joan Whitman.

of his recipes for single persons. Before her death in 1975, Jeannette Rattray, a regal and jolly woman who was publisher of The East Hampton Star, was a regular. But the number is small.

Those who have come to eat and to participate include chefs of great distinction. Mr. Bocuse was there last summer. André Soltner of Lutèce is always welcome, as are Roger Fessaguet of La Caravelle, Jean Vergnes of Le Cirque, René Verdon, President Kennedy's chef, Pierre Laverne of La Côte Basque and Jacques Pépin.

Among the hundreds of notables who have been guests are Alfred A. Knopf, the publisher and oenophile; Edward Giobbi, Jimmy Ernst, Robert Gwathmey and Alfonso Ossorio, the artists; Muriel Oxenburg Murphy, the salonnière; Art Buchwald, Irwin Shaw, Willie Morris, Berton Roueché, Gloria Emerson and Jean Stafford, the writers; Betty Friedan, the feminist leader; Eleanor Perry, the screen writer; Betty Comden and Adolph Green, the comedy writers, and Peter Stone, the dramatist.

At the "initiation" party at my new house in East Hampton, the guests in the kitchen included Shirley Heller, Gloria Jones, Gael Greene, the food critic, and Kay Leroy.

Guests seldom sing for their supper, but for Burton Lane, the composer and lyricist, Mr. Claiborne rented a piano, and Mr. Lane led a sing-along of his compositions.

Saturday evening begins Saturday morning, when Mr. Claiborne (and sometimes Mr. Franey) does the shopping for a menu planned days ahead. If the dinner is to have a fish course, Mr. Claiborne will journey to David Catena's in Southampton, stopping for fresh vegetables (in season) at The Green Thumb in Water Mill. Or he may go to Stuart's Fish Market in Amagansett. It all depends on the availability of local fish. For groceries and meats, it's to Gristedes. And for table flowers, to Buckley's in East Hampton.

Serious work on the various dishes starts after a late lunch and reaches its peak from 7:30 to 8 o'clock. By then the guests have arrived and Mr. Creel will have set the table, the wine glasses polished to a sparkle and the silverware burnished to a gleam. Dress, except for feast-day galas (when it is black tie), is informal. Mr. Claiborne greets his guests aproned and in slacks. Mr. Creel conflates his margaritas. He and the guests generate small talk as Mr. Claiborne vanishes into the kitchen.

But soon, as on a recent Saturday evening, the guests, too, make their way to the spiritual center of the house. To the uninitiated, it may seem like the Tower of Babel in the midst of Chaos.

Music—anything from Verdi's *Requiem* to *Porgy and Bess*—floats from recessed stereo speakers. Mr. Franey, who came to the United States with Henri Soulé in 1939, is chopping, measuring, cooking—and tasting with a forefinger. Simultaneously, he keeps up a running conversation with Mr. Claiborne and with the guests, swinging effortlessly between French and English. Mr. Claiborne, meanwhile, is noting ingredients and precise amounts in notebooks equal to the number of dishes on the menu—and talking in French or English.

Mr. Franey's hands are so practiced that he can mince onions or garlic, skin a fish, or cut the meat reflexively while conducting several animated conversations at once. Just as skilled, Mr. Claiborne, when it is required, can duplicate the feat.

Although Mr. Franey is precise in his measurements—virtually everything is weighed or meted out by fractions of a tablespoon—he remarked the other evening as aromas emerged from the oven:

"That's what it's all about—you cook with your nose."

He is also adept at creating dishes from Mr. Claiborne's descriptions of them. Mr. Claiborne had partaken of a fish soup in Halifax, N.S., a few weeks ago, and Mr. Franey recreated it as provençale fish soup.

Some time before dinner Mr. Claiborne selects the wines from a capacious cellar maintained at 56 to 57 degrees. For the recent Saturday, he chose Rioja Clarete 1971, a Spanish red, and Pinot Chardonnay (Mâcon-Luguy) 1974, a French white.

Finally, there is a semblance of order in the kitchen, and Mr. Claiborne calls out, "On mange," or "À table," and he and Mr. Franey and their guests sit down—Mr. Claiborne last, because he serves.

The evening this writer was present eight were at the table, all intimate friends, so the conversation spun from politics to publishing to cooking to jokes and in-house gossip. When the table is larger, it resembles a free forum.

As usual, although the dishes were many, the portions were modest —the better, Mr. Claiborne believes, to appreciate their subtleties. He rarely serves anything "minceur," or slimming, but there is no gourmandizing. And only a simple dessert of fresh fruit or sherbet. The meal, over which guests tend to linger, concludes with coffee and a digestif—usually a stinger.

§ § §

I am passionately fond of New Year's Eve. I love that night like a warm blanket, a roaring log fire, and an extra-dry martini. It is the only festival at the year's end about which I am sentimental. It is a time of abandon and forgetfulness, good will, good wine, and good food. In times past, when I have been unbearably poor, I have on that one night felt colossally rich, the grandest of pashas, the epicure's epicure.

This euphoria first gripped me when I had just moved into a tiny one-room apartment in midtown Manhattan. I had invited a few chefs —close friends—and others into my home for a sit-down dinner on New Year's Eve. Within a day or so the guest list had swelled to thirty.

A sit-down dinner for thirty? In a telephone booth? Indeed. We simply moved the bed and set up folding tables and chairs. The main course of the evening was, as it has often been over the years, suckling pig.

From that first celebration, a few things have been constant on New Year's Eve, not the least of which is Roger Fessaguet, chef of La Caravelle in Manhattan. I should add that these celebrations have now taken on, in other respects, the form of a "covered dish supper." The chefs, who arrive with their wives or friends, generally have a pâté or two tucked under the arm.

The other seeming imperatives at the gatherings are oysters on the half shell; that incomparable salt-cod mousse called *brandade de morue;* and two kinds of *boudins*—black and white sausages cooked on a grill and served with mustard. There are, inevitably, magnificent pâtés and terrines, some baked in pastry, and as far back as I can remember, baked country ham, generally fancified at the insistence of one French chef or another and served with a Madeira or Port wine sauce. There is always a purée of chestnuts, another of celery root. Brie cheese is always there as well as fruitcakes, mincemeat pies, pumpkin pies, and, on a few occasions, a *bûche de Noel.*

As I have mentioned, for many years I have kept a journal of menus and guests who have dined in my home, and the New Year's Eve dinners hold a pre-eminent spot in these books. Thumbing through them recently I noted that on the last day of 1974 we feasted on, among other things, suckling pig stuffed with apples and roast goose stuffed with chestnuts and a venison ragout.

On the ultimate evening of 1970 we dined on a coulibiac of salmon, another stuffed goose, and a purée of celery root. That was also the year we splurged and had a pound or so of caviar. The wines that year included a Pouilly-Fuissé, 1969; a Chassagne-Montrachet, 1966; and Pommery Brut Champagne, 1961.

Thumbing still further through those wine-stained pages, I find among the appetizers or first courses, in addition to those oysters on the half shell (often served with small grilled sausages), oysters Rockefeller, a mousse of pigeon, taramosalata, hog's head cheese, smoked salmon, a terrine of venison liver, *celeri rémoulade,* a hot pâté in crust with a *beurre blanc* and "Ed Giobbi's bathtub tuna." Ed always blends his tuna in the bathtub before processing it in olive oil.

Main courses have included striped bass stuffed with oysters, a leg of lamb baked in pastry, paella *à la valenciana,* a Mediterranean fish stew, pheasant braised in red wine, civet of rabbit, a truffled roast capon, and garlic sausages with lentil salad.

By the way, I can recall only one catastrophe in all those years, the day when a neighbor's enormous German shepherd made away with the Brie cheese in one yawning gulp.

If there is one celebration that is even more joyous to my mind, it is New Year's Day. That, too, has become a ritual, but for a smaller group—those who have driven great distances plus close neighbors of many years' standing. That régale is much simpler. Less preparation is involved and the champagne generally flows freely. The menu consists of *les restes,* meaning the leftovers from the night before—cold roast goose, cold roast suckling pig, and so on. Plus a baker's dozen of great cold foods.

I have a standing annual order of good things at the year's end from Murray's Sturgeon Shop in Manhattan—lox, bagels, Nova Scotia salmon, smoked brook trout, schmaltz herring, matjes herring, smoked sturgeon, cream cheese, kosher pickles, sour cream, and more.

And no matter how many disasters have occurred since last January 1, I always go to bed on New Year's night knowing that "last year was, indeed, a very good year." Perhaps the best.

§ § §

It is no confession to say that the greatest share of my income derives not from a salary but from cookbook royalties. I point this out because, while I have stated that I regard my former profession, public relations, with disdain, I am well aware of the effects of publicity on the sale of merchandise. And books are merchandise.

Ergo, the more often a "merchant's" name appears in print, the larger the sale of his product.

If I have enjoyed a certain amount of "fame" in my profession within the past few years, it was relatively slow in materializing. Although I had been with *The New York Times* for several years, I am of the opinion that any "celebrity" that I now enjoy dates largely from a picnic that took place in 1965 and is elaborately outlined in my menu books.

When I moved into my home in East Hampton, I used to sit in a swing chair in my glass-paneled living room gazing out across often calm, sometimes turbulent bay waters at a marvelous, mysterious stretch of land called Gardiners Island. To those of us who lived facing it, it was five acres of fascinating legend. We all knew that Captain Kidd had plied the waters of that bay and had buried treasure on the island. It was a place with hordes of deer, wild turkey, and pheasant. Through binoculars from a distance, one can see the osprey birds, once nearly extinct, wheeling in large arcs above their nests made of twigs. There are three thousand privately held acres that, we had been told, had been held in the Gardiner family since 1635 when Lion Gardiner came here from England, fifteen years after the arrival of the *Mayflower*. This Lion Gardiner was made "lord of the manor" by Charles I, the Stuart king.

The island is now controlled by Robert David Lion Gardiner, a direct descendant and the present lord of the manor.

On the days that I would visit the Franeys' (their cottage also faced the island) we would sit around grilling fish or feasting on freshly harvested littlenecks and cherrystones taken only moments before from Pierre's "back yard," another small bay called Accabonac, or on steamed lobsters taken in traps in that very Gardiners Bay. As we would sip our white wine, someone would muse, "Maybe we could sneak over during the week when he's not around."

"Oh no," another would caution, "he has a caretaker."

One day in midsummer, Pierre and I decided to have a picnic on the beach and invite a few close friends, all French chefs who worked in Manhattan, and their wives. We talked in vague terms of menu and dates.

That evening I sat down with a scotch and soda in that swing chair and gazed out again. And then an inspiration.

"If we gave a picnic on that island," I mused to myself, "and if Robert David Lion Gardiner likes to eat, maybe he could be persuaded . . ." What the hell, I thought, I have nothing to lose.

The next morning I telephoned Gardiner and got the usual, not unanticipated response, "Craig who?" I explained that I was food editor of *The Times,* that I knew all these famous chefs, that we wanted to give a lavish picnic, and we would like him and his wife, Eunice, to join us. Preferably we would make it easy on them. We'd give the picnic on his private island.

His reply was not ecstatic. Nor did he refuse. Rather, he proposed that I come to his office. Understandably. He didn't know me from Adam's off ox (another of my mother's often used expressions) and, I was quite certain, had never seen my by-line or read my column. Which did not disqualify him in my mind as a *fin bec* or connoisseur.

As it turned out, he did relish fine food and belonged to one or another wine and food society. And he agreed to let us come to the island for the picnic. He even offered us the use of his boat.

That is the genesis of what turned out to be one of the most glorious days and feasts of my life. No meal at the grandest restaurant ever tasted so good, nor was it ever consumed with more warmth, good grace, and friendship.

Pierre was as joyful as I that we would finally make it to the island and our plans became more elaborate. We called the White House and asked for René Verdon, the chef. I had, several years earlier, broken the story—to the dismay of the White House—that Jacqueline Kennedy had engaged a Frenchman to head the presidential kitchen. It made the front page of *The Times*.

The news about René had been "leaked" to me by our very good friend Roger Fessaguet, one of the greatest chefs in America. Roger had been one of the first "invitées." The other chefs were Jacques Pépin, former chef to Charles de Gaulle and today a cookbook author and roving cooking teacher; and Jean Vergnes, former chef of the Colony. They would come with their wives and friends, almost all of whom, with the exception of the Gardiners and myself, were French.

The chefs arrived at my house Friday night and were up until two in the morning preparing food for the occasion.

The next morning, the equipment and supplies for the *pique-nique* nearly filled a Land Rover and the back of a station wagon. There were two dozen Baccarat wine glasses; a small grill; a large grill that weighed 120 pounds; two cases of wine; ten crates of food; a giant clamshell to be used as a service piece; and, to hold a mélange of fresh-cut fruit in liqueurs, two hand-carved watermelons.

Once on the island, we boarded the Gardiners' battered four-wheel-drive truck and drove through acres of rolling fields covered with wild grapes, raspberries, blackberries, elm, and oak. As the party descended from the truck at Bostwick Point, white egrets flapped their wings in the distance and disappeared into the oak forest.

The Gardiners had brought Dom Pérignon Champagne, and it gurgled into the Baccarat glasses.

"Isn't it delicious in this crystal?" Mr. Gardiner asked. "You can feel the bubbles through the glass."

Within minutes of arrival the chefs had collected massive tree trunks, driftwood planks, and a weathered piece of jetsam, an old cable wheel. All were put together to create a fabulous dining area.

Close by, a fire was built for the small grill to cook the striped bass, and the charcoal was started in the massive grill to hold the fifteen squabs, later to be cooked with mustard and bread crumbs.

The grandest picnic of my life, a fine day in August 1965, on Gardiners Island, which I could sight from my house on Gardiners Bay. Five chefs and I prepared the food. In the background approaching the camera are Jean Vergnes, chef of the old Colony restaurant, and Jacques Pépin, the cooking authority; sitting are Pierre Franey, Roger Fessaguet, then chef now a partner at La Caravelle, and René Verdon, then chef of the White House and now owner of Le Trianon in San Francisco.

A Feast Made for Laughter

The giant clamshell was unloaded to receive seviche, the raw fish appetizer made from a recipe concocted by Pierre after a visit to Mexico two years earlier. Mussels in a delicious herbed *sauce ravigote;* a piquant salad of beef vinaigrette; the pâté in its terra cotta container; and freshly caught bluefish from the bay, cooked with white wine and onions, were set out. So were a giant wheel of Brie, a large wedge of goat cheese, and small wheels of Camembert to get to the proper temperature.

The wine appeared to the accompaniment of accordion music played by Armand Innocenti, a printer at the French Embassy.

The picnic wines, bought from a local liquor store, were (in this day and age one would add "incredibly") inexpensive and ideal for the occasion. There were a $16.20 case of Almadén Mountain White Chablis, well chilled, and a $16.50 case of light and fine, fruity Beaujolais Supérieure. The white wine was in portable carrying cases of shaved ice.

To the tune of *"Auprès de Ma Blonde," "Le Petit Vin Blanc," "Boire un Petit Coup,"* and *"À la Bastille,"* the bluefish was poached, squabs were grilled, and the children arrived with a net to sweep in the sea for thousands of small whitebait. The whitebait were batter-fried in hot oil to a crisp, succulent, and delectable turn and eaten out of hand while the music played on.

M. Fessaguet prepared cold lobster with egg stuffing, and Mr. Gardiner noted that at one time a fisherman rented a shack on the island and paid for his rent with lobsters.

"I wish someone were doing that now," Mrs. Gardiner added.

The party was scheduled to depart at 5 P.M., but by then children, grandmothers, and all were holding hands and moving in a circle, dancing and singing. So word was sent to the boats that there would be a slight delay, and we didn't shove off until seven.

"Gardiners Island," the owner remarked, "hasn't seen a feast like this since Captain Kidd ate suckling pig with my forebears nearly three hundred years ago."

One small segment of that story has never been told in print.

Having a mind geared to public relations, I telephoned *Life* magazine, at that time in its heyday, and asked if they would like to cover the picnic. They answered eagerly in the affirmative.

With a photographer from that august publication on hand, I decided that pure crystal goblets were in order.

I was certainly in no position to invest in crystal for the affair and I was sure that *The Times* would never foot a bill for, what would seem to them, such a frivolous occasion.

Therefore, I telephoned Baccarat Crystal on Fifty-seventh Street. I had over the years made many modest purchases of Baccarat whenever I felt my budget could afford it.

I was blunt and to the point when I explained the nature of my call. A few chefs and I were going on a picnic on one of the legendary islands of America, just off Long Island. The chefs, including the chef of the White House, were internationally known. *Life* magazine would cover the outing. Would Baccarat like to lend us two dozen crystal goblets? The ones I had in mind cost, in that long-lost age, fifteen dollars a glass.

The first reply was an unequivocal "No." Baccarat would never "lend" merchandise.

Someone in the organization then called again.

"The company has reconsidered and they will lend you the glasses *provided* you return them without a flaw. There must be no sign of lint and, of course, no chips or other signs of breakage."

The glasses arrived and they were taken to the picnic.

They were put to good and frequent use and the chefs were photographed holding their glasses on high in a toast.

And at picnic's end, they were treated like so many fragile eggs.

They were brought into my kitchen and put in the dishwasher. They were removed in all their pristine crystal purity. Any trace of detergent spot was conscientiously wiped dry with paper toweling to avoid any suspicion of lint.

They were then lined up on a pass-through between my kitchen and dining area.

That evening I went to bed with that fine feeling of bliss that comes from good food, good wine, and an outing in the open air. The picnic had been an uncompromising success; *Life* magazine was obviously pleased and, what's more, I had a good and entertaining article in my notebooks.

About 3 A.M. I was awakened by a crash reminiscent of the buzz-bombs I once heard long ago in London during the war. A shattering bang followed by splintering.

A heavy Provençale platter, one that I treasured and one that had been used on the picnic, had been rehung in its usual place over the pass-through.

It had dropped from the nail and onto that exaltation of Baccarat.

There isn't much more to tell except *The Times* suddenly found itself confronted with an unanticipated bill for crystal that had been used for a "frivolous" occasion.

Another pleasant outdoor feast came about in 1970 when the producers of a television program, "Camera Three," telephoned me from CBS, to ask if I would create and orchestrate a meal that would celebrate American cooking. It would be shown on July Fourth in full color.

I agreed to it with considerable enthusiasm for only a few years

At a second picnic on Gardiners Island, the champagne flowed freely. The guests included Clifton Daniel (standing just to my right, back to camera) and his wife, Margaret Truman.

earlier I had discovered the pleasures of the East Coast institution known as a clambake. I am convinced to this day that it happens to be the most colorful, joyous, and festive of American feasts.

I had become familiar with the awesome fascination of clambakes under the tutelage of a man named Stanley Surozenski, who worked for a nursery on Long Island. He moonlighted weekends by staging clambakes from one end of the island to the other, so many in fact that he was often referred to as Stanley Steamer.

I had been invited to the clambake by a friend on Shelter Island and, when I arrived, Stanley was in the process of peeling onions with a tear or two falling here and there on the sand. Actually, Stanley was in fine spirits because the sun was shining.

"We're lucky to have sun," he told me, "after all the rain this year. That's one thing about a clambake; a lot of rain can be a disaster.

"We gave one last year and when we started to build the fire the skies looked threatening. We went ahead anyway and put the seaweed on those fired-up rocks and covered it with tarpaulin like always.

"Then the rains came and it poured for four hours solid. You couldn't believe it. When the time came to eat, we took off the tarpaulin and nothing had happened. The lobsters on top of the clambake had crawled away. All the guests had to eat that day was watermelon and beer."

I learned that in addition to sun, a properly made clambake takes protean labor and boundless enthusiasm and over the years Pierre Franey and I have supervised a dozen or so on his rocky beach or mine. You start by gathering wood. Any wood so long as it burns, driftwood, logs, kindling, broken-down furniture, no-matter-what, as long as it is combustible. But there must be enough to keep the fire burning incessantly for six hours or longer.

Next, you must gather enough rocks, stones, and small boulders measuring at least a foot across to fill a newly dug pit in the sand, about six feet in diameter. And then comes the most difficult part, the search for nearly six hundred pounds of fresh seaweed, the better to steam the clams and other food.

The proceedings begin by filling the pit with rocks, covering them with firewood and firing it, taking care that more ignitables are added as the wood burns away. As the fire burns you prepare the assorted foods, each category of which is carefully tied in squares of cheesecloth to make packages. These include (at our clambake for 60 persons, at any rate) 2 bushels of cherrystone clams, 60 one-and-one-quarter-pound lobsters, 10 pounds of small peeled onions, 120 ears of freshly shucked corn, and 200 pieces of chicken that has been cut into quarters. It is important for flavor that the chicken pieces be sprinkled with paprika and grilled over charcoal until slightly charred on the outside and not cooked in the center. When cooled, the pieces, a dozen at a time, are tied inside the cheesecloth squares.

When the fire has burned for six hours, you hastily rake the remnants of burning wood and ashes away from the fired-up stones. To doubly assure their cleanliness, you sweep further with wet brooms. With bullet-like precision, you cover the stones with the soggy seaweed, and over it place a large damp cloth, preferably a clean bed sheet. Make a rim over the seaweed bed with packages of clams. Make a rim inside this with bags of chicken, a third inner rim of corn, and atop this mass, the onions, the live, unfettered lobsters, quickly keeping them intact and in place with a second wet bed sheet. This in turn is covered with two massive, wet tarpaulins. Then you shovel enough sand from the beach to cover the tarpaulins and clambake.

At this point, the participants at a clambake can revel in four hours of what the Italians call *dolcefarniente,* my favorite phrase for idleness, meaning sweet doing nothing. At our gatherings this has taken the form of water skiing, reading, boating, fishing, swilling gin and tonic or, more to the occasion, ice cold beer.

When the clams and the other foods have steamed for four to four-and-one-half hours, the feast is ready to begin. The sand is carefully removed with rakes and brooms from atop the tarpaulins, the tarpaulins are lifted with great care to prevent sand from falling into the food. And as the upper sheet is torn away there always is that mouth-gaping, ecstatic moment of seeing that riot of color—the burning red of the lobsters engulfed in great gusts of steam (the clambake is in effect a pressure cooker), the gray-white bags of corn and chicken—and then the rush to the jerry-rigged tables, the planks on sawhorses, where the lobsters are cut in half, the bags untied, and the food distributed along with butter in cups plus Worcestershire sauce and Tabasco sauce and lemon wedges. The clams are eaten first, then the lobsters, chicken, corn, and onions. All of it downed with quantities of beer or sodas or iced tea. And for dessert, watermelon, poundcake, and lemon meringue pie.

When the producers from CBS approached me to propose a classic but traditional feast with which to herald the Fourth of July, I naturally volunteered clambakes. They had contacted me in mid-May and thus there were two months before the actual showing.

With no want of alacrity, I informed them that we would demonstrate not only the preparation of the clambake from the laying of the fire to the hauling back of the tarpaulin, but the vital first steps as well. This, I added, would include the gathering of clams and the harvesting of the lobsters from our own lobster pots in Gardiners Bay.

They were desirous of shooting the film within one week's time. I did not indicate to them that our lobster pots were not yet in place but that was a small matter.

On the day before they were to arrive, Pierre and I got into his small boat with our lobster traps aboard and ready to be sunk. To ensure our catch before the cameras, we had also had the foresight to go to our local fish market to purchase six lobsters, which we intended to plant in the traps.

How the camera crew would marvel at our good fortune when they discovered that we *did* have such co-operative lobsters in our local waters.

The crew arrived on schedule the next morning and, with us in one boat and the crew in another, we set out into the bay to the other side of Gardiners Island where the traps were floating under the surface, the cork markers bobbing up and down on the water.

We pulled up a lobster pot, heaved it aboard, and opened the small trap door. Sure enough it contained a couple of real, live crustaceans, the camera zooming in and whirring away.

Just great. The crew broke into applause. The problem was that we'd foolishly blown our cover. We had forgotten to remove the rubber bands that the fish market had put around the claws to make them stable.

We admitted our fraud, removed the bands, put the lobsters back in the pots, resank them, and hauled them in again.

The public never knew and the clambake proceeded as scheduled.

§   §   §

One of the greatest pleasures during my stay at *The New York Times* has been the ability to travel around the world, as well as in all of America, to dine on the finest foods offered by any restaurant that I deemed to my liking or even idle curiosity. I was also privileged on these trips to be a guest in private homes and to spend time in the kitchens of local cooks par excellence.

I once traveled to Alaska to investigate the Brower Café in Barrow, where I was introduced to mukluk, made from the skin and the fat of the whale, and reindeer stew. I had been curious to meet Thomas Paneahtak Brower, a half Eskimo whose father, Charles Dewitt Brower, was born in Brooklyn in 1863. His father had come to Alaska in 1884, the first white settler in Point Barrow, to establish a whaling and fur trading company. He married an Eskimo girl, became wealthy and widely known as the "King of the Arctic," and wrote one book, *Fifty Years Below the Arctic,* which enjoyed considerable fame over a several-year period.

Much later I sampled a dish in Paris called *cha gio,* a delicate Vietnamese version of egg roll. My enthusiasm for the dish was boundless and I persuaded *The New York Times* to let me travel to Vietnam to write about native cooking. I arrived in that country seven months before the end of the heartbreaking hostilities.

It was curious to be writing about food when a war was going on, but I was reminded of Graham Greene's *The Quiet American* of twenty years before, when he had written of life in Saigon: "Ordinary life goes on—that has saved many a man's reason." There were certainly terse indexes everywhere of a nation at war. Up and down the streets of Saigon were soldiers with their guns and walkie-talkies and jeeps and many of the cross sections had rolls of barbed wire on the side and at the ready, but after a day or so both the soldiers and the barbed wire became another random part of the landscape. I certainly did not find Saigon a somber place and, to my great surprise, I found a deep-rooted respect for good food conscientiously prepared. It might be a traditional and well-seasoned pork soup or perhaps prawns in tomato and chili sauce sold at small open-air street markets or more elaborate dishes such as an elegant and delectable curried eel soup or deep-fried crab or chopped shrimp grilled on sugar cane skewers. During one memorable meal consisting of *oc nhoi thit,* delicately seasoned snails stuffed in the shell lined with fresh ginger leaves, and *cha ca,* filleted fish with dill eaten with noodle pancakes, artillery fire sounded somewhere north of the restaurant, which was harbored in the middle of a lotus pond. Everyone turned to look and without comment returned to the meal at hand.

It was in the home of an ingenious Saigonese, Mrs. Doan the Hon, that I learned the fine points of making *cha gio,* that savory fragment I had first tasted in a few of the flourishing Vietnamese restaurants of Paris. *Cha gio* consists basically of morsels of ground meat, sometimes with chopped crab, shrimp, or chicken, wrapped in pastry and deep-fried. These morsels, cooked to a golden brown, crisp without, tender within, are served hot at table with an assortment of fresh herbs, including mint, basil, and coriander, cold Boston lettuce leaves, and that ubiquitous Vietnamese spicy fish sauce, *nuoc nam. Cha gio* are as irresistible as peanuts, popcorn, new radishes, fresh cider, and caviar. And *cha gio* are but one small savory fragment from the Vietnamese kitchen, which surely must rank among the most outstanding on earth.

§   §   §

I have made several trips to Japan, reveling in sushi, sashimi, yakitori, and tempura long before Japanese restaurants became commonplace in the United States, and dining at the Akahane in Tokyo, where gastronomic luxury was heaped on gastronomic luxury but in the most delicate manner possible. There were fiddlehead ferns served in sesame seed sauce and a tender beanlike vegetable known as *aiko* prepared in a bean curd sauce. Wild vegetables that grow in water, dozens of green leaves, each with its own delicate flavor, and small mushrooms with long stems that resemble hat pins. The predominant specialty of the restaurant, however, is game—cormorants and wild duck when I was there.

One memorable meal in Tokyo was enjoyed in the company of one of Japan's most famous surgeons, Tokuji Ichikawa. He took me to a restaurant to eat *fugu,* or globefish, a much-coveted specialty from Japanese waters and available only from the time of the autumn equinox to the spring equinox. Globefish, the doctor explained on the way, is sometimes toxic, a thought that did not do a great deal to stimulate the appetite. But, he added, they wash it well in cold water and this sluices away all the poisonous substances. That was indeed comforting and, after all, a little game of Japanese roulette never hurt anybody. We quickly downed a diminutive bottle of sake before the first course, a tiny individual tray with three items—salmon caviar on a lemon slice, a small, whole, uncleaned fish salted, grilled, and designed to be eaten in one piece, and something in a fishy-tasting pastelike sauce. The "something" was cold and cooked and a little firm—like rubber bands that had been cut into bite-size lengths. We asked the doctor what it was, though by now we should have known better.

"Fish bowels," he said without a smile.

At about this point the kimono-clad waitress brought in another part of the *fugu* ritual, piping hot sake in beautiful porcelain glasses. And inside each glass was a burnt *fugu* fin. And I must add that the rest of that meal was delicious. The delicacies that followed began with sashimi—beautiful, almost transparent slices of raw *fugu* served with soy sauce, grated radish with hot pepper and chives; shimmering, tender lengths of globefish cartilage and skin; batter-fried *fugu.* After that a large ceramic cauldron of boiling stock was placed on the table and into it went even larger pieces of globefish, bean curd, mushrooms fluted in a most elegant manner, sections of Japanese leeks, and, finally, fresh, tender chrysanthemum leaves. Then came rice with egg and chopped scallions, pickles, and persimmons for dessert. If you should be in Japan between the autumn and spring equinox, you shouldn't miss *fugu.* It is a rare treat and delicious, and the meat tastes like American blowfish, sometimes called chicken of the sea.

§   §   §

In Taipei in 1968 I dined on some of the best and most diverse Chinese food I had ever experienced. One dinner for eight included Taiwan ham baked in clay, sliced in a honey-sweet sauce, and served in rectangles of bread, sandwich-style, as an appetizer. This was followed by an extraordinary, mousselike dish of ground chicken livers and chopped fresh water chestnuts baked in bamboo and served in silver ramekins. Taipei has some of the best shrimp in the world and they are used lavishly everywhere. On this occasion they were sautéed with white mushrooms, ginger, and scallions, a fairly common combination, but they were served on a bed of pea pod leaves and somehow on that evening the flavor seemed more subtle and elusive than usual. Then came spicy ancestor's chicken, the best carp in creation in a sweet and sour sauce made with vinegar, sugar, ginger, garlic, and scallions, an excellent dish of shredded pork lightly tinged with garlic, and a fantastic production called sliced fish in chicken soup.

Another banquet in Taipei, offered me by the directors of the National Museum, began with four extraordinary eel dishes. One consisted of thin steamed slivers of eel in a rich oil sauce seasoned with garlic, shredded ginger, and fresh coriander; a second of crisply fried shredded eel with chopped fresh ginger; third, braised sections of eel with bamboo shoots and pork fat; and, lastly, sautéed eel with transparent noodles seasoned to a subtle but obvious point with freshly ground pepper.

§　§　§

I dined in one of the most intriguing restaurants in the world in Old Delhi—the Moti Mahal—which specialized in tandoori chicken. The tandoors, or ovens, in this open-air dining spot resembled very large, sunken Grecian urns made of clay. They are fired at the bottom with charcoal or wood to white heat when they are ready to receive the various foods to be cooked. Tandoori chicken is made by brushing a paste of spices and red vegetable dye all over a skinned chicken that is impaled on skewers and lowered into the burning hot tandoor. The chicken roasts in fifteen minutes or thereabouts and it comes out with an utterly delicious, slightly smoked flavor. The chicken, to be eaten with fingers, is served with slices of lime.

After this trip, I had a tandoor shipped to my home in East Hampton so we could re-create this national dish of India.

§　§　§

One memorable Easter season in Athens, I found myself a most willing participant in a celebration of the holiday with my friends Leon

Lianides, the proprietor of New York's much-esteemed Coach House restaurant, and his wife, Aphrodite. It was Holy Saturday and a night of brilliant stars and moonlight, and as midnight approached we strolled through otherwise darkened streets to a tiny church. Hundreds of other "pilgrims" had preceded us to the small plaza in front of the church, to await the tolling of the bells that would signify the arrival of Easter morning. In the darkness someone handed us candles and as bells were tolled the priest emerged bearing a candle with which he kindled the candle of the closest member of those assembled.

"Christos anesti," he declared. "Christ is risen." The second candle illuminated a third, the third a fourth, individual to individual, until moments later that entire square was awash with light.

The second event of that evening remains equally vivid in memory. The Lianideses and I joined a Greek artist, Jannis Spyropolous, and his wife for a traditional Greek Easter feast. It consisted merely of soup and bread, but it was an incredibly delicious meal, including one dish of which I had had no prior knowledge. I had, of course, dined on avgolemono soup, that typical Hellenic specialty made of an abundantly rich broth thickened and flavored with lemon and eggs. But on this occasion I was told that the soup was named *mayeritsa* avgolemono and that at that moment in thousands and thousands of households throughout Greece, celebrants would be dining on this particular soup made with the head of lamb and assorted other parts of the animal including the neck, knuckles, and liver, all bones removed and the meat chopped fine. The Easter bread was made with a lightly sweetened egg and yeast dough of surpassing flavor and texture. Red-dyed Easter eggs were offered the guests and these, too, are traditional, representing both the rebirth of the season and the resurrection of Christ. And those three elements were the sum and substance of that meal. Earlier, when asked why the *mayeritsa* soup was so traditional in Greek homes at the beginning of Easter, Leon explained that roast baby lamb is the almost inevitable main dish for the principal feast of Easter day.

"In Greece," he said, "nothing is wasted. Tomorrow," he said, "we will dine here again and they will use the tripe of the lamb in another soup, avgolemono-style."

§   §   §

I have dined on spider crab in Madrid, the best *rijsttafel* I have ever eaten in Bali, roast suckling pig in Segovia and Puerto Rico, wild boar in Nova Scotia, and I once spent five days in Rio de Janeiro going from restaurant to restaurant searching in vain for a menu that listed *feijoada*, the national dish of Brazil. I learned that it is traditionally served only on Saturday at noon and my time schedule had not permitted my remaining over the weekend. A short while after this trip, in New York, I had my first full experience with that marvelous and inspired blend of black beans, salted meats, beef, and assorted parts of the pig, and those wonderful Portuguese sausages, *linguiça* and *paio*. It was at the home of Dona Dora Vasconcellos, Brazilian consul-general in New York, and a splendid hostess. Since that experience, I have indulged an incurable appetite for *feijoada* on numerous occasions in the home of a friend and native of Rio, Dorotea Elman, who makes what may well be the finest *feijoada* to be found in the United States. Dorotea also came to my home one summer day and re-created, with all the dexterity and authority of a cowboy, that Brazilian feast known as *churrasco à gaucha,* which I had first sampled in Rio.

The feast is actually a barbecue, gaucho-style, and includes beef ribs, chicken, pork, lamb, and sausages grilled over hot ashes. We began with morsels of spicy Brazilian sausages (purchased in Manhattan) wrapped in foil and buried in hot coals. These were taken with a seemingly innocent, superficially innocuous and irresistible but potent Brazilian drink known as caipirinha made with the clear distillate of sugar cane, lime and sugar over ice. The meats, cooked over searing coals which burned in an open, newly dug, slit-trench, were served amber and sizzling hot from the fire with a seductively seasoned salad of mixed vegetables in a tangy mayonnaise. That plus a platter of buttery farofa, a splendid dry cereal dish cooked with banana. To bind the meal together, to give it an exceptional and uncommon fillip, a spicy onion sauce make of oil and vinegar, chopped parsley, and coriander was served on the side.

That meal was consumed one September 7, which just happened to be the National Day of Brazil.

§ § §

And, of course, I have made many business trips to Europe, particularly to France. The first was in 1959 in the company of Frank Schoonmaker, in that era the most celebrated and by far the most knowledgeable wine expert in America. I was much in awe of the gentleman inasmuch as he was well established in his field long before I joined *The New York Times.* Frank disarmed me early in our travels, however, by repeating the history of his initial interest in wines. Early in his career he had written a guidebook called *Through Europe on $2 a Day,* and intended to become a serious travel writer. In his early days in France he lived with the family of a wine merchant.

"During our first meal," he said, "the father of the house put two glasses at my place and poured a different wine into each.

" 'Which do you prefer?' he asked.

" 'The one on the left,' I proposed.

"He snatched the glasses from my place and admonished me, 'No more wine for you, young man.' He kept up that nonsense for a week and during that time I did learn to tell the difference."

That trip with Frank brings back the memory of an embarrassing incident that began with a telephone call one morning in late October 1959. There was a stranger on the other end who professed to have "the most revolutionary invention where wine is concerned of the twentieth century . . . an automatic corkscrew."

I was intrigued and asked him to stop by *The Times*.

When he arrived he asked if I had an unopened bottle of wine. I led him back to *The Times* test kitchen and pulled a bottle of wine out of a cabinet. He pulled out an aluminum cigar-shaped gadget with rounded ends. He unscrewed it at mid-point and withdrew one half with a needle-like object protruding from it like a hypodermic needle.

He ran a knife around the foil near the mouth of the bottle and pulled off the top of the foil enclosure. He inserted the needle in the bottle, gave it a twist, and quicker than you can say Trockenbeerenauslese, the cork flipped up and out.

I was enchanted.

He replaced the cork in the bottle and handed me the gadget. I plunged it in and out came the cork. I called other reporters and editors into the kitchen to show them this marvel, this *merveille d'ingéniosité*. As they gathered around, I kept pushing the cork in and pumping it out.

The visitor had already explained to me how the gadget worked. There was a CO_2 cartridge attached to the needle. This is the same cartridge that introduces carbon dioxide into seltzer bottles to make carbonated water. When the needle goes through the cork, the cartridge releases a tiny fraction of CO_2, just enough to expel the cork.

I told my visitor that I was about to embark on a tour of Burgundy and Bordeaux with Frank Schoonmaker and that I would be inordinately pleased if I might take along his miracle worker.

He said no, that this was only a prototype and the only one in America. He could not part with it. However, he said, if I would go to the factory outside London, they would be able to let me take one on a temporary basis.

That I agreed to do within a week or so and emplaned for London before traveling on to France to meet Frank in Burgundy. I went to the factory, picked up the cork extractor, and shortly thereafter joined Frank at the Hotel Splendid in Bordeaux. I did not mention my secret.

That evening we went to the Dubern restaurant where we dined on, among other things, shrimp *bordelaise* and woodcock with *foie gras.*

I asked Frank not to allow the sommelier to open the wine when it arrived. I wanted to do that myself.

When the waiter arrived with a bottle of white Haut-Brion, I asked him to cut away the round of foil from the top. I then took the bottle and inserted the needle. The cork was extracted in a trice, as they say. Both Frank and the waiter were wide-eyed. So the cork was pushed back in over and over again as Frank and the waiter took turns in using the needle. Within minutes, the entire staff of the restaurant, including the owner, came over to examine the needle-pointed wonder.

Within an hour, Frank had "annexed" the gadget. At vineyard after vineyard he would amaze and delight the owners and workers with the new extractor. First through Bordeaux and then through Burgundy. Several of them expressed an interest in investing in the English concern that manufactured the cork extractor.

The day came when I had to go back to England to return the gadget. In London I was alone on my last evening and decided to make the best of it by dining at the fashionable Mirabelle restaurant.

I well recall the fare. The meal began with Scotch salmon and fat oysters from the English coast. I dined on turtle soup and, as a main dish, roast grouse, which was superb.

I had finished my meal when I glanced at the entrance. Alexis Lichine was walking to a center table in the dining room with a magnificent-looking blonde on his arm, a few yards of ermine trailing behind her.

Alexis spotted me and asked me to join them. I still had the fantastic cork extractor in my pocket. I would return it the next morning before taking my plane.

I told Alexis that I had finished my meal but that I would join them with a glass of Cognac. By this time I was plotting. I could scarcely wait to see the look of *étonnement* in Lichine's eyes when I did my magic with the needle.

When he ordered wine I asked him, as I had Frank, not to allow the sommelier to open the bottle. I would do that myself.

The sommelier arrived, the top of the foil was carved away and I took the bottle.

I plunged in the needle and, *voilà!* The damn thing exploded, sending wild splashes of red wine upward to the ceiling and drenching the lady's ermine coat.

Do you know, to this day I can't recall the remainder of that evening? I have total amnesia. I don't recall apologies. I don't recall wiping off the coat, which must have been spoiled. Total oblivion. Someday I must summon the courage to ask Alexis.

Funny, I haven't thought of that cork extractor in years. It did enjoy a large popularity in America and then disappeared from the market. Perhaps too many ermines and ceilings had to be repaired, too many suits for damages.

One further thing. I recently glanced through my files and looked up that column on the Mirabelle, the one that outlined the food on which I dined. It appeared on November 4, 1959. I found this paragraph amusing:

"The Mirabelle is expensive but it is estimated that one can dine splendidly with four courses and a bottle of wine for about $15."

§ § §

I have come to know in depth the perils and pleasures of my unruly enthusiasms, but where dining in Europe is concerned they are totally justified. I have always considered Taillevent to be the greatest restaurant in Paris. On all three levels that restaurants are judged—the kitchen, the service, and the physical appeal of the dining room—Taillevent soars.

Comme Chez Soi in Brussels is another culinary treasure that I return to frequently. One particularly cherished meal there was on the occasion of the restaurant's fiftieth anniversary in 1976, and a more distinguished roster of gastronomic geniuses will rarely be assembled. There was Jean-Claude Vrinat, proprietor of Taillevent, and Jean-Pierre Haeberlin of the treasured Auberge de l'Ill in Alsace, Pierre Troisgros of the restaurant that bears his family name in Roanne, and Paul Bocuse, whose name is synonymous with the restaurant in Lyon. Royalty arrived at eight-eleven—eleven minutes late—in the person of Prince Albert, brother of the King. The champagne flowed for all assembled. The celebration dinner, which began promptly at eight-thirty was a model of simplicity, and all the more laudable because of it.

The first course was a total novelty to most of those at the gathering. It consisted of a consommé of locally harvested baby shrimp, each shrimp not much larger than a man's thumbnail. Each serving of consommé, a long-simmered clear, rich broth made with the shells of the shrimp, contained, in addition to a score or more of the tiny shrimp, shreds of citronelle, an uncommon herb with a pungent, lemony aroma. The soup was followed by a terrine of vegetables—green beans, peas, carrots, and artichoke bottoms—held together with a delicate aspic with chopped parsley and tarragon, sliced and served with a gossamer sauce of watercress. With a slice of fresh *foie gras* on the side.

The sole dish was a marvel of sorts, the fresh fillets bathed in a frothy, savory sabayon sauce that smacked lightly of lemon and pepper, with a garnish of small fresh asparagus tips and poached oysters. The principal course of the evening was baby partridge wrapped in vine leaves and oven-cooked in open casseroles. They were served with a fine accompaniment, rounds of duchesse potatoes containing fresh sweet corn kernels, a splendid idea for roast wild birds. The last courses of the meal were a Brie blended until smooth with Roquefort, and a marvelously perfumed dessert of woodland strawberries, blackberries, and morsels of peach served with ice cream. Plus coffee, of course, and fine Cognacs. Most of the wines for the meal were of the same vintage as the restaurant, which is to say they were laid down in 1926.

§ § §

There honestly is nothing in all the world to compare with fresh *foie gras,* and it should be sampled at least once in a lifetime. It is a paragon among foods with the finest texture and flavor. And the Auberge de l'Ill in the small Alsatian town of Illhaeusern is a prime source. One ultimate fantasy that I dined on there is called *"la fameuse truffe sous la cendre."* It is wild and wonderful, a whole fresh truffle packed with fresh *foie gras* into a ball of thin pastry and deep-fried. And if that were not enough of an embarrassment of riches, it was served with a thin, beautifully perfumed sauce of fresh truffles.

§ § §

I had the rare good fortune in 1974 of sitting next to Mado Point, the elegantly styled widow of Fernand Point, at a dinner in her honor. M. Point was, of course, patron-chef of the celebrated Pyramide restaurant in Vienne and one of the undisputed geniuses of French cookery. After his death in 1954, Mme. Point ruled the restaurant with an unswerving allegiance to her husband's memory and her dedication was acknowledged at this spectacular fete given by Paul Bocuse at his restaurant in Lyons. Mme. Point was wearing a simple, floor-length silk dress set off with a diamond-studded silk brooch. On one arm she wore a modest, single-chain diamond and silver bracelet and on the other a diamond and silver watch, all gifts from her late husband.

"M. Point," she told me, "spent his life giving me jewelry and I kept protesting, don't buy, don't buy, Fernand, we don't have the money, but he insisted. He was a very shy man and was never comfortable with people who didn't care about, or didn't understand food. He'd talk about casseroles, then talk about wines. Then talk about casseroles,

At my fiftieth birthday, a surprise party aboard the S.S. France. *Standing beside me are the various cooks and the master chef, Henri Lehuédé, second from my right.*

then talk about wines. In his own home he was pasha, monarch, and king. Away from home he was speechless."

Paul Bocuse, almost without question the most famous chef in the world today, was but one of fifteen chefs at the dinner who had worked under M. Point. But of them all, it was Bocuse who seemed to occupy a special niche in Mme. Point's affection. Of him, she said, his is the *fils spirituel* of Fernand and they are very much alike in their talents and invention.

§ § §

And then there was a succession of meals in what I termed in 1969 "the finest French restaurant in the world." This was, of course, the first-class dining room of the late S.S. *France,* on which I traveled from Le Havre to New York. (The following year I celebrated my fiftieth birthday at a party on that marvelous ship.) In that leisurely voyage, not one of the ship's headily composed menus was repeated, and each menu for lunch and dinner was a veritable cornucopia of things to amuse, beguile, and conquer the palate. Hors d'oeuvre? Caviar almost every night. Or, if one wished, fresh *foie gras* baked in a crust. Or, if one coveted more earthly things, cold *langouste* with freshly made mayonnaise, or a handsome ballottine of duckling, or a pâté of veal, or a fancifully marbled terrine of chicken. Among the courses that followed, a cream of *petits pois Lamballe* or a double consommé, then a *médaillon* of brill with *sauce perinette* followed by roast saddle of lamb, stuffed squab with truffle sauce, or perhaps something more prosaic such as steak with maître d'hôtel butter or superb pasta dishes tossed with sauce at the last moment from a movable wagon next to the table. If one still hungered, there was always a splendid cold buffet with turkey and more terrines and Italian hams and Paris hams. And cheeses and desserts of myriad patterns and forms.

Aboard the S.S. France *when Pierre and I gave cooking lessons during a cruise. Sam Aaron, the wine merchant, close friend, and owner of Sherry Lehmann, and Burgess Meredith lectured on wine. 1971.*

An incredible thing about the *France* was that if there was nothing on any given menu to tempt the palate, almost any dish of classic or regional cooking could be commanded a few hours in advance and it would be made with brilliance and no particular ceremony. It was not at all uncommon to see an unlisted rack of hare being carved in the dining room or a venison stew being ladled out or an intricately put together chartreuse of pheasant or a heaping platter of snails being served.

Salvador Dali was on board ship during this trip with his ocelot, Babou. Babou ate boiled fish in the morning, grilled meat at night. He also enjoyed fresh lettuce, raw French beans, and raw whole carrots. He dined at times with his master.

§ § §

In 1976 Pierre and I had been told of what was conceivably the greatest French restaurant on the European continent. So we set out for the tiny Swiss town of Crissier, three miles from Lausanne, to investigate the phenomenon called Fredy Girardet. On the night that we dined on an elaborate succession of dishes at Restaurant Girardet, the meal was bliss. Not a dish to be faulted, a genuine feast for the season, a *repas luxueux*. The proceedings began with a fragile hors d'oeuvre, bite-size pastry tarts filled with small crawfish tails in a delicate Nantua sauce with sorrel, this accompanied by a light, dry, nicely chilled local white wine.

We were richly regaled with Girardet's much-talked-about cassolette of duck livers, the slices of liver quickly sautéed so that they were crisp on the outside, melting within, and with a hot vinegar and shallot sauce. There were glorious slices of *loup de mer* with oysters and a fine julienne of vegetables in a cream sauce; that plus a celestial lobster dish with basil, a *poularde de Bresse* with truffles studded beneath the skin, roasted and served on a bed of finely chopped leeks and truffles in a cream sauce, and an exceptional high-standing soufflé made with a purée of fresh passion fruit.

Afterward, we talked to Fredy Girardet about his rise to fame among the likes of Bocuse, Troisgros, and Guérard. Although he is very much his own man and his inspirations are pure Girardet, his thinking follows closely the precepts of *la nouvelle cuisine*.

"La nouvelle cuisine," Mr. Girardet noted, "is nothing more than good taste. It is to prepare dishes to preserve their natural flavors and with the simplest of sauce."

La nouvelle cuisine is not, incidentally, what many people mistakenly presume it to be—calorie-free but nonetheless delectable. To the contrary, the vast majority of the Girardet sauces, just as in the kitchens of Bocuse, Vergé, et al., are based primarily on cream.

"I don't love cream like those Lyonnaise chefs," Mr. Girardet observed, but added that he does use 100 quarts each week as well as 160 pounds of butter.

When we returned home, Pierre re-created the dishes we had dined on for the readers of *The Times,* substituting striped bass for the *loup de mer,* which is not found in American waters. And on subsequent trips to Crissier we have found Mr. Girardet to be one of the great creative forces in the world of chefs today.

§ § §

Incidentally, I did go to several spas during my travels, most notably to Montecatini in Italy and Eugénie-les-Bains in France. But with all due respect to Michel Guérard's considerable talents as a chef, his *cuisine minceur* left me cold. It was not until I went to the Golden Door in California in 1981 that I learned to love abstinence—at least for one week.

§ § §

It has been my great good fortune that many of the finest chefs of Europe and America were generous enough to drive out to my home on Long Island and spend a day or an evening confecting the dishes for which their restaurants are noted. In fact, these are some of the most agreeable reminiscences of my life.

On a typical visit, Pierre acts as sous-chef, helping in the preparation and questioning the visitor as to techniques and ingredients. I stand at my typewriter in the kitchen, watching the chef and talking to him, taking down each step in his preparation of a dish (he frequently has three or four going at once). On a later day, Pierre and I make the dishes again to assure ourselves that the recipes are clear. Incidentally, it took time in the beginning to persuade Pierre that it was vital to measure ingredients accurately if readers were going to be able to follow recipes easily and with assurance. Now he does this reflexively.

There was a joyous two-day visit in 1978 with Jean Troisgros, who, with his brother Pierre, created the cuisine that gave their restaurant in Roanne a three-star rating in the *Guide Michelin* and international esteem. Jean reveled in our local produce—tomatoes, fresh corn on the cob, clams, fish, mussels—and gorged himself on a two-and-one-half-pound lobster at a nearby restaurant. His only reservations about the American kitchen were our cream (not enough body) and our flour (too much milling). He cooked an unforgettable meal for Pierre and

Sharing a pleasantry with James Beard, the cookbook author and friend of many years, at a luncheon in Manhattan, 1978.

me and our guests that started off with a salad, a concept that I had always thought was very unsophisticated. But this was no mundane tossing together of *quelques feuilles vertes.* It was an inspired orchestration of greens and herbs and quickly sautéed thin medallions of chicken, the whole anointed with a celestial sauce, the soul of which was oil of walnut.

With the salad came a splendid, dry, full-bodied white Burgundy. It was followed by mixed steamed fish fillets with a *beurre nantais,* accompanied by a young, red, slightly chilled Beaujolais. That's right. Red with fish. As Jean Troisgros asks, why not? Later there were scallops of veal, lightly coated with Dijon mustard and whole mustard seeds, sautéed quickly, and served with a fresh tomato sauce. That, plus a fine wheel of Brie with crusty French bread and fresh local strawberries with a dry white champagne.

A Feast Made for Laughter

§ § §

And there was the day Chef Tsung Ting Wang came out from New York, where he is the major force behind three of the city's best-known restaurants—the Shun Lee Palace, the Shun Lee Dynasty, and the Hunam Restaurant. He enlightened us on the operation of a Chinese restaurant kitchen, in addition to preparing a twelve-course banquet that included a sauté of duck feet and a soup served with one duck tongue embedded and steamed in one spoonful of fish mousse for each guest. Chef Wang, which he prefers, although his family name is Tsung, was an apprentice in a Shanghai kitchen at the age of eleven. His principal duties were to keep the kitchen clean, make the chef's bed, and draw warm water for his bath. He also made the rice and warmed the wine. In the traditional Chinese kitchen, he told us, there are five principal stations—one for cooking, one for steaming, one for cutting, another for making pastry, and, finally, one for making cold platters. Back in the old days, he said, there were some chefs who did nothing but act as cutting chef for an entire lifetime. A cutting chef is one of the most important people in the kitchen because the size of a dice, slice, or strip of meat before it is cooked is one of the essential refinements of the finest Chinese cookery. A good cutter knows within a fraction of an ounce, or the Chinese equivalent, precisely how much meat he will deliver with one slice of his cleaver.

§ § §

Another skilled and inventive Chinese chef is Wen Dah Tai, better known as Uncle Tai, then of the Hunan Yuan in New York. In addition to dining on several of his restaurant's most prestigious dishes, we learned on his visit to my home how he judges a Chinese restaurant. If a meat dish is prepared with 70 per cent meat and 30 per cent vegetables, he said, the restaurant is propably first class, all else being equal. If the ratio is fifty-fifty, the place is probably mediocre. If the meat to vegetable ratio is reversed, stay away.

Uncle Tai attributes the association of hot, spicy food and Hunan to the province's climate, which is very damp. And I know it to be empirically true that spicy food pleases the body and appetite in other hot humid climates of the world.

§ § §

If you must be trapped in a blizzard, there are far less comfortable ways to do it than in your own home, the snow slashing against the panes and a roaring fire in the fireplace. And to have as company one of New York's finest chefs, who had committed himself to cook a half a dozen of his specialties. For a dedicated chef, a promise is a commitment, even if the power fails, the furnace is kaput, and the cooking must be done by the light of candles and a kerosene lamp. It happened during the Great Blizzard of 1978, when Josef Renggli, chef of The Four Seasons restaurant, showed up one February morning after a five-hour drive on the Long Island Expressway, a trip that usually takes about two hours. Brushing snow and ice from his hair, he entered my kitchen with crate after crate of choice victuals that included veal and beef, salmon, striped bass, oysters, red snapper, and a mass of fresh herbs and vegetables from the restaurant's larder.

Seppi, as he prefers to be called, doffed his heavy outer coat and donned an apron. For the next eight hours, he chopped herbs and vegetables with the staccato precision of a sewing machine; he confectioned a dazzling assortment of dishes including leek leaves stuffed with trout mousse, striped bass in phyllo pastry, a consummately good court bouillon of salmon and oysters, and an uncommonly sophisticated version of steak *au poivre*. By 7 P.M., four guests invited to share the meal had telephoned to say that their cars were stalled in their driveways. Mine was impassable. At eight o'clock, Seppi and I sat down to that several-course collation. With the court bouillon of salmon and oysters and the paupiettes of trout mousse, we toasted our friends in absentia with a chilled bottle of marquis de Goulaine muscadet, 1976. With the steak *au poivre* and its accompaniments, sautéed green and red peppers and sautéed mushrooms with herbs, a bottle of Nuits St. Georges, 1949. As the fire dwindled we ended the meal with pears stewed and stuffed with gorgonzola cheese and served with a sauce containing fresh ginger slices and chopped pistachios spooned over.

If you have to sit out a storm, you might as well do it at the elbow of a great chef.

§ § §

When Alain Chapel, generally acknowledged to be one of the ten or twelve finest chefs of France, was invited to my home, he telephoned early one morning, his voice alive with excitement, to state he had found a fantastic source for calves' ears and thus would be pleased to prepare one of the dishes most in demand at his restaurant, La Mère Charles, twenty kilometers from Lyons. It was good news, for I knew the dish by reputation to be one of his finest and most talked-about creations. Well, he didn't bring his calves' ears—they sent him three cows' heads instead. But he did prepare many other fine dishes, including what surely must be his ultimate triumph, one of the absolute cooking glories of this generation. It is his *gâteau de foies blonds,* a

---

blissfully silken, creamy, mousselike creation made with puréed chicken livers and beef marrow. It is indecently rich and is served with a sinfully seductive sauce of lobster and cream. Come to think of it, we didn't even miss the calves' ears.

§ § §

I have a very fond memory of watching a spectacularly colorful young Italian chef standing on a step stool in my kitchen preparing a fantasy of spun sugar to be served on a dessert called *zuccotto alla Michelangelo.* Spun sugar looks like angel hair and it is made by tossing a hot sugar syrup into the air. By the time Mariano Vizzotto, pastry chef of La Pace Hotel and restaurant in Montecatini, had finished bandying about his forked whisk, my kitchen did indeed resemble the remains of a dismantled Christmas tree.

§ § §

When Paul Bocuse made his presence known in my kitchen, he had in his satchel a kilogram of Stygian-black truffles, valued at slightly in excess of two hundred dollars. He combined these with cubes of truffled *foie gras,* a hastily made but rich and full-bodied chicken consommé, and a topping of butter-layered puff pastry, to make a soup that he had created for the occasion of his being awarded the Legion of Honor by France's president, Valéry Giscard d'Estaing. Before M. Bocuse arrived, we had spent the morning shopping for the finest and freshest vegetables available at our local market, plus fresh chickens and lobster, which would be turned into a navarin—a sort of stew based on the traditional and more common navarin of lamb.

The chef was obviously impressed with the fare, which was in all respects of first quality. "Impeccable," he stated, a word that he uses with enthusiasm and cunning abandon as he works. He sipped the lobster sauce from a wooden spoon. "Impeccable!" (pronounced *am-pay-KAH-bluh!*) he exclaimed. The sauce for the chicken pleased him. "Impeccable." But when he broke into the puff pastry that glorified the truffle soup, I beat him to the draw. "Impeccable," I said.

§ § §

Some of my pleasantest moments have been spent in the company of amateur chefs—both in my home and theirs—and many have become close friends. I count among them Diana Kennedy, with whom I share a love of Mexican cooking. Diana is ebullient and extremely knowledgeable and set, before she left and moved to Mexico as her

The air-cooled wine cave with its hand-assembled floor-to-ceiling racks serves a double purpose at times—in this case, storing a country ham.

permanent home, what must have been the best Mexican table in all of Manhattan.

The word amateur should not have a pejorative connotation. It stems from *amare,* meaning, of course, to love. It is a fine and flattering thing to be called an amateur in French, to indicate that you have a special enthusiasm toward one pursuit or another. It is inevitable that in any profession one is notably influenced by amateurs. One of my most prized acquaintances is Ed Giobbi, who is a true amateur of the kitchen in the finest sense of the word. It is not an exaggeration to say that he is a creative genius, particularly in the cuisine of his family and ancestry. Ed is a successful artist, but he also "puts up" his own tuna, raises his own pigeons, makes his own pasta, and grows a wonderful array of good things in his garden.

Another expert on Italian cuisine who has frequently visited my kitchen is Marcella Hazan. It was she who instructed me in how different pastas should be sauced. Generally speaking, she says, sauces that contain pieces of things—like chopped meat, peas, ham, and so on—go well with a pasta that has a hole, or a shape that catches pieces, like spirals and shells. Very thin sauces are destined for pasta like spaghetti or vermicelli. But there is one exception. If the sauce has a base of olive oil and contains clams, scallops, chopped fish, or seafood, pasta strands such as spaghetti would be quite suitable. Homemade pastas go best with sauces that must be absorbed, which is to say sauces that cling. Like the cream and cheese sauce tossed with fettucine and known as Alfredo. You would never, according to Marcella, serve packaged spaghetti with that sauce. She also is firm in her belief that homemade pasta rolled by hand is superior to that prepared by machine.

§ § §

For years I had heard of Danny Kaye's prowess as a chef, particularly in the province of Chinese cooking, but I tended to regard it with at least a touch of skepticism. One more touch of Hollywood, I mused. But when I visited his Beverly Hills home in 1975 my scoffing quickly turned to awe as he proceeded to bone a chicken or two with surgical skill and, at the moment of cooking, wield his cleaver, wok scoops and spoons with maestrolike dexterity. Danny learned to cook in one of the best-known restaurants in San Francisco's Chinatown, and he has what is undoubtedly the finest Chinese kitchen of any private home in America and as far as we know the world. When he entertains—and he regaled me and other guests with a banquet that would have pleased the palate of the Dowager Empress—he never sits at table until after the end of the meal. He presides over the woks, preparing one course at a time, each of which is served in succession on a lazy susan permanently placed in the middle of a large round table.

§   §   §

My life from its very outset has seemed to me one enormous mass of ironies and not the least of these has had to do with my interest in Chinese cooking.

This interest was germinated, I suspect, during my childhood when my aunt Elizabeth returned to America after twenty years as a missionary in China. Shortly thereafter, when I was seven or eight years old, my family took me to Birmingham to visit another aunt or relative. In that time and place anyone's idea of excitement or genuine adventure was a trip to a big town like Birmingham or Memphis. I remember— to tell the truth, it is the only thing I do remember about that trip— being taken to a Chinese restaurant. There were hanging Chinese lanterns and foreign waiters and real Chinese china and chopsticks and very hot and exotic tea. I cannot recall the menu in precise detail, but I did eat won ton soup and a dish that contained bean sprouts. I marveled over those bean sprouts. What an odd, enticing-looking vegetable! To this day I have not got over an inordinate fondness for won ton soup, and I have retained an all but insatiable appetite for any dish—even a mediocre dish—made with bean sprouts. It is reasonable to suppose that the food I ate then was quite spurious, adapted to the southern palate, and dreadful. But it kindled a flame.

Yet while I am hopelessly infatuated with all forms of cookery, I never intended in a serious sense to "cook Chinese." My reasoning went something like this: I had trained in depth in French cookery in a Swiss hotel school, and it appealed to me from the beginning as a form of cookery that could be, let us say, wholly embraced. It is true that the French kitchen is without end in its variations, and yet the techniques are such that, with enough foundation, there is nothing that can't be mastered—be it brioche dough, puff pastry, or the most elegant mousse, omelet, or soufflé. It seems so logical.

On the other hand, the Chinese kitchen seemed as involved and interwoven as a bucket of boiling noodles. I love fried *jao-tze* (fried filled meat dumplings), for example, but who other than a Chinese could accomplish the technique of a simultaneous steaming-frying process? And who could master those myriad seasonings that blend so marvelously—ginger and garlic, scallions and chives, dark and light soy, and the slightest trace of vinegar and sugar? Having heard so much over the years of the many "schools" of Chinese cooking and the seemingly endless nature of each, I was blindly in awe of Chinese cookery and therefore—with rare exceptions—avoided trying my hand

In the kitchen of my new home in East Hampton, 1980.

at it. It seemed to me simply too vast to undertake. "If I cannot master the sum," I told myself, "I choose to ignore the parts."

Happily, I came around to "cooking Chinese" in a most felicitous and roundabout way.

There is probably no author on earth who has not, in the odious midst of finishing a book, sworn that he would never write another. That was my attitude while dotting i's and crossing t's for the final chapter of an international cookbook. "Never again," I vowed. Vehemently. And I meant it.

At that time I was also on the brink of leaving *The New York Times* after thirteen mostly happy, always hectic years as that newspaper's food news editor and restaurant critic. I had just returned from a long and somehow frustrating tour of the world. I was tired. I needed rest and a respite from cooking.

And then I met Virginia Lee.

Several letters had arrived on my desk extolling in a most laudatory fashion the lady's virtues and talents, and I reacted with the usual skepticism in the face of such high-flown praise. But why not pursue an interview? There was, after all, another column to fill.

I met Virginia in the autumn of 1970. When I arrived for that interview with the usual pad, pencil, and photographer, I was met by a strikingly handsome, smiling, and dignified Chinese woman who looked much too grand and refined ever to have handled a cleaver. I wondered if a lady with that style and elegance had ever washed a wok. Who, I wondered, really did the cooking behind those closed kitchen doors?

In any event it was just another assignment and, if she wasn't doing the cooking, I could enjoy the company and never write about the meal. And then we sat at a table and a procession of foods of a most exceptional nature began—an incredibly good feather-light scallop dish on a bed of crisp fried greens; delicately spiced beef slices coated with rice powder and steamed until marvelously tender on a bed of dried lotus leaves; an elegant steamed flounder; a piping hot and sour soup with its appealing, intriguing contrasts in flavor; the most gossamer of chicken dishes, called chicken velvet; and, as a vegetable, a delectable creation my hostess had labeled cabbage Koo. I learned later the genesis of that most admirable dish.

It seems that when Mrs. Lee first came to this country, she remarked that wherever she went she heard someone speak of or was served beef Wellington. She decided to create a Chinese dish along the same lines and wrapped Chinese cabbage in pastry. She baked it. It was splendid —so good, in fact, that she named it after her long-time friends, Dr. and Mrs. Wellington Koo.

I soon discovered, of course, that there was no hidden genie in Virginia Lee's kitchen turning out those miracles. It was Virginia herself.

On that morning Virginia decided to give cooking classes and allowed me to announce this in *The Times.* I did and listed her phone number. She was besieged with requests, and among them she found my own.

For the next few months, once a week, I took that long subway ride from Times Square to her simple kitchen above her daughter's thriving store in New York's Chinatown. And all my solemn vows about writing another book went by the board. I was hopelessly trapped. I agreed to join with her in writing *The Chinese Cookbook,* and together we worked for months testing recipes in my East Hampton kitchen.

At a book-signing in a department store, to herald the publication of The Chinese Cookbook *in 1972. Virginia Lee is wearing spectacles and standing to my left.*

I would not have traded my upbringing in Chinese cooking with Virginia for—to coin a phrase—all the tea in China. I learned an endless number of things about seasonings and flavors and the countless virtues of the wok. I even learned to use a Chinese cleaver with a certain flair and expertise. But most important, I learned that Chinese cooking is by no means an impossible art. It can be done with ordinary Western cooking utensils, including skillets and kitchen scissors and quite ordinary knives. Although it is equally as sophisticated as the French, I find it to be far less complicated. The greatest French sauces at times take hours to prepare; a simple sauce like hollandaise or béarnaise can curdle at a most crucial moment; many French desserts—*gâteau St. Honoré* comes to mind—require three or four distinct and involved preparations; and so on.

And by contrast, once you have mastered cutting, slicing, and chopping techniques, the vast majority of Chinese dishes are quite basic and simple. The advance preparation is at times tedious and time-consuming, but it is not difficult. Many dishes can be made in advance—the cold appetizers, steamed dishes, and casseroles; other entries, such as soups, can be prepared earlier and finished at the last moment; and even the stir-fry foods can be—indeed, must be—cooked in seconds. Besides that, it is fun—more so, I have found, if you work in pairs, one person doing the stirring, the other handing him or her the ingredients.

I have spent many pleasant hours in the company of Dr. Wellington Koo, the distinguished Chinese statesman and scholar, who has a fine sense of humor about the Chinese table (he is also fond of Western wines, and I have always been amused that he serves a red Bordeaux with special dinners in his home). He told me once that there is a Chinese saying, "There are only two things we don't eat, a nine-headed bird in the sky and a Hupei man on the ground." And indeed, Chinese cooks are nothing if not frugal.

Dr. Koo spoke of an enormous banquet given by Marshal Chang Tso-ling, the famous Manchurian general, when the soup turned out to be inordinately good.

"Do you know what you are eating?" his host asked.

"It is a bit unusual," Dr. Koo replied, "but delicious."

"It is the nose of the sturgeon." One nose had served the entire party of thirty guests.

Food has always been scarce in China, and hunger has been an ever-present threat throughout its history. A Chinese friend of mine avers that this is why the Chinese, under whatever dynasty or regime, have always treated food with such scrupulous respect and care. It is precious.

"Although my family in China," he said, "never suffered from want of food, I grew up to learn not to waste a single grain of rice. I have vivid childhood memories of my father, born as a peasant and worker in the rice fields, asking me at the end of a large meal to turn up my rice bowl to show him that not a grain was left uneaten."

That same acquaintance also associates the delicacy with which Chinese food is served to the peasant's reverence for his daily rice or wheat. "He knows that food is not to be gobbled, but savored; not to be chopped up in chunks, but sliced into delicate pieces; not to be haphazardly served to the tune of rattling metal, but ceremoniously presented." I count that a bit poetic and attribute the use of bite-size morsels to the practical but aesthetic nature of the Chinese in their ancient and honorable use of chopsticks. And I have never been more serious about the aesthetics and philosophy of eating in my life than when I say that to my mind Chinese food tastes better when eaten with chopsticks. Anyone who has tasted Chinese food only with a knife and fork has never really savored or understood it. In this connection I once overheard someone ask a Chinese why his people used chopsticks. "We would prefer," was the reply, "not to butcher at table."

I would not trade my experiences with Virginia Lee for any of my most prized material possessions. And the book that came out of that association in 1972, *The Chinese Cookbook,* was a tribute to the Chinese genius. And a testament to Virginia, one of the great natural cooking experts of this or any age. It was a book, I felt, that had to be written. I was only the midwife.

§ § §

At one point in my career I became an absolute "hero" to the entire Chinese community in New York.

As I have stated before, when I first joined *The Times,* a decent Chinese meal in midtown was almost impossible to find. You had to travel to Chinatown for any meal that might be called memorable and the best of the lot down there was Bo-Bo's on Pell Street. Not one could be spoken of or written about as having style. Szechwan and Hunanese cooking were unheard of in Manhattan.

In late 1965 a restaurant opened on Second Avenue at Forty-eighth Street and it was called the Shun Lee Dynasty. On my first visit it was, to my astonishment and pleasure, a wholly new concept in Chinese dining. It was light-years removed from the standard egg roll and *wor shu opp* makeup of menus. The menu was daring and inspired. I came to know chicken *soong,* or chicken in lettuce packages, marvelous dumplings called *jao-tze, pon pon* chicken, cold spiced eggplant, cold noodles with sesame sauce, and dozens of other delights. I awarded it three stars (that was before I instituted four stars as the top restaurant rating in *The New York Times*). And suddenly I was the darling of the Chinese population. It was only the first of the "great" Chinese restaurants to open in the city, the first of many to be praised while I was restaurant critic. When I retired for two years in 1972, I was honored with an enormous banquet sponsored by the Chinese restaurant owners, cooking teachers, and others. I was awarded a sum of money equal to that of a round-trip ticket to China. That trip I finally took in 1978. It afforded me the opportunity to evaluate at great length the restaurants of Peking and Shanghai and I wrote of those gustatory experiences in an extensive magazine article, but my feelings could be summed up in one sentence: I found little to fault and much to praise.

I parted company with *The New York Times* in the middle of May in

"Four stars from Craig Claiborne, raves from Mimi Sheraton, and a clean bill from the Department of Health."

Cartoon.

1972 to the considerable consternation of the management and the general puzzlement of the readers of the paper's food columns.

To use a cliché, there is rarely a single reason for any of our most critical acts in life and my departure was certainly no exception.

Primary among my reasons was an overriding guilt that I had felt over the years about Pierre's role as a contributor to the food columns and the inconsequential credit that he was given in print. He shared no by-line, he was an unpaid contributor, and his only compensation was an occasional mention in my columns. For years he gave unstintingly of his time, working side by side with me in my kitchen, and a hefty per cent of the recipes that appeared, especially in the Sunday *Magazine,* were produced by his hands.

It was also true that the restaurant column of *The Times* had become for me an intolerable burden on several counts. The public concept of that assignment is that it would be one of the sweetest of pleasures to dine day after day, night after night, in the greatest restaurants of the greatest restaurant city in America. And all of it on an expense account. Not only that, but the added perquisite of traveling around the world feasting on glorious tidbits.

The awful truth is that, to my mind, at least, restaurant criticism under the best of circumstances is by no means all cakes and ale, champagne, truffles, and caviar. I disliked the power. It burdened my conscience to know that the existence or demise of an establishment might depend on the praise or damnation to be found in *The Times.* Although I reasoned, correctly, that the judgment of the food critic did not invariably determine whether a restaurant would prosper or suffer mortal decline.

Let me cite an example or two. When Lutèce opened in 1961 and La Grenouille approximately two years later, I greeted them with an enthusiasm that was, at best, hesitant. Both restaurants subsequently became and are today considered—justifiably—two of the brightest ornaments on the Manhattan restaurant scene. Other restaurants— The Forum of the Twelve Caesars and La Fonda del Sol—to which I tossed verbal bouquets with abandon, died within less than ten years.

But my role as restaurant critic—Cassandra or no—weighed heavily on my soul. Many's the sleepless night I've lain in bed worrying about the stellar worth of one restaurant or another, about whether I was justified in referring to a chef's mornay sauce as pure mucilage, or whether that unaccustomed flavor in the hollandaise was actually basil or rosemary as I had judged it to be.

And, to tell the truth, I was bored with restaurant criticism. At times I didn't give a damn if all the restaurants in Manhattan were shoved into the East River and perished. Had they all served nightingale tongues on toast and heavenly manna and mead, there is just so much that the tongue can savor, so much that the human body (and spirit) can accept, and then it resists. Toward the end of my days as restaurant critic, I found myself increasingly indulging in drink, the better to endure another evening of dining out. I had become a desperate man with a frustrating job to perform.

On a safari in Kenya with a guide.

Part of that frustration had come about through an almost irrational desire to sustain anonymity. It is difficult for someone who has not worked as a critic to comprehend that earnest desire to pass unrecognized in the eyes of those being judged. To observe, as they used to say in college, without being observed as observing.

In the case of a restaurant critic there are many reasons to cultivate anonymity. In my own instance, I maintain a natural, lifelong shyness. I do not enjoy being fawned over and I would most certainly distrust the fawning of a restaurant owner or his staff.

I became, also, inordinately tired at that particular period of my life.

I had recently traveled through Ethiopia, Kenya, an island called Lamu, and other points of the globe. It had been a particularly frustrating trip, perhaps the most frustrating of my years with the newspaper. With the exception of Ethiopia, the food had been dreadful and the writing of copy had been particularly hard going. It has been my cardinal rule in my profession that if you can't engineer enough enthusiasm about one meal or another to make it entertaining, it is best to ignore it. I have never relished damning, for the sheer sake of damning. And, therefore, on this particular hegira I found myself reporting more about the elephants and other four-legged beasts that I had encountered rather than what I had eaten. This had been conspicuously true in an account I had written about a game farm I had visited in Kenya that was owned by the late William Holden, the actor. I talked about the flora and fauna and the cultivated fish in the streams and mentioned only casually what I had eaten in the hotel dining room.

When I came back, I felt depleted, if not to say dejected and slightly morose. I returned to my home in East Hampton, desperately in need of a respite and retreat from my frustrations. On the second day, the phone rang. It was a copy reader from the news desk telling me that I had to rewrite the game farm article to make it "more food-y." It gave me a nasty jolt. For better or for worse, over the years my copy had always been edited with a very light hand. I felt as if I were being punished. But I wrote two more paragraphs, both manufactured to fit the demands, and telephoned them in.

At that point in my life I had published five cookbooks plus a dining guide to Manhattan, all of them profitable. For what must have been the first time in my life I had money in the bank, an ongoing income from my books, and my only major debt was a mortgage on my house. I consulted my accountant, who assured me that I could sustain myself if I resigned from *The Times*. With a conscience that was more than a little burdened, I offered my resignation.

As I have said, my primary concern was the incredibly small credit that Pierre Franey was being given for his contributions to the food columns of *The Times*. Although I had been cursed with a small ego throughout my life, I had been encouraged by disinterested parties to start a newsletter about food. And in this I visualized a partnership with Pierre in which we would be successful publishers, share and share alike. And thus, *The Craig Claiborne Journal* was born. It was, to my mind then and still is to this day, a nifty idea.

The first issue was dated March 15, 1972, and it had style. It consisted, as it did for the two years of its existence, of recipes, restaurant reviews, anecdotes about gastronomy, and "news" of food and gadgets. In those pages we were the first to write about the food processor —the Magimix from France—imported and re-christened, Cuisinart.

We interviewed internationally known chefs and printed jokes that seemed pertinent. Some of them a trifle off-color.

It was a handsomely styled publication. A colleague from *The Times,* Arnold Hoffmann, Jr., who had for years been art director of the Sunday *Times,* resigned and joined us as art director. The newsletter was printed on first-rate paper; the type and art were stylish; and it was expensive. Perhaps too much so. It cost thirty-six dollars a year for twenty-four issues. Within a year we had more than one thousand subscribers and the number increased monthly. Alas, not hurriedly enough.

We engaged a West Coast consultant to prepare in-depth research on circulation matters, promotional ideas, future costs, and so on. The entire project cost in the vicinity of sixty thousand dollars, a sum that seemed and was exhorbitant, given the prospects and the state of our bank account. Within a very short while it became apparent that our

The advertisement that was displayed around New York when I returned to The New York Times *in 1974 following a two-year "retirement."*

reach had exceeded our grasp by a long shot and there was no choice but to fulfill our obligations and to fold.

News of our tattered and torn financial condition at the newsletter had traveled fast and I had a telephone call from *The New York Times* asking me if I would return to the paper. I told them yes, if they would get us out of these grievous circumstances. They agreed to let us have an advance of enough money to pay off our creditors, the advance to be repaid over four years by way of books to be published by *The Times* subsidiary Times Books. It was also agreed that I would not resume restaurant criticism. And, equally important, that I would not have to work out of *The Times* office in Manhattan. I could work out of my own kitchen and off my own typewriter in East Hampton. I was scheduled to return to *The Times* the first week in January, 1974.

On the last Sunday in December Pierre and I decided to say farewell to the newsletter (the final edition had been put to bed, as they say, although it would not reach subscribers until March 1, 1974) and to the staff. At least, we felt, we should say good-by in style—with a champagne lunch of striped bass with *sauce gribiche*. We iced the champagne and said our adieus over a few pre-prandial bloody marys. The more bloody marys we drank the more painful and consequential the demise of that newsletter seemed to be. I think there were a few tears. A couple of hours later we sat down to that fish and the iced champagne. And an hour or so later, I stood on my feet somewhat unsteadily and raised a toast to the passing. The staff left.

What I wanted most but needed least in life at that point was one more drink. But I was depressed and the worst was over. I decided to drive to the neighboring village of Bridgehampton, home of Bobby Van's, unquestionably the best-known and most fashionable bar in the Hamptons. It has catered to a good many writers like William Styron, Wilfred Sheed, John Knowles, Truman Capote, and Willie Morris, who is, of course, a fellow Mississippian. Halfway to Bobby's I KNEW I did not need one more drink, but on I drove and arrived about four in the afternoon. Willie was sitting at the bar. I sat beside him and over a scotch and soda I engaged him in a good bit of Mississippi talk.

"I just received a photograph from Sunflower and you know what? It's a picture of an intersection of two streets in town—Claiborne Street and Craig Avenue. Also the town library called. They're doing an oral history of famous people from Sunflower and they want me to participate."

"Hell," Willie remonstrated, "you and B. B. King are the only two people anybody ever heard of outside Sunflower County."

And so it went, through William Faulkner for the hundred and eleventh time, Willie's memories of his football team, and on and on. A couple of professional Southerners at play.

The real catastrophic decision came about seven o'clock. Willie asked me to join him for dinner and I switched to extra-dry martinis, straight up with a twist. At nine that evening I drove back to East Hampton and at the stop light in the center of town I was stopped by the police for drunken driving. I was handcuffed, fingerprinted, and tossed into a cell like all the other criminals. It was the most demeaning and miserable moment of my adult life. One further humiliation. Along about midnight I asked to use the telephone. I wanted to call *The New York Times*. After all, I would be back on their payroll in less than two weeks.

I called the news desk and got Arthur Gelb, an old friend and an assistant managing editor, at home.

"Arthur," I said, "I'm in jail."

"You're WHAT?"

"In jail. Send help!"

A local lawyer arrived two hours later. And at 8 A.M. I was driven from the jail to court, where the least sympathetic of judges handed down his decree: a six-hundred-dollar fine and deprivation of my driver's license for six months. Plus another scar on my psyche that is likely not to heal. Ever.

§ § §

I have known and interviewed countless chefs over the years but I have never known any chef with such an extraordinary capacity to improvise and rectify when working in the kitchen as Pierre Franey. He is a veritable Merlin when it comes to changing failed sauces into triumphs, in knowing precisely how to make a culinary catastrophe into a thing of genius. It may be as seemingly simple as turning a curdled hollandaise into a masterpiece of silken homogeneity or whisking in a little cold water to revitalize and reconstitute a mayonnaise. I have seen a bar chocolate that would become unmeltable in an average man's saucepan suddenly flow like heavy cream when Pierre adds his whisk.

And once, but only once, have I been witness to his wrath and bewilderment when he discovered himself in a kitchen circumstance for which he had no answer. It started a chain of events that eventually became a *cause célèbre*, celebrated throughout East Hampton as The Case of the Severed Head, a case that was the principal topic of conversation at a few score dinner parties in the Hamptons.

In 1977 he and I were commissioned to write a veal cookbook, a book that would become unique as the only cookbook to deal exclusively with the subject of veal, one of the most elegant of meats. As we plotted it, the book would deal with all aspects of veal cookery from roasts and scallopine through ground veal, veal shanks, and stews.

Pierre Franey performs an act of prestidigitation with a wire whisk as I apply mustard to a dish of veal.

Plus, of course, the use of all the oddments that the calf can yield; including the heart, sweetbreads, brains, kidneys, liver, and tongue. And that classic dish of bourgeois French cookery, *tête de veau* vinaigrette and mock turtle soup, both of which are made with calf heads. I personally would rank *tête de veau,* or calf's head vinaigrette, one of the greatest creations of French chefdom. The whole head, cooked with the brains and tongue intact, offers a combination of textures and flavors that are unequaled when served with a splendid, well-made vinaigrette sauce.

In order to perfect the recipes that would appear in the book, we had access to some of the finest veal in the country, which we could order fresh for immediate shipment from a distributor in New Jersey to be delivered direct to my kitchen in East Hampton.

When the day arrived to prepare the calves' head dishes, an enormous package arrived at my doorstep and inside were four mammoth calf heads, each of which weighed in at something like fifty pounds.

It should be stated with utmost clarity that calf heads were by no means an unknown experience for Pierre. In his day in restaurant

On one occasion during a power failure in my home, I resorted to my stenographic pad to take notes as Pierre sieved a soup or sauce.

kitchens both in America and France, he has dealt with hundreds if not a thousand or more. But the difference between the heads he had encountered in restaurants and the heads in my kitchen that morning was vast.

Meat dealers in metropolitan areas prepare the heads with the care of surgeons. They remove all the hairs from the head and deliver the heads to the chefs in all their pristine beauty.

Not so those heads that arrived from the New Jersey wholesaler. Those heads needed a shave and badly. I might add at this point that, unlike me, Pierre is not much given to profanity.

And on the morning when those paper crates containing the heads were unpacked I had gone to town. It was a cold snowy, wind-blown day in late March or early April and Pierre was in the kitchen with his young son, Jacques. My kitchen overlooked Gardiners Bay and it was our custom to toss a good many bits and pieces of clean garbage over the side of my cliff to feed the seagulls, which circled overhead in profusion. Guests often remarked that they must be the best-fed seagulls on earth.

When I arrived from town and walked into the kitchen that morning I heard Pierre mutter something like "Godddd-Am," and in his fury and frustration removed his apron and threw it with unaccustomed violence onto the counter.

He turned to Jacques and said, "Take those goddd-am heads and throw them to the gulls." Jacques dutifully obeyed. Pierre had tried unsuccessfully for more than an hour to remove the hairs from those calf heads. He had used knives and razors and scissors to no avail. He had tried to singe them off over the gas burners.

Once the heads had been removed we transferred our thoughts to other cuts of veal and resumed testing dishes.

A day or so later I did an unaccustomed thing. I had gone to bed in midafternoon and was lying peacefully asleep when the telephone rang. It was Helen Rattray, daughter-in-law of Jeannette and the editor of the East Hampton *Star,* one of America's finest and most progressive small-town newspapers.

I grabbed the phone, my brain fogged with sleep.

"Craig," she said, "is something funny going on in your kitchen?"

"What do you mean?" I asked. "What's funny?"

"Some local people have found calves' heads washed up on your beach."

"For God's sake, Helen, those heads didn't wash up from anywhere, we threw them over the side."

At that point it was a bit late to still the furor and alarm that had been loosed in town over the heads.

The next week's edition of the *Star* explained it all in a lengthy article that began on the front page and extended to the centerfold.

The news account reported that a neighbor had found "the severed heads lying in the sand, not many feet apart, lapped by the water of Gardiners Bay."

More neighbors came with a shovel and several plastic bags and filled them with the heads. Speculation ran rife about the origins of the death of the animals. It was surmised that the calves had been smuggled from someplace, that they had come off ships that hauled them around for their own use to be slaughtered and butchered for mealtimes. Perhaps they came from Soviet trawlers that had been seen in local waters or they had been stolen from a local farm. "Hijacked meat for black market sale appeared to be the more likely motive. . . ."

"Was there," a reporter mused, "somewhere in East Hampton, a sub-rosa abattoir? Had this been a ritual slaughter of drug-crazed hippies?"

Eventually the U.S. government was brought into the act. Tags had been found on each of the calves' tongues and a federal inspector had been called. He traced the heads to the butcher in New Jersey who had shipped the heads to us in the first place, the butcher gave him our name, and we were contacted once more. The great slaughterhouse mystery had come to an end.

§ § §

In that same issue of the *Star* there was an amusing culinary footnote.

Pierre Franey writes a column for *The New York Times* called "60-Minute Gourmet" and these recipes have appeared in book form using the same title.

A column in the *Star* was headed "24-Hour Gourmet" and under it appeared this recipe:

"Calf's Head Vinaigrette: Expecting company? Bone four calves' heads, remove brains and tongues. Soak heads and tongues for two hours; soak brains separately, minus membranes, in water with juice of three dozen lemons.

"Cook heads and tongues separately; ten-gallon stockpot may accommodate heads, add onions, cloves, carrots, and salt to taste. Tongues will simmer until tender, perhaps an hour and a half. Heads should simmer an hour after coming to a boil. Skim.

"Cook brains separately, poaching briefly with herbs. Cut head and tongue into serving pieces, arrange on your largest platter with boiled potatoes, accompanied by sauce vinaigrette. Serves 24 hungry people."

§ § §

By far the most theatrical (and a host of readers declared the most audacious and cynical) thing I've ever done had to do with a dinner at a restaurant called Chez Denis that cost $4,000.00.

At this distance, I can declare that the episode was not entered into without a certain amount of guile and a touch of artifice. The genesis of the affair was an evening spent quietly alone in my home in East Hampton in June 1975.

I do not turn reflexively to television in idle moments. But this particular evening was an exception. I had been approached some weeks earlier by a spokesman for Channel 13 in New York, the local public television station, to ask if I would donate a dinner for two in my home to be cooked and served by Pierre Franey and myself. I had agreed to this and now the time had come to witness the winners. I was, of course, curious to know who the guests in my home would be.

Along about 7:30 P.M. the announcer stated without a great deal of fanfare or flourish of trumpets that American Express was offering

Pierre at the wedding of his oldest daughter, Claudia, July 1975.

dinner for two, a sky's-the-limit meal anywhere in the world, and it would be awarded to the highest bidder. That part of my brain that was trained in public relations was vigorously triggered. Quicker than you can say Georges Auguste Escoffier I thought that I could turn this offer to my own profit. I did not bid on that meal with visions of caviar and *foie gras* racing through my brain. My vision was, and cynicism be damned, that I could capture a few inches of space in one newspaper or another if I played the game right.

And my sole source of anxiety on that evening (I had comforted myself with a scotch and soda or two) was that I could not afford to make a great monetary offer in my bidding. I knew that my offer had, because of the nature of my bank balance, to be limited.

I was not poor at that moment but I was also not in a position to spend money with anything that might approach gay abandon. I decided to extend myself, however, to the tune of three hundred dollars.

I telephoned the station and made an *initial* bid of three hundred dollars. I believe that the routine of the offers that evening was that the winners of each category would be announced at the end of the hour in which they were made. My interest at that point had shifted largely from who was coming to dinner to where *I* would go to dinner with Pierre. Anywhere in the world.

There was also a financial limitation here, on the remote chance that I would win that offer even if I increased my top bid to five hundred dollars. I simply could not afford at that point in my life to spend a vast sum on air travel to, let us say, some exotic and therefore newsworthy spot on the globe like Japan or Australia or Fiji or Samoa. My destination would have to be no more costly where air fare was concerned than Europe.

I was also aware that the cost of such an expedition would fall out of my own pocketbook and that the transportation would not be paid by American Express or *The New York Times.* I had no intention of informing *The Times* of my plans and did not mention my scheme to a soul on the newspaper then or later. The first that anyone on *The Times* knew of my journey with Pierre was when I cabled the newspaper from Sweden to inform them that I would be filing a story on the most expensive meal in the world on the following morning. For reasons having to do with time, I did not file the article in Paris but rather from Stockholm, where a restaurant, Operakällaren, that had figured in my original plans was situated.

When the American Express offer was flashed on the television screen toward the end of the hour, my *initial* offer of three hundred dollars was included. I had won the prize. I was dazzled and awed and ecstatic over my good fortune. I telephoned Pierre and described the details. He was less than impressed. He had heard of more than one harebrained adventure that had been spawned in my cranium.

As for myself, I got down every guide to restaurants around the world that I had ever accumulated. The restaurant had to be dramatic in one way or another. For example, it should not be in America. For reasons of air fare, as noted, it had to be in Europe and not halfway around the world. It should not be in a celebrated, often acclaimed dining room with kitchen such as that of Paul Bocuse in Lyon or Troisgros in Roanne. And the entire enterprise was as fascinating as a game of gastronomic chess. But the prize was mine. And for a mere three hundred dollars.

After a time I had drawn up a list of thirty or forty contenders; some of the restaurants were well known, others were obscure. They included restaurants in Belgium and Stockholm as well as in France. A general on the field of battle has never been more careful in his tactics.

What had not entered my consciousness or reasoning in the very beginning was a stipulation that the restaurant, to meet the terms specified by the donor, had to accept the American Express credit card. That, when I read the fine print, was a little dispiriting.

A Feast Made for Laughter

It eliminated, for example, a visit to my favorite restaurant in Paris, Taillevent, and my favorite in Alsace, the Auberge de l'Ill in Illhaeusern.

My interest in a little-known restaurant in Paris called Chez Denis had been sparked several months before I made my bid during a meeting with Carl Sontheimer, the man who introduced the food processor to America. He imported a machine called Magimix by the French firm of Robot Coupe. Carl changed the name to Cuisinart, the name that became synonymous with food processors in this country.

Shortly after the introduction of that machine to the American public, I had lunch with Carl. He told me that he had a sensational meal at a restaurant called Chez Denis and that he had been especially delighted with a first course called a chiffonade of lobster. He added that Chez Denis was practically unknown to the public at large because it was not listed in the *Guide Michelin*. It was not listed in the guide that most people consider the absolute bible when it comes to a choice of restaurants in France because the owner of the restaurant did not wish to be included. It seems that some months or years before, the members of the jury who decide who will and who will not be included in that sacred tome had come to the owner, Denis Lahana, a septuagenarian, and informed him that they would award him three stars if he "cleaned up the place." That is if he made his dining room more elegant and stylish; it was, in all honesty, in need of refurbishing. The then present décor included plastic ivy and plastic flowers woven here and there in the not-too-fancy iron grillwork.

Denis, it is said, became more than a little choleric, ordered the inspectors out of his dining room, and asked them to delete his name from their august volumes, now and forever. He did have loyal supporters in the two other best-known restaurant guides in France, the *Guide Kleber* and *Gault and Millau.*

The *Kleber* inspectors praised his cuisine *"fastueuse,"* meaning sumptuous, and *Gault and Millau* stated that Denis "is capable of everything. He is the *cuisiner* who is open to all creations *culinaire,* the most knowledgeable of what is old-hat in cooking, the most attentive to the *alimentation* of his clients."

Denis, when I first heard of it, also had the reputation of being conceivably the most expensive restaurant in Paris. All these facts appealed to my sense of drama in eating. Not in the *Guide Michelin,* the most expensive, and so on.

I was also curious to taste that chiffonade of lobster on which my friend Sontheimer had lavished so much praise.

And thus one day, I found myself reconnoitering the establishment with Pierre and two friends in Paris. We dined on several things, including the chiffonade of lobster (a salad of cold lobster, cubed *foie*

---

gras, a touch of Cognac and cayenne and tarragon mayonnaise flavored with tomato, tossed with lettuce); braised sweetbreads with a light truffle sauce; roast quail; andouillettes served with an outstanding truffle sauce; and those delectably tiny birds from the Landes region of France, ortolans. The wine was a Pommard. The entire experience engendered feelings of exultation and well-being, if not to say euphoria.

I was traveling with my usual anonymity but was well aware that M. Denis was in our presence. He was strutting about the dining room with an air of unimpeachable authority, a bit of a pouter-pigeon and martinet rolled into one.

When we finished our meal, I gestured to ask him to stop by our table and I said, in French, "M. Denis, I have a curious question to ask you." I spoke quite cautiously, my heart racing, the beginning of my theatrical episode.

"I have recently passed my fiftieth birthday," I lied, that birthday having occurred five years earlier. "I have an acquaintance in America, a crazy, incredibly rich friend [meaning American Express] who wants to give me a gift. The most expensive meal that can be created on the continent of Europe. But of course, I would want it to be in France." I paused to let him absorb this. In the beginning he had not been impressed with my presence.

"I wonder," I said, "if you could conceive of a meal that would cost say, about nine thousand francs," which was then about the equivalent of two thousand dollars. This put a shine in those Gallic eyes and suddenly he was all attentive enthusiasm.

He replied with such sudden assurance and elaborate thought, it was almost as though his answer had been in his mind for a long, long time.

"Oui, monsieur," he answered, "I could make you a *repas de vins,* a classic based around some of the finest vintages in my far from modest cellar. We could have caviar and *foie gras* and truffles in many dishes. There would be a first service of appetizers and soups, fish and a chartreuse of partridge, a second service of game and *salmis* and *foie gras* aspics, a third service of desserts." And as he mentioned each service, his eyes glazed over as he spoke in perfect English of the wines to accompany each, some of them more than a hundred years old.

It was a highly seductive speech and, a creature of impulse, I decided then and there to go along with Denis, the remainder of the restaurants on the list to be visited in a relaxed and totally detached manner. The main part of the lark was a *fait accompli.*

I told M. Denis that I was spending one more day in Paris, that I was then traveling to Belgium in our quest, but I would be happy to give utmost consideration to his proposed menu. And would he please send me a complete outline of the menu, including all the dishes plus wines

---

and the cost thereof. We would be staying at the Amigo in Brussels.

We arrived in Brussels, checked into the hotel, and, to my great disappointment, not a line from Denis. In the day or two following we dined in several restaurants, including the Villa Lorraine and Comme Chez Soi, which is to my mind one of the four or five greatest restaurants in the world. I was becoming apprehensive but the communication from Denis finally arrived. He proposed a menu—it was all there in clear outline—and the cost?—17,600 new francs, or the equivalent of $4,000. I did not gasp. I smiled, savoring the reaction of American Express when they got the bill. If it had been $6,000 I would not have been disturbed. This lark, I reflected, was turning out to be some bird!

But even with his letter in hand, I was to be left with some anxiety. To fulfill the meal, M. Denis needed a deposit of $2,000 to ensure my goodwill! I was disturbed because to raise that sum on such brief notice would be exceedingly difficult.

I hit upon a quick solution.

I had at that time, a friend of long standing named Yanou Collart, one of the dearest, warmest, and to my eyes, most beautiful of women. She is a seductive bundle of enthusiasm who has been, in her time, a press spokesperson for many of the greatest chefs in Europe, including Paul Bocuse, the Troisgros brothers, Michel Guérard, and so on.

On my earlier stay in Paris, I had told her of my plans to stage that dinner for two at Chez Denis. I knew that she was an acquaintance of the owner.

And thus, I telephoned her. I explained that I had agreed to the menu and the cost. Would she please act as my intermediary, call M. Denis and inform him of my good credentials, explain that I was food editor and a restaurant critic of *The Times.* Tell him the whole story about the TV show and American Express and guarantee him that we would arrive on time.

And that, more or less, is all there was to the preface of dining at Chez Denis for an uncommon amount of money.

Was it worth it? It was grand. There was endless caviar and *foie gras* and truffles and ortolans; a superb dish made of hundreds of fillets of *sots l'y laisse* or the "oysters" that occur in chickens just above the thigh bones; a *chaud-froid* of woodcock with Chambertin wines; oysters with white butter sauce; a parfait of truffled sweetbreads; charlottes and pears Alma and floating islands and a dozen other delectables.

And the wines, of course, were the factor responsible for the cost. A Château Latour, 1918; a Château Mouton-Rothschild, 1928; a Romanée-Conti, 1929; a Château d'Yquem, 1928; a Madeira dated 1835; a Calvados, 1865, a Champagne Comtesse Marie de France, Cuvée Denis, 1966; a Montrachet Baron Thénard, 1969; a Château Lafite Rothschild, 1947; a Château Petrus, 1961; and Cognac hors d'age Denis.

And when it was over, Pierre and I left the restaurant in a state of pleasant euphoria.

As I mentioned earlier, Pierre and I were scheduled to leave Paris the next morning, having arranged to dine at Operakällaren in Stockholm the next evening. I had heard so much about the smörgåsbord at that restaurant, I refused to change our plans, even though the grand prize of our journey was over. And thus, I did not write the details of that meal until we arrived in Stockholm, where we were staying at the Grand Hotel. I cabled *The Times* to expect an article on the greatest meal and the price we had paid for it.

When the article had been filed, I had no earthly idea how *The Times* would greet it. They might, I felt, ignore it as a fatuous caprice and relegate my copy to the wastebasket. I learned the next day that the dinner had been headlined on the front page. And it did, of course, make headlines around the world.

The question we have been most often asked, and it has happened hundreds of times both in this country and Europe: did you leave a tip?

No. The tip, we figured, was included.

The dinner was not without its barbs. Subsequently, almost a thousand letters arrived on the desks of editors of *The New York Times,* half of them amused by the episode, the other half damning the vulgarity and cold-bloodedness and heartlessness of Pierre and me dining in such luxury while half the world starves. We were put down by the Vatican as having committed a "scandalous" act. And, all in all, some of the most cherished of my possessions is that vast accumulation of letters, pro and con, tear sheets from magazines and newspapers all over the world.

And for the four thousand dollars, logic and several thousand readers asked if it was a perfect meal in all respects. The answer is no.

The crystal was Baccarat and the silver was family sterling, but the presentation of the dishes, particularly the cold dishes such as the sweetbread parfait and quail mousse tart, was mundane.

The foods were elegant to look at, but the over-all display was undistinguished, if not to say shabby. The food itself was generally exemplary, although there were regrettable lapses there, too. The oysters in the shells, which should have been piping hot, were almost lukewarm when they reached the table, and so was the chartreuse of pheasant. The lobster in the gratin was chewy and even the sauce could not compensate for that. When an account of the meal was included in a book titled *Guide des Meilleurs Restaurants de France* by Nicholas de Rabaudy (1976, Editions J.-C. Lattes, Paris) it came out that I had reported the lobster as being "Chewingommeux." The chef, Claude Mornay, replied to this criticism. "I had too little time to prepare for that meal and besides, there were other customers that had to be served that evening."

The $4,000 dinner
November 9, 1975

REPAS DE VINS
A WINE DINNER

On being seated at our table there were two things served,
small Parmesan cheese toasts and
a small dish with toasted almonds from Mallorca.

LE MENU

HORS SERVICE
CHAMPAGNE COMTESSE MARIE DE FRANCE, CUVÉE DENIS, *1966*
Caviar Beluga d'Iran
Beluga caviar from Iran served in a bowl of shaved ice.
With toast.

PREMIER SERVICE

Consommé Denis
A rich, full-bodied clear consommé of wild duck with shreds
of fine crêpes *and herbs.* The soup had been clarified
with raw duck and duck bones and then lightly
thickened, as many classic soups are, with fine tapioca.

Germiny froid
A cream of sorrel soup.

Velouté à l'andalouse
An outstanding cream of tomato soup with shreds of sweet
pimiento and fine herbs, including fresh chives and chervil.

* * *

CHÂTEAU LATOUR, *1918*
Tartelettes Montglas
Individual tarts of Italian ham and mushrooms with a
border of truffles.

CRAIG CLAIBORNE

Parfait de ris de veau Denis
A parfait of sweetbreads.

Tartelettes de mousse de cailles
Individual tarts of quail mousse.

* * *

MONTRACHET BARON THÉNARD, *1969*
Huîtres de Belon au buerre blanc
*Belon oysters heated in the shell and served with a pure
buerre blanc, a creamy, lightly thickened butter sauce.*

Gratin de homard
*Lobster in a cardinal-red sauce heavily laden with chopped
truffles.*

Rougets en pie
*A startling but excellent dish, a sort of Provençal pie of red
mullet baked with tomato, black olives, and herbs, including
fennel seed, rosemary, sage, and thyme.*

* * *

CHÂTEAU MOUTON-ROTHSCHILD, *1928*
Suprême et sot l'y laisse de volaille de Bresse
*Fillets of chicken breasts (the tender thin strip found on
each breast) plus the "oysters" of Bresse chickens found in
the after-backbone of chicken, blended in a cream sauce
containing sliced wild mushrooms. The term* sot l'y laisse
is a jocular phrase meaning "Only a fool would leave it."

Chartreuse de perdreaux
*Pieces of roast partridge nestled in a bed of cabbage and
baked in a mosaic pattern, intricately styled, of carrot and
turnip cut into fancy shapes.*

Filet de boeuf Olla Palinkas
*Tender, rare-roasted fillet of beef from the Limousin region
with a rich truffle sauce.*

SECONDE SERVICE

CHÂTEAU LAFITE ROTHSCHILD, *1947*
CHÂTEAU PETRUS, *1961*
ROMANÉE-CONTI, *1929*
CHÂTEAU D'YQUEM, *1928*

Ortolans en brochettes
Small birds, which dine on berries throughout their brief lives, roasted whole on skewers with head on and without cleaning except for the feathers. The birds are fat as butter. Even the bones, except for the tiny leg bones, are chewed and swallowed. There is one bird to one bite.

Aiguillettes de canard sauvage in a red wine sauce
Fillets of wild duck en salmis *in a rich brown game sauce.*

Rognonade de veau Denis
Roast boned loin of veal wrapped in puff pastry with fresh black truffles about the size of golf balls.

Pommes Anna
Potatoes cut into small spheres and baked in butter.

Purée Rachel
A purée of fresh artichokes.

Truffes de Sarlat
Baked sliced potatoes with truffles.

Aspic de foie gras d'oie
A butter-rich fresh foie gras *in clear aspic.*

Chaud-froid de bécasse au Chambertin
Breast meat of woodcock cooked until rare and served with a natural chaud-froid, *another aspic.*

Salmis de faisan aux noix
A cold platter of sliced pheasant with hazelnuts covered with a clear aspic.

TROISIÈME SERVICE

VIN DE MADÈRE, *1835*
CALVADOS, *1865*
COGNAC *hors d'age Denis*
Charlotte glacée aux fraises, sauce cardinal
A cold glazed charlotte with strawberries.

Île flottante
Poached egg-shaped meringues floating in a vanilla custard.

Poires Alma
Cold pears poached in a Port wine syrup with zest of orange, sprinkled with praline powder and crowned with whipped cream.

Adieu to salt and no regrets. A total farewell to sodium in its commonest, most widely used form.

Even as a child I had almost an addiction to salt. It was customary in my home to make fresh ice cream every Sunday in a hand-cranked freezer. To prepare it, the dasher would go into the freezer barrel, the custard would be added, and the barrel set to turn, surrounded by a heavy packing of ice and rock salt. When the ice cream was ready and the lid lifted from the canister, a rock salt crystal would occasionally drop into the ice cream. I would hastily scoop up a spoon of the ice cream with the salt chunk and taste it, letting the salt melt slowly in my mouth after the ice cream was gone.

For as long as I can remember, I could sit down to a plate full of anchovies with only olive oil, lemon juice, or vinegar to dress it, and have a feast. A single salty sour pickle has never been enough for me. I prefer margaritas to other cocktails because of the rim of salt on the glass. Years ago in Japan I learned the pleasure of foods dipped in soy sauce (almost 100 per cent salt) and lime juice. I have at times drunk that potion straight. A platter of salty, sour sauerkraut can almost be my undoing, and I have a craving for straight sauerkraut juice over ice.

And then one day in 1979 I felt some disorientation while strolling down Fifty-seventh Street in Manhattan. My balance was off and the sun suddenly seemed unbearably bright. An acquaintance familiar with my bizarre appetite for salt suggested I might be suffering from hypertension. He sent me to a well-known diet specialist, Dr. Joseph Rechtschaffen, who confirmed the hypertension. When I described my salt-consuming habits, he frowned and handed me a diet sheet that I followed for the next few weeks. There was absolutely no salt, and he also advised me to eschew sugar, fats, and beef in any and all forms. He offered me the same latitude he allows himself—a small amount of alcohol and "if some day you feel like a whole bottle of wine, go ahead and enjoy it, but don't touch a drop for the next couple of days.

And I have followed this diet faithfully now for three years and longer, with only occasional lapses. Truth to tell, I have not found adherence to a sodium-restricted diet a bane of any sort. From the beginning, it seemed like a somewhat perverse test of character. Do I feel better? Immeasurably. Not only did I pass the character test, but within a few short months I had lost twenty pounds and my blood pressure dropped from 186 over 112 to 140 over 80, which is considered normal. I continue to dine well, but on foods that contain a minimum of sodium. I have also modified my intake of fat, sugar, and foods high in cholesterol.

And with the help of Pierre, who was not in the beginning particularly amused at the thought of cooking without salt, we came up with hundreds of recipes that we included in a book called *Craig Claiborne's Gourmet Diet.* They are the dishes of a sort that I will continue to eat

My birthplace, Sunflower, Mississippi, today.

for the remainder of my days. I no longer crave salt, I am enormously content with my loss of weight, but primarily, perhaps, I take understandable pride and pleasure in my feeling of well-being and in the knowledge that my new regime is an altogether positive way of living.

My Recommended Cookbook Library

M any people over the years have asked me to investigate or at
least browse through their cookbook collections. I have found very few
that are not simply assortments of books selected at random and without pattern, aggregations of volumes that are not cohesive in their
span of subjects. The following is my proposal for an all-inclusive,
consciously well-rounded collection of books on food.

Those marked with an * are my recommendations for the ultimate
basic library, which may be added to at random according to individual
whim and interest.

Modesty prevents my listing all the books authored by Pierre Franey
and/or myself in the essential cookbook shelf. While I have included
two books edited by me, one in collaboration with Virginia Lee, I have
done so with the feeling that they are indispensable to any cookbook
library. Here are all the others, however, and I trust that if this autobiography is of interest to you, so these books will be.

The New York Times Cook Book, *Harper & Row, 1961*
The New New York Times Cookbook, *with Pierre Franey, Times Books,*
1979
The New York Times Menu Cook Book, *Harper & Row, 1966*
The New York Times International Cook Book, *Harper & Row, 1971*
Cooking with Herbs and Spices, *Harper & Row, 1963*
Craig Claiborne's Kitchen Primer, *Knopf, 1969*
Pierre Franey's 60-Minute Gourmet, *Times Books, 1979*
Pierre Franey's More 60-Minute Gourmet, *Times Books, 1981*
Veal Cookery, *with Pierre Franey, Harper & Row, 1978*
The Chinese Cookbook, *with Virginia Lee, Lippincott, 1972*
Craig Claiborne's Gourmet Diet, *with Pierre Franey, Times Books, 1980*
Craig Claiborne's Favorites, *Quadrangle/The New York Times Book Com-*
pany, 1975
Craig Claiborne's Favorites, *Volume 2, Quadrangle/The New York Times*
Book Company, 1976
Craig Claiborne's Favorites, *Volume 3, Times Books, 1977*
Craig Claiborne's Favorites, *Volume 4, Times Books, 1978*

General

The Joy of Cooking, Irma S. Rombauer and Marion R. Becker, Bobbs-Merrill,
1951. paperback, New American Library, 1979.
This was the first cookbook that I ever owned. It was given to me by
my sister in 1946 and, because of the excellence of the recipes and the

---

clarity with which they are outlined, I became a reasonably inspired cook during my early years in Chicago. To my mind it is unique, the finest of all-inclusive, comprehensive basic American cookbooks. It goes well beyond mere primer techniques, however, and should be indispensable to any good cook's library. It is a marvelous reference book not only for recipes but for cooking techniques, temperatures, baking times, and so on.

*The New York Times Cook Book, Craig Claiborne, Harper & Row, 1961. Of all the books I have written, this is the one that has been most praised (and I am told the most used). Most of the recipes were tested by Ruth P. Casa-Emellos, for eighteen years home economist of The Times. She was a genuinely inspired woman and great friend. It is difficult to be detached about this book, but I consider it to be one of the finest basic cookbooks and one of the best rounded. International in scope, many of the recipes were enthusiastically adapted from my textbooks at the Professional School of the Swiss Hotel Keepers Association.

The Gourmet Cookbook, Volume I, the Editors of Gourmet Magazine, 1959. This was one of the first "comprehensive" and most impressive of all international cookbooks. It is vast and, in its day, was one of the most informative books in its field. It is still worthwhile having in any kitchen library that pretends to be definitive. Many of the recipes were tested in the Gourmet test kitchen. I worked at Gourmet for ten months once and have personal knowledge, however, that not all the recipes that appeared in the Gourmet cookbooks were tested. Many of them were rearranged in the typewriter and were promptly issued therefrom. Whether all the recipes were tested or not, Volume I in particular is a fine reference work.

The James Beard Cookbook, James Beard, Dutton, 1959. paperback, Dell, 1959.
This is one of the first and best "basic" cookbooks to be published in the present age. It was first published in 1959. Some of the observations in the book may seem a bit dated ("In France, Austria and Italy veal is extremely popluar") but the recipes are excellent for beginning cooks. In preparing the book, James Beard had the invaluable assistance of Isabel E. Callvert.

*The Complete Asian Cookbook, Charmaine Solomon, McGraw-Hill, 1976. This is one of the finest, if not the finest, book on Asian cooking I have ever found. It is all-embracing (as much as you could expect a nonencyclopedic cookbook to be) and awesome in content. There are thirteen nations or regions involved and they include India and Pakistan, Sri Lanka, Indonesia, Vietnam, China, Korea, and Japan. There are excellent sources listed for the various uncommon ingredients. The recipes are clearly detailed and the results are first rate.

The New James Beard, Knopf, 1981.
This is an excellent cookbook although it is hard to categorize. It has some of the most basic recipes ever created—corn pudding, boiled cauliflower, buttered white turnips, sautéed eggplant, braised short ribs of beef, carrot cake, and so on—but it is more than a general, basic cookbook. It has scores of recipes for standard international fare, most of it familiar to the new generation of adventurous cooks in America, things like ratatouille, Greek salad, blanquette of lamb, bollito misto, and cassoulet. There are not a lot of innovations and altogether new creations but it makes a nice reference book for home entertaining. At least one genuinely different or little-known recipe in the book is not explained in prefatory notes. There is no mention, for example, that a tian is a fine casserole dish that derives from Provence. It is, nonetheless, a worthwhile book for experienced as well as novice cooks.

Paula Peck's Art of Good Cooking, Simon & Schuster, 1966. paperback, Fireside, 1970.
Five years after her admirable and highly successful *The Art of Fine Baking* was published, Paula Peck wrote a companion book, the *Art of Good Cooking,* which was equally inspired. Mrs. Peck had impeccable taste and both her books remain remarkably valid and worthwhile.

**Better Than Store-Bought, Helen Witty and Elizabeth Schneider Colchie, Harper & Row, 1979.*
In its own way I consider this book a small masterpiece. The title is thoroughly explicit and the book offers recipes for foods to be made in the home kitchen all of which will be the equal of and probably superior to anything you may find on your supermarket or grocery shelf. There are things like ketchup and breads and mustards and pickles, marshmallows, breakfast sausages, bean curd, even certain liqueurs and vanilla extract.

**The Chez Panisse Menu Cook Book, Alice Waters, Random House, 1982.*
Although this book had not been published at the time I wrote this

---

manuscript, I had the good fortune of perusing the work in its original form. Alice Waters is one of the two chefs and restaurant owners with an international reputation and I can testify to the superior nature of her cuisine through interviews and visits to her fine restaurant Chez Pannise in Berkeley. She is a magician in the kitchen and her cookbook reflects the best of her talents. The recipes are inspired and carefully written and edited.

American

James Beard's American Cookery, Little, Brown, *1972*.
There is no such thing as a definitive dictionary or encyclopedia of American cookery but James Beard's book seems to come as close as any. It is a lengthy volume and to a degree well researched. The origins of recipes, such as they are, are admirably covered and for the most part accurate. Anyone conversant with the entire scope of American cookery will find numerous omissions, however. Lane cake, dirty rice, and crab Norfolk to name a few. Whatever its omissions, it is still the best book of its kind and essential for any library that pretends to be complete in the American field.

The Boston Cooking-School Cook Book, Fannie Merritt Farmer, *1896*. *Facsimile edition, Crown, published 1973*.
This book is, to my mind, one of the glories of American cookery. It is the first of many cookbooks that were called *The Boston Cooking-School Cook Book* and, in later years, *The Fannie Farmer Cook Book*. Mrs. Farmer was no meat-and-potatoes cooking instructor, but astonishingly sophisticated, and hers was the first cooking school in America to gain nationwide recognition. As well it should have. This is more than a fantastic collection of American recipes; it includes such "un-American" dishes as sweetbreads *à la poulette, vol-au-vents,* tripe in many ways, tutti-fruitti, and charlotte russe. I consider it an absolute must for anyone who considers serious cookbook collecting.

The Fannie Farmer Cookbook, Twelfth Edition, Revised by Marion Cunningham with Jeri Laber, Knopf, *1979*.
Except for the name there is little about this excellent work that would relate it to the original and dated masterpiece of American cookery *The Boston Cooking-School Cook Book*. This is an altogether well researched and modern all-purpose book that is cordially recommended

for brides, serious cooks, and collectors. It is in all respects a sound volume for home cookery.

American Food: The Gastronomic Story, Evan Jones, Putnam, 1975.
One of the great historical lacks in the field of food is a definitive volume detailing the origins and recipes for all-American cookery, which is for the most part regional. Hamburgers, hot dogs, and chili con carne are three of the few dishes I know that could claim to be quintessentially all-American and universal on this continent. Evan Jones has written a highly readable and informative volume and this is an important book despite its several limitations. There are scores if not hundreds of American dishes that are ignored in this volume, including such seemingly obvious things as Harvard beets and spoon bread.

The American Heritage Cookbook, Simon & Schuster (American Heritage Publishing Co.), 1969.
This work was first published in 1964 and included many of the best-known writers in the field of food and specialists in other areas. They included Cleveland Amory, the late and much admired Lucius Beebe, Russell Lynes, and the foremost "Historical Food Consultant" Helen Duprey Bullock. It is a worthwhile compilation of prose and recipes but falls far short of being definitive. What is included is interesting and of considerable research value.

The West Coast Cook Book, Helen Evans Brown, Ward Ritchie Press, 1952. paperback, Ballantine, 1974.
The late Helen Evans Brown was one of the first American cookbook writers to compile books with serious and wholly imaginative intent and content. Her *West Coast Cook Book* is a collector's item and for very good reason. It is broad-ranging, written with acute intelligence and enthusiasm, and is highly representative of that form of regional cookery ascribed to the West Coast. There are recipes plus anecdotes, histories of various dishes (including Hangtown Fry and cioppino). Essential in a library of regional American cookbooks.

The International Chili Society Official Chili Cook Book, Martina and William Neely, St. Martin's Press, 1981.
Chili, it is my personal contention, is America's favorite cook-at-home dish. Anyone, no matter whether a talented cook or not, can turn out

a bowl or kettle of chili that is, to the cook's own taste, the finest in the world. This is the best book on chili cooking that I have ever read. It contains the selections of the International Chili Society plus the recipes of a few chili fanciers, including myself. There is a lot of mishmash and odd ingredients in some of the recipes, including goat cheese, but if you are a chilihead you should have this book on your shelves.

The Cotton Country Collection, The Junior Charity League of Monroe, Louisiana, 1972. Cotton Country Collection, P.O. Box 7138, Monroe, Louisiana 71202

Charleston Receipts, The Junior League of Charleston, South Carolina, 1950. Charleston Receipts, P.O. Box 177, Charleston, South Carolina 29402

River Road Recipes Volumes I and II, The Junior League of Baton Rouge, Louisiana, 1978. River Road Recipes, The Junior League of Baton Rouge, Louisiana, Inc., 4950-E, Government Street, Baton Rouge, Louisiana 70806

Bayou Cuisine, St. Stephen's Episcopal Church, Indianola, Mississippi, 1970. Bayou Cuisine, St. Stephen's Episcopal Church, P.O. Box 1005, Indianola, Mississippi 38751

The Memphis Cook Book, The Junior League of Memphis, Inc., Memphis, Tennessee, 1952. The Junior League House, 2711 Union Extended, Memphis, Tennessee 38112

Some of the finest, most exacting regional cookbooks to be found in America are recipe collections printed by private organizations such as Junior Leagues, church groups, and charities. Five of the best are those listed above. Within the past couple of decades the books contain far more than regional recipes but have taken on an international tone. They are the "favorite" home-style recipes of the good cooks in each area. Many of the recipes may border on the banal, but over all they are a fine addition to a kitchen library. Many of them have spiral bindings, most of them are soft-cover, and the cost is generally lower than most cookbooks printed by established publishing houses.

Caribbean and Latin America

The Flavors of the Caribbean & Latin America, Alex D. Hawkes, Viking Press, 1978.

I knew Alex Hawkes and interviewed him many years ago for one of my columns in *The New York Times.* I know how dedicated he was to the cooking of the Caribbean and Latin America. He was an accomplished cook, an outstanding researcher who knew how to write recipes with clarity. This is probably the best of the regional cookbooks dealing with Caribbean and Latin American cookery.

Chinese

The Chinese Cookbook, Craig Claiborne and Virginia Lee, Lippincott, *1972.* paperback, Harper & Row, *1976.*
I have noted elsewhere that one of the most fortuitous events of my life was meeting Virginia Lee, perhaps the greatest nonprofessional cook I have ever known. I worked with her for two years in producing this book (she practically lived in my kitchen during the period). I am prejudiced, of course, but I think it is the best Chinese cookbook in print. That is not self-praise. As I have stated, the book is a testament to the genius of Virginia. I acted only as mid-wife.

Pleasures of Chinese Cooking, Grace Zia Chu, Simon & Schuster, *1962.* paperback, Cornerstone, *1974.*
Grace Zia Chu, who, incidentally, was taught by my aunt Elizabeth when Grace was in the equivalent of kindergarten in Shanghai, was *the* pioneer missionary in introducing Chinese cooking into the American home, demonstrating that Chinese cooking can be done on American stoves. She has been a dedicated cook and this was the first *great* Chinese cookbook for the American audience. It is as valid today as it was when first printed in 1962.

The Great Tastes of Chinese Cooking, Jean Yueh, Times Books, *1979.*
Florence Lin's Regional Cookbook, Hawthorn Books, *1978.*
These are two outstanding books that deal with Chinese cooking. Jean Yueh is a native of Shanghai who learned her techniques from chefs in Hong Kong. She has a cooking school in Berkeley Heights, New Jersey.
   Florence Lin is an undisputed authority on Chinese cookery who taught for many years at the China Institute in Manhattan. The recipes are first rate, authentic, and detailed.

The Thousand Recipe Chinese Cookbook, Gloria Bley Miller, Grosset & Dunlap, *1970.*

When this book appeared in 1966 it seemed like a rearrangement and re-editing of all the recipes to be found in every Chinese cookbook then in print, plus a great deal of information about Chinese cooking techniques and an explanation of the ingredients of a Chinese kitchen. It was massive in size and, even today, what it may lack in originality is more than made up for in total content. It is an impressive and fine reference work.

French

*Mastering the Art of French Cooking, Simone Beck, Louisette Bertholle, Julia Child, Knopf, Volume I, 1961, Volume II, 1970.
Giving a critique of Julia Child at this late date is like explaining all about motherhood and the American flag. Julia, more than any other, has given meaning to French cookery for the American kitchen. These, her first two books, produced in collaboration with Simone Beck and Louisette Bertholle, are by far her finest works. They precede a whole spate of books, most of which seem to have been ground out by whirling dervishes off camera.

Simca's Cuisine, Simone Beck, Knopf, 1972.
Simca, otherwise known as Simone Beck, collaborated with Julia Child on the two classic volumes of Mastering the Art of French Cooking, and was thereby launched into the international world of cookbook writing. She is an enormously imaginative cook and has a good deal to offer in this book, much of it highly original and inspired. The recipes are easy to follow, too.

The Art of Charcuterie, Jane Grigson, Knopf, 1968.
Good books on charcuterie and sausage-making in general are hard to come by for some reason that I have never been able to divine. This is conceivably the best book on charcuterie-making that is available in the English language. I have never prepared a recipe from it but I have often used the book in research on sausage-making and the like. There is something off-putting about some of the recipes. The recipes for confits or preserved meats, such as confit d'oie (preserved goose), are too general and vague for my own taste in recipe writing. It is, however, an important book for reference.

A French Chef Cooks at Home, Jacques Pépin, Simon & Schuster, *1975.*
paperback, Fireside, *1980.*
This is one of the finest basic books on French cooking ever written.
Jacques Pépin is nationally known and has demonstrated cooking from
one coast to the other. He is a master chef and one of the most
dextrous and talented in the kitchen. The recipes are totally comprehensive, choice in their categories, and almost fail-safe in their outline.

Greek

Greek Cooking for the Gods, Eva Zane, *101* Productions, *1970.*
There are times when I cannot pinpoint precisely why I prefer one
cookbook in a national category over another. I happen to think that
this book on Greek cookery is quite special. The recipes are easy to
follow and trustworthy. At times, I feel that Eva Zane has oversim-
plified (to cater to American tastes, as in the case of the Easter soup
called mayeritsa, which calls for lungs and tripe of lamb, which she
ignores) but the dishes are simple and tasty.

Greek Cooking, Lou Seibert Pappas, Harper & Row, *1973.*
Cooking and Baking the Greek Way, Anne Theoharous, Holt, Rinehart &
Winston, *1977.*
Greek Islands Cooking, Theonie Mark, Little, Brown, *1974.*
These are three of the best Greek cookbooks designed for the Ameri-
can audience. I find them equally valuable as reference works. I have
lumped them together quantitatively because I find them to be strik-
ingly similar in their recipes and cooking techniques.

Hungarian

The Cuisine of Hungary, George Lang, Atheneum, *1971.*
George Lang, restaurateur, amateur cook, historian, man about town,
was born in Hungary and takes enormous delight in his origins. This
is by far the finest book ever written in English on the subject of
Hungarian cooking. The recipes are outlined in detail (I sometimes
think too much detail) but George can't resist his erudite nature. If you
are interested in the foods of Hungary (historically or otherwise), this
is the one best book to own in English.

Indonesian

*The Indonesian Kitchen, Copeland Marks with Mintari Soeharjo, Atheneum,
1981.*
This is, to my taste, by far the finest cookbook available on Indonesian
cooking. It is comprehensive. The techniques and flavors of Indonesia
are outlined in admirable detail. And, as far as I know, the recipes are
as authentic as you could hope for, only slightly tailored for the American kitchen to make them wholly workable. Although Copeland Marks
is an American who has lived off and on over many years in Indonesia,
he is wholly conversant with the cooking of the region and has had the
inestimable help of Mintari Soeharjo, a formidably good Indonesian
cook.

Indian

An Invitation to Indian Cooking, Madhur Jaffrey, Knopf, 1973.
Classic Indian Cooking, Julie Sahni, Morrow, 1980.
*Cooking of the Maharajas, Shivaji Rao and Shalini Devi Holkar, Viking
Press, 1975.*
An Invitation to Indian Cooking by Madjur Jaffrey has long been considered the finest Indian cookbook in English for the simple reason that
it was first to outline Indian recipes that were comprehensive, easy to
follow, and as authentic as possible given the markets and ingredients
available to Americans.

Since her book appeared in 1973, two more books on Indian cookery
have appeared and they have a great deal to recommend them. They
are Classic Indian Cooking, which is wholly admirable in its authenticity,
and Cooking of the Maharajas, which seems to be only slightly less so.
If you are interested in the preparation of excellent Indian meals, all
three books would be of considerable value in the kitchen.

International

Foods of the World Series, Time-Life Books.
This is the most important collection of international cookbooks ever
assembled in America and will quite likely remain so for many years.
It almost goes without saying that the wholly comprehensive series of

books on international cuisines would be enough to fill more volumes than the twenty-nine volumes of the Encyclopaedia Britannica. But the twenty-six-volume Time-Life series (do not confuse this with the more recent Time-Life series *The Good Cook/ Techniques and Recipes*) is startlingly well researched and remarkably selective of the foods and recipes of the representative cooking of regional America, China, Russia, Scandinavia, Africa, and so on. There are some curious omissions (the African volume, for example, astonishingly enough does not even mention couscous) but over all the series is a tour de force and one of the most laudable publishing efforts in the history of cookbooks. The poorest of the volumes is titled *The Cooking of Provincial France,* which is actually a badly muddled bouillabaisse of regional as well as traditional classic cookery.

Elizabeth David Classics, Knopf, 1980.
Elizabeth David has long been one of my favorite cookbook authors and writers on food since I first read her book *Mediterranean Food* more than two decades ago (I found it in a secondhand book store in the 1950s). This volume contains reprints not only of her *Mediterranean Food* but *French Country Cooking* and *Summer Cooking.* You may never produce one dish from any volume, but they are a joy to browse through. These books are enduring classics.

The Four Seasons, 250 Original Recipes from One of the World's Great Restaurants, Tom Margittai and Paul Kovi, edited by Barbara Kafka, Simon & Schuster, 1980.
This is a superb collection of recipes from the kitchen of Chef Josef (Seppi) Renggli, one of America's foremost chefs, who presides over the menus and the range of The Four Seasons Restaurant in Manhattan, which has catered for many years to some of the world's foremost tastemakers. Renggli is a genius in the kitchen. He contributed the recipes for this book to Barbara Kafka, an outstanding cook and recipe author. The recipes are converted from mass cookery, such as is found in a great restaurant, to home use. The results are wholly admirable. The recipes are inspired and have such names as sorrel vichyssoise, salmon escalopes with caviar, and chopped lamb steak with pine nuts.

Cooking for One Is Fun, Henry Lewis Creel, Times Books, 1976.
Cooking On Your Own, Henry Lewis Creel, Times Books, 1980.
Henry Lewis Creel has been one of my closest friends for more than twenty-five years. During that time he has spent endless hours in my

kitchen watching Pierre Franey and me devise and prepare recipes that would eventually find their way into *The New York Times,* both daily and Sunday. We gave Henry permission years ago to adapt these recipes to his own uses in cooking for one. These books are, to my way of thinking, the finest books dealing with that subject that you can find. The recipes are sound, accurately tested, and are international in scope. This is a sort of single person's guide to good cooking.

A Treasury of Great Recipes, *Mary and Vincent Price, Grosset & Dunlap, 1965.*
This is a fascinating book, an exceptional personal collection of recipes by the author and his first wife. The recipes were collected over a period of years from the owners and chefs of many of the world's most famous restaurants including the Baumanière in Les Baux, the Pyramide in Vienne, Harry's Bar in Venice, the Jockey in Madrid, and La Crèmaillère in Banksville, New York. The recipes are interesting and include such fare as a Mediterranean fish soup, roast pork Castilian style, German meatballs with capers and sardellen sauce, and excellent desserts. The recipes were tested by Ann Seranne, who gave me my start as a food writer when she was managing editor of *Gourmet* magazine more than a quarter of a century ago.

The Dumpling Cookbook, *Maria Polushkin, Workman Publishing, 1976.*
This is an engaging little book that should be of special interest to anyone who is fond of dumplings. I am, in depth. The book is dedicated to the author's mother "whose delicious vareniki, piroshki and chebureki inspired a lifelong love of dumplings, and to my father, whose robust appetite inspired me to learn to make them." Maria Polushkin is a neighbor in East Hampton, an outstanding cook. The recipes include, among many, dropped dumplings, Polish dumplings, Mexican meat dumplings, meat-filled Siberian dumplings, and so on.

The Saucier's Apprentice, *Raymond Sokolov, Knopf, 1976.*
This is one of the finest and most informative books on French sauces ever printed. It is comprehensive and easy to understand. Sokolov, who succeeded me as food editor of *The New York Times* during my two-year absence starting in 1972, carefully outlines the progression of making the most basic sauces and demonstrates the manner in which a basic sauce can be converted into a classic and more elaborate one. You start off, for example, with a recipe for a demi-glace and

convert it into a *sauce poivrade* for game. The book encompasses brown sauces, white sauces, oil and egg sauces like mayonnaise, and butter and egg sauces like hollandaise. It is an elaborate primer. The book has, curiously enough, never had the large audience that it deserves. The title is, unfortunately, a bit too flippant for comfort and may account for the book being underrated by serious cooks.

Great Sausage Recipes and Meat Curing, *Rytek Kutas, Richard S. Kutas Co., Buffalo, 1976.*
For some inexplicable reason, a good, reliable, and comprehensive sausage cookbook is hard to come by. To my way of thinking this is the best available. The author is of Polish descent and began sausage-making when he transferred from the East Coast to Las Vegas. His hunger for kielbasa was overpowering and so he made his own. He branched out into international sausage-making and returned to Buffalo where he sells all the necessary equipment, including spices and casing, for home sausage-makers. The book includes, in addition to recipes (for cooked or smoked sausages), total advice on the theories of sausage-making.

Italian

*The Classic Italian Cookbook: The Art of Italian Cooking and the Italian Art of Eating, Marcella Hazan, Knopf, 1976.
*More Classic Italian Cooking, Marcella Hazan, Knopf, 1978.
There is no disputing Marcella Hazan's role as the veritable queen of Italian cooking in America. It is she who has done most through her books to prove that there is more to *la cucina italiana* than spaghetti and meatballs and lasagne. She has successfully preached the gospel of delicate, irresistible sauces for pasta, for spectacularly good and innovative dishes like tripe with beans and swordfish with salmoriglio sauce (a simple sauce of lemon juice, oregano, and olive oil). Her sections on Italian desserts may be a bit too brief, but if you want to cook Italian in classic style, Marcella is your source.

*The Fine Art of Italian Cooking, Giuliano Bugialli, Times Books, 1977.
Mr. Bugialli is one of the best instructors in Italian cooking to be found in America. He is enormously literate, a patient, kindly man who has done much to spread the gospel of how fine the best Italian cooking

can be. His is also one of the best cookbooks on the subject. The recipes, whether for sausage bread, tortellini in meat sauce, or polenta, are expertly and clearly detailed. I like his dedication: "To my mother, still the worst cook in the family, but the best everything else."

Italian Regional Cooking, Ada Boni, Bonanza Books, 1969.
For reasons wholly unfathomable to me, Ada Boni's *Italian Regional Cooking* has never achieved anywhere near the fame that it deserves. I find it wholly admirable, an inspiration to read, a joy in its diversity, wholly laudable in its authenticity, highly enlightening in its outline and detail of Italian regional specialties and, with a few alterations here and there, recipes that are easily reproduced in the home. For some reason, many book stores have remaindered (marked down the cost) the books within recent memory. It should be in the kitchen of anyone who wants to "cook Italian."

The Complete Book of Pasta, Jack Denton Scott, Morrow, 1968. paperback, Bantam, 1979.
This is a very good book and of special value because it is one of the few books on Italian cookery that outlines with sketches and words some of the best-known, and many that are not so well-known, shapes of pasta that should be understood by anybody who cares about dining well, Italian-style. The recipes are also carefully detailed and of general interest.

Italian Family Cooking, Edward Giobbi, Random House, 1971. paperback, Vintage, 1978.
Although Edward Giobbi, a friend of long standing, is a serious painter and sculptor, he has an incredible knowledge of cooking, mainly Italian. He has passed many hours in my kitchen, sharing the stove with Pierre and me, and many are the happy days we have spent in his home for one special feast or another. This is an excellent, down-to-earth volume. The recipes are inspired and easy to follow.

Italian Food, Elizabeth David, Knopf, 1958. paperback, Penguin, 1970.
I have noted elsewhere that there is a collection of Elizabeth David's works that is available in a single volume. *Italian Food* is not included in that compilation. This is, to me, one of David's most interesting

books and, if you are a devotee of the lady, you will find it imperative to add this book to your collection. It ranks with her best and that is high praise, indeed. It will make you hunger for another visit to Italy, no matter how recently you returned.

Japanese

*Japanese Cooking: A Simple Art, Shizuo Tsuji, Kodansha International, 1980.
In praise of this book I can only quote the paragraph used on the dust jacket and signed by me. "As far as I know there has never been an all-embracing and authentic cookbook relating to Japanese food in English. Shizuo Tsuji's volume fills that void with distinction and there is a bonus in having a lovely and affectionate introduction by my favorite writer on food, M. F. K. Fisher. This is a volume . . . [that I would ever] be loath to part with." Tsuji is the owner and director of the Tsuji Hotel School in Osaka, the largest in all of Japan. He is an intense, sensitive, and brilliant gastronome. He is the author of many volumes on French as well as Japanese cooking. I feel certain that he knows more about the cooking of his native land than anyone else in the world.

*At Home with Japanese Cooking, Elizabeth Andoh, Knopf, 1980.
One of the very best and most comprehensive books on Japanese cooking. Elizabeth Andoh is an American, born and raised in New York. She lived in Japan and studied at the Yanagihara School of Classical Japanese Cooking. She taught cooking in Japan for many years. This is a fine work tailored to home cooks in this country who want the taste of Japanese cooking on their table. The recipes are forthright and accurate.

Mexican

*The Cuisines of Mexico, Diana Kennedy, Harper & Row, 1972.
Although British-born, Diana Kennedy is the prima donna assoluta when it comes to Mexican cooking. A library without her volume on Mexican

cookery is like a meal in Mexico without tortillas. I like to believe that I inspired her to produce this work, the first of several. Once she encouraged me to write a Mexican cookbook when I visited her in Mexico. She was then married to Paul Kennedy, the late Central American correspondent for *The New York Times*. I demurred. Having just finished a devastatingly good meal in her home, I said I would wait for her to produce the definitive volume. And she did.

Middle East

*The Complete Middle East Cookbook, Tess Mallos, McGraw-Hill, *1980*. This is one of the grandest and most ambitious of cookbooks and all the more remarkable that it is available in English. Americans are simply not all that well acquainted with the food of the Middle East, which deserves a great deal more popularity than it is accorded. It is some of the most varied and tempting in all creation. This book is a tour de force, amply illustrated and as close as any book could come, to my way of thinking, to the definitive recipes of Greece, Turkey, Armenia, Israel, Lebanon, and so on. It is astonishing in its scope.

Moroccan

*Couscous and Other Good Food from Morocco, Paula Wolfert, Harper & Row, *1973*.
I have noted that couscous for very good reasons (it was the first "foreign" dish I ever sampled) is one of my favorite dishes. There is far more than couscous in Moroccan cooking, as Paula Wolfert so ably points out in this estimable volume. One of the great main courses in this world is something called *b'steey* (or *b'stilla, bsteeya,* and so on), a pigeon pie. That dish and scores of others, all tempting and stimulating to the soul as well as the taste buds, are included in this volume, the best of its kind on Moroccan cookery in English.

Scandinavian

The Great Scandinavian Cook Book, Karin Fredrikson, Crown, *1967.*
I consider this book a "must" for those who care about the cooking
of Scandinavia. But it is, and has been for years, more a reference book
than a cookbook. The outline of each recipe is a bit too vague, but the
book, over all, is informative and worth browsing through for source
material.

**The Swedish Princesses Cook Book (from the original Swedish "Prinses-
sornas Kokbok"),* Jenny Åkerström, Albert Bonnier, *1936.*
This is generally considered by the finest Swedish cooks in this country
to be the best recipe book dealing with Swedish cooking ever printed
in English. It is not generally available in bookstores and, as of this
writing, can only be procured at secondhand sources that deal in
cookbooks. The recipes are well outlined and easy to follow. Jenny
Åkerström owned and managed the most famous cooking school in
Stockholm, or for that matter all of Sweden. It was customary in some
parts of Europe for the children of royalty to learn the art of cooking
and housekeeping and the three princesses who attended her school
and to whom the book is dedicated are Princess Margaret of Denmark,
Crown Princess Martha of Norway, and Crown Princess Astrid of Belgium.

Spanish

*The Foods and Wines of Spain, Penelope Casas, Knopf, *1982.*
I have for a good long while been the friend of the author of this book.
I have dined several times at her table and can testify that I have never
eaten finer Spanish food in Barcelona or Madrid. I have, at my own
request, been privileged to read the manuscript of her book and can
declare it to be without question by far the finest and most comprehensive book on Spanish food ever written in English. I consider it invaluable for anyone who pretends to have anything approaching a well-
rounded cookbook collection. The book will be published in October
1982.

Turkish

The Art of Turkish Cooking, Neşet Eren, Doubleday, *1969*.
Years ago I dined in the home of Neşet Eren, the wife of Nuri Eren, then the Turkish Deputy Ambassador to the United Nations. The food was magnificent ·from the snow almonds and cheese boereks to the chicken walnut and baklava. I was one of the first to purchase her book on Turkish cuisine and have found it to be a source of happy memories ever since. Mrs. Eren is an excellent cook and her expertise is reflected in this volume.

Vietnamese

* *The Classic Cuisine of Vietnam,* Bach Ngo and Gloria Zimmerman, Barron's Educational Series, *1979*.
I am convinced that the cooking of Vietnam is one of the glories of gastronomy, more limited in scope but equal in the extravagant goodness of its flavors to that of China. It is unfortunate that Vietnamese cuisine is so little known in America and all because of that traumatic, unspeakable war that debased us all. This is no doubt the finest book on Vietnamese cooking to have been written in English. It is excellent.

Vegetarian

* *World-of-the-East Vegetarian Cooking,* Madhur Jaffrey, Knopf, *1981*.
I have never given serious thought to becoming a food faddist. I have too long cherished the likes of meat and fish and poultry ever to consider becoming a vegetarian. If, through some miracle, I decided to resort to a vegetable diet forever, this new book by Madhur Jaffrey, who is to my mind the finest authority on Indian cooking in America, would be my bible. It is by far the most comprehensive, fascinating, and inspired book on vegetable cookery that I have encountered. Whether or not you are a vegetarian, it is a valuable work offering an incredible number of good recipes to appeal to any cook. The recipes are adapted from the cuisines of India, Bali, Japan, China, the Far Eastern and Middle Eastern countries "where vegetarian cookery is an age-old tradition."

Baking

__English Bread and Yeast Cookery__, Elizabeth David, Penguin Books, London, 1977.
__English Bread and Yeast Cookery__, Elizabeth David, Introduction and Notes for the American Cook by Karen Hess, Viking Press, 1980.
This book in its original edition is far more valuable than the American version with its notes by Karen Hess, who also translated or mistranslated some of the recipes. The book contains a wealth of information about the subject at hand but it is by far the dullest of all Elizabeth David's works. Reading the book from cover to cover would, for me at least, be an impossible task. The facts about English breads and yeast cookery are covered in unmerciful detail. But the British edition of the book should be in any library that pretends to be definitive where food and cooking are concerned. Some of the recipes tried in the American edition were a culinary disaster.

__Art of Fine Baking__, Paula Peck, Simon & Schuster, 1961. paperback, Fireside, 1970.
Historians have indicated that the cooking revolution in America first took hold in the 1950s. One of the pioneers in the field was a woman named Paula Peck, who was a genuinely inspired cook with remarkable taste and imagination. This was her first book and it still stands as a culinary landmark for home baking.

__Beard on Bread__, James Beard, Knopf, 1973.
James Beard's volume is small and personal, containing many fine bread recipes that he has discovered in his travels about the world or borrowed from friends.

__The Complete Book of Breads__, Bernard Clayton, Jr., Simon & Schuster, 1973.
This is one of the finest and most complete books to deal with bread making. The recipes are clearly outlined and thoroughly tested by the author in his Bloomington, Indiana, kitchen-studio. There are basic loaves and variations on many breads which are international in scope. This is the volume that I would recommend most highly on overall bread making.

__The Complete Book of Pastry, Sweet and Savory__, Bernard Clayton, Jr., Simon & Schuster, 1981.

This is to me the "classic" book on pastry making and its range is indeed broad, including as it does such international pastries as empanadas, cream puffs, turnovers, kipfel, and cannolis, Danish pastries, pizzas, tarts, and quiches. The recipes are outlined just as clearly and as comprehensibly detailed as in his earlier book, *The Complete Book of Breads*. This is, in fact, in my mind, an essential companion book to that one.

Canning, Drying, and Preserving

* The Ball Blue Book, *the Ball Corporation, Muncie, Indiana, 1975.*
If I had to own but one book on canning and preserving, this would be it. It is a no-nonsense guide to the ins and outs of "putting things up" for future use. I can scarcely imagine a summer passing by without referring to the ways of storing my excess tomatoes or turning them into juice, ketchup, and so on, without at least one reference to *The Ball Blue Book*. This is an all-American production and if you want to know how to make and put up Dixie Relish, apple and other fruit butter, even lye hominy, this is the place you'll find it.

* The Pleasures of Preserving and Pickling, *Jeanne Lesem, Knopf, 1975.*
The Green Thumb Preserving Guide, *Jean Anderson, Morrow, 1976.*
These books may not be as basic as *The Ball Blue Book* but they are certainly inspired. Jeanne Lesem's book ranges from marmalades and grape preserves to ratafias (an old-fashioned drink) and rose geranium. Jean Anderson offers "The Best and Safest Way to Can and Freeze, Dry and Store, Pickle, Preserve and Relish" vegetables and fruits.

Cheese

French Cheese, *Pierre Androuet, Harper's Magazine Press, 1973.*
When this book was published I would have said it was absolutely indispensable for the complete kitchen library. It seems a little dated, now, however, because of the tremendous change in the cheese situation in France and in this country. We have become so cheese con-

scious and the kinds of cheese produced in France and all over Europe have so increased in variety because of the demand, Androuet's contribution is somewhat diminished in authority. It is still worth having.

Desserts

*Maida Heatter's Book of Great Desserts, Maida Heatter, Knopf, 1974. paperback, Warner Books, 1977.
*Maida Heatter's Book of Great Cookies, Knopf, 1977.
*Maida Heatter's Book of Great Chocolate Desserts, Knopf, 1980.
The publisher has not been at all modest in dubbing all three of these books as "great" in their title. And he has been accurate, for Maida Heatter is an inspired and dedicated cook who knows what she is about, principally in the field of desserts and cookies. One of my favorite stories has to do with the first volume outlined here. Maida had tested with patience and great care over a long period of time all the desserts contained in that volume. Shortly before publication, a stove repairman arrived in her kitchen and announced that the thermostat was faulty and that the oven temperature was twenty or so degrees less than it should have been. With infinite care she returned to the kitchen and retested every recipe second time around to ensure their accuracy. I cringe in contemplation of that ordeal! These books are of the essence for anyone with a sweet tooth.

*The Joy of Cheese Cake, Dana Bovbjerg and Jeremy Iggers, Barron's, 1980. I have long been convinced that the expression should be "As American as cheesecake" rather than as apple pie. For cheesecake, at least in the world I inhabit, seems to be by far the preferred dessert of most Americans. This is the ultimate book on cheesecake-making, taking into account scores of good recipes for that rich and delectable confection.

Foraging and books on the out-of-doors

Stalking the Wild Asparagus, Euell Gibbons, McKay, 1962.
Stalking the Blue-eyed Scallop, Euell Gibbons, McKay, 1964.

The late Euell Gibbons was indefatigable in his quest for foods to nourish mankind that could be found free by foraging around the countryside. He was a good writer, a joy to visit, and an amusing conversationalist. These are both fascinating volumes, which I once told him should be titled *The Best Things in Life Are Free.*

Wine

Alexis Lichine's New Encyclopedia of Wines & Spirits, Knopf, 1974.
Frank Schoonmaker's Encyclopedia of Wine, Hastings House, 1964, revised 1973.
The New York Times Book of Wine, Terry Robards, Times Books, 1976.
These books are not described separately because they are all essential for any bookshelf that pretends to be complete and authoritative. They are all written by the finest experts in the field and they all have special merit. Physically the Lichine book is more "showy" and elaborate-looking, otherwise all three volumes are, in my book, equally authoritative.

The Joys of Wine, Clifton Fadiman and Sam Aaron, Abrams, 1975.
This is an impressive book, another essential for the "complete" wine library. It is not an encyclopedia or a dictionary but it makes for fascinating reading and is highly enlightening in many respects whether you are considering the wines of America or Europe. There are "maps of great wine regions, vintage charts, and expert selections of outstanding wine" as the dust jacket declares. It delivers that and much more. Cocktail table in size and appearance.

Reference

Dictionnaire de l'Académie des Gastronomes, Aux Éditions Prisma, 2 volumes, 1962.
I have never divulged in print or otherwise the book that I have prized and relied on most heavily in writing about the classic dishes of France. It is this dictionary. It was given to me many years ago by Vincent Bourrel, who was then president of the Academy of Gastronomes in

CRAIG CLAIBORNE

Paris, and the book has been an invaluable reference work where my writings are concerned.

It lists words that are essential to the French kitchen, describes the ingredients to be used in the preparation of foods as well as the origins of the names of dishes. Let me choose one name to illustrate my dedication and enthusiasm for the two volumes. Let us say I am familiar with one dish that bears the name salade Bagration and am curious to know how the name came about. I learn that the name is given in homage to an Armenian prince named Pierre Bagration who lived from 1765 to 1812. He was chiefly celebrated as an adversary of Napoleon. His name is applied chiefly to a soup and a salad. The common ingredient in these dishes is the presence of macaroni. The salad also includes a julienne of artichoke bottoms and celery root in mayonnaise garnished with tomato. The soup is made with veal broth and cream. I also learn that there is a dish called eggs Bagration and it is made with cooked eggs garnished with macaroni, cream, and black truffles.

Larousse Gastronomique, Prosper Montagné, Crown, 1961.
If I could not read French and if I were to be permitted one dictionary or encyclopedia on food, French cooking in particular, this is the book that I would select, hands down. Praising *Larousse Gastronomique* in this wholly estimable translation by Charlotte Turgeon and Nina Froud is tantamount to saying a few nice words about the finest wines of Champagne, Burgundy, and Bordeaux. The task of translation was mammoth and Mmes. Turgeon and Froud have never received the share of praise that is their due. The one book that I would least like to do without as a serious food writer.

La Technique, Jacques Pépin, Times Books, 1976.
La Méthode, Jacques Pépin, Times Books, 1979.
These are two exceptional and, for serious cooks, indispensable books by one of the foremost master chefs of America, Jacques Pépin. They outline in intricate but wholly understandable detail with photographs and text the basic and not-so-basic concepts of French and European cooking. The photographs are in black and white and color. Within the pages of these books you will learn how to bone poultry, joints of meat, and fish; how to slice smoked salmon; how to create aspics; how to prepare pâtés; and so on. If there is any technique or method missing, I have yet to discover it. Elaborate and easily comprehended.

Cooking Techniques, Beverly Cox with Joan Whitman, Little, Brown, 1981. This excellent book shows in clear and logical sequence how to do almost everything called for in Western cookery—from seeding a tomato to butterflying a leg of lamb, from how to fill a pastry bag to rolling your own pasta, from filleting a fish to forming a turnip flower, and on and on in more than 2,000 black and white and color photographs. Its value is that it is not limited to French cuisine and should be in the reference library of every novice and expert cook who wants to perfect or expand his or her skills.

Chinese Technique, Ken Hom with Harvey Steinam, Simon & Schuster, 1981.
This is an admirable, illustrated guide to the fundamental techniques of Chinese cooking. It does for Chinese cooking what Jacques Pépin's *La Technique* does for French. It contains hundreds of photographs showing step-by-step techniques in the preparation of such dishes. There are notes on such matters as seasoning woks and cleavers, using bamboo steamers, techniques of stir frying, and so on. There are many recipes. Ken Hom is a wholly qualified expert cook who teaches cooking in California. This book should be in the library of any one who is seriously interested in Chinese cookery.

The Wise Encyclopedia of Cookery, Wise, 1948. Revised edition, David B. Wise, Grosset & Dunlap, 1971.
This encyclopedia has been an invaluable source of information for me. I am not at all certain how it was put together and some of the information seems to have been lifted without alteration from other books. The attributed contributors to the volume, organizations such as the Wheat Flour Institute and National Canners Association, figure in the hundreds in the acknowledgments section. It is sound in the information offered and at times quite amusing. The entries range from *"à la mode,"* described as "Literally, following the fashion," to zythum, "an ancient beverage made from malt and wheat; a kind of beer." Over the years I have noted one or two minor errors but they have been negligible. There are many recipes in the book and they seem quite in order. It is the best over-all encyclopedia on food that I have found for everyday research.

The Food of France, Waverley Root, Knopf, 1958. paperback, Random House, 1977.

This is one of the best and most informative books on the food of France ever written in any language. Mr. Root has a brilliant explanation of the three principal domains of French cookery. The book is divided into The Domain of Butter (Paris, Normandy, Burgundy, and so on), The Domain of Fat (Alsace-Lorraine with its Germanic influence, Perigord and the Auvergne, where geese flourish, and Languedoc), and The Domain of Oil (Provence, the Côte d'Azur, and Corsica, where olive trees flourish). It is a painstakingly researched book and one of the proudest additions to my kitchen library.

Food, Waverley Root, Simon & Schuster, 1980.
This is the best, most readable book on the history of food in my library because the author is Waverley Root, the author of the celebrated *The Food of France,* which also happens to be the best book in English on *that* subject. When I reviewed *Food* in *The New York Times* I pointed out that this is not the definitive encyclopedia that I had hoped it would be (there had been rumors of the impending publication of the work, years before it came off the presses). It does not contain, I noted, explanations for what aardvark and Aaron's rod are, only that they do exist and are edible. There are, in my distinct opinion, glaring omissions such as lox and bagels. I had a note in return from Waverley explaining why this book was not the definitive encyclopedia that both he and I had hoped it would be. "I thought you might be interested in knowing why Food is not the definitive encyclopedia which both you and I wanted. I won't say that the 'definitive' encyclopedia came out of my typewriter, but didn't get published, but at least I did write a million words of which the publisher used about a third. I do not reproach them for this; indeed, I think they did nobly, since they had contracted to print only 150,000 words, but the point is that there *were* articles on aardvark and Aaron's rod, which you mention, and many others which are still here, in my files." Waverley added that he had wanted another title, *Food: An Informal Dictionary.*

The Food of the Western World, Theodora FitzGibbon, Times Books, 1976.
This is one of the most important reference works where food is concerned ever published in English. I have found it invaluable since its publication in checking and double-checking facts about food. And I have learned a lot of amusing things about which I knew nothing. *Macreuese,* for example, I discovered to be "French for widgeon." Looking up widgeon, I found that a widgeon is "a wild duck, larger than the teal but smaller than the mallard." The author states that

small English scallops are better than the U.S. version and I would dispute this. You will find numerous American regional dishes explained in the book—Caesar salad and johnnycake, for example—but there are many omissions in this area. Perhaps it is far too much to expect that she would include such things as "red eye gravy" and "dirty rice," but they are valid foods in their own right. *Food of the Western World,* however, is an essential book for the complete kitchen shelf.

Bouquet de France, Samuel Chamberlain, Gourmet Magazine, 1966.
Samuel Chamberlain was a gentleman and scholar and one of the few people I have ever known worthy of the name gourmet. A connoisseur of wine and food. He was an architect and brilliant etcher. He wrote a column for many years for *Gourmet* magazine titled "An Epicurean Tour of the French Provinces." I doubt that any American knew more about the subject. The material in this book is largely a collection of those essays. The book first appeared in 1952, almost thirty years ago. It still makes good reading.

* The Encyclopedia of Fish Cookery, A. J. McClane *(photography by Arie de Zanger), Holt, Rinehart & Winston, 1977.*
This is the finest encyclopedia relating to fish in the English language. I find it remarkable in most details and wholly enlightening in many respects. For instance, I learned that there is a category of clams, littlenecks, which are "properly spelled as one word as opposed to the trade term for the small eastern Little Neck). Littlenecks are found in Pacific waters. There are some definitions that could have been more elaborate. He does not, to choose one example, note the pronunciation of the oddly named clams (gooey-ducks or gwe-ducks) or that the clam's name derives from a Nisqualli Indian word meaning "dig-deep." These are trivial criticisms, however, and the book is invaluable as a reference work. It also has fine photographs by Arie de Zanger, including step-by-step pictures that show how to dress soft shell crabs, how to open clams, how to fillet a fish, and so on.

* Le Repertoire de la Cuisine, Louis Saulnier, De Luxe Edition, translated from *the original French edition by E. Brunet, Barron's, 1967.*
I first bought this book in its original as a textbook while a student at the École Hôtelière in Lausanne, Switzerland, a few years before I joined *The New York Times.* It has been invaluable as a handy reference

work for more than a quarter century. The book was first published in Paris in 1916 and, as noted in the preface, "rapidly became internationally famous as a standard work of reference in the culinary world." It puts the entire work of Auguste Escoffier at your fingertips. There is an explanation of French culinary terms. The main parts of the book range from the basics of classic cookery, garnishes and sauces, hors d'oeuvres, soups, eggs, fish, main courses, salads, and so on, through sweets and savories. If you want to learn the basic components of a classic dish you might spot on a menu, you simply turn to the category of food and look up the name. To choose one example, chicken Richelieu. You dip breast of chicken in egg, coat it with bread crumbs, and cook it in butter. You put truffle slices on top and pour maître d'hôtel butter over all.

Composition of Foods, Agricultural Handbook No. 8, United States Department of Agriculture, Bernice K. Watt and Annabel L. Merrill, 1963.
This is the best and most basic book outlining in charts the composition of foods (sodium, potassium, calcium, protein, fat, and so on) from abalone to zwieback. The composition is listed for foods of 100 gram weight and also for 1 pound weight. Unfortunately, the volume of the foods is not given (that is, half a cup of celery, a cup of carrots and so on) and there are some omissions. Generally speaking, however, it has been of enormous benefit to me, particularly as to the sodium content of foods. The volume should be of particular interest to anyone on a diet.

*Beeton's Book of Household Management, A First Edition Facsimile, Isabella Beeton, Jonathan Cape, London, 1968.
*Book of Household Management, Isabella Beeton, editor, Farrar, Straus & Giroux, 1977.
I can no more conceive of a food library without the complete *Book of Household Management* by Isabella Beeton than I could conceive of a general library without Shakespeare and the Bible. It is an incredible reference work and a historic, remarkable achievement. Isabella Beeton was a bride of twenty-one when she began the book and only twenty-eight when she died. If you can find it, by all means buy the facsimile edition printed in London.

*Escoffier's Le Guide Culinaire (in English), Auguste Escoffier, translated by H. L. Cracknell and R. J. Kaufmann, Mayflower Books, 1980.

The Escoffier Cook Book, *A. Escoffier, Crown, 1941.*
A few of the finest cooks I know, those who do not read French, have
told me that they learned to cook "in a classic manner" by using *The
Escoffier Cook Book* published by Crown. It is a good translation but
almost every recipe refers you to another recipe and I find it bother-
some.

The finest, most authentic translation of the Escoffier work is that
by Messrs. Cracknell and Kaufmann. They have been true in all respects to the master, who was to many generations of chefs what Hoyle
was to game playing. Their translation is an outstanding, distinguished
work and indispensable for a complete library.

*Encyclopaedia Britannica, Eleventh Edition, *Encyclopaedia Britannica
Company, 1910.*
The eleventh edition of the Encyclopaedia Britannica is generally considered among the world's thinkers to be superior to all subsequently
published editions. I am the proud possessor of all twenty-nine
volumes of that edition. It has been invaluable to me in food research
in that I am interested in the details of the lives of many famous people
for whom chefs have chosen to name various dishes.

Reading

*The Physiology of Taste, *Jean A. Brillat-Savarin, translated by M. F. K.
Fisher, Knopf, 1971.*
M. F. K. Fisher, my favorite writer on food in the English language,
must have been born to translate Brillat-Savarin's historic book of
dissertations on dining. The book is essential for a fine library concerning food but you may find certain sections of it a little tedious, a bit
like *War and Peace* or the works of Marcel Proust. There are many
enchanting sections, however. His chapters about hunting in Connecticut during a visit to America (he played piano in a Manhattan theater
during his days of exile here) and his essays on oysters would make the
volume worth owning for their sake alone.

*The Art of Eating, *M. F. K. Fisher, Random House, 1976.*
Of all the books on food that are dedicated to the art of eating, this
is the one volume that has given me the most pleasure. My reaction

to the book is about summed up in the introduction by Clifton Fadiman, who calls Mrs. Fisher "the most interesting philosopher of food now practicing in our country." He also speaks of the one line about food that I most wished I had written: "There is a communion of more than our bodies when bread is broken and wine is drunk. And that is my answer, when people ask me: Why do you write about hunger, and not wars or love." *The Art of Eating* is a collection of works by the author. They include *Serve it Forth, Consider the Oyster, How to Cook a Wolf, The Gastronomical Me,* and *An Alphabet for Gourmets.*

The Glorious Oyster, *Edited by Hector Bolitho, Horizon Press, 1960.*
This is an enchanting book about oysters, perhaps the best book I know that is dedicated to a single item of food. It is a cunning collection of the author's own experiences in dining on oysters, essays concerning the reproduction and growth of oysters, oyster culture, the anatomy and physiology of oysters, plus an anthology. I could quote many passages that illustrate my enthusiasm for the book but this will suffice: "We came upon a place where the oysters grew, packed together, close as grapes. My companion put the basket on the ground, and took out two bottles, two glasses, two plates and two forks. I produced nothing but a chisel. I broke the oysters off, one by one, choosing the big ones of tidy shape. The outside of their shells were still wet from the sea. We pried them open, carefully, to save the liquor from spilling. Then we placed them, eighteen upon each plate. My friend produced lemon and red pepper and I began to eat.
" 'Wait,' he said. He opened the bottles, one of champagne and one of stout and filled the glasses. Thus I came to the eating of oysters with black velvet, sitting on a beach, with the blue ocean stretched before me."

Table Topics, Julian Street, Knopf, 1959.
Julian Street was a remarkable man and one of this century's great epicures and writers on gastronomy among other things. He had been a drama critic, collaborated with Booth Tarkington on a play called *The Country Cousin,* and was a founder of the New York branch of the Wine and Food society. He died in 1947. For many years he wrote a pamphlet for a wine and liquor importer and it was called "Table Topics." The pamphlets contained hundreds of essays, poems, and anecdotes about food and wine. Plus recipes. This is a highly selective assortment of pieces from those pamphlets. It was here that I first discovered a favorite and often repeated anecdote about wine.

"A gourmet ordered with dinner in a restaurant a bottle of magnificent old vintage Burgundy. The waiter who brought it handled the bottle carelessly.

"Look here," exclaimed the gourmet, "you haven't shaken that bottle, have you?"

"No, sir," replied the waiter, "but I will."

The Alice B. Toklas Cookbook, *paperback, Doubleday Anchor, 1954.*
This book, since its publication, has been the darling of the food-and-wine congregation. I find it amusing for occasional reading and as a conversation piece, but it is not as consequential where recipes are concerned as some declare it to be. On the other hand, I feel that my bookshelves would be poorer without it.

Food in History, *Reay Tannahill, Stein & Day, 1973.*
A fascinating, highly readable book on the history of food. The book is scholarly without being boring and pedantic.

*The Taste of Country Cooking, *Edna Lewis, Knopf, 1976.*
This is, to my mind, one of the most engaging and best of family cookbooks. The author, a Virginian, descended from slaves, offers a warm, inspired approach to good, regional cooking.

*Culture and Cuisine: A Journey Through the History of Food, *Jean-François Revel, Doubleday, 1982.*
This is one of the most extraordinary books on the art of dining—well or poorly—I've ever had the pleasure to read. Jean-François Revel's work (originally titled *Un Festin en paroles*), as translated in English, puts him in the ranks of the finest writers on food and that includes M. F. K. Fisher and Elizabeth David. I cannot praise his work too highly. It is a masterpiece, an absolute delight to read. The fact that the author will fill your cranium—educate you as he did me—with hundreds of hitherto unobserved facts about the history and enjoyment of food may be secondary to the sheer pleasure of simply feasting on his words.

Any or all cookbooks written by Ann Seranne are cordially recommended.

My One Hundred
Favorite Recipes

D uring the course of a single year, more than three hundred recipes that have been tested in my home kitchen (many of which may have resulted from interviews with amateur or professional cooks) are printed in the daily and Sunday *New York Times*. I estimate that in the course of my tenure as food editor of *The Times* over the past quarter century, more than eight thousand recipes have run with my imprimatur.

The following recipes, the vast majority of which are the creation of Pierre Franey, are those I consider the hundred best to have appeared during my years as food editor.

Recipes

Scallop Seviche
Shrimp Baratin
Jane Berquist's Timbales au Roquefort
    Crème fraîche
Brandade de morue
Oysters Rockefeller
Clams with Blini
    Blini
Punch à la Jacques Pépin
David Eyre's Pancake
Grits and Cheddar Cheese Casserole
Oeufs à la chimay
Les oeufs en cocotte à la reine
Mock Eggs Benedict
Scotch Eggs
Salade de boeuf gribiche
    Boeuf bouilli
Grilled Beef and Romaine Salad Thai-style
Salade gourmande

Chiffonade of Lobster Chez Denis
Shrimp, Oranges, and Anchovies
    Sauce Vinaigrette with Rosemary
Turkey Soup
Cream of Pumpkin Soup
Philadelphia Pepper Pot
Long Island Bouillabaisse
Billi Bi
Tomato Soup
Reuben Sandwiches
    Russian Dressing
Côtes de veau belles des bois
Veal Chops Beauséjour
Stuffed Breast of Veal
Ossobuco Milanese
Black Pepper Veal Loaf
    Tomato Sauce
Breaded Veal Scallops
Paillard of Veal

Ann Seranne's Rib Roast of Beef
   Roasting Chart
Steak au poivre
   Fond brun
Hamburger
Mexican Flank Steak
   Corn Bread
Chili con Carne with Cubed
   Meat
Chili con Carne with Ground
   Meat
Home-cured Corned Beef
Home-cured Pastrami
Janice Okun's Buffalo Chicken
   Wings
   Blue Cheese Dressing
Broiled Racks of Lamb
Butterfly Lamb with Rosemary
Couscous
   Hot Pepper Sauce
   Chou vert farci
Lettuce Package
Ham and Sauerkraut Balls
Paupiettes de sole aux poireaux
   Beurre blanc
Pigs' Feet Sainte-Menhould
   Sauce Diable
Rognons de veau à la moutarde
Tripes lyonnaise
Gâteau de foies blonds
   Homard au court bouillon
   Beurre de homard
Cervelles de veau maréchale
Chicken with Noodles Pari-
   sienne
   Tomato Sauce
Chicken Cutlets Pojarski
   Paprika Sauce

Lemon Chicken
Charcoal-grilled Duck, French
   Style
Stuffed Squabs Derby
   Perfect Rice
   Brown Sauce for Poultry
Shad Stuffed with Roe
Fish Mousse
   Sauce Portugaise
Fish or Seafood Orly
   Fritter Batter
   Sauce Orly
Striped Bass tout Paris
   Lobster Sauce Américaine
   Fish Broth
   Fish Velouté
Whole Salmon Baked in Foil
   White Wine Sauce
   Dill and Cucumber Mayon-
   naise
Saumon à l'Oseille
Coulibiac of Salmon
   Salmon and Mushrooms with
   Velouté
   Brioche Dough
   Crêpes
   Rice and Egg Filling
   Vésiga
A Smoked Fish and Bagel
   Brunch
Broiled Kippered Herring
Pilaf of Mussels
Mussels Marinière
Moules frites
   Tartar Sauce
Batter-fried Shrimp
   Beer Batter
   Hot Mustard

Marmalade and Mustard
  Sauce
Mrs. Reardy's Shrimp and Arti-
  choke Casserole
Garides mi Feta
Coquilles Saint-Jacques
Jean Vergnes' Seafood Crêpes
  Crepes with fines herbes
  Curry Sauce
  Sauce Piquante
Chinese Fire Pot
  Shrimp Balls
  Fish Balls
  Pork Balls
Braised Endive
Deep-fried Mushrooms
Le Cirque's Spaghetti Primavera
Fettuccine alla Romana
Curried Sweetbreads with Fet-
  tuccine
Pesto with Pistachios
My Mother's Chicken Spaghetti

Crème Brûlée
Lemon Lotus Ice Cream
Grapefruit Sherbet
Granité de fruits au cassis
Granité au citron
Ann Seranne's Pumpkin Cream
  Pie
Soufflé au gingembre
Minetry's Miracle
Charlotte Russe with Kirsch
Hazelnut Cheesecake
French Bread-and-butter Pud-
  ding
Crème renversée au caramel
Bavarois à la vanille
  English Custard
Oeufs à la neige
Mousse au chocolat
Viennese Crescents
Lora Brody's Chocolate Cherry
  Torte
Chocolate Glaze

Scallop Seviche

1 ½ pounds (about 2 cups) fresh bay scallops
⅓ cup chopped onion
⅔ cup fresh lime juice
¼ cup tomato juice
1 tomato, skinned and chopped
¼ cup olive oil
⅓ cup finely diced seeded green pepper
⅛ teaspoon Tabasco sauce, or to taste
1 clove garlic, finely chopped
1 tablespoon finely chopped parsley
½ teaspoon dried thyme
Salt and freshly ground pepper to taste

Rinse scallops and pat dry. Place in a bowl with remaining ingredients, cover, and allow to stand in refrigerator several hours or overnight. The lime juice does all the "cooking" that is necessary. Serve in scallop shells.

YIELD: 6 to 8 appetizer servings.

Shrimp Baratin

4 tablespoons butter
36 medium-size or 18 extra-jumbo-size shrimp, shelled and deveined
Salt to taste
2 tablespoons finely minced shallots
Freshly ground pepper to taste
1 teaspoon lemon juice
3 tablespoons warm Cognac

1. Melt the butter in a chafing dish and, when hot, add the shrimp in one layer. Sprinkle with salt. Cook shrimp until pink on one side, then turn to cook other side, a total of about 4 minutes.

2. Sprinkle shrimp with shallots, pepper, and lemon juice and continue cooking, stirring. Sprinkle with warm Cognac and ignite. Spoon sauce over and over shrimp as flame burns. Serve immediately on warm plates as a first course.

YIELD: 4 or more servings.

Jane Berquist's Timbales au Roquefort

¼ cup Roquefort cheese
2 tablespoons butter
¼ cup Philadelphia cream cheese
Freshly ground pepper to taste
Paprika to taste
3 eggs
2 to 3 tablespoons crème fraîche (see following recipe)
1 tablespoon finely chopped chives
Fried croutons
Puréed spinach or braised spinach in butter, optional

1. Preheat oven to 350 degrees.

2. Break up the Roquefort cheese and cream it with the butter and cream cheese. Season with pepper and paprika.

3. Beat the eggs and crème fraîche together and add to the preceding mixture. The resulting mixture should not be lumpy; if so, strain through a sieve. Add the chopped chives.

4. Butter 4 baba timbale molds well. Add the mixture to each and place in a pan of hot water. Bake 15 to 20 minutes. The crème is done when it begins to pull away from the mold.

5. Unmold timbales on fried croutons and arrange on a plate with a border of puréed spinach or on a bed of braised spinach in butter.

YIELD: 4 servings.

NOTE: This first course dish is even better when it is served with a sauce made by reducing 1 cup of fresh cream perfumed with ½ tablespoon chopped chives.

Crème fraîche

1 cup heavy cream
1 tablespoon buttermilk

Put 1 cup heavy cream in a screw-top jar with 1 tablespoon buttermilk. Shake for 1 minute. Let stand at room temperature at least 24 hours, then refrigerate 24 hours before using.

Brandade de morue
Mousse of Salt Cod

1 ½ pounds salt cod
¾ pound potatoes, freshly baked
1 cup heavy cream, at room temperature
¼ cup warm olive oil
½ teaspoon cayenne pepper, or to taste
3 large cloves garlic, finely chopped
1 truffle, sliced, optional

1. Soak the salt cod in cold water for several hours, changing the water three times. Drain and cut it into 3-inch squares. Place the fish

in a skillet and add cold water to cover. Bring to a boil and simmer not more than 8 minutes. Drain the cod and carefully remove the bones.

2. Slice the hot baked potatoes in half and scoop the flesh into the bowl of an electric mixer. Discard the potato skins. Start the mixer on low speed and add the cod. Continue beating while adding the cream and olive oil, a little at a time. (The oil must be warm or it will not homogenize properly.)

3. Add the cayenne pepper and garlic and finish whipping briefly on high speed. The mixture should have the consistency of creamy mashed potatoes. The brandade should be served lukewarm, garnished with slices of truffle, if desired. Serve with toast triangles fried in butter.

YIELD: 6 to 8 servings.

Oysters Rockefeller

36 oysters
2 pounds or 2 (10-ounce) packages fresh spinach
1 cup finely chopped scallions
½ cup finely chopped celery
½ cup finely chopped parsley
1 clove garlic, finely minced
1 (2-ounce) can anchovies, drained
8 tablespoons butter
2 tablespoons flour
½ cup heavy cream
Tabasco sauce to taste
1 or 2 tablespoons Pernod, Ricard, or other anise-flavored liqueur
⅓ cup grated Parmesan cheese

1. Preheat the oven to 450 degrees.

2. Open the oysters, leaving them on the half shell and reserving the oyster liquor.

3. Pick over the spinach and remove any tough stems and blemished leaves. Rinse well and put in a saucepan. Cover and cook, stirring, until spinach is wilted. Cook briefly and drain well. Squeeze to remove excess moisture. Blend or put through a food grinder. There should be about 2 cups.

4. Put the scallions, celery, and parsley into the container of a food processor or an electric blender and blend. There should be about 1 cup finely blended.

5. Chop the garlic and anchovies together finely.

6. Heat 4 tablespoons of butter in a skillet and add the scallion and celery mixture. Stir about 1 minute and add the anchovy mixture. Cook, stirring, for about 1 minute and add the spinach. Stir to blend.

7. Heat the remaining 4 tablespoons of butter in a saucepan and add the flour. Blend, stirring with a wire whisk, and add the oyster liquor, stirring vigorously with the whisk. Stir in the cream. Season with Tabasco. Do not add salt. Add the spinach mixture and Pernod. Let cool.

8. Spoon equal amounts of the mixture on top of the oysters and smooth over the tops. Sprinkle with Parmesan cheese. Bake for about 25 minutes, or until piping hot.

YIELD: 6 servings.

NOTE: The same spinach topping is equally good (some think it is better) with clams on the half shell.

Clams with Blini

36 littleneck clams
2 tablespoons finely chopped shallots
½ cup dry white wine
Freshly ground pepper
3 tablespoons butter
3 tablespoons flour
2 tablespoons Pernod, Ricard, or other anise-flavored liqueur
2 egg yolks
3 tablespoons heavy cream
4 teaspoons finely chopped fresh parsley
1 tablespoon finely chopped fresh tarragon, or half the amount dried
A few drops Tabasco sauce
18 blini (see following recipe)

1. Open the clams or have them opened. Save the clams and liquid in separate batches. There should be about 1¼ cups clams and 1⅓ cups clam liquid. Chop the clams coarsely and set aside. Do not chop the clams too fine.

2. Add the chopped shallots and wine to a small skillet and cook down until almost all the wine has evaporated. Add the clam liquid. Add a generous amount of pepper and bring to the boil.

3. Blend the butter and flour until smooth.

4. Remove the saucepan from the heat and gradually add the butter-

flour mixture, a little at a time, stirring constantly with a wire whisk. When thickened, add 1 tablespoon of the Pernod and return to the heat.

5. Blend the yolks and cream and add gradually to the sauce, stirring constantly. Do not boil or the eggs will curdle. You must heat it, however, so that the yolks lose their raw taste.

6. Add the parsley and tarragon. Add Tabasco, remaining Pernod, and pepper to taste.

7. Add the clams and heat without boiling. The more the clams cook the more they toughen.

8. Serve 3 blini on each of six plates and spoon equal portions of the clams in sauce over them.

YIELD: 6 servings.

NOTE: The above recipe specifies, for a very good reason, the use of littleneck clams. When purchasing the clams, select the smallest ones available. The smallest clams are much more tender than, say, the larger cherrystones. Chowder clams would not be acceptable.

Blini

1 cup buckwheat or rye flour
½ cup all-purpose flour
2 eggs, separated
4 teaspoons granular yeast
1 ½ cups milk
Salt
4 tablespoons heavy cream
4 tablespoons chopped dill

1. Combine the flours in a mixing bowl and add the egg yolk. Dissolve the yeast in the milk and add it, stirring with a wire whisk. Add salt to taste. Set in a warm place and let stand for about 2 hours, covered with a towel.

2. When ready to cook, add the cream and chopped dill. Beat the egg white and fold it in. Cook in a crêpe pan as with ordinary crêpes.

YIELD: 18 blini.

Punch à la Jacques Pépin

1 ½ cups sugar
2 tablespoons peppercorns
1 piece dried ginger
2 bay leaves
2 cardamom seeds
3 pieces mace
1 teaspoon shaved nutmeg, or ¼ teaspoon grated
1 cinnamon stick
1 (1-inch) piece vanilla bean, or 1 teaspoon pure vanilla extract
3 strips lemon peel, yellow part only
3 strips orange peel, orange part only
2 cups water
3 cups orange juice
1 cup lemon juice
2 bottles light rum
1 cup Cognac
1 cup Cointreau
3 ½ to 4 quarts ice cubes
2 orange wedges, seeded, for garnish
1 pint strawberries, washed and drained, sliced or left whole, for garnish

1. Combine the sugar, peppercorns, ginger, bay leaves, cardamom seeds, mace, nutmeg, cinnamon, vanilla, lemon and orange peels, and water in a saucepan. Bring to a boil and simmer 25 minutes. Let the infusion stand until cool. Chill, if desired. Strain.

2. Combine the infusion with the orange and lemon juices, rum, Cognac, and Cointreau and stir to blend. When ready to serve, pour the punch into a bowl and add the ice. There should be about one and one-half times as much ice as there is punch. Immediately garnish the bowl with the orange wedges and strawberries and serve.

YIELD: 40 to 50 servings.

David Eyre's Pancake

½ cup flour
½ cup milk
2 eggs, lightly beaten
Pinch of nutmeg

---

4 tablespoons butter
2 tablespoons confectioners' sugar
Juice of ½ lemon

1. Preheat the oven to 425 degrees. In a mixing bowl, combine the flour, milk, eggs, and nutmeg. Beat lightly. Leave the batter a little lumpy.

2. Melt the butter in a 12-inch skillet with heatproof handle. When very hot, pour in batter. Bake in oven 15 to 20 minutes, or until golden brown.

3. Sprinkle with sugar and return briefly to the oven. Sprinkle with lemon juice, then serve with jelly, jam, or marmalade.

YIELD: 4 to 6 servings.

Grits and Cheddar Cheese Casserole

4 cups water
1 teaspoon salt
1 cup uncooked quick grits
¼ pound butter plus butter for greasing casserole
¾ pound Cheddar cheese, grated
Freshly ground pepper
2 tablespoons Worcestershire sauce
1 or 2 cloves garlic, minced
Tabasco sauce (see note)
2 egg whites

1. Bring water to the boil and add salt. When it is boiling vigorously, add grits slowly. Return to the boil and cook over direct heat, stirring, for 2½ minutes. While still hot, stir in remaining ingredients, except egg whites. Let cool.

2. Meanwhile, preheat the oven to 400 degrees.

3. Beat whites until stiff and fold them into grits mixture. Pour into a buttered 1½-quart casserole or soufflé dish and bake until puffed and lightly browned on top, about 20 minutes. Serve immediately with meat or poultry.

YIELD: 8 or more servings.

NOTE: 1 tablespoon or more chopped mild chilies (Ortega or El Paso brands) may be used instead of the Tabasco.

Oeufs à la chimay
Eggs with Mornay Sauce

6 hard-cooked eggs
5 tablespoons butter
1 tablespoon olive oil
1 tablespoon minced onion
¼ pound mushrooms, finely chopped
2 tablespoons tomato purée
1 teaspoon chopped fresh parsley
½ teaspoon salt
¼ teaspoon pepper
2 tablespoons flour
½ cup milk
½ cup light cream
2 tablespoons grated Swiss cheese
3 tablespoons freshly grated Parmesan cheese
Dash of cayenne pepper
½ teaspoon Dijon mustard

1. Preheat the oven to 425 degrees.
2. Halve the eggs lengthwise and remove yolks.
3. Melt 1 tablespoon of the butter, add the oil, and sauté the onion until tender but not browned. Add the mushrooms and cook quickly 2 or 3 minutes.
4. Add the tomato purée, parsley, ¼ teaspoon of the salt, and ⅛ teaspoon of the pepper. Sieve the egg yolks and add.
5. Fill the egg whites with the mushroom mixture and place in a greased baking dish.
6. Melt 2 tablespoons of remaining butter and blend in the flour. Stir in the milk and cream slowly. Bring to the boil, stirring.
7. Stir in the grated Swiss cheese and 2 tablespoons of the Parmesan cheese. Add the remaining salt and pepper, the cayenne, and mustard.
8. Finish the mornay sauce by whirling in the remaining 2 tablespoons of butter until it is just blended.
9. Coat the stuffed eggs with the mornay sauce and sprinkle with the remaining Parmesan cheese.
10. Bake to reheat the eggs, 5 to 10 minutes.
YIELD: 3 or 4 servings.

Les oeufs en cocotte à la reine

Eggs in Ramekins with Creamed Chicken

½ chicken breast with skin and bones intact
1 carrot, scraped and sliced
1 rib celery with leaves, sliced
1 small onion, peeled and left whole
Fresh or canned chicken broth or water
Salt and freshly ground pepper
4 tablespoons (approximately) butter
2 tablespoons flour
Cayenne pepper to taste
¾ cup heavy cream
⅛ teaspoon freshly grated nutmeg, or to taste
12 eggs

1. Place the chicken breast in a small saucepan and add the carrot, celery, onion, chicken broth to cover, salt and pepper to taste. Bring to the boil and simmer partly covered for about 20 minutes. Let the chicken cool in the broth.

2. Preheat the oven to 400 degrees.

3. Remove the chicken and reserve the broth. Remove and discard the skin and bones. Cut the chicken meat into ½-inch or slightly smaller cubes. Reserve.

4. Melt 2 tablespoons of butter in a saucepan and stir in the flour. Add 1 cup of the reserved chicken broth, stirring rapidly with a wire whisk. Cook, stirring, until thickened and smooth. Add the cayenne.

5. Heat 1 tablespoon of butter in a skillet and add the cubed chicken, salt and pepper to taste. Cook, stirring gently, about 1 minute. Add the sauce and stir gently, just enough to blend. Add ¼ cup heavy cream and nutmeg and bring just to the boil. Keep warm.

6. With the remaining butter, lightly grease 12 ramekins, or cocottes. Sprinkle with salt and pepper to taste.

7. Spoon about 2 tablespoons of the chicken sauce into the bottom of each ramekin.

8. Break 1 egg into each ramekin and spoon about 2 teaspoons of heavy cream on top of each egg. Sprinkle with salt and pepper to taste.

9. Arrange the ramekins in a baking dish and pour boiling water around them. This will keep them from baking too rapidly. Bake 10 to 12 minutes. When cooked, the whites should be firm and the yolks liquid or just starting to firm. Do not overcook. Serve 2 to each guest along with French bread or buttered toast.

YIELD: 6 servings.

Mock Eggs Benedict
Eggs and Ham on Toast with Cheese Sauce

4 tablespoons butter
2 tablespoons flour
1 cup milk or half milk and half cream
Salt and freshly ground pepper to taste
Tabasco sauce to taste
½ teaspoon Worcestershire sauce
⅛ teaspoon freshly grated nutmeg
¼ pound cheese, such as Cheddar, Swiss, or Gruyère, grated
¼ cup white vinegar
4 eggs
4 slices cooked ham
4 slices hot buttered toast
Paprika

1. Melt 2 tablespoons butter in a saucepan and add the flour, stirring with a wire whisk.

2. When blended, add the milk, stirring rapidly with the whisk. Season with salt, pepper, Tabasco sauce, Worcestershire sauce, and nutmeg. Remove from the heat and add the cheese, stirring until melted.

3. In a skillet bring enough water to the boil to cover the eggs when added. Add the vinegar and salt to taste. Carefully break the eggs into the water, one at a time, and cook gently until the white is set and the yolk remains runny. Carefully remove and drain on paper toweling.

4. Meanwhile heat the ham in remaining 2 tablespoons butter, turning once.

5. Arrange the toast on four hot plates. Cover each slice with a slice of ham and add a poached egg to each serving. Bring the sauce to the boil and spoon it over. Sprinkle each serving lightly with paprika and serve hot.

YIELD: 4 servings.

Scotch Eggs

8 large eggs
1 pound ground lean pork
¾ cup fresh fine bread crumbs, preferably made from untrimmed English muffins
Salt and freshly ground pepper to taste
1 ½ teaspoons crushed dried marjoram
1 tablespoon chopped fresh parsley
2 tablespoons heavy cream
Flour for dredging
¾ cup fresh fine bread crumbs, made from trimmed day-old sandwich bread
Fat for deep frying

1. Place 6 of the eggs in a saucepan and add lukewarm water to cover. Bring to the boil and simmer 12 to 15 minutes. Drain the eggs and run them immediately under cold water. Drain once more. Peel the eggs and set aside.

2. Combine the pork, bread crumbs made from English muffins, 1 raw lightly beaten egg, salt and pepper to taste, marjoram, parsley, and cream. Blend well with the hands.

3. Divide the pork mixture into 6 equal portions. Place 1 portion on a sheet of plastic wrap. Cover with another sheet of plastic wrap. Press down evenly and smooth the meat into a flat oval large enough to enclose 1 hard-cooked egg. Remove top sheet of plastic wrap.

4. Dredge the hard-cooked eggs in flour, shaking off excess. Place 1 egg in the center of the meat. Bring up the edges of the bottom sheet of plastic wrap so that the meat encloses the egg, pinching the seams together and pressing so that the egg is neatly and evenly enclosed. Remove the plastic wrap.

5. Continue until all the eggs are wrapped in the pork mixture.

6. Dredge the wrapped eggs once more in flour.

7. Break the remaining raw egg into a rimmed dish and beat lightly. Dip the flour-coated Scotch eggs in this, turning to coat evenly. Dredge the eggs in the fresh fine bread crumbs made from sandwich bread.

8. Heat the fat for frying in a deep skillet. Add the eggs and cook about 5 minutes, turning often until the meat is cooked and golden brown. Drain the eggs on paper toweling. Serve the eggs hot or lukewarm, sliced in half.

YIELD: 6 servings.

Salade de boeuf gribiche
Beef Salad with Herb Mayonnaise

24 to 36 thin slices freshly cooked boiled beef (see following recipe)
1 hard-cooked egg, put through a sieve
1 egg yolk
1 tablespoon imported mustard, preferably Dijon or Düsseldorf
1 tablespoon white vinegar
3 tablespoons finely chopped onion
2 tablespoons finely chopped shallots
1 tablespoon finely chopped fresh parsley
1 tablespoon chopped fresh tarragon, or use half the amount dried
1 cup peanut, vegetable, or corn oil
3 drops Tabasco sauce
½ teaspoon Worcestershire sauce
Salt and freshly ground pepper to taste
1 tablespoon cold water
1 hard-cooked egg, chopped, for garnish
Finely chopped fresh parsley for garnish

1. Arrange the meat neatly with overlapping slices in a symmetrical pattern.
2. To prepare the sauce, put the sieved egg, egg yolk, mustard, vinegar, onion, shallots, parsley, and tarragon in a mixing bowl.
3. Using a wire whisk, stir to blend, then gradually add the oil, stirring vigorously and continuously. It should thicken like mayonnaise.
4. Season the sauce with the Tabasco, Worcestershire sauce, salt and pepper to taste, and thin it by beating in the water.
5. Spoon all or part of the sauce over the meat. Garnish with chopped egg and parsley and serve cold.
YIELD: 4 to 6 servings.

Boeuf bouilli
Boiled Beef for Summer Salads

5 pounds lean brisket or boneless shin of beef
5 pounds beef bones, such as shin bones, cracked
1 large onion stuck with 4 cloves
3 to 6 carrots, trimmed and scraped, but left whole

3 large ribs celery, trimmed and broken in half
2 or 3 leeks, trimmed and tied together, optional
6 sprigs fresh parsley
4 cloves garlic, peeled
2 bay leaves
Salt and freshly ground pepper to taste
½ teaspoon dried thyme
2 small turnips, peeled, optional

1. Combine all the ingredients in a large kettle and add water to cover (about 1 gallon). Cook, carefully skimming the surface as necessary to remove foam and scum. After about 1 hour cover closely and continue cooking 1½ hours longer, or until the meat is tender.

2. Slice the beef for salad while the meat is still lukewarm. Use broth for soups.

YIELD: About 6 servings.

Grilled Beef and Romaine Salad Thai-style

THE GREENS
1 large head (about 1½ pounds) romaine lettuce, rinsed and cut up or broken with fingers as for salad
1 large or 2 medium-size cucumbers, peeled and thinly sliced (about 1 cup)
1 red onion, thinly sliced
10 to 12 firm radishes, trimmed and thinly sliced (about 1 cup)
2 ripe red tomatoes, cored and cut into eighths, or sliced
1 bunch scallions, trimmed and cut into 1-inch lengths (about ¾ cup)
16 fresh mint leaves
16 fresh basil leaves
½ cup loosely packed fresh coriander leaves (also known as Chinese parsley and cilantro)

THE SAUCE
1 cup (more or less) oriental fish sauce (see note)
½ to 1 teaspoon powdered hot red chilies (see note)

THE MEAT
8 thin slices (about 1½ pounds) top round, sirloin, or club steak
Salt and freshly ground pepper to taste
¼ cup peanut, vegetable, or corn oil

1. Prepare a charcoal or other grill for cooking the meat. This should be done before starting to prepare the ingredients.

2. Prepare all the greens as indicated and combine in a salad bowl.

3. Combine the ingredients for the sauce and set aside.

4. Brush meat with oil. Sprinkle with salt and pepper. Grill meat on both sides, about 2 minutes to a side or longer, depending on the desired degree of doneness.

5. Quickly, while the meat is still hot, cut the slices into ½-inch strips and add them to the greens. If there are any accumulated meat juices, add them to the sauce. Pour the sauce over all and toss. Serve immediately with hot rice or long loaves of bread.

YIELD: 8 servings.

NOTE: Either Vietnamese fish sauce (nuoc nam) or Thai fish sauce (nam pla) may be used in this recipe. Fish sauce and powdered red chilies are widely available in Chinese markets.

Salade gourmande
Foie Gras Salad

THE BASIC SALAD
½ pound green beans, the fresher and smaller the better
Salt
24 asparagus spears
2 ripe, firm, unblemished avocados
Lettuce leaves, preferably from red leaf or Boston lettuce, although other lettuce
    such as endive or watercress could be used
1 (½-pound) can pure foie gras
1 large or 2 small black truffles, sliced and cut into fine (julienne) strips

THE DRESSING
1 teaspoon imported mustard, preferably Dijon or Düsseldorf
Salt and freshly ground pepper
2 tablespoons cider vinegar
¼ cup peanut oil
¼ cup olive oil
⅛ teaspoon sugar

1. Snip off and discard the tips of the green beans. Cut the beans into uniform 2-inch lengths. Drop the pieces into boiling salted water to cover and cook 5 to 8 minutes, depending on size. Do not overcook.

When done, the pieces should be crisp-tender. Drain and let cool to room temperature.

2. Cut the tips, about 2 inches in length, from the asparagus. Set the remaining sections of the asparagus aside for another use such as in soups, salads, and so on. Rinse the asparagus tips well under cold running water. Drain and drop them into boiling salted water to cover. Cook 3 to 7 minutes, depending on thickness. When done, the pieces should be crisp-tender. Drain and let cool to room temperature.

3. When you are ready to serve, peel, halve, and pit the avocados. Cut the halves into eighths.

4. Arrange a few lettuce leaves on six chilled salad plates. If red lettuce is available, arrange it so that the red perimeter of the lettuce will show as a border for the salads.

5. Arrange equal portions of the green beans in the center of each salad, then a layer of asparagus tips and avocado wedges over the beans. If the foie gras comes in a terrine or crock, spoon equal amounts of it in the center of the vegetables. If it is a "bloc" or tunnel-shape of foie gras, cut it into 12 portions. Arrange equal amounts of foie gras on each salad. Sprinkle each serving with the shredded truffles.

6. Place the mustard in a mixing bowl and add salt and pepper to taste. Add the vinegar, stirring with a wire whisk. Gradually add the oils, stirring rapidly with the whisk. Add the sugar and blend. Spoon the sauce over the salads and serve, preferably with buttered, toasted French bread.

YIELD: 6 servings.

Chiffonade of Lobster Chez Denis

2 (1 ½-pound) live lobster, or 2 cups cubed cooked lobster meat
1 egg yolk
1 tablespoon white wine vinegar
1 tablespoon imported mustard, such as Dijon or Düsseldorf
1 tablespoon tomato paste
Salt and freshly ground pepper
⅛ teaspoon cayenne pepper, or Tabasco sauce to taste
1 cup olive oil
Juice of ½ lemon
1 teaspoon chopped fresh tarragon, or ½ teaspoon dried
2 teaspoons Cognac
½ cup cubed pure foie gras, optional
¾ cup cubed, seeded tomatoes
6 to 12 leaves fresh, crisp, romaine lettuce

1. If live lobster are used, drop them into enough vigorously boiling salted water to cover. Put a lid on. Cook 10 minutes and remove from the heat. Let stand covered about 15 minutes. Drain and let cool.

2. When the lobster are cool enough to handle, crack them and remove the meat from the claws and tail. Reserve and set aside any red coral. There should be about 2 cups of meat and coral. Refrigerate until ready to use.

3. Place the yolk in a mixing bowl and add the vinegar, mustard, tomato paste, salt and pepper to taste, and cayenne. Gradually add the oil, beating vigorously with a wire whisk. Beat in the lemon juice, tarragon, and Cognac.

4. Add the lobster, foie gras, and tomatoes to the mayonnaise and fold them in with a rubber spatula. This may be done in advance and refrigerated for an hour or so.

5. When ready to serve, stack the romaine lettuce leaves and cut them into the finest possible shreds, using a heavy sharp knife. There should be about 2 cups loosely packed shreds. Add this to the salad and fold it in. Serve immediately before the shreds wilt.

YIELD: 6 to 8 servings.

Shrimp, Oranges, and Anchovies

24 raw shrimp in the shell
6 whole allspice
Salt
2 small onions, preferably the red skin variety
3 or 4 seedless navel oranges
8 flat anchovy fillets
½ cup sauce vinaigrette with rosemary (see following recipe)
Black olives, preferably imported Greek olives

1. Put the shrimp in a saucepan and add the allspice and salt to taste. Add cold water barely to cover and bring to the boil. Turn off heat and let the shrimp stand until they are at room temperature. Drain, shell, and devein. Set aside.

2. Peel and cut the onions into ¼-inch slices. Place them in a small bowl and pour boiling water over them. Stir for about 15 seconds and drain immediately. Drop them into a small bowl containing cold water and a few ice cubes. When thoroughly chilled, drain and set aside.

3. Peel the oranges and slice them. Arrange an equal number of slices on four salad plates. Arrange the shrimp on the oranges and

scatter onion rings over each serving. Garnish each with 2 anchovy fillets. Spoon the sauce vinaigrette with rosemary over each serving and add the black olives. Serve immediately.

YIELD: 4 servings.

Sauce Vinaigrette with Rosemary

2 teaspoons imported mustard, preferably Dijon or Düsseldorf
Salt and freshly ground pepper
½ teaspoon chopped garlic
4 teaspoons red wine vinegar
½ cup peanut, vegetable, or corn oil
1 teaspoon chopped fresh rosemary, or half the amount dried

1. Place the mustard in a small mixing bowl and add salt and pepper to taste, garlic, and vinegar.

2. Use a wire whisk and gradually add the oil, stirring vigorously with the whisk. Stir in the rosemary.

YIELD: About ½ cup.

Turkey Soup

1 turkey carcass
1 cup ½-inch cubes leftover cooked turkey meat, optional
16 cups water
Leftover giblet gravy, if any
1 cup coarsely chopped onion
1 bay leaf
Salt and freshly ground pepper to taste
2 whole cloves
4 sprigs fresh parsley
2 sprigs fresh thyme, or ½ teaspoon dried
3 whole carrots, trimmed and scraped
3 whole ribs celery, trimmed and scraped
½ cup broken vermicelli, cappelini, or spaghettini

1. Pick over the carcass and reserve any tender morsels of meat. Use this, if desired, for the cup of meat indicated, adding more meat as necessary.

2. Place the carcass in a kettle and set the meat aside. Add to the kettle any jellied gravy that may have accumulated on the turkey platter.

3. Add the water to the kettle. Add the leftover giblet gravy if there is any. Add the onion, bay leaf, salt, pepper, cloves, parsley, thyme, carrots, and celery. Bring to the boil and simmer partially covered 1 hour, skimming the surface as necessary.

4. Strain the soup through a sieve lined with a clean kitchen towel or a double thickness of cheesecloth. Discard all the solids except the carrots and celery.

5. Pour about 2 cups of the soup into a saucepan and add the vermicelli. Cook until just tender.

6. Add this to the soup. Cut the carrots and celery into ½-inch cubes and add them. Add the 1 cup of cubed turkey meat. Bring to the boil. Serve piping hot.

YIELD: About 14 cups.

Cream of Pumpkin Soup

1 small (about 4 pounds) pumpkin
2 tablespoons butter
½ cup coarsely chopped onion
4 tablespoons flour
4 cups chicken broth
1 teaspoon sugar
1 cup heavy cream

1. Cut off and discard the stem of the pumpkin. Split the pumpkin in half and scoop out the seeds and inner fibers. Discard. Cut the pumpkin into eighths. Cut off and discard the tough skin. Cut the pumpkin meat into 1-inch cubes. Set aside.

2. Heat the butter in a saucepan and add the onion. Cook until wilted and sprinkle with flour, stirring with a whisk. When blended, add the broth, stirring rapidly with the whisk. When blended and smooth, add the pumpkin. Simmer about 30 minutes or until pumpkin is quite tender.

3. Purée the soup in the container of a food processor or blender or put it through a food mill. Return the purée to a saucepan. Add the sugar and cream and bring just to the boil. Serve piping hot.

YIELD: 12 servings.

Philadelphia Pepper Pot

1 pound fresh honeycomb tripe
½ cup diced salt pork
½ cup chopped onion
1 green pepper, cored, seeded, and chopped
½ cup chopped celery
½ cup chopped carrots
2 cloves garlic, finely minced
1 small, hot green pepper pod, trimmed and chopped
12 cups water
5 pounds veal knuckles
Salt and freshly ground pepper
1 bay leaf
1 sprig fresh thyme, or ½ teaspoon dried
1 cup diced raw potatoes
1 teaspoon paprika
2 tablespoons butter
2 tablespoons flour
½ cup heavy cream

1. Rinse the tripe under cold running water and drain it.

2. Place the tripe on a flat surface and cut it into thin shreds. Chop the shreds into 1-inch lengths. Set aside.

3. Heat the salt pork in a kettle and, when it is rendered of fat, add the onion. Cook, stirring, until onion is wilted. Add the tripe shreds, green pepper, celery, carrots, and garlic and cook briefly. Stir in the hot pepper and water and add the veal knuckles, salt, pepper, bay leaf, and thyme. Bring to a boil and simmer partially covered 3 hours.

4. Add the potatoes and continue to cook about 1 hour or until the tripe is thoroughly tender. It should not be chewy. Sprinkle with paprika.

5. Blend the butter with the flour and stir it, bit by bit, into the soup. When the mixture is thickened slightly and boiling, stir in the cream.

YIELD: 12 servings.

Long Island Bouillabaisse

3 tablespoons olive oil
1 cup finely chopped leeks
3 cloves garlic, finely minced
1 cup chopped onion
1 ¾ cups chopped tomatoes
2 sprigs fresh thyme, or ½ teaspoon dried
2 sprigs fresh parsley
1 bay leaf
1 cup dry white wine
2 cups water
1 large teaspoon crumbled leaf saffron
Salt and freshly ground pepper
¼ teaspoon Tabasco sauce, or to taste
1 (1 ½-pound) lobster
3 tablespoons butter
1 ½ teaspoons flour
1 pound fresh red snapper, striped bass, porgy, or other white fish, cut into serving
  pieces
1 quart fresh mussels, scrubbed well
2 dozen cherrystone clams
12 raw shrimp, peeled and deveined
1 tablespoon Pernod, Ricard, or other anise-flavored liqueur, optional

1. Heat the olive oil in a large saucepan and add the leeks, garlic, and onion. Cook until wilted, then add the tomatoes, thyme, parsley, bay leaf, wine, water, saffron, salt, pepper, and Tabasco. Simmer 10 minutes.

2. Plunge a knife into the center point of the lobster where tail and carcass meet. Split tail and carcass. Cut carcass in half lengthwise. Scoop out the liver and coral and place in a small mixing bowl. Cut tail section into 4 pieces crosswise.

3. Add the carcass and any scraps of lobster to the tomato mixture. Cover and simmer 30 minutes.

4. Meanwhile, blend the butter and flour with the fingers, then mix with the reserved coral and liver.

5. Strain the tomato mixture through a sieve, pushing through as many solids as possible. Return mixture to saucepan, bring to the boil and add the red snapper, mussels, clams, shrimp, and reserved lobster tail. Simmer uncovered 15 minutes. Stir in the coral mixture and bring to the boil. Add the Pernod. Scoop into hot soup plates and serve.

YIELD: 4 servings.

Billi Bi

2 pounds mussels
2 shallots, coarsely chopped
2 small onions, quartered
2 sprigs fresh parsley
Salt and freshly ground pepper to taste
Pinch of cayenne pepper
1 cup dry white wine
2 tablespoons butter
¼ bay leaf
½ teaspoon dried thyme
2 cups heavy cream
1 egg yolk, lightly beaten

1. Scrub the mussels well to remove all exterior sand and dirt. Place them in a large kettle with the shallots, onions, parsley, salt, pepper, cayenne, wine, butter, bay leaf, and thyme. Cover and bring to a boil. Simmer 5 to 10 minutes, or until the mussels have opened. Discard any mussels that have not opened.

2. Strain the liquid through a double thickness of cheesecloth. Reserve the mussels for another use or remove them from the shells and use them as a garnish for the soup.

3. In a saucepan bring the liquid to the boil and add the cream. Return to the boil and remove from the heat. Add the beaten egg yolk and return to the heat long enough for the soup to thicken slightly. Do not boil. Serve hot or cold.

YIELD: 4 servings.

Tomato Soup

¾ cup butter
2 tablespoons olive oil
1 large onion, thinly sliced (about 2 cups)
2 sprigs fresh thyme, or ½ teaspoon dried
4 fresh basil leaves, chopped, or ½ teaspoon dried
Salt and freshly ground pepper to taste
2 ½ pounds ripe, fresh tomatoes, cored, or 1 (2-pound 3-ounce) can imported
    Italian tomatoes

3 tablespoons tomato paste
¼ cup all-purpose flour
3 ¾ cups chicken stock or canned chicken broth
8 slices crusty, day-old French bread
1 large clove garlic, split
8 teaspoons (approximately) olive oil
1 teaspoon sugar
1 cup heavy cream

1. Heat ½ cup of the butter in a kettle and add the 2 tablespoons olive oil. Add the onion, thyme, basil, salt, and pepper. Cook, stirring occasionally, until the onion is wilted.

2. Add the tomatoes and tomato paste and stir to blend. Simmer uncovered 10 minutes.

3. Place the flour in a small mixing bowl and add about 5 tablespoons of the stock, stirring to blend. Stir this into the tomato mixture. Add the remaining chicken stock and simmer 30 minutes, stirring frequently all over the bottom of the kettle to make certain that the soup does not stick.

4. Preheat the oven to 400 degrees.

5. To make croutons rub the bread slices on both sides with the garlic, then brush generously with the 8 teaspoons olive oil. Place the bread on a rack or baking sheet and bake until golden, turning once if necessary.

6. Put the soup through the finest sieve or food mill possible. Return it to the heat and add the sugar and cream. Simmer, stirring occasionally, about 5 minutes. Add the remaining butter, swirling it around in the soup.

7. Top each portion of soup with a crouton.

YIELD: 8 servings.

Reuben Sandwiches

8 slices fresh rye bread or pumpernickel
8 teaspoons melted butter
½ cup Russian dressing (see following recipe)
½ pound very lean corned beef, cut into the thinnest possible slices
¼ pound uncooked drained sauerkraut
⅓ pound Gruyère or Swiss cheese, thinly sliced

1. Preheat the oven to 400 degrees.

2. Place the bread slices on a flat surface and brush one side of each with the melted butter.

3. Turn the slices over and spread the other side with Russian dressing. Arrange equal amounts of corned beef on 4 of the slices smeared with Russian dressing. Add equal amounts of sauerkraut over the corned beef. Arrange an equal number of slices of cheese over the sauerkraut. Cover the layered slices with the remaining 4 slices of bread, Russian dressing side touching the filling.

4. Place the sandwiches on a hot griddle or a large skillet in the oven and bake briefly, just until the cheese is melted.

YIELD: 4 sandwiches.

Russian Dressing

½ cup mayonnaise
1 tablespoon chili sauce or ketchup
1 teaspoon finely grated or chopped onion
½ teaspoon horseradish
¼ teaspoon Worcestershire sauce
1 tablespoon finely chopped parsley
1 tablespoon black or red caviar, optional

Combine all the ingredients in a mixing bowl. Blend well.
YIELD: About ½ cup.

Côtes de veau belles des bois
(Veal Chops with Morels)

⅓ ounce dried morels
6 (½ pound each) veal chops
Salt and freshly ground pepper
14 tablespoons butter
2 tablespoons finely chopped shallots
Juice of ½ lemon
6 tablespoons dry white wine

1 cup heavy cream
1 tablespoon Madeira or dry sherry
¼ cup flour
1 cup chicken broth

1. Place the morels in a mixing bowl and add hot (not boiling) water to cover. Let stand until cool. Drain well and pat dry.
2. Sprinkle chops with salt and pepper; set aside.
3. Heat 4 tablespoons of butter in a skillet and add the shallots. Cook briefly, stirring, and add the morels. Cook, shaking the skillet, about 3 minutes and add the lemon juice. Cover and çook about 5 minutes. Add 2 tablespoons white wine and cover. Simmer 5 minutes. Add the cream, cover, and cook over relatively high heat about 15 minutes. At this point the cream should be fairly well reduced and thickened. Add salt and pepper to taste and the Madeira wine. Swirl 2 tablespoons of butter into the sauce.
4. Dredge the chops in flour. Heat remaining 8 tablespoons of butter in a large skillet and add the chops. Cook over high heat about 5 minutes or until nicely browned on one side. Turn and cook about 15 minutes on the other side. Do not overcook, or the chops will dry out.
5. Remove the chops to a warm serving platter. Pour off most of the fat. Add remaining 4 tablespoons white wine and cook briefly. Add the chicken broth and cook over relatively high heat until reduced to about ¼ cup. Return the chops to the skillet. Spoon and scrape the morels over all. Stir. Serve the chops with the morels in sauce spooned over.
YIELD: 6 servings.

Veal Chops Beauséjour

6 veal chops, preferably cut from the rack, each 1 ½ inches thick
Flour
¼ cup salad oil
4 tablespoons butter
6 whole cloves garlic
2 medium-size bay leaves
½ teaspoon dried thyme
Salt and freshly ground pepper
2 tablespoons wine vinegar
½ cup chicken stock
¼ cup water

1. Dredge the chops lightly on all sides in flour. Heat the oil and 3 tablespoons of the butter in a skillet large enough to hold all 6 chops. Brown the chops.

2. Scatter the garlic cloves around the chops. Cut the bay leaves into 3 pieces. Place 1 piece on each chop. Add thyme, salt, and pepper. Cook the chops, tightly covered, over moderate to low heat about 30 minutes, or until they are cooked through and the natural sauce in the skillet is syrupy. Transfer the chops to a hot serving dish and keep warm. Leave garlic and bay leaves in the skillet.

3. Add the vinegar to the skillet and cook, stirring, until it has evaporated. Add the stock and water and cook, stirring, about 5 minutes. Check seasonings. Turn off the heat and swirl in the remaining tablespoon of butter. Pour the sauce over the chops and garnish each chop with 1 clove of garlic and a piece of bay leaf. Serve immediately.

YIELD: 6 servings.

Stuffed Breast of Veal

1 (4-pound) breast of veal
1 pound spinach
1 pound ground pork
½ pound mushrooms
2 cups chopped onion
2 cloves garlic, chopped
6 shallots, chopped
2 bay leaves, chopped
½ teaspoon dried thyme
2 eggs
Salt and freshly ground pepper
4 slices white bread, made into bread crumbs
Peanut oil
1 carrot, scraped and chopped
3 sprigs fresh parsley, chopped
1 sprig fresh rosemary, optional, or ½ teaspoon dried and chopped
1 rib celery, coarsely chopped
1 to 2 cups water

1. Have the butcher trim the veal breast and reserve the bones. Have him slit a pocket in the veal.

2. Trim and rinse the spinach and cook briefly in boiling water to cover. Drain and press well.

3. Heat the oven to 400 degrees.

4. Grind the spinach, pork, mushrooms, half the onion, half the garlic, shallots, half the bay leaves, and half the thyme together. In a mixing bowl, combine the mixture with the eggs, salt, pepper, and bread crumbs. Mix with the hands and stuff the veal breast. Sew up the opening. Sprinkle with salt and pepper. Brush with oil.

5. Line a large roasting pan with veal bones and place the stuffed veal breast on them, boned side up. Scatter the remaining onion, garlic, bay leaf, thyme, carrot, parsley, rosemary, and celery over the veal. Reduce the oven heat to 350 degrees and cook the veal 30 minutes.

6. Turn breast to other side. Baste frequently. Cook 1½ hours and pour off fat.

7. Add 1 cup of water and cover with aluminum foil. Continue cooking approximately 1 hour longer, adding water if necessary. Remove aluminum foil for the last 15 minutes of cooking.

8. Transfer the meat to a serving platter and remove string. Strain the sauce from pan and heat. Serve separately with sliced veal.

YIELD: 10 to 12 servings.

Ossobuco Milanese

3 veal shanks, sawed into 3 pieces, 2 inches thick
⅓ cup flour
1 teaspoon salt
½ teaspoon freshly ground black pepper
3 tablespoons olive oil
3 tablespoons butter
½ teaspoon ground sage
1 teaspoon rosemary
1 medium-size onion, finely chopped
3 cloves garlic, minced
2 small carrots, scraped and diced
1 stalk celery, diced
1 ½ cups dry white wine
1 ¼ cups chicken stock
2 tablespoons tomato paste
1 ½ tablespoons chopped parsley
1 tablespoon grated lemon peel

1. Dredge the prepared veal shanks in the flour, which has been seasoned with the salt and pepper.

2. In a large skillet heat the olive oil and the butter. Over medium heat, cook the pieces of meat on all sides until they are golden brown. If necessary, add a little more oil or butter.

3. Arrange the meat in a Dutch oven. Stand each piece on its side so that the marrow found in the bones does not fall out as the meat cooks. Sprinkle the veal with the sage and the rosemary. Sprinkle the onion, one third of the minced garlic, the carrots, and the celery over the meat. Season with salt, if desired. Cover closely and braise for 10 minutes.

4. Remove the cover and add the wine, chicken stock, and the tomato paste. Cover the Dutch oven and simmer the dish on top of the stove for 2 hours.

5. Combine the chopped parsley, the remaining 2 cloves of minced garlic, and the lemon peel. Sprinkle mixture over the veal.

YIELD: 6 to 8 servings.

Black Pepper Veal Loaf

2 cups chopped fresh parsley (stems removed)
2 cups diced celery
½ cup water
2 pounds ground veal
1 to 2 tablespoons black peppercorns, crushed with mortar and pestle
1 egg, beaten
2 ½ teaspoons salt
¾ cup (about 2 slices) soft bread crumbs
Butter for greasing pan or mold
Tomato sauce (see following recipe)

1. Preheat the oven to 300 degrees.

2. Blend the parsley with celery and water in a food processor or blender until fine. Add mixture to veal. Add pepper, egg, salt, and crumbs. Mix well.

3. Turn mixture into a greased 9×5×3-inch loaf pan or a greased 1-quart gelatin mold. Bake 2 hours, or until meat shrinks from sides of pan. Serve with tomato sauce.

YIELD: 8 servings.

Tomato Sauce

2 *small white onions, sliced*
1 *clove garlic, halved*
3 *tablespoons olive oil*
2 *cups thinly sliced celery*
1 *cup thinly sliced carrots*
1 *bay leaf*
1 *teaspoon salt*
2 *cups (1-pound 1-ounce can) tomatoes*
¾ *cup tomato purée*
1 *cup water*
½ *teaspoon sugar*
½ *teaspoon chopped fresh basil leaves*
½ *teaspoon crumbled, dried oregano*

1. Sauté the onion and garlic in the oil in a saucepan. Add the celery, carrots, bay leaf, salt, tomatoes, purée, and water. Cover and cook slowly 1 hour.

2. Add the sugar, basil, and oregano to the saucepan. Cover and cook 15 to 20 minutes. Put through a sieve or food mill or blend in a food processor. Reheat and serve over black pepper veal loaf.

YIELD: 2¼ cups.

Breaded Veal Scallops

4 *(6-ounce) veal scallops, preferably cut from the leg*
Salt and freshly ground pepper
Flour
1 *egg*
1 *teaspoon water*
1 *cup fresh bread crumbs*
½ *cup butter*
Lemon wedges

1. Place each scallop between pieces of plastic wrap and pound with a flat mallet or the bottom of a small, heavy skillet until thin. Sprinkle lightly on both sides with salt and pepper. Dredge them lightly but thoroughly in flour.

2. Beat the egg lightly with the water and dip the floured veal in the mixture. Turn the veal in the crumbs until well coated. Pat them lightly

with the side of a heavy kitchen knife. This will help the crumbs adhere. Transfer the meat to a wire rack. Refrigerate 1 or 2 hours. This, too, will help the breading to adhere to the cutlets.

3. Heat the butter in a large skillet and, when it is hot but not brown or smoking, sauté the veal in it until golden brown on both sides.

4. Arrange the veal on a heated serving platter and garnish with lemon wedges. Serve immediately.

YIELD: 4 servings.

NOTE: If the breaded scallops are garnished with anchovies and chopped egg, they are known as veal scallops viennoise.

Paillard of Veal

½ pound thinly sliced veal steak
Salt and freshly ground pepper to taste
Oil for brushing meat
1 teaspoon butter
Lemon wedge

1. The crucial elements in cooking this dish are speed and high heat. Ideally, the paillard should be cooked on a hot grill, but a very hot skillet will do.

2. Place the veal between sheets of plastic wrap and pound it with a flat mallet until it is about ¼ inch thick.

3. Sprinkle the meat with salt and pepper and brush with about 1 tablespoon of oil on both sides.

4. Meanwhile, if a grill is to be used, fire it well. It must have an intense heat. Or heat a heavy iron skillet large enough to hold the meat so that it will cook quickly and evenly. The skillet must be very hot.

5. If a grill is used, place the steak diagonally on the grill and cook it about 10 seconds on one side. Give it a half turn on the grill (on the same side) in order to give it a diamond pattern. Cook 10 seconds and turn the meat over. Cook 10 seconds and give it a half turn to make a pattern on the other side. Cook 10 seconds.

6. If a skillet is used, add the meat when the skillet is very hot and cook about 30 seconds. Turn the meat over and cook 15 seconds on the other side.

7. Place the meat on a hot plate and rub the butter over it. Serve with the lemon wedge.

YIELD: 1 serving.

Ann Seranne's Rib Roast of Beef

1 (4 ½- to 12-pound) 2- to 4-rib roast of beef, short ribs removed
Flour
Salt and freshly ground pepper

1. Remove the roast from the refrigerator 2½ to 4 hours before cooking.
2. Preheat the oven to 500 degrees.
3. Place the roast in an open shallow roasting pan, fat side up. Sprinkle with a little flour and rub the flour into the fat lightly. Season with salt and pepper.
4. Put the roast in the preheated oven and roast according to the roasting chart, timing exactly. When cooking time is finished, turn off the oven. Do not open the door at any time.
5. Allow the roast to remain in the oven until oven is lukewarm, or about 2 hours. The roast will have a crunchy brown outside and an internal heat that will be suitable for serving as long as 4 hours.

YIELD: 2 servings per rib.

NOTE: To make thin pan gravy, remove excess fat from the meat drippings, leaving any meat pieces in the pan. Stir in ½ to 1 cup of beef stock or broth. Bring to the boil, scraping the bottom of the pan to loosen the meat pieces. Simmer for 1 minute and season to taste.

Roasting Chart

RIBS	WEIGHT WITHOUT SHORT RIBS	ROAST AT 500 DEGREES
2	4 ½ to 5 lbs.	25 to 30 min.
3	8 to 9 lbs.	40 to 45 min.
4	11 to 12 lbs.	55 to 60 min.

Steak au poivre

4 (1-pound) boneless sirloin steaks, each about 1 inch thick
¼ to ⅓ cup peppercorns
Salt
5 tablespoons butter
3 tablespoons finely chopped shallots
3 tablespoons finely chopped onion
2 tablespoons Cognac
1 cup dry red wine
1 ¼ cups brown sauce (see following recipe)
Chopped fresh parsley for garnish

1. Trim steaks of all but ¼-inch rim of fat.
2. Crush the peppercorns with mortar and pestle or crush them on a flat surface with the bottom of a heavy skillet. The peppercorns must not be too fine. Dip steaks, one at a time and on both sides, into crushed peppercorns. Press pepper into steaks with the heel of the hand. Sprinkle lightly on both sides with salt.
3. Heat 3 tablespoons butter in a skillet large enough to hold steaks, or divide butter between two smaller skillets. Brown steaks on both sides and cook to desired degree of doneness.
4. Remove steaks to a warm platter. Add shallots and onion to the skillet. Stir quickly and add Cognac and wine. Bring to a boil and stir in the brown sauce. Cook briefly, stirring. Add salt to taste. Pour in any drippings from the steak platter. Swirl the remaining butter into the sauce and pour sauce over steaks. The whole steaks may be served or they may be cut in half for 8 servings. Dot center of each steak with a generous pinch of chopped parsley.

YIELD: 4 to 8 servings.

Fond brun or demi-glace
Brown Sauce

3 pounds veal bones, cracked
1 cup coarsely chopped celery with a few leaves
½ teaspoon thyme
1 cup thinly sliced carrots
1 ½ cups coarsely chopped onion
16 cups water

16 parsley stems tied in a bundle with 1 bay leaf
16 peppercorns, crushed

1. Preheat the oven to 400 degrees.

2. Arrange the bones in one layer over a baking dish (a dish that measures about 18 × 12 × 2½ inches is suitable). Place the dish on the floor of the oven and bake for about 20 minutes, or until bones start to take on color. Stir to redistribute them.

3. Bake for 10 minutes longer and scatter the celery, thyme, carrots, and onion over the bones. Continue baking for 15 minutes, or until the bones are nicely browned.

4. Remove the pan and spoon and scrape the bones and vegetables into a kettle. Pour off any fat that may have accumulated in the pan, but do not wash it.

5. Add to the pan 2 cups of the water and stir to dissolve the brown particles that cling to the bottom and sides of the pan. Add this to the bones. Add the remaining 14 cups of water and the parsley bundle with bay leaf and peppercorns. Bring to the boil and simmer for about 5 hours. Skim the surface of scum and fat as it accumulates.

6. Strain the sauce. There should be about 5 cups. Chill. Scrape off the surface fat. Return the sauce to a saucepan and bring to the boil. Cook for about 45 minutes or until reduced to about 3 cups.

YIELD: About 3 cups.

NOTE: Leftover brown sauce can be frozen.

Hamburger

1 ½ pounds ground round steak
Salt and freshly ground pepper
4 tablespoons butter
1 teaspoon Worcestershire sauce
¼ cup chopped parsley
Juice of ½ lemon

1. Divide the meat into 4 portions and shape each portion into a round patty. Handle the meat lightly, just enough so that it holds together.

2. Sprinkle a heavy skillet with a very light layer of salt and heat the skillet until very hot. Add the patties and sear well on one side. Turn the patties and reduce the heat. Cook to the desired degree of doneness, 3 minutes or longer.

3. When the hamburgers are done, sprinkle them with salt and pepper and top each patty with 1 tablespoon of butter. Transfer the hamburgers to a hot serving platter and sprinkle with Worcestershire sauce, parsley, and lemon juice. Serve on buttered toast or on toasted buns.

YIELD: 4 servings.

Mexican Flank Steak

1 flank steak
2 tablespoons bacon fat or lard
1 ½ cups finely chopped onion
¾ cup chopped celery
½ cup finely chopped green pepper
3 cloves finely minced garlic
2 teaspoons chopped fresh thyme, or 1 teaspoon dried
Salt and freshly ground pepper to taste
Tabasco sauce to taste
4 cups crumbled corn bread (see following recipe)
2 eggs, lightly beaten
2 tablespoons hot green chili peppers (available in cans)
2 tablespoons finely chopped parsley
3 tablespoons peanut oil
½ cup chopped tomatoes
½ cup chopped carrots
1 bay leaf
1 cup beef broth
Chili powder to taste

1. Preheat the oven to 350 degrees.
2. Lay the flank steak on a flat surface and, using a long, sharp knife, slice it lengthwise in half, or have it done by a butcher.
3. Heat the bacon fat and add 1 cup of onion, ½ cup of celery, the green pepper, and one third of the garlic, finely chopped. Cook slowly until the vegetables are wilted, about 15 minutes, and add 1 teaspoon of fresh thyme, salt and pepper, and Tabasco to taste.
4. In a mixing bowl combine the corn bread with the eggs, chilies, and parsley. Add the vegetable mixture and mix well.
5. Spread equal parts of the filling on each portion of meat. Roll the meat up jelly-roll style and tie both rolls in several places with string. Sprinkle with salt and pepper and brown on all sides in the peanut oil.

Pour off most of the fat and add the remaining onion, celery, garlic, and thyme, the tomatoes, carrots, and bay leaf. Add the broth.

6. Cover closely and bake about 1 hour, or until tender. Transfer the meat to a serving platter and remove the string. Slice the meat. Strain the gravy remaining in the pan into a saucepan. Remove surface fat, add the chili powder, bring to a boil, and serve hot with the meat.

YIELD: 8 or more servings.

Corn Bread

1 (8½-ounce) can cream-style corn
1 cup yellow corn meal
3 eggs
1 teaspoon salt
½ teaspoon soda
¾ cup milk
⅓ cup melted lard, butter, or vegetable oil
½ cup grated sharp cheese
2 tablespoons butter

1. Preheat the oven to 400 degrees.

2. In a mixing bowl combine the corn, corn meal, eggs, salt, soda, milk, lard, and half the cheese. Beat well.

3. Meanwhile, put the 2 tablespoons of butter in a 1½-quart casserole (preferably a glazed Mexican earthenware casserole) or a 9-inch skillet. Place the casserole in the oven until butter is hot but not brown. Immediately pour in the corn bread mixture. Sprinkle with remaining cheese and bake 40 minutes.

YIELD: 8 servings.

Chili con Carne with Cubed Meat

5 pounds lean chuck roast
½ cup olive oil
½ cup flour
½ cup chili powder, more or less to taste
2 teaspoons cumin seeds
2 teaspoons dried oregano

6 to 10 cloves garlic, finely minced
4 cups fresh or canned beef broth
Salt and freshly ground pepper

1. Trim the meat and cut it into 1-inch cubes. Heat the oil in a deep kettle and add the cubed meat. Cook, stirring, just until the meat loses its red color.

2. Sift together the flour and chili powder and sprinkle the meat with it, stirring constantly so that the pieces are evenly coated.

3. Place the cumin and oregano in the palm of one hand. Rub the spices between the palms, sprinkling over the meat. Add the garlic and stir. Add the broth, stirring the meat constantly. Add salt and pepper and bring to the boil. Partly cover and simmer for 3 to 4 hours, or until the meat almost falls apart. If necessary, add more broth as the meat cooks. This chili should not be soupy, however. Serve with pinto beans, if desired, and chopped lettuce, sour cream, grated Cheddar cheese, chopped fresh coriander leaves, and hot pepper flakes.

YIELD: 8 to 12 servings.

Chili con Carne with Ground Meat

¼ pound beef suet from the kidney, or 3 tablespoons bacon fat
3 cups chopped onion
1 ½ cups finely chopped green pepper
3 pounds ground beef
3 tablespoons finely chopped garlic
¾ teaspoon ground pepper
6 tablespoons chili powder
1 tablespoon crushed dried oregano
1 teaspoon ground cumin
1 teaspoon celery salt
1 tablespoon red wine vinegar
1 (35-ounce) can tomatoes with tomato paste and basil leaf or use 4 cups canned imported tomatoes and three tablespoons tomato paste
1 cup water
Salt and freshly ground pepper to taste
1 tablespoon chili paste with garlic, available in Chinese and oriental groceries, optional

1. Put the suet in a large deep casserole or Dutch oven. Cook until rendered of fat. Scrape out solids. Pour off all but 3 tablespoons of fat.

2. Add the onion and green pepper. Cook until the onion is wilted.

3. Add the meat. Using a heavy metal spoon, cook, chopping down with the spoon to break up lumps in the meat.

4. Add the garlic and black pepper and stir to blend. Add the chili powder, oregano, cumin, and celery salt. Stir and add the vinegar. Add the tomatoes with tomato paste, water, salt, pepper, and, if desired, chili paste with garlic. Bring to the boil, stirring to break up tomatoes. Cook uncovered over low heat for about 30 minutes.

YIELD: 8 servings.

Home-cured Corned Beef

7 quarts water
3 cups (approximately) kosher salt
1 raw egg in the shell for testing brine
1 (6- to 9-pound) brisket of beef
3 whole cloves garlic, peeled
20 cloves
20 peppercorns
1 bay leaf
6 sprigs fresh thyme, or 1 teaspoon dried
½ tablespoon saltpeter, available in drugstores

1. To cure the brisket, you will need a large earthenware, enamel, or stainless steel crock. Pour the water into the crock and add the salt, stirring to dissolve it. Add the egg. The egg is used to test the salt content of the brine. If the egg floats in the solution, it is ready. If it does not float, continue adding salt a little at a time, stirring to dissolve, until the egg floats. Remove the egg.

2. Add the brisket to the brine. Add the garlic, cloves, peppercorns, bay leaf, thyme, and saltpeter. Stir well. Place a clean, heavy weight on the meat to make certain it is covered. Place a lid on the crock and refrigerate for from 8 to 12 days. Turn the brisket occasionally, but keep it weighted down.

3. When ready to cook the corned beef, remove it from the brine and rinse it well. Put it in a kettle with water to cover and add 1 bay leaf, 1 sliced onion, 6 sprigs fresh thyme, 16 peppercorns, 1 clove garlic, 1 carrot, cut into pieces, and 2 ribs celery, cut into pieces. Bring to the boil and simmer partially covered for 2 to 3 hours.

4. Remove the corned beef and cut it into the thinnest possible slices. Serve with rye bread, mustard, and garlic pickles.

YIELD: 12 or more servings.

Home-cured Pastrami

1 (4 ½-pound) slab of beef flanken
½ cup salt, preferably kosher
2 tablespoons sugar
2 teaspoons ground ginger
1 teaspoon saltpeter, available in drugstores
1 tablespoon coriander seeds
¼ cup peppercorns
1 clove garlic, finely chopped

1. Pat the meat dry.

2. Combine the salt, sugar, ginger, and saltpeter in a mixing bowl.

3. Coarsely crush the coriander seeds and peppercorns, using a mallet or the bottom of a clean, heavy skillet. Or grind coarsely. Add them to the bowl along with the garlic. Blend well. Rub the mixture into the meat.

4. Place the seasoned meat in a plastic bag and seal tightly. Place in a tray large enough to hold it. Refrigerate and turn the bag over once a day so that the meat seasons evenly. Let the meat cure for 7 or 8 days.

5. Remove the meat and drain the liquid that accumulated. Save the solid seasonings and discard the liquid. Rub the solid seasonings back into the meat. Use a needle to run a string through the meat. Tie the ends of the string together. Suspend the meat on the string and let it dry in a cool, windy place or use an electric fan. Dry for about 24 hours.

6. Hang the meat in a smoker and smoke 2½ to 3 hours at about 150 to 160 degrees, or smoke according to the manufacturer's instructions.

7. To cook, cover with unsalted cold water and simmer partially covered 2 hours or until meat is tender.

8. Remove the pastrami and cut it into the thinnest possible slices. Serve with rye bread, mustard, and garlic pickles.

YIELD: 8 to 12 servings.

Janice Okun's Buffalo Chicken Wings

24 (about 4 pounds) chicken wings
Salt, optional
Freshly ground pepper to taste
4 cups peanut, vegetable, or corn oil
4 tablespoons butter
2 to 5 tablespoons Frank's Louisiana Red Hot Sauce
1 tablespoon white vinegar
2 ½ cups blue cheese dressing (see following recipe)
Celery sticks

1. Cut off and discard the small tip of each wing. Cut the main wing bone and second wing bone at the joint. Sprinkle the wings with salt, if desired, and pepper to taste.

2. Heat the oil in a deep-fat fryer or large casserole. When it is quite hot, add half of the wings and cook about 10 minutes, stirring occasionally. When the chicken wings are golden brown and crisp, remove them and drain well.

3. Add the remaining wings and cook about 10 minutes or until golden brown and crisp. Drain well.

4. Melt the butter in a saucepan and add 2 to 5 tablespoons of the hot sauce and vinegar. Put the chicken wings on a warm serving platter and pour the butter mixture over them. Serve with blue cheese dressing and celery sticks.

YIELD: 4 to 6 servings.

Blue Cheese Dressing

1 cup homemade mayonnaise
2 tablespoons finely chopped onion
1 teaspoon finely minced garlic
¼ cup finely chopped parsley
½ cup sour cream
1 tablespoon lemon juice
1 tablespoon white vinegar
¼ cup crumbled blue cheese
Salt to taste, optional
Freshly ground pepper to taste
Cayenne pepper to taste

1. Combine all of the ingredients in a mixing bowl.
2. Chill for an hour or longer.
YIELD: About 2½ cups.

Broiled Racks of Lamb

1 double rack of lamb
1 tablespoon (approximately) peanut, corn, or vegetable oil
Salt and freshly ground pepper
4 tablespoons fresh fine bread crumbs
2 tablespoons finely chopped parsley
½ teaspoon finely minced garlic
3 tablespoons melted butter

1. Choose a double rack of lamb, consisting of 2 racks joined together.
2. Down the center of the double rack is the backbone. You should have this hacked totally away. If you ask your butcher to do this, tell him that you want the "chine" bone of the rack or racks of lamb hacked away.
3. There is a thin, lean layer of meat with a small amount of fat on the top of the rack. Using the fingers and a paring knife, carefully remove this layer.
4. With a sharp knife, preferably a boning knife, cut away all the fat from the tops of the ribs. There is a small layer of fat covering the meaty loin at the top of the ribs. Cut away most of this fat, but leave a very thin layer.
5. Preheat the broiler to high. If the oven unit is separate from the broiler, preheat the broiler to high and *also* preheat the oven to 475 degrees. Arrange the racks of lamb, meaty side down, in a shallow baking dish. Sprinkle the lamb with about 1 tablespoon peanut, vegetable, or corn oil, salt and freshly ground pepper to taste.
6. Place the baking dish under the broiling unit so that the racks are about 3 inches from the source of heat. Cook 4½ to 5 minutes.
7. Turn the racks meaty side up. Return to the broiler. Leave the broiler door open. Broil about 2½ minutes.

8. Meanwhile, combine the bread crumbs, parsley, and garlic in a small bowl. Blend well.

9. Remove the racks and sprinkle the parsley mixture over the top. Spoon the melted butter over all. If the broiler and the oven are a single unit, turn off the broiler and lower the oven temperature to 475 degrees as soon as racks are removed from the broiler. Otherwise remove the baking dish and transfer it to the preheated oven. Bake the racks 4 to 5 minutes (or longer if you insist on well-done lamb). If the lamb is not brown enough on top, run it briefly under the broiler. Carve the lamb between each 2 ribs and serve.

YIELD: 4 to 6 servings.

Butterfly Lamb with Rosemary

1 (5 ½- to 6-pound) boned leg of lamb in 1 piece
¼ cup olive oil
1 tablespoon lemon juice
1 tablespoon dried, crumbled rosemary
2 teaspoons coarsely ground black pepper
1 bay leaf

1. Trim off most of the surface fat and tough outer coating of the lamb. Place the lamb in a shallow pan that will hold it snugly.

2. Combine the oil, lemon juice, rosemary, pepper, and bay leaf. Blend well and rub the mixture all over the lamb. Cover and let stand for 2 hours or longer, unrefrigerated but in a cool place. Turn the meat occasionally as it stands.

3. Prepare a charcoal fire or preheat the broiler. Place the lamb on the fire or under the broiler, as far from the broiler heat as the rack allows. Grill or broil the meat to the desired degree of doneness. Turn the meat several times as it cooks. Cooking time will depend on whether the grill is covered. It should vary from about 20 minutes for rare meat to 40 minutes for medium well done. Let stand for 20 minutes covered with foil. Serve sliced with a little melted butter and lemon juice spooned over the lamb.

YIELD: 8 servings.

Couscous

¾ cup butter, at room temperature
4 pounds very lean leg of lamb, cut into 1 ½- to 2-inch cubes
Salt to taste
1 teaspoon grated fresh ginger, or ½ teaspoon ground ginger
Freshly grated pepper to taste
1 teaspoon crumbled stem saffron, or more to taste
¼ teaspoon ground cinnamon
3 cloves
¼ teaspoon freshly grated nutmeg
7 cups water or lamb broth (see note)
1 pound couscous
1 ½ pounds onions, cut into 1-inch slices
5 (about 1 pound) white turnips, peeled and halved or quartered, depending on size
3 carrots, scraped and quartered
3 medium zucchini, trimmed and cut into 1-inch lengths
½ cup raisins
1 cup cooked fresh or canned chick-peas
½ cup blanched almonds
6 tablespoons hot pepper sauce (see following recipe)

1. It is best to use a specially made couscous cooker (couscoussière), although one can be improvised by placing a steamer with a perforated bottom or a colander over a kettle. The steamer must be close-fitting, however.

2. Melt ½ cup of the butter in a kettle and add the meat, salt, ginger, pepper, saffron, cinnamon, cloves, and nutmeg. Turn the meat in the mixture without browning. Add the water or lamb broth. Do not add the steamer, but cover the kettle and bring to a boil. Simmer covered about 1 hour (this time may have to be decreased if the meat is unusually tender).

3. Meanwhile, line a colander with cheesecloth and add the couscous. Run cold water over the couscous until it is thoroughly dampened and let stand about 30 minutes.

4. Crumble the couscous with the fingers to get rid of any lumps. Place the steamer over the boiling stew. Do not cover. Let steam 15 minutes.

5. Remove the steamer and set it aside. Combine ¼ cup of water with salt to taste. Sprinkle this over the couscous and let stand.

6. Meanwhile, add the onions, turnips, carrots, zucchini, raisins, and chick-peas to the stew. Cover and cook 15 minutes.

7. Stir the couscous once more to break up any lumps. Return the steamer to the kettle and continue to steam 15 minutes longer.

8. The couscous is now ready to be served. Empty the cereal into a large hot bowl and stir in the remaining ¼ cup butter. Arrange the meat, vegetables, and raisins over the couscous, but do not add the liquid. Garnish with almonds. Serve the hot broth and hot pepper sauce separately.

YIELD: 6 servings.

NOTE: Lamb broth is made by placing a few meaty lamb bones in a kettle and adding 8 cups of water and salt to taste. Simmer, covered, about 1 hour.

Hot Pepper Sauce

12 dried hot red pepper pods
Salt to taste
3 tablespoons olive oil
1 tablespoon boiling water

1. Place the pepper pods in a saucepan and add water to cover. Bring to a boil and set aside. Let stand until the water is cold.

2. Drain the pepper pods and split them in half. Remove and discard the seeds. Place the pods, skin side down, on a flat surface and scrape off and accumulate the pulp in a small mixing bowl.

3. Add salt to taste and gradually beat in the oil with a wire whisk. Finally beat in the boiling water.

YIELD: About 6 tablespoons.

Chou vert farci
Stuffed Cabbage

1 (3 ½-pound) firm, unblemished cabbage
1 tablespoon butter
2 cups finely chopped mushrooms, about ½ pound
1 cup finely chopped onion
1 tablespoon finely chopped garlic
1 ½ bay leaves, finely minced
1 ½ teaspoons chopped fresh thyme or ½ teaspoon dried
½ pound chicken livers, picked over to remove any tough fibers
1 pound ground pork (with a small amount of fat included)
Salt, if desired
Freshly ground pepper
2 eggs, lightly beaten
½ cup finely chopped parsley
1 cup fine fresh bread crumbs
⅛ teaspoon freshly grated nutmeg
⅛ teaspoon allspice
1 ½ pounds chicken wings
¾ pound pork bones, chopped into two-inch pieces
½ cup coarsely chopped onion
½ cup coarsely chopped carrots
½ cup coarsely chopped celery
1 whole clove garlic
6 peppercorns
½ cup dry white wine
2 cups fresh or canned chicken broth
¼ cup tomato paste
1 cup chopped, red, ripe tomatoes or imported canned tomatoes
1 teaspoon arrowroot or cornstarch
2 tablespoons dry white wine

1. Preheat oven to 375 degrees.
2. Using a sharp knife, cut off the stem end of the cabbage. Cut out the core of the cabbage.
3. Bring a large quantity of water to the boil in a kettle. Add the cabbage and cover. Let it boil, turning the cabbage so that it cooks evenly all over. As the cabbage cooks, separate the leaves at intervals and cook from 10 to 15 minutes. Drain thoroughly.
4. Heat the butter in a skillet and add the mushrooms and finely chopped onion. Cook, stirring, until onion is wilted and mushrooms have given up their liquid. Continue cooking until liquid evaporates.

Add the finely minced garlic, half a bay leaf, and half of the thyme and stir.

5. Finely chop the livers or purée them in an electric blender or food processor. Add the livers and pork to the mushroom-and-onion mixture. Cook, stirring, about 30 seconds. Add salt and pepper to taste.

6. Spoon and scrape the mixture into a mixing bowl. Let cool briefly. Add the eggs, parsley, bread crumbs, nutmeg, and allspice. Add salt and pepper to taste and blend well.

7. Lay out a large square of cheesecloth on a flat surface. Arrange six or seven of the large cabbage leaves in the center of the cheesecloth, the edges of the leaves slightly overlapping in a circular fan shape. The stem ends of the leaves should point outward and not to the center. Cover the middle of the circle of leaves with another large leaf.

8. Spoon about one-third of the pork mixture into the center of the round layer of cabbage leaves. Spoon it almost but not quite to the outer edges of the leaves.

9. Add another layer of slightly smaller leaves. Spread this with another third of the filling. Add another layer of leaves and a final third of the filling. Put the smallest leaves in the center of the final layer of filling.

10. Bring up the edges of the cheesecloth so that the leaves and filling are returned to a whole cabbage shape. Press the large cabbage together compactly and tighten the cheesecloth all around. Tie the cheesecloth into a tight bag and cut off the excess cheesecloth at the ends.

11. Select a heavy casserole large enough to hold the stuffed cabbage. Add the chicken wings and pork bones and cook, stirring, until nicely browned. Add the coarsely chopped onion, carrots, celery, whole clove of garlic, peppercorns, and the remaining bay leaf and thyme. Cook, stirring, about one minute. Pour off most of the fat.

12. Add the wine, chicken broth, salt and pepper to taste. Add the tomato paste and stir. Add the tomatoes.

13. Arrange the cabbage tied side down and cover closely. Place in the oven and bake 2 hours.

14. Remove the cabbage from the sauce. Untie and discard the cheesecloth. Arrange the cabbage on a baking dish. Return it to the oven and bake 10 minutes.

15. Meanwhile, cook down the sauce remaining in the casserole over moderately high heat 5 minutes. Strain the sauce, pressing the solids to extract as much liquid as possible. Put the sauce in a saucepan. Blend the arrowroot or cornstarch and wine and add it to the sauce, stirring.

16. As the cabbage bakes for 10 minutes, baste it occasionally with the sauce. Serve with parsleyed potatoes.

YIELD: 10 to 12 servings.

Lettuce Package

1 large firm head iceberg lettuce
½ cup shredded bamboo shoots
12 to 16 water chestnuts, preferably fresh
6 to 8 dried black mushrooms
¾ pound coarsely ground pork
1 egg, lightly beaten
1 ½ tablespoons dark soy sauce
1 tablespoon plus 1 teaspoon cornstarch
2 tablespoons dry sherry or shao hsing wine
½ cup chicken broth
1 ½ teaspoons sugar
¼ teaspoon monosodium glutamate, optional
2 teaspoons salt
5 ½ tablespoons peanut, vegetable, or corn oil
1 cup finely diced celery

1. Peel away 16 to 20 leaves from the lettuce. If leaves are extremely large, slice in half top to bottom. Place on a serving dish. Set aside in the refrigerator.

2. Cut and chop the shredded bamboo shoots and the water chestnuts into very fine dice. Combine. Pour enough hot water over the mushrooms to cover. Let stand for 15 to 30 minutes, then drain, squeezing to extract most of the liquid. Trim off the stems and shred the mushrooms fine, then cut and chop into very fine dice.

3. Combine the mushrooms with the bamboo shoots and water chestnut mixture and set aside.

4. Combine the pork with the egg, soy sauce, and 1 tablespoon of the cornstarch. Mix well and set aside.

5. Combine the wine, half the chicken broth, the sugar, monosodium glutamate, if desired, and salt and set aside.

6. Blend the remaining teaspoon of cornstarch with the remainder of the chicken broth and set aside.

7. Heat 4 tablespoons of the oil in a wok or skillet and, when almost smoking, add the pork mixture, stirring quickly and constantly to separate the bits of pork. When the pork is cooked, add the mushroom

mixture and cook about 2 minutes, stirring. Add the wine, broth, and sugar mixture and cook about 15 seconds, stirring. Stir the cornstarch mixture to make certain it is properly blended and stir into the pork. Cook, stirring rapidly, about 15 seconds. Add the celery and stir just until the celery is heated through. Add the remaining 1½ tablespoons of oil, stirring to distribute it. This will glaze the dish.

8. Turn the dish out onto a serving platter and accompany the meat with the platter of lettuce leaves. To serve, let guests help themselves to a cold lettuce leaf, the cup of which is then filled with a spoonful of the pork. It is wrapped between the fingers, and eaten while the pork is still hot.

YIELD: 4 to 8 or more servings.

Ham and Sauerkraut Balls

4 teaspoons butter
1 ½ tablespoons flour
½ cup milk
½ pound cooked ham
½ pound sauerkraut
¼ cup finely chopped onion
½ teaspoon caraway seeds
2 teaspoons dry mustard
Freshly ground pepper
2 egg yolks
1 egg
¼ cup water
Salt
Flour for dredging
1 ½ cups fresh bread crumbs
Oil for deep frying
Lemon wedges
Hot mustard, optional, see note

1. Melt 3 teaspoons butter in a very small saucepan and add the flour, stirring with a wire whisk. Add the milk, stirring rapidly with the whisk. When blended and smooth, the sauce should be quite thick. Remove from the heat.

2. Chop the ham finely on a flat surface or grind, using the medium blade of a food grinder or food processor.

3. Press the sauerkraut to extract most of the liquid.

4. Heat the remaining 1 teaspoon of butter and add the onion. Cook, stirring, until wilted. Add the sauerkraut and cook briefly, stirring. Add the ham, caraway, dry mustard, and pepper to taste. Add the white sauce. Blend thoroughly. Add the egg yolks, stirring rapidly. Cook about 1 minute, stirring, and remove from the heat.

5. Spoon the mixture into a mixing bowl and smooth over the top. Cover with foil or plastic wrap and chill.

6. Using the fingers, shape the mixture into 28 or 30 balls.

7. Beat together the egg, water, and salt and pepper to taste. Set aside.

8. Dredge the balls lightly all over with flour. Dip them into the egg mixture to coat well and, finally, in the bread crumbs. Arrange on a rack.

9. When ready to cook, heat the oil for deep frying and cook the balls, turning as necessary, until golden brown and piping hot throughout. Drain and serve hot with lemon wedges and, if desired, hot mustard.

YIELD: 6 servings.

NOTE: To prepare hot mustard, blend ⅓ cup dry mustard with 2 tablespoons cold water, white wine, or beer. Let stand at least 15 minutes to allow the flavor to develop.

Josef ("Seppi") Renggli's
Paupiettes de sole aux poireaux
Sole Mousse in Leek Leaves

1 ¼ pounds skinless, boneless sole fillets
3 or 4 very large leeks
2 eggs
1 cup heavy cream
⅛ teaspoon freshly ground nutmeg
4 drops Tabasco sauce
Salt to taste, if desired
Freshly ground pepper to taste
2 tablespoons butter
5 tablespoons fish broth (bottled clam broth diluted with a little water may be used as a substitute)
1 cup white butter sauce (see following recipe)

1. Preheat the oven to 400 degrees.
2. Cut the sole into 1-inch cubes and chill well.
3. You will need 12 large outer leaves of leeks, the larger the better. Remove the leaves from the leeks and rinse them thoroughly. Drop the leaves into a kettle of boiling water and add salt to taste. Let simmer 2 minutes and drain. Run cold water over the leaves until well chilled. Drain. Pat dry on clean toweling.
4. Put the sole into the container of a food processor. Start blending and add the eggs while blending. Gradually add the cream, nutmeg, Tabasco sauce, salt, and pepper.
5. Open up the leek leaves and arrange them on a flat surface. Neatly trim off the top and bottom of each leak to make a rectangle about 9 inches long.
6. Place about 3 tablespoons of the mousse mixture near the base of each leek leaf. Roll up each to enclose the mousse neatly and compactly.
7. Butter a metal baking dish (a dish that measures about 14 × 8-inches) and arrange the rolls, seam side down, on the dish. Dot the rolls with any remaining butter. Pour the broth over all.
8. Cover closely and bring to the boil on top of the stove. Place in the oven and bake 15 minutes.
9. Transfer the stuffed leeks to a serving dish. Spoon the butter sauce over and sprinkle with black pepper. Serve hot.
YIELD: 6 servings.

Beurre blanc
White Butter Sauce

2 tablespoons vinegar
2 tablespoons water
2 tablespoons finely chopped shallots
½ pound butter at room temperature

Combine the vinegar and water in a saucepan and bring to the boil. Add the shallots and cook until most of the liquid evaporates. Add the butter, bit by bit, stirring rapidly with a wire whisk over moderate heat. The sauce may boil gently but you must stir rapidly. When ready, the sauce should be thickened and creamy.
YIELD: About 1 cup.

Pigs' Feet Sainte-Menhould

4 large pigs' feet (preferably with the knuckles; if not, select 4 pigs' feet and 4
pigs' knuckles)
2 ribs celery
1 tablespoon salt
Coarsely ground pepper to taste
1 onion, studded with 2 cloves
1 carrot, scraped and quartered
1 piece French bread about 5 inches long, or 3 slices ordinary bread
4 tablespoons imported mustard, preferably Dijon
Oil for baking dish
1 cup sauce diable (see following recipe)

1. Put the pigs' feet in a large saucepan and add water to cover. Add the celery, salt, pepper, onion, and carrot. Bring to the boil and simmer 2 hours. Remove the meat from the broth and cool. Reserve ½ cup of cooking liquid.

2. Meanwhile, bake the bread in a 400° oven until it is dried out and browned, but do not let it burn. Grate the bread on an ordinary cheese grater or blend it to make crumbs. Put the crumbs in a sieve and shake them to obtain crumbs of uniform size.

3. Blend the reserved ½ cup of cooking liquid with the mustard and dip the cooled pigs' feet in it. Coat well and chill.

4. Preheat the oven to 425 degrees.

5. Coat the pigs' feet with bread crumbs. Oil a baking dish and place the pigs' feet on it. Bake 30 minutes. If the pigs' feet start to burn, reduce oven heat. At the end of 30 minutes, turn pigs' feet and continue cooking 5 to 10 minutes longer, or until crisp on the outside and tender within. Serve with sauce diable.

YIELD: 4 servings.

Sauce diable
Devil Sauce

2 tablespoons coarsely chopped onion
2 shallots, finely chopped
1 clove garlic, finely chopped
15 crushed peppercorns
Pinch of thyme
½ bay leaf
¼ cup wine vinegar
1 cup beef stock
1 tablespoon cornstarch
1 tablespoon water
1 tablespoon butter
2 teaspoons imported mustard, such as Dijon or Düsseldorf

1. Cook the onion, shallots, garlic, peppercorns, thyme, bay leaf, and wine vinegar in a small saucepan until almost all the liquid has evaporated.

2. Add the beef stock and simmer 10 minutes. Blend the cornstarch with the water and stir into the simmering liquid.

3. Strain the mixture through a sieve, pushing as much of the solids through as possible. Return to the heat and bring to a boil. Remove the sauce from the heat and stir in the butter. Stir in the mustard and serve.

YIELD: About 1 cup.

Rognons de veau à la moutarde
Veal Kidneys in Mustard Sauce

2 pair (about 1 ½ pounds) veal kidneys
2 tablespoons peanut, vegetable, or corn oil
3 tablespoons butter
¼ pound mushrooms, thinly sliced
2 tablespoons finely chopped shallots
1 tablespoon Cognac
1 cup heavy cream
1 tablespoon imported mustard, such as Dijon or Düsseldorf
Toast

---

1. Pull off and discard the outer coating of fat, if there is any, from the kidneys.

2. Split the kidneys in half lengthwise. Cut away most of the tough white center core but leave a small layer intact. Cut the kidney halves into cubes, 1 inch or slightly smaller.

3. Heat the oil until hot and almost smoking in a heavy skillet. Add the kidneys and cook, stirring often, about 3 minutes. Cook only until the rare stage. Remember, they will be cooked once more. If over-cooked at any point they will become dry. Pour the kidneys into a sieve and set aside to drain.

4. Add 2 tablespoons of butter to another heavy skillet and add the mushrooms. Cook, stirring often, about 2 minutes, and add the shallots. Cook 3 minutes, stirring often, and sprinkle with Cognac. Add the cream and cook, stirring, about 3 minutes.

5. Add the kidneys, bring to the boil, and add the mustard, stirring to blend. Swirl in the remaining butter and serve hot on toast.

YIELD: 4 servings.

Tripes lyonnaise
Tripe Sautéed with Onions

1 ¾ pounds cleaned, ready-to-cook tripe
Salt and freshly ground pepper to taste
4 whole allspice
2 whole cloves
2 sprigs fresh thyme, or 1 teaspoon dried
1 bay leaf
3 small ribs celery, trimmed
1 carrot, trimmed and scraped
3 sprigs fresh parsley
1 large onion
3 tablespoons butter
1 clove garlic, finely minced
1 or 2 tablespoons red wine vinegar
2 tablespoons finely chopped fresh parsley

1. Cut the tripe into 3 or 4 pieces and place them in a kettle. Add water to cover, salt, pepper, allspice, cloves, thyme, bay leaf, celery, carrot, and parsley sprigs. Bring to the boil. Partly cover and simmer until tender. This may vary from a few minutes to an hour depending on the tripe. Test often. When cooked, the tripe should be quite tender but not mushy. Drain.

2. When the tripe is cool, shred it with a knife.

3. Chop the onion. There should be about 3 cups.

4. Heat the butter in a heavy skillet and add the tripe, salt, and pepper. Cook, stirring often, about 10 minutes. Add the onion and continue cooking and stirring, shaking the skillet to prevent sticking, until nicely browned or golden. Sprinkle with garlic, salt, and pepper and stir. Sprinkle with vinegar and serve garnished with chopped parsley.

YIELD: 2 to 4 servings.

Gâteau de foies blonds
Baked Mousse of Chicken Livers

THE MOUSSE OF CHICKEN LIVERS
¼ pound firm, fresh marrow (see note)
⅔ pound chicken livers, picked over to remove any veins and connective tissues
1 small clove garlic
1 cup (about 4) whole eggs
⅔ cup (about 8) egg yolks
2 ⅔ cups heavy cream
Salt and freshly ground pepper to taste

THE SAUCE
1 (2- to 2 ½-pound) cooked lobster (see following recipe)
¼ cup butter, preferably lobster butter (see following recipe)
Salt and freshly ground pepper to taste
3 tablespoons Cognac or Armagnac
1 cup heavy cream
¼ cup whipped cream
3 egg yolks
2 tablespoons water
½ pound butter, melted

1. Preheat the oven to 350 degrees.

2. It will take about 1½ pounds of marrow bones to produce about ¼ pound of marrow. To make the mousse, blend the marrow with the chicken livers and garlic in a food processor. Beat lightly the whole eggs and egg yolks and stir the chicken liver mixture into the egg mixture. Add the cream and salt and pepper to taste and strain the mixture through a very fine sieve.

3. Butter a 6-cup mold and pour in the mousse. Line a deep baking dish large enough to hold the mold with a layer of paper. Pour in boiling water. Put the mold in the dish and place in the oven. Bake for 1 hour, or until the custard is slightly firm in the center. A straw inserted in the center will come out clean when withdrawn.

4. As custard cooks, prepare the sauce.

5. Remove the meat from the tail and claws of the lobster and cut the meat into slices.

6. Heat the butter in a saucepan and add the lobster slices, salt, and pepper. Add the Cognac and ignite. Add the heavy cream and whipped cream and bring just to the boil.

7. Prepare the egg yolks like a hollandaise. Place them in a saucepan and add the water. Cook, beating vigorously, over high heat or hot water until they are thickened and pale yellow. Gradually spoon the clear liquid from the melted butter into the sauce, beating constantly. Discard the white milky residue. Stir sauce into the lobster and heat without boiling.

8. Unmold the mousse and spoon the lobster sauce over each serving.

YIELD: 8 to 10 servings.

NOTE: If you wish to butcher your own, buy 1½ to 2 pounds marrow bones and carefully crack them with a cleaver so that they break in half and the marrow can be easily removed.

Homard au court bouillon
Boiled Lobster

4 quarts water
3 onions, peeled and quartered
3 carrots, scraped and quartered
4 cloves garlic, unpeeled and crushed
6 sprigs fresh parsley
2 sprigs fresh thyme, optional
Salt to taste
12 peppercorns, crushed
1 bottle (3 cups) dry white wine
1 (2- to 2½-pound) live lobster

1. Combine the water, onions, carrots, garlic, parsley, thyme, salt, and peppercorns in a kettle large enough to hold the lobster and bring to the boil. Simmer 10 minutes.

2. Add the wine and return to the boil. Cook 5 minutes.

3. Add the lobster and simmer 20 minutes, covered. Remove from the heat and let stand 10 minutes longer. Drain.

YIELD: 1 lobster.

Beurre de homard
Lobster Butter

1 cooked lobster carcass plus any excess trimmings, coral, and so on
¼ pound butter, at room temperature
2 cups (approximately) water

1. Pound the carcass with a mallet and/or chop it with a cleaver. Add it to the container of a food processor. Add the butter. Blend well.

2. Scrape the mixture into a saucepan. Cook, stirring, until a nice nutty smell comes from the saucepan. Add water to cover to a depth of about 1 inch over the top of the butter mixture. Bring to the boil and remove from heat.

3. Strain the mixture through a fine sieve, using a wooden spoon to extract as much liquid from solids as possible.

4. Let cool, then chill. The butter will harden on top. Remove the butter and discard the water. This butter will keep for more than a week in the refrigerator and can be frozen.

YIELD: About ¼ pound.

Cervelles de veau maréchale
Breaded Calves' Brains with Asparagus

3 or 4 sets (about 1 ¼ pounds) calves' brains
2 cups cold water
2 tablespoons white vinegar
1 bay leaf
1 sprig fresh thyme, or ½ teaspoon dried
6 peppercorns
½ cup flour
2 eggs
3 tablespoons olive oil
¼ cup water

Salt and freshly ground pepper to taste
2 cups fresh bread crumbs
¼ cup peanut, vegetable, or corn oil
6 tablespoons butter
18 asparagus tips, each about 4 inches long
6 to 10 thin black truffle slices, optional

1. Soak the brains in cold water to cover for several hours. Drain and pick over the brains. Remove and discard all the fiberlike threads and membranes. Place the brains in a saucepan and add the water, vinegar, bay leaf, thyme, and peppercorns. Bring to the boil and simmer about 1 minute. Remove from the heat and let stand until cool. Drain.

2. Dredge the brains in flour. Shake off excess. Beat the eggs with oil, water, salt, and pepper. Dip the pieces of brain in egg, then in bread crumbs.

3. Heat the oil and 2 tablespoons of butter in a large skillet and add the breaded brains. Cook about 5 minutes, or until golden brown on one side. Turn and cook until golden on the other.

4. Place the asparagus tips in a skillet and add cold water to cover and salt to taste. Bring to the boil and simmer 30 seconds. Drain.

5. Transfer the pieces of brains to a hot platter and garnish between the pieces with asparagus tips. Cover each piece with a slice of truffle. Heat the remaining butter until foamy and pour over all.

YIELD: 6 servings.

Chicken with Noodles Parisienne

1 (4-pound) chicken
Chicken stock or water
1 carrot, scraped and sliced
2 ribs celery, broken in half
1 onion stuck with 2 cloves
12 peppercorns
1 ½ cups tomato sauce (see following recipe)
4 tablespoons butter
¼ cup flour
Salt and freshly ground pepper
¾ cup heavy cream
Tabasco sauce
½ pound broad noodles
3 tablespoons chopped chives

1 egg yolk
¾ cup grated Parmesan cheese

1. Place the chicken in a kettle and add chicken stock or water to cover, carrot, celery, onion, and peppercorns. If water is used instead of stock, season with salt. Bring to the boil and simmer partially covered until chicken is tender, about 45 minutes.

2. Prepare the tomato sauce.

3. Remove the chicken and continue boiling the broth until it is reduced to about 2 cups. Strain the broth and reserve. When chicken is cool enough to handle, remove and discard the skin and bones. Pull or cut the meat into strips.

4. Melt 2 tablespoons of butter and add the flour. When it is blended, add the reserved chicken broth, stirring vigorously with a wire whisk. When blended and smooth, simmer over low heat, stirring occasionally, for about 30 minutes. This is called a velouté.

5. Preheat the oven to 350 degrees.

6. Melt 1 tablespoon of butter in a skillet and add the strips of chicken. Sprinkle with salt and pepper. Blend ½ cup of the cream with 1 cup of the velouté. Add a touch of Tabasco and stir this sauce into the chicken. Remove from heat.

7. Cook the noodles in 6 cups boiling salted water until they are tender, but do not overcook. Drain and rinse in cold water. Heat the remaining tablespoon of butter and toss the noodles in it just long enough to warm them.

8. Generously butter a baking dish and add a layer of noodles and a layer of the tomato sauce. Continue making layers until all the noodles and sauce are used. Sprinkle with chives and spread the chicken in cream sauce over all.

9. Blend the remaining velouté with the remaining cream and the egg yolk. Heat but do not boil. Spread this over the chicken layer and sprinkle with the cheese. Bake 30 to 45 minutes, or until golden brown.

YIELD: 4 to 6 servings.

Tomato Sauce

2 large ripe tomatoes
3 tablespoons butter
3 tablespoons finely chopped onion
Salt and freshly ground pepper
½ bay leaf
2 sprigs fresh thyme, or ½ teaspoon dried

---

1. Spear the stem end of the tomatoes, one at a time, with a two-pronged fork. Dip into boiling water for about 9 seconds. Remove and pull away the peel with a paring knife. Pare away the stem end. Chop the tomatoes coarsely.

2. Melt the butter in a saucepan and add the onion. Cook until onion is wilted and add the tomatoes and remaining ingredients. Simmer about 5 minutes. If fresh thyme sprigs are used, discard them and discard the bay leaf.

YIELD: Approximately 2 cups.

Chicken Cutlets Pojarski

2 large whole chicken breasts, skinned and boned
Salt and freshly ground pepper, preferably white
¼ teaspoon grated nutmeg
11 tablespoons butter
½ cup flour
1 egg, lightly beaten
1 teaspoon oil
1 tablespoon water
1 ½ to 2 cups fresh bread crumbs
1 ½ cups paprika sauce (see following recipe)
Chopped fresh parsley

1. Chill a mixing bowl in the freezer.

2. Place the boned chicken meat on a board and chop with a sharp knife, or grind the meat, using a fine blade. There should be about 1½ cups chopped or ground meat. Place meat in the chilled bowl. Add salt and pepper to taste, nutmeg, and 5 tablespoons of the butter, melted. Beat well or blend thoroughly but quickly with the fingers. Chill in the freezer, but do not freeze.

3. Season the flour with salt and pepper and place on a length of waxed paper.

4. Beat the egg in a pie plate with the oil and water.

5. Place the bread crumbs on another length of waxed paper.

6. Divide the chicken mixture into 8 portions and shape each portion into a ball. Flatten each ball to ½-inch thickness and mold each into the shape of a small cutlet or pork chop. Dip 1 cutlet at a time into flour, then into egg, then into bread crumbs. Press gently to make crumbs adhere. Chill briefly.

7. Heat the remaining butter in a large skillet and carefully add the cutlets. Cook until golden brown on one side. Turn and cook on the other. Arrange on a hot platter with paprika sauce on the side or spooned over the cutlets. Garnish the platter with parsley and serve immediately with buttered noodles and sautéed carrots.

YIELD: 4 servings.

Paprika Sauce

2 tablespoons butter
3 tablespoons chopped onion
2 teaspoons paprika
1 tablespoon flour
½ teaspoon thyme
½ cup chicken stock
½ cup heavy cream
2 teaspoons lemon juice
Salt and freshly ground pepper
1 teaspoon Cognac
¼ cup sour cream

1. Melt 1 tablespoon of butter in a small saucepan and cook the onion until wilted. Sprinkle with paprika, flour, and thyme, stirring. Stir in the chicken stock, using a wire whisk, and simmer about 3 minutes.

2. Add the cream and bring to the boil. Add the lemon juice, salt, pepper, and Cognac. Strain the sauce through a sieve. Return to the heat and stir in the remaining butter and the sour cream. Bring just to the boil, but do not boil.

YIELD: 1½ cups.

Lemon Chicken

4 whole chicken breasts, boned and skinned
2 tablespoons light soy sauce
¼ teaspoon sesame oil
1 teaspoon salt

1 tablespoon gin or vodka
3 egg whites, beaten until frothy
1 cup water chestnut flour or powder
Peanut or salad oil
¾ cup sugar
½ cup white vinegar
1 cup chicken broth
1 tablespoon cornstarch
2 tablespoons water
1 teaspoon monosodium glutamate, optional
Juice of 1 lemon
Thin yellow rind of 1 lemon, finely chopped
¼ head iceberg lettuce, finely shredded
3 small carrots, cut into thinnest possible strips
½ large green pepper, seeded and cut into thinnest possible strips
3 scallions, cut into thinnest possible strips
½ cup shredded canned pineapple
1 (1-ounce) bottle lemon extract

1. Place the chicken in a shallow earthenware dish or bowl. Combine the soy sauce, sesame oil, salt, and gin and pour over the chicken. Toss to coat and let sit 30 minutes.

2. Drain the chicken and discard the marinade. Add the chicken pieces to the beaten egg whites and toss to coat. Place the water chestnut flour on a plate and use to coat the chicken pieces.

3. Add peanut oil to a skillet to a depth of ½ inch and heat to 365 degrees. If no thermometer is available, drop a 1-inch cube of bread into the fat and, if the temperature is correct, the bread will brown in sixty seconds. Add the chicken pieces, a few at a time if necessary, and brown on both sides. Drain.

4. Meanwhile, place the sugar, vinegar, broth, cornstarch mixed with water, monosodium glutamate, if desired, lemon juice and rind in a small pan. Bring to a boil and cook, stirring, until the mixture thickens.

5. Cut the drained chicken into 1-inch crosswise slices and place it on top of the shredded lettuce on a serving platter. If necessary, keep warm in a 200-degree oven.

6. Add the vegetables and pineapple to the sauce. Remove from the heat and stir in the lemon extract. Pour over the chicken.

YIELD: 4 servings.

Charcoal-grilled Duck, French Style

1 (4 ½- to 5-pound) whole, cleaned duck with giblets
½ bay leaf
Salt and freshly ground pepper to taste
¼ teaspoon dried thyme
1 tablespoon peanut, vegetable, or corn oil
3 tablespoons butter
1 clove garlic, peeled and crushed
2 tablespoons chopped parsley

1. In this method of grilling duck, the breast is cut away in 2 neat, flat pieces without skin or bone. The legs and thighs are left more or less intact with skin on and bones in. The legs and thighs are cooked first because they require the longest cooking, about 30 minutes or longer. The breast meat is grilled just before serving, for it cooks quickly like a small, thin steak or scaloppine.

2. First, place the duck, backside down, on a flat surface. Run a sharp knife, such as a boning knife, along the breast bone, cutting through the skin and down to the bone. Carefully run the knife between the skin and the meat, pulling the skin with the fingers to expose the smooth breast meat. Cut off and discard the skin. Now carefully run the knife between the breast meat and the carcass, using the fingers as necessary. Remove the 2 pieces of breast meat.

3. Carve off the 2 thighs, leaving the legs attached. Use the carcass for soup. Place the legs and thighs on a flat surface, skin side down, and carefully cut away the excessive peripheral skin fat that borders the thigh.

4. Sever the bone joint between the legs and thighs, but do not cut the legs and thighs in two. This will facilitate cooking.

5. Chop together the bay leaf, salt, pepper, and thyme, chopping until the bay leaf is quite fine. Rub this mixture into the legs and thighs and over the breast and giblets. Brush all with oil.

6. Arrange the breast pieces, ends touching, in a flat dish. Cover with giblets and neatly arrange the legs and thighs, skin side up, over all. Let stand until ready to cook.

7. Prepare a charcoal grill and have it ready. The coals must be white hot but not too plentiful or the meat will cook too fast. Arrange the bed of coals about 6 inches from the grill that will hold the duck for broiling. Arrange the giblets on a skewer and add them to the grill.

8. Place the legs and thighs, skin side down, on the grill. Grill the legs and thighs, turning as often as necessary, until skin is crisp and flesh is cooked, about 30 minutes. If necessary, brush the food with a

little more oil as it cooks. Grill the giblets until done, turning often. About 5 minutes before these foods are done, add the breast meat and cook, 1 or 2 minutes on each side, until done. Ideally, the breast meat should be served a bit rare.

9. Transfer the pieces to a small serving skillet. Slice the breast meat on the bias and cut legs and thighs in half where they join.

10. Heat the butter and garlic and pour over the grilled pieces. Sprinkle with chopped parsley and serve immediately.

YIELD: 2 to 4 servings.

Stuffed Squabs Derby

8 (each about ¾-pound cleaned weight) squabs (see note)
2 cups (approximately) baked rice (see following recipe)
5 tablespoons butter
8 squab livers, each cut in half
1 ¼ ounces pure foie gras
1 tablespoon chopped truffles
Salt and freshly ground pepper
3 tablespoons Cognac
1 ½ cups brown sauce for poultry (see following recipe)
8 truffle slices

1. The squabs should be cleaned and ready for roasting, but reserve the necks, feet, and gizzards for the brown sauce. Reserve the livers for the stuffing.

2. Preheat the oven to 425 degrees.

3. Prepare the rice and set it aside.

4. Heat 1 tablespoon butter in a small skillet and add the livers. Cook over high heat, shaking the skillet and stirring, about 1 minute. The livers must cook quickly or they will be tough. Add the livers to the rice.

5. Cube the foie gras. Add the foie gras and the truffles to the rice and stir to blend.

6. Sprinkle the inside of the squabs with salt and pepper to taste and stuff them with the rice mixture. Truss the squabs. Sprinkle with salt and pepper.

7. Melt 3 tablespoons of butter in a heavy roasting pan large enough to hold the squabs in one layer. Turn the squabs in the butter until coated on all sides. Place squabs on their sides and bake 15 minutes.

Baste often. Turn on to other side and bake 15 minutes, basting frequently. Place squabs on their backs and continue roasting for another 10 to 15 minutes.

8. Remove the squabs to a warm platter and cover with foil.

9. Skim off all the fat from the roasting pan, leaving the squab drippings. Add 2 tablespoons Cognac and ignite it. Pour in the brown sauce and stir to blend. Put the sauce through a fine sieve into a saucepan and bring it to the boil. Swirl in the remaining butter. Add the remaining Cognac and serve piping hot with the squabs. Garnish each squab with a truffle slice before serving.

YIELD: 8 servings.

NOTE: The squabs may be boned before stuffing and roasting. Squabs are available in fine poultry and meat markets.

Perfect Rice

2 ½ tablespoons butter
2 tablespoons minced onion
¼ teaspoon minced garlic
1 cup rice
1 ½ cups chicken stock
2 sprigs fresh parsley
1 sprig fresh thyme, or ¼ teaspoon dried
½ bay leaf
⅛ teaspoon cayenne pepper, or Tabasco sauce to taste

1. Preheat the oven to 400 degrees.

2. Melt 1 tablespoon of the butter in a heavy ovenproof saucepan and cook the onion and garlic, stirring with a wooden spoon, until the onion is translucent. Add the rice and stir briefly over low heat until all the grains are coated with butter.

3. Stir in the stock, making sure there are no lumps in the rice. Add the parsley, thyme, bay leaf, and cayenne. Cover with a close-fitting lid and place in the oven.

4. Bake the rice or cook it on top of the stove exactly 17 minutes. Remove the cover and discard the parsley and thyme sprigs and the bay leaf. Using a two-pronged fork, stir in the remaining butter.

YIELD: About 2½ cups.

Brown Sauce for Poultry

1 tablespoon oil
Necks, feet, and gizzards from the 8 squabs (see note)
Salt and freshly ground pepper
¼ cup chopped celery
½ cup chopped onion
½ cup chopped carrots
3 sprigs fresh thyme, or ½ teaspoon dried
3 sprigs fresh parsley
½ bay leaf
2 tablespoons flour
½ cup dry white wine
1 cup chicken broth
1 cup water
1 tablespoon tomato paste

1. Heat the oil in a small heavy saucepan and add the necks, feet, and gizzards. Sprinkle with salt and pepper. Cook, stirring frequently, until parts are nicely browned all over. Drain.

2. Return the squab pieces to the saucepan and add the celery, onion, carrots, thyme, parsley, and bay leaf. Continue cooking, stirring occasionally, about 5 minutes.

3. Sprinkle with flour and stir until all pieces are well coated. Cook, stirring occasionally, about 5 minutes. Add the remaining ingredients and stir rapidly until blended. Bring to the boil and simmer uncovered for 1½ hours. Put through a fine sieve, pressing the solids with the back of a wooden spoon to extract as much of the liquid as possible. Discard the solids. Put the sauce in a small saucepan and simmer, uncovered, about 30 minutes longer.

YIELD: 1½ cups.

NOTE: If the squabs have been trimmed of their necks, feet, and so on, bony chicken parts such as necks may be substituted.

Shad Stuffed with Roe

¾ pound boneless scrod or cod
3 shallots, finely chopped
¼ cup finely chopped parsley
1⅔ cups heavy cream
⅔ cup fresh bread crumbs

CRAIG CLAIBORNE

Salt and freshly ground pepper to taste
Cayenne pepper to taste
2 boneless fillets fresh shad
1 pair shad roe
5 tablespoons butter
1 ½ cups thinly sliced mushrooms
1 cup dry white wine
1 tablespoon flour
1 teaspoon lemon juice

1. Preheat the oven to 400 degrees.
2. Cut the scrod or cod into small cubes and place in the container of an electric blender or food processor. Blend well, stirring down the sides of the container with a rubber spatula.
3. When the fish is blended, add 1 tablespoon chopped shallots and 1 tablespoon of the parsley. Gradually add ⅔ cup of the cream. Carefully scoop the mousse into a mixing bowl. Stir in the bread crumbs and season with salt, pepper, and cayenne.
4. Lay one of the shad fillets, skin side down, on a flat surface. There are two "flaps" on either side of the fillet where the bones were removed. Open these flaps and spread half the scrod mixture down the center of the fillet. Split the pair of shad roe in two and place the 2 parts tip to tip down the center of the mousse.
5. Spread the remaining mousse mixture over the roe.
6. Open the flaps on the other shad fillet and place this fillet, skin side up, over the stuffed fillet. This will in effect form a box with the mousse and roe enclosed. Tie the fish crosswise in about four places with string. Place in a baking dish.
7. Sprinkle the fish with salt and pepper and spread it generously on top with 4 tablespoons of the butter. Sprinkle it with the remaining parsley and shallots and scatter the mushrooms all around. Pour the wine around and cover with aluminum foil. Bake 40 to 50 minutes, lifting the foil and basting occasionally with the wine.
8. Remove the fish to a warm platter. Remove the string and keep the fish warm.
9. Pour the sauce into a saucepan and reduce it over high heat to about two thirds of its original volume. Add the remaining cup of cream and cook about 10 minutes. Blend together the remaining tablespoon of butter and flour and stir bit by bit into the sauce. When thickened, add the lemon juice.
10. Peel the skin from the top of the shad and pour a little of the sauce over and around the fish. Serve the remaining sauce separately.
   YIELD: About 6 servings.

Fish Mousse

1 ½ pounds skinless, boneless, fresh fish fillets, such as flounder, gray sole, lemon sole, weakfish, red snapper, or salmon
Salt and freshly ground pepper to taste
¼ teaspoon cayenne pepper
⅛ teaspoon nutmeg
1 egg yolk
2 cups heavy cream
Sauce portugaise (see following recipe)

1. Preheat the oven to 375 degrees.
2. There may be a fine bone line running down the center of each fillet. If so, cut it away and discard. Cut the fish into 1- or 2-inch cubes and put into a bowl. Place the bowl with fish in it in the freezer briefly until very cold. Do not freeze.
3. Remove from freezer and put the pieces into the container of a food processor. Add salt, pepper, cayenne, nutmeg, and egg yolk.
4. Start processing and, when the mixture is coarse-fine, gradually add the heavy cream, pouring it through the funnel.
5. Butter the bottom and sides of a 4-cup mold.
6. Spoon and scrape the mousse into the mold and pack down, smoothing over the top. Cover closely with foil, pressing the foil closely around the sides of the mold.
7. Set the mold in a heat-proof baking dish and pour boiling water around it. Bring the water back to the boil on top of the stove.
8. Place in the oven and bake 1 hour, or until internal temperature registers 130 degrees on a meat thermometer. The mousse can now be served, or the mold may be set aside and reheated before serving. To reheat, place the mousse back in the oven (sitting in its water bath) and bake about 10 minutes.
9. Remove the foil, wipe bottom of mold, and unmold the mousse on a round dish. Serve sliced with sauce portugaise.
   YIELD: 6 servings.

Sauce Portugaise
A Cream and Tomato Sauce

2 cups fish broth
½ cup dry white wine
½ pound tomatoes

CRAIG CLAIBORNE

2 *tablespoons butter*
¼ *cup finely chopped onion*
Salt and freshly ground pepper to taste
1 *cup heavy cream*
2 *tablespoons finely chopped parsley*

1. Put the fish broth and wine in a saucepan and bring to the boil. Cook down to about ¼ cup. Set aside.

2. Peel and core the tomatoes. Cut each tomato in half and squeeze to extract and discard most of the seeds and juicy pulp. Chop the tomatoes. There should be about 1¼ cups.

3. Heat half the butter in a saucepan and add the onion. Cook until wilted.

4. Add the tomatoes, salt, and pepper. Cook down until most of the liquid has disappeared, about 10 minutes. Set aside.

5. Add the cream to the cooked-down fish broth. Cook over high heat about 5 minutes.

6. Add the cooked tomato mixture. Cook down about 1 minute. Set aside closely covered until ready to serve.

7. When ready to serve, reheat and swirl in the remaining butter. Stir in the chopped parsley.

YIELD: 6 servings.

Fish or Seafood Orly

2 *pounds flounder or other fish fillets, or 50 medium-size raw shrimp*
Salt and freshly ground pepper
Fritter batter (see following recipe)
Fat for deep frying
2 *cups sauce Orly (see following recipe)*

1. If fillets are used, cut away the tiny bone line running lengthwise down the center of each. Cut the fillets diagonally into strips about 4 inches long and ¾ inch wide. If shrimp are used, shell and devein them. Sprinkle the strips or shrimp with salt and pepper.

2. Prepare the fritter batter and add the fish strips or shrimp.

3. Heat the fat to 365 degrees and, using a fork, drop the batter-coated fish strips, one at a time, into the hot fat. If no thermometer is available, drop a 1-inch cube of bread into the fat and, if the temperature is correct, the bread will brown in 60 seconds. Do not crowd the

fish in the pan. When the fish strips are brown on one side, turn and brown on the other. Drain on absorbent toweling. Continue cooking until all the fish has been cooked. If the fish is not to be served immediately, it may be kept hot in a warm oven for 5 or 10 minutes. Serve with sauce Orly.

YIELD: 8 to 12 servings.

Fritter Batter

1 cup flour
¼ teaspoon grated nutmeg
⅛ teaspoon cayenne pepper
2 eggs, separated
Salt and freshly ground pepper
⅔ cup milk

1. Place the flour, nutmeg, and pepper in a mixing bowl and make a well in the center. Add egg yolks, salt, and pepper and stir with a fork. Gradually add the milk, stirring.

2. Beat the whites until stiff and fold them into the batter mixture.

YIELD: Enough batter to coat 50 strips of fish fillets or 50 shrimp.

Sauce Orly

2 tablespoons olive oil
6 tablespoons butter
1 ½ cups finely chopped onion
2 cloves garlic, finely minced
3 sprigs fresh thyme, or ½ teaspoon dried
1 bay leaf
1 teaspoon sugar
Salt and freshly ground pepper
2 cups chopped fresh tomatoes or canned Italian plum tomatoes
6 tablespoons tomato paste

1. Heat the oil and 2 tablespoons butter in a saucepan. Cook the onion and garlic in it, stirring occasionally, until onion is wilted. Add the thyme, bay leaf, sugar, salt, pepper, tomatoes with their liquid, and tomato paste. Simmer, stirring occasionally, 20 minutes.

2. Strain the sauce into another saucepan. Return to the boil. Remove the sauce from the heat and swirl in the remaining butter.

YIELD: About 2 cups.

Striped Bass tout Paris

4 cups lobster sauce américaine (see following recipe), approximately
2 cups fish velouté (see following recipe), approximately
4 pounds striped bass fillets
2 tablespoons butter
4 tablespoons finely chopped shallots
Salt and freshly ground pepper
½ pound thinly sliced (about 4 cups) mushrooms
1 cup brut champagne
1 cup heavy cream
Juice of ½ lemon

1. Prepare the lobster sauce américaine and the fish velouté.
2. Preheat the oven to 450 degrees.
3. While the velouté simmers, cut the fish into 8 equal portions.
4. Select a heatproof baking dish large enough to hold the fish in one layer. Grease the dish with half the butter. Sprinkle the shallots, salt, and pepper to taste over the bottom of the dish. Arrange the fish pieces over all and scatter the sliced mushrooms over the fish. Sprinkle lightly with salt and pepper. Sprinkle with champagne.
5. Cut a square or round of waxed paper to fit over the fish. Cover the fish with the waxed paper and bring to the boil on top of the stove. Place the dish in the oven. Bake 20 minutes.
6. Remove the waxed paper and carefully pour the cooking liquid into a saucepan. With a spoon, remove most of the mushroom slices from the baking dish and add them to the liquid. Cook over high heat until the cooking liquid is reduced to about 1 cup, about 12 minutes. Add the velouté and stir briskly with a wire whisk until well blended and smooth. Add the cream and lemon juice. Swirl in the remaining tablespoon of butter. Spoon the hot sauce over the fish. Spoon the lobster sauce around the fillets.

YIELD: 8 servings.

Lobster Sauce Américaine

2 (1 ½-pound) lobster
6 tablespoons salad oil
10 tablespoons butter
½ cup finely chopped onion
½ cup finely chopped carrots
⅓ cup finely chopped celery
6 shallots, finely chopped
6 tablespoons Cognac
2 cloves garlic, finely minced
2 sprigs fresh thyme, or ½ teaspoon dried
2 bay leaves
24 peppercorns
4 sprigs fresh tarragon, or 2 teaspoons dried
8 sprigs fresh parsley
1 (6-ounce) can tomato paste
1 ½ cups dry white wine
1 ½ cups fish broth (see following recipe)
Salt
4 teaspoons flour
Cayenne pepper

1. Place lobster on a chopping block and plunge a knife through the center of the body cavity where body and tail meet to kill the lobster.

2. Break off the large claws and crack each claw on two sides with a heavy knife. Break off the tail and cut it crosswise into 2 pieces. Chop off the small claws. Split the body of the lobster lengthwise and remove the tough sac near the eyes. Remove the liver and coral of the lobster and reserve them in a small bowl.

3. Heat the oil and 4 tablespoons of butter in a large heavy skillet and add the lobster. Cook, stirring with a wooden spoon, until shell is bright red. Add the onion, carrots, celery, and shallots. Cook, stirring, until vegetables start to brown. Sprinkle with 4 tablespoons of warm Cognac and ignite. When the flame dies, add the garlic, thyme, bay leaves, peppercorns, tarragon, parsley, tomato paste, wine, and fish broth. Add salt to taste. Cover and simmer 15 minutes.

4. Remove the lobster from the sauce and let cool slightly. When cool enough to handle, remove the meat from the shell and cut into small cubes and reserve.

5. Add 2 tablespoons of butter and the flour to the reserved liver and coral. Blend well. Bring the sauce to a boil and stir in the liver-coral mixture. Rinse out the vessel that contained the liver-coral mixture with 2 tablespoons of Cognac and add it to the sauce.

6. Put the sauce through a sieve, pressing with the back of a spoon to extract as much sauce from the solids as possible. Season the sauce with a little cayenne and add the lobster meat. Just before serving, heat the sauce to the boil. Take off the heat and swirl in 4 tablespoons of cold butter.

YIELD: About 4 cups.

Fish Broth

1 ½ pounds fish bones with the head, if available
1 cup dry white wine
3 cups water
⅓ cup chopped celery
1 whole clove garlic
2 sprigs fresh thyme, or ½ teaspoon dried
1 bay leaf
6 sprigs fresh parsley
Salt to taste
10 peppercorns

1. Combine all the ingredients in a saucepan and let simmer 15 minutes, skimming to remove foam and scum.

2. Put stock through a strainer.

YIELD: About 4 cups.

NOTE: Leftover broth can be frozen.

Fish Velouté

4 tablespoons butter
8 tablespoons flour
2 cups fish broth (see preceding recipe)

1. Melt the butter in a saucepan and add the flour, stirring with a wire whisk.

2. Add the broth, stirring rapidly with the whisk until the mixture is thickened and smooth. Continue cooking over low heat, stirring frequently, about 45 minutes.

YIELD: About 2 cups.

Whole Salmon Baked in Foil

1 (6- to 8-pound) cleaned whole salmon, preferably with head left on
1 cup thinly sliced carrots
1 cup thinly sliced onion
¼ cup thinly sliced shallots
1 cup thinly sliced celery
½ teaspoon dried thyme
Salt
8 peppercorns, crushed
1 clove garlic, unpeeled and crushed
1 bay leaf
2 cups dry white wine
About 3 cups white wine sauce (see following recipe) or 3 cups dill and cucumber mayonnaise (see following recipe)

1. Preheat the oven to 400 degrees.

2. Select a baking sheet large enough to accommodate the fish.

3. Lay out a long double length of heavy-duty aluminum foil on top of the baking sheet. Place the salmon in the center of the foil and add the carrots, onion, shallots, celery, thyme, salt to taste, peppercorns, garlic, bay leaf, and wine. Bring up the edges of the foil and seal as compactly and tightly as possible.

4. Place the fish in the oven and bake 50 minutes to 1 hour. At the end of 50 minutes, loosen the foil and test for doneness. The fish is cooked when the back center fin can be easily removed when pulled with the fingers.

5. Serve hot with white wine sauce or cold with dill and cucumber mayonnaise.

YIELD: 8 to 12 servings.

White Wine Sauce

2 cups of the liquid with which the salmon was baked
Vegetables and seasonings with which the salmon was baked
1 cup heavy cream
2 tablespoons butter, at room temperature
2 tablespoons flour
4 tablespoons cold butter
Juice of ½ lemon
Salt
Cayenne pepper

1. Strain the liquid from the foil in which the salmon baked into a saucepan. Add the chopped or sliced vegetables with which the salmon was baked. Bring this mixture to the boil and let it simmer about 15 minutes, or until it is reduced to 1½ cups when strained.

2. Strain the sauce and return it to the saucepan. Add the cream.

3. Prepare a beurre manié by blending the room-temperature butter and flour until they form a smooth paste. Bring the sauce to the simmer and gradually add the butter-flour mixture, stirring constantly. When the blend is thick and smooth, add the cold butter bit by bit, stirring. Add the lemon juice, salt, and cayenne to taste. Remove from the heat.

YIELD: About 3 cups.

Dill and Cucumber Mayonnaise

1 cup peeled, seeded, and diced cucumber
Salt
2 egg yolks
Freshly ground pepper
2 teaspoons imported mustard, such as Dijon or Düsseldorf
2 teaspoons vinegar or lemon juice
2 cups peanut, vegetable, or olive oil
¼ cup finely chopped fresh dill

1. Put the cucumber in a bowl and sprinkle with salt to taste. Refrigerate 30 minutes.

2. Meanwhile, place the yolks in a mixing bowl and add salt and pepper to taste, mustard, and vinegar or lemon juice. Beat vigorously for a second or two with a wire whisk or electric beater.

3. Start adding the oil gradually, beating continuously with the whisk or electric beater. Continue beating and adding oil until all of it is used.

4. Drain the cucumbers. Add the cucumbers and dill to the mayonnaise and blend well.

YIELD: 3 cups.

Saumon à l'Oseille
Salmon with Sorrel Sauce

1 ¼ pounds skinned and boned fillets of salmon
7 teaspoons butter
2 tablespoons finely chopped shallots
¼ cup dry vermouth
½ cup dry white wine
1 cup fresh fish broth (see recipe, page 337) or clam broth
1 cup heavy cream
1 tablespoon flour
2 tablespoons finely chopped fresh sorrel
Salt and freshly ground pepper
Juice of ½ lemon

1. Place the salmon fillets on a flat surface and cut on the bias, against the grain, into 8 slices of equal weight.

2. Place the slices between sheets of freezer paper and pound with a flat mallet to make thin steaks about the thickness of veal scaloppine.

3. Melt 3 teaspoons butter in a saucepan and add the shallots. Cook briefly and add the vermouth and wine. Cook until reduced by half and add the fish broth. Cook about 5 minutes and strain the liquid, using a fine sieve and pushing the solids with the back of a wooden spoon to extract their juices. Discard the solids.

4. Add the cream to the juices and simmer about 5 minutes.

5. Blend 1 teaspoon of butter with the flour and add this bit by bit to the sauce, stirring. Add the chopped sorrel, salt and pepper to taste, and lemon juice.

6. Swirl in the remaining 3 teaspoons of butter. Do not boil, but keep hot while cooking the salmon.

7. Use a nonstick pan to cook the salmon. Do not add fat. Place the salmon pieces in the pan and cook until delicately golden on one side about 30 seconds. Turn and cook on the other about 15 to 30 seconds. Do not overcook or the salmon will have a dry texture.

8. Spoon equal portions of the sauce in the center of eight hot plates. Place 1 piece of the cooked salmon in the center of the sauce and serve.

YIELD: 8 servings.

Coulibiac of Salmon

THE ASSEMBLY AND BAKING OF COULIBIAC OF SALMON
Salmon and mushrooms with velouté (see following recipe)
Brioche dough (see following recipe)
½ cup flour, approximately
14 (7-inch) crêpes (see following recipe)
Rice and egg filling (see following recipe)
2 egg yolks
2 tablespoons cold water
2 tablespoons butter, at room temperature
¾ pound plus 4 tablespoons hot melted butter

1. Remove the salmon and mushrooms with velouté from the refrigerator. Using a knife, cut it in half lengthwise down the center. Set aside.

2. Remove the brioche dough from the bowl and, with floured fingers, shape it into a thick, flat pillow shape. Place the brioche dough on a lightly floured board and roll it into a rectangle measuring about 21 × 18 inches. The rectangle, of course, will have slightly rounded corners. Arrange 8 crêpes, edges overlapping in a neat pattern, over the center of the rectangle, leaving a border of brioche dough.

3. Sprinkle the crêpes down the center with a rectangle of about one third of the rice and egg mixture. Pick up half of the chilled salmon and carefully arrange it, mushroom-sauce side down, over the rice mixture. Sprinkle with another third of the rice mixture.

4. Top this, sandwich-fashion, with another layer of the chilled salmon filling, mushroom-sauce side up. Sprinkle with remaining rice. Cover with 6 overlapping crêpes.

5. Bring up one side of the brioche. Brush it liberally with a mixture of beaten yolks and water. Bring up the opposite side of the brioche dough to enclose the filling, overlapping the two sides of dough. Brush all over with egg yolk. Trim off the ends of the dough to make them neat. Brush with yolk and bring up the ends, pinching as necessary to enclose filling. Butter a baking dish with 2 tablespoons of butter. This

will keep the seams intact. Brush the coulibiac all over with yolk. Using a small, round, decorative cookie cutter, cut a hole in the center of the coulibiac. This will allow steam to escape. Brush around the hole with yolk. Cut out another slightly larger ring of dough to surround and outline the hole neatly. Roll out a scrap of dough and cut off strips of dough to decorate the coulibiac. Always brush with beaten yolk before and after applying pastry cutouts.

6. Roll out a 6-foot length of aluminum foil. Fold it over into thirds to make one long band about 4½ inches in height. Brush the band with 4 tablespoons of melted butter. Arrange the band neatly and snugly around the loaf, buttered side against the brioche. The purpose of the band is to prevent the sides of the loaf from collapsing before the dough has a chance to firm up while baking. Fasten the top of the band with a jumbo paper clip. Run a cord around three times and tie the ends. Make certain the bottom of the loaf is securely enclosed with foil. Set the pan in a warm, draft-free place for about 30 minutes. Meanwhile, preheat the oven to 400 degrees. Place the loaf in the oven and bake 15 minutes. Reduce the oven heat to 375 degrees and bake 10 minutes longer. Cover with a sheet of aluminum foil to prevent excess browning. Continue baking 20 minutes (a total baking time at this point of 45 minutes). Remove the foil and continue baking 15 minutes more. Remove the coulibiac from the oven. Pour ½ cup of the melted butter through the steam hole into the filling. Serve cut into 1-inch slices with hot melted butter on the side.

YIELD: 16 or more servings.

Salmon and Mushrooms with Velouté

2 skinless, boneless (each weighing about 1 ½ pounds) salmon fillets, preferably center cut
4 tablespoons butter
2 tablespoons finely chopped onion
2 tablespoons finely chopped shallots
Salt and freshly ground pepper to taste
¾ pound fresh mushrooms, thinly sliced
¼ cup finely chopped fresh dill
2 cups dry white wine
3 tablespoons flour
⅛ teaspoon cayenne pepper
3 tablespoons lemon juice
5 egg yolks

1. Preheat the oven to 400 degrees. Using a sharp knife, cut each fillet, one at a time, on the bias into slices about ⅓ inch thick. Each fillet should produce about 12 slices. Select a heatproof rectangular baking dish. It should be just large enough to hold two rows of slightly overlapping slices (a dish measuring 13½×8½×2 inches is appropriate). Rub the bottom of the dish with 2 tablespoons butter and sprinkle with onion, shallots, salt, and pepper. Arrange two parallel rows of salmon slices, the slices slightly overlapping, over the onion and shallots. Sprinkle with salt to taste. Sprinkle somewhat liberally with pepper. Scatter the mushrooms over the salmon.

2. Sprinkle the mushrooms with fresh dill and pour the wine over all. Cover with aluminum foil and bring to the boil on top of the stove. Place the dish in the oven and bake 15 minutes.

3. Remove the dish, uncover, and pour any accumulated liquid into a saucepan. Carefully spoon off most of the mushrooms and transfer them to another dish. Bring the cooking liquid to the boil over high heat. Tilt the dish containing the salmon. More liquid will accumulate as it stands. Spoon or pour this liquid into the saucepan containing the cooking liquid.

4. For the velouté, melt 2 tablespoons butter in a saucepan and stir in the flour, using a wire whisk. When blended, add the cooking liquid, stirring rapidly with the whisk. Cook about 5 minutes, stirring often. Add the mushrooms and continue cooking about 20 minutes, adding any liquid that accumulates around the salmon. Add the cayenne pepper and lemon juice. Beat the yolks with a whisk and scrape them into the mushrooms, stirring vigorously. Cook about 30 seconds, stirring, and remove from the heat. Add salt and a generous amount of pepper to taste.

5. Spoon and scrape this mushroom sauce—it should be quite thick —over the salmon. Using a spatula, cover the salmon with an even layer of the sauce but try to avoid having it spill over the sides of the salmon.

6. Let the sauce-covered salmon cool. Grease a neat rectangle of waxed paper with butter. Arrange this, buttered side down, on the sauce-covered salmon and refrigerate until thoroughly cold.

YIELD: Filling for 1 coulibiac.

Brioche Dough

¾ cup milk
¼ teaspoon sugar
3 tablespoons (packages) dry yeast
4 to 4 ½ cups flour
Salt to taste
1 cup (about 12) egg yolks
8 tablespoons (1 stick) butter, at room temperature

1. Pour the milk into a saucepan and heat it gradually to lukewarm. Remove from the heat. If milk has become too hot, let it cool to lukewarm.

2. Sprinkle the milk with sugar and yeast and stir to dissolve. Cover with a towel. Let stand about 5 minutes and place the mixture in a warm place (the natural warmth of a turned-off oven is good for this) about 5 minutes. It should ferment during the period and increase in volume.

3. Place 4 cups of flour with salt to taste in the bowl of an electric mixer fitted with a dough hook, or use a mixing bowl and wooden spoon. Make a well in the center and pour in the yeast mixture, the cup of yolks, and butter. With the dough hook or wooden spoon gradually work in flour until well blended. Then beat vigorously until the dough is quite smooth and can be shaped into a ball.

4. Turn the dough out onto a lightly floured board and knead until it is smooth and satiny, about 10 to 15 minutes. As you work the dough, continue to add flour to the kneading surface as necessary to prevent sticking, but take care not to add an excess or the finished product will be tough.

5. Lightly butter a clean mixing bowl and add the ball of dough. Cover with a clean towel and let stand in a warm place about 1 hour, or until double in bulk. Punch down the dough. Turn it out once more onto a lightly floured board. Knead it about 1 minute and return it to the clean bowl. Cover closely with plastic wrap and refrigerate overnight.

6. The next morning, punch the dough down again and continue to refrigerate, covered, until ready to use.

YIELD: Enough dough for 1 coulibiac.

Crêpes

1 ½ cups flour
3 large eggs
Salt and freshly ground pepper
1 ¾ cups milk
3 tablespoons melted butter
1 tablespoon finely chopped parsley
1 tablespoon finely chopped dill

1. Place the flour in a mixing bowl and make a well in the center. Add the eggs, salt, and pepper and gradually stir in the milk.

2. Put the mixture through a sieve, running the whisk around the inside of the sieve to remove lumps. Add 2 tablespoons of the melted butter, the parsley, and dill.

3. Melt the third tablespoon of butter and use this to brush a 7-inch pan each time or as necessary before making a crêpe.

4. Brush the crêpe pan lightly and place it on the stove. When the pan is hot but not burning, add 2 tablespoons of batter (it is preferable if you use a small ladle with a 2-tablespoon capacity), and swirl it around neatly to completely cover the bottom of the pan. Let cook over moderately high heat about 30 to 40 seconds or until lightly browned on the bottom. Turn the crêpe and cook the second side only about 15 seconds longer. Turn the crêpe out onto a sheet of wax paper.

5. Continue making crêpes, brushing the pan lightly as necessary to prevent sticking, until all the crêpes are made. As the crêpes are made turn them out, edges slightly overlapping, onto the wax paper.

YIELD: 14 (7-inch) crêpes.

Rice and Egg Filling

3 hard-cooked eggs
1 ¾ cups firmly cooked rice
¼ cup finely chopped parsley
1 tablespoon finely chopped dill
Salt and freshly ground pepper to taste
1 ½ cups chopped cooked vesiga (see following recipe), optional

1. Chop the eggs and add them to a mixing bowl.
2. Add the remaining ingredients and blend well.
YIELD: Filling for 1 coulibiac.

Vésiga

One of the classic—but optional—ingredients for a coulibiac of salmon is called vésiga. It is a ropelike, gelatinous substance, actually the spinal marrow of sturgeon. The vésiga, after cleaning, must be simmered for several hours until tender. It is then chopped and looks like chopped aspic. It has a very mild, bland flavor and its principal contribution to the dish is its slightly tender but chewy texture.

½ pound vésiga
Salt to taste

1. Wash the vésiga in cold water. Split it as necessary for thorough cleaning. Drain the vésiga and place it in a saucepan. Add water to cover and salt to taste. Bring to the boil. Partially cover.
2. Simmer 4 hours, replacing the liquid as it evaporates. Drain the vésiga and chop it. It will be translucent and resemble chopped aspic.
YIELD: 1½ cups.

A Smoked Fish and Bagel Brunch

1 ½ pounds smoked salmon or lox
1 pound smoked sturgeon
1 whole smoked whitefish fillet
¾ pound pickled salmon in cream sauce
2 matjes herring fillets in natural sauce, cut into bite-size pieces
2 matjes herring in wine sauce, cut into bite-size pieces
4 pickled herring fillets in cream sauce, cut into bite-size pieces
½ pound genuine caviar, optional
10 bagels
5 bialys
1 pound cream cheese
¼ pound black olives packed in brine

½ cup drained capers
1 large (about ¾ pound) Bermuda or Spanish onion, sliced (about 15 slices)
Sprigs fresh dill or parsley to garnish platters
Lemon halves or wedges for garnish
A pepper mill
Sour cream for caviar, optional
Chopped hard-cooked eggs for caviar, optional
Chopped onion for caviar, optional
Butter for bagels

1. Combine the various components for the brunch on platters, in sauce boats and plates as desired. Garnish with dill, lemon wedges, and so on.
2. Serve with a pepper mill on the side.
3. If desired, make sandwiches as follows: 1 slice of toasted, buttered bagel smeared with cream cheese, an onion slice, sturgeon and/or salmon, capers, a few drops of lemon juice, and a grind of black pepper. Caviar is best if eaten separately. It makes the sandwich too rich.
YIELD: 10 servings.

Broiled Kippered Herring

2 kippered herring, available in cans and also packed in plastic
3 tablespoons butter
2 lemon wedges or halves
Fresh parsley for garnish

1. Preheat the broiler.
2. Place the herring skin side down on a baking dish and dot with 1 tablespoon of butter.
3. Place the herring under the broiler and let cook long enough to become piping hot throughout. Do not overcook. Remove when lightly browned. Heat remaining butter and pour over the herring.
4. Place 1 herring on each of two plates and garnish with lemon wedges and parsley. Serve, if desired, with scrambled eggs, grilled tomato halves, and pickled walnuts, available in jars in supermarkets and in food specialty shops.
YIELD: 2 servings.

Pilaf of Mussels

1 ½ cups rice, cooked in chicken broth rather than water (see recipe for Perfect
   Rice)
3 pounds well-scrubbed mussels
2 tablespoons finely chopped onion
1 tablespoon chopped shallots
5 tablespoons chopped parsley
7 tablespoons butter
½ cup dry white wine
3 tablespoons flour
1 ½ cups thinly sliced mushrooms
½ teaspoon each minced onion and shallot
½ cup heavy cream
Salt and freshly ground pepper to taste

1. Prepare the rice.

2. Meanwhile, scrub the mussels well to remove all exterior sand
and dirt. Place the mussels in a kettle and add the 2 tablespoons
chopped onion, 1 tablespoon chopped shallots, 3 tablespoons parsley,
1 tablespoon butter, and white wine. Cover and bring to the boil. Cook
until mussels open, 5 to 10 minutes. Discard mussels that do not open.

3. Strain the cooking liquid and reserve. Remove each mussel from
the shell. Pull off and discard the tough, stringlike band attached to
each mussel. Reserve the mussels in a small covered container.

4. Melt 2½ tablespoons butter in a small saucepan and add the
flour. Stir with a whisk until blended. Add 1¾ cups of the liquid from
the mussels, stirring vigorously with the whisk until mixture boils.

5. Heat 2 tablespoons butter in a skillet and cook the mushrooms
until they are wilted. Add the minced onion and shallot and stir. Cook
briefly and add this, liquid and all, to the sauce. Simmer uncovered
over very low heat 45 minutes. Add the cream and continue cooking
about 10 minutes. Add salt and pepper to taste.

6. Meanwhile, preheat the oven to 300 degrees.

7. Butter a 1-quart heatproof bowl and add 2 cups of the cooked
rice. With the fingers or a spoon press the rice against the bowl, leaving
a well in the center to receive the mussels.

8. Spoon ½ cup of the sauce and 1 tablespoon of parsley onto the
mussels and blend. Heat thoroughly and spoon the mussels into the
rice-lined bowl. Top with remaining rice and press down to enclose the
mussels.

9. Cover with aluminum foil and place in the oven just to heat
through, about 5 minutes. Discard the foil and unmold onto a round,
warm serving platter.

10. Add the remaining parsley to the sauce and bring to a boil. Remove from the heat and swirl in the remaining 1½ tablespoons butter. Spoon a little sauce around the rice mold and serve the remainder separately.

YIELD: 4 to 6 servings.

Mussels Marinière

2 pounds mussels
2 shallots, coarsely chopped
2 small onions, quartered
2 sprigs fresh parsley
Salt and freshly ground pepper to taste
Pinch of cayenne pepper
1 cup dry white wine
2 tablespoons butter
½ bay leaf
½ teaspoon dried thyme

1. Scrub the mussels well to remove all exterior sand and dirt. Place them in a large kettle with the shallots, onions, parsley, salt, pepper, cayenne, wine, butter, bay leaf, and thyme. Cover and bring to a boil. Simmer 5 to 10 minutes, or until the mussels have opened. Discard any mussels that have not opened.

2. Serve the mussels and broth in hot soup plates with crusty French bread.

YIELD: 4 servings.

Moules frites
Deep-fried Mussels

48 mussels, cooked as for mussels marinière (see preceding recipe)
½ cup flour
3 eggs, lightly beaten
2 cups fresh bread crumbs
Fat for deep frying
Tartar sauce (see following recipe)

1. Remove the mussels from the shells. Dredge the mussels lightly in flour and shake off excess. Dip the mussels in beaten egg and then roll each mussel in bread crumbs.

2. Heat the fat to 375 degrees. If you do not have a deep-fat thermometer, drop a 1-inch cube of white bread into the fat and if the fat is at the proper temperature, the bread will brown in about 45 seconds. Deep fry the mussels, a few at a time, until golden brown. Drain on absorbent toweling. Serve hot with tartar sauce.

YIELD: 6 to 8 servings.

Tartar Sauce

1 cup freshly made mayonnaise
2 tablespoons finely chopped parsley
1 tablespoon finely chopped chives
1 tablespoon finely chopped tarragon
1 tablespoon finely chopped chervil, optional
1 teaspoon finely chopped onion, optional
1 tablespoon finely chopped capers
1 small sour pickle, finely chopped

Combine all ingredients and blend well. If desired, add a little minced garlic.

YIELD: About 1¼ cups.

Batter-fried Shrimp

1 ½ pounds shrimp
Beer batter (see following recipe)
1 ½ tablespoons cornstarch
1 tablespoon dry sherry
2 tablespoons finely chopped parsley
Salt
Peanut, vegetable, or corn oil for deep frying
Lemon wedges, optional
Hot mustard (see following recipe), optional
Chopped chutney, optional
Marmalade and mustard sauce (see following recipe), optional

1. Peel and devein the shrimp but leave the last tail segment intact. Refrigerate until ready to use.

2. Prepare the beer batter well in advance.

3. Combine the shrimp with the cornstarch, sherry, parsley, and salt to taste.

4. When ready to cook, heat the oil. Add a few shrimp at a time to the batter and, using a two-pronged fork, drop them, one at a time, into the hot oil. Cook, turning as necessary, to brown evenly. Drain on paper towels. Sprinkle with salt.

5. Serve immediately with lemon wedges or any of the desired sauces.

YIELD: 4 to 6 servings.

Beer Batter

¾ cup flour
½ cup flat beer, at room temperature
Salt to taste
1 teaspoon peanut, vegetable, or corn oil
1 egg, separated

1. Place the flour in a bowl and stir in the beer, salt, and oil. Stir to blend roughly. There should be a few small lumps. Cover the bowl with plastic wrap and let stand in a warm place about 3 hours.

2. Stir in the egg yolk.

3. When ready to cook, beat the white until stiff and fold it in.

YIELD: Enough batter for 1½ pounds shrimp.

Hot Mustard

Combine 6 tablespoons of powdered mustard in a mixing bowl with 3 tablespoons beer or water. Add salt to taste. Let stand 20 minutes to develop flavor.

YIELD: About ⅓ cup.

Marmalade and Mustard Sauce

½ cup orange marmalade
1 teaspoon prepared or homemade hot mustard (see preceding recipe)
1 teaspoon Grand Marnier

Combine all the ingredients and serve.
YIELD: About ½ cup.

Mrs. Reardy's Shrimp and Artichoke Casserole

6 ½ tablespoons butter
4 ½ tablespoons flour
¾ cup milk
¾ cup heavy cream
Salt and freshly ground pepper to taste
1 (Number 2) can artichoke hearts, drained, or 1 (10-ounce) package frozen
    artichoke hearts, cooked according to package directions
1 pound shrimp, cooked, shelled, and deveined
¼ pound mushrooms, sliced
¼ cup dry sherry
1 tablespoon Worcestershire sauce
¼ cup freshly grated Parmesan cheese
Paprika

1. Preheat the oven to 375 degrees.
2. Melt 4½ tablespoons of the butter and stir in the flour. When blended, gradually add the milk and cream, stirring constantly with a wire whisk. When the mixture is thickened and smooth, season to taste with salt and pepper.
3. Arrange the artichokes over the bottom of a buttered baking dish. Scatter the shrimp over the artichokes.
4. Cook the sliced mushrooms in the remaining 2 tablespoons of butter for 6 minutes. Spoon the mushrooms over the shrimp and artichokes.
5. Add the sherry and Worcestershire to the cream sauce and pour it over the contents of the baking dish. Sprinkle with Parmesan cheese and paprika and bake 20 to 30 minutes.
YIELD: 4 to 6 servings.

Garides mi Feta
Shrimp Baked with Feta Cheese

3 cups imported canned Italian plum tomatoes
1 pound (about 24) shrimp
¼ cup olive oil
1 teaspoon finely chopped garlic
¼ cup fresh fish broth or bottled clam juice
1 teaspoon crushed dried oregano
1 teaspoon dried hot red pepper flakes
2 tablespoons drained capers
Salt and freshly ground pepper
3 tablespoons butter
¼ pound feta cheese
¼ cup ouzo, optional, a Greek anise-flavored liqueur widely available in wine and spirits shops

1. Preheat the oven to 350 degrees.
2. Put the tomatoes in a saucepan and cook until reduced to about 2 cups. Stir often to prevent burning and sticking.
3. Shell and devein the shrimp and set aside.
4. Heat the olive oil in another saucepan or deep skillet and add the garlic, stirring. Add the tomatoes, using a rubber spatula to scrape them out.
5. Add the fish broth, oregano, pepper flakes, capers, and salt and pepper to taste.
6. Heat the butter in a heavy saucepan or skillet and cook the shrimp briefly, less than 1 minute, stirring and turning them until they turn pink.
7. Spoon equal portions of half the sauce into four individual baking dishes and arrange 6 shrimp plus equal amounts of the butter in which they cooked in each dish. Spoon remaining sauce over the shrimp.
8. Crumble the cheese and scatter it over all. Place the dishes in the oven and bake for 10 to 15 minutes, or until bubbling hot.
9. Remove the dishes from the oven and sprinkle each dish with 1 tablespoon ouzo, if desired, and ignite it. Serve immediately.
YIELD: 4 servings.

Coquilles Saint-Jacques

1 ½ pounds (about 2 cups) scallops, preferably bay scallops
2 sprigs fresh thyme, or ½ teaspoon dried
1 bay leaf
1 sprig fresh parsley
8 peppercorns
Salt
½ cup water
½ cup dry white wine
7 tablespoons butter
3 tablespoons flour
2 egg yolks
1 teaspoon lemon juice
Cayenne pepper
Grated Parmesan cheese

1. Preheat the oven to 400 degrees.
2. Combine the scallops, thyme, bay leaf, parsley, peppercorns, salt, water, and wine in a small saucepan and bring to the boil. Cover and simmer exactly 2 minutes. Remove parsley, bay leaf, and thyme sprigs and drain but reserve the cooking liquid. Let the scallops cool. If bay scallops are very large, cut them in half. If sea scallops are used, cut them into thin slices. Set aside.
3. Melt 2 tablespoons butter and stir in the flour with a wire whisk. When blended, add the scallop liquid (about 1½ cups), stirring vigorously with the whisk.
4. Remove the sauce from the heat and beat vigorously with an electric beater. Add the remaining butter a little at a time. It must be added very gradually. Beat in the egg yolks and continue beating until cool. Add the lemon juice and cayenne.
5. Spoon a little of the mixture into twelve to sixteen small scallop shells or six to eight large scallop shells or ramekins. Top with equal parts of scallops. Cover with the remaining sauce and sprinkle with Parmesan cheese.
6. Bake 5 to 10 minutes, or until bubbling and golden brown. If necessary, glaze at the last minute under the broiler.

YIELD: 4 to 6 servings.

Jean Vergnes' Seafood Crêpes

20 crêpes with fines herbes (see following recipe)
1 ½ cups (approximately) curry sauce (see following recipe)
1 ½ cups (approximately) sauce piquante (see following recipe)
3 tablespoons butter
2 tablespoons finely chopped shallots
⅓ cup dry white wine
1 tablespoon each finely chopped fresh chives, parsley, and tarragon or half the
   amount dried
1 cup finely diced lobster meat
1 cup finely diced shrimp
1 cup lump crab meat
Salt and freshly ground pepper
Butter for brushing crêpes

1. Prepare crêpes.
2. Start sauces. While they are simmering, prepare the filling.
3. Place the 3 tablespoons of butter in a saucepan and add the shallots. Cook briefly, stirring, and add the wine. Cook to reduce by half. Add the herbs and seafood and stir to blend. Sprinkle with salt and pepper to taste and cook briefly, stirring, until heated through.
4. Preheat the oven to 200 degrees.
5. Spoon equal portions of the mixture into the center of each crêpe and roll. Arrange the crêpes on an ovenproof platter and brush with melted butter. Butter a sheet of waxed paper and place it buttered side down over the crêpes. Cover and bake until heated through.
6. Serve on hot plates, spooning a little of the curry sauce on half of each crêpe, a little of the sauce piquante on the other half.
YIELD: 8 to 10 servings.

Crêpes with fines herbes

1 ½ cups sifted all-purpose flour
2 eggs
¼ teaspoon salt
2 ½ cups milk
1 tablespoon each chopped fresh tarragon, parsley, and chives or half the amount
   dried
4 tablespoons melted butter

1. Combine the flour, eggs, and salt in a mixing bowl. Gradually add the milk, stirring constantly with a wire whisk.

2. Strain the batter into a mixing bowl, then add the herbs and 3 tablespoons melted butter.

3. Heat a 6- to 7-inch seasoned crêpe pan and brush it lightly with a little remaining butter. Ladle a little of the batter in, swirling the pan around until the bottom is thoroughly covered with a thin coating. Cook until lightly browned on one side. Flip and cook briefly on the other side. The crêpe should not be brown on the second side. Repeat the procedure until all the batter is used.

YIELD: About 20 crêpes.

Curry Sauce

4 ½ tablespoons butter
1 clove garlic, finely minced
⅓ cup finely chopped onion
⅓ cup finely chopped celery
3 tablespoons chopped carrot
2 tablespoons flour
2 tablespoons curry powder
½ bay leaf
2 sprigs fresh parsley
2 sprigs fresh thyme, or ½ teaspoon dried
1 ¾ cups chicken broth
Salt and freshly ground pepper

1. Heat 3 tablespoons of butter in a saucepan and add the garlic, onion, celery, and carrot. Cook, stirring, until onion is wilted. Add the flour and cook, stirring, about 3 minutes. Stir in the curry, bay leaf, parsley, and thyme.

2. Using a wire whisk, continue to stir briskly while adding the broth. Simmer, covered, stirring occasionally, about 30 minutes. Put the mixture, including soft vegetables, through a fine sieve, using a wooden spoon to push the solids through. Swirl in the remaining butter and add salt and pepper to taste.

YIELD: About 1½ cups.

Sauce Piquante

2 tablespoons Dijon or Düsseldorf mustard
3 tablespoons bottled sauce Robert (see note)
4 tablespoons bottled sauce Diable (see note)
¼ teaspoon Worcestershire sauce
¼ teaspoon Tabasco sauce
1 ¼ cups heavy cream
Salt and pepper

In a saucepan, combine all the ingredients. Simmer, uncovered, stirring occasionally, about 10 minutes.

YIELD: About 1½ cups.

NOTE: These sauces with the Escoffier label are available in many supermarkets and in most fine food outlets.

Chinese Fire Pot

1 small head Chinese cabbage (bok choy)
2 ounces bean thread (sometimes called Chinese vermicelli or cellophane noodles)
Shrimp balls (see following recipe)
Fish balls (see following recipe)
Pork balls (see following recipe)
16 small shrimp in the shell
8 large dried black mushrooms
1 large or 2 small bamboo shoots
16 littleneck or cherrystone clams
Chicken broth

1. Trim off and discard the root end of the Chinese cabbage. Cut the leaves into 3-inch pieces. Drop into boiling water to cover and cook about 8 minutes. Remove the pieces but reserve the liquid for cooking bean thread. Set cabbage aside.

2. Drop the bean thread into the boiling liquid in which the cabbage cooked. Simmer 3 minutes. Add cold water to the kettle to stop the cooking. Set aside.

3. Prepare the shrimp, fish, and pork balls.

4. Drop the shrimp in the shell into boiling water to barely cover and let the water return to the boil. Simmer 1 minute and let cool in the cooking liquid.

---

5. Place the dried mushrooms in a mixing bowl and pour boiling water over them. Let stand until cool. Drain. Squeeze out most of the moisture. Cut or trim off the tough stems. Slice diagonally and set aside.

6. Cut the bamboo shoots in thin bite-size slices. Reassemble the slices and set aside.

7. Scrub the clams and set aside.

8. Arrange a layer of Chinese cabbage on the bottom of the round food and liquid basin of a Chinese fire pot (see note). Arrange drained bean thread over this. Arrange groups of precooked shrimp balls, fish balls, pork balls, shrimp in the shell, black mushrooms, and bamboo shoots. Unless the fire pot is quite large, do not add all the ingredients at once, but add more as the portions are eaten.

9. When ready to cook, add a well-seasoned chicken broth to barely cover the ingredients. Add the clams. Cover with the fire pot lid. Add burning charcoal to the fire pot chimney and let the broth come to a boil.

10. Serve the cooked ingredients with small bowls of rice and chopsticks.

YIELD: 8 servings.

NOTE: Authentic fire pots are available in Chinese shops. Make certain the room in which you cook is well ventilated because of the fumes from the charcoal. Also make certain the fire pot is placed on a heatproof pad. Do not place it directly on a fabric or wooden surface. The commercial pad known as Flame-Tamer makes an excellent insulation for the fire pot.

Shrimp Balls

½ pound shrimp in shells
1 tablespoon cornstarch
½ egg white (empty white into a bowl, beat it lightly and measure it, or simply use your own judgment; use remainder of egg white in making pork balls—see following recipe)
1 teaspoon salt
½ teaspoon sugar
1 tablespoon shao hsing or dry sherry wine

1. Peel and devein the shrimp. Combine all the ingredients in the container of a food processor. Blend thoroughly. Or finely chop with a knife or cleaver on a flat surface.

2. Fill a casserole about 2 inches deep with cold water. Gather a mass of the shrimp mixture between the thumb and forefinger. Transfer this into a wet spoon, shaping it neatly to form a more or less round ball. Drop the balls, as they are made, into the cold water. Continue until all the balls are formed.

3. Bring the water to the boil slowly. When the balls rise to the surface, remove them with a slotted spoon and drop them into a bowl of cold water. Let stand until ready to use in the fire pot. These balls can be refrigerated in cold water for a day or longer and, when drained, may be served in clear chicken soup.

YIELD: About 10 to 12 balls.

Fish Balls

½ pound fresh fish fillets, preferably yellow pike, or use another white-flesh, nonoily fish
1 ½ teaspoons salt
¼ cup water
1 egg white
1 tablespoon lard, at room temperature, optional
1 tablespoon shao hsing or dry sherry wine
1 tablespoon finely chopped scallions
2 tablespoons finely minced cooked ham, preferably Smithfield
½ tablespoon chopped fresh ginger
Freshly ground pepper to taste

1. The flesh of the fish should be firm. Trim away and discard any thin, flabby stomach flesh. Cut the fish into cubes and blend it thoroughly in a food processor. Or finely chop with a knife or cleaver on a flat surface.

2. Add the salt, water, egg white, and lard and blend.

3. Scrape the mixture into a mixing bowl and add the wine, scallions, ham, ginger, and pepper.

4. Follow the instructions for shrimp balls for shaping and cooking. These balls may be kept refrigerated in cold water for a day or longer and may be used in soup.

YIELD: About 10 to 12 balls.

Pork Balls

½ pound ground pork
1 egg yolk
½ egg white (empty white into a bowl, beat it lightly and measure, or simply use
    your own judgment; use remainder of egg white in making shrimp balls)
3 tablespoons finely chopped water chestnuts
1 tablespoon grated fresh ginger
1 tablespoon finely chopped scallion
1 ½ teaspoons salt
1 tablespoon shao hsing or dry sherry wine
½ teaspoon sugar
1 tablespoon cornstarch

1. Place the pork in a bowl and add the remaining ingredients. Stir in a circular fashion to blend. The more the mixture is stirred, the looser the meat will become and the pork balls will be more tender when cooked.

2. Follow the instructions for shrimp balls for shaping and cooking. These balls may be kept refrigerated in cold water for a day or longer and may be used later in soup.

YIELD: About 10 to 12 balls.

Braised Endive

16 heads Belgian endive
Juice of 1 lemon
4 tablespoons butter
Salt to taste
½ cup water
1 tablespoon sugar

1. Preheat the oven to 450 degrees.

2. Trim off and discard any discolored leaves from the endive. Place the endive in an ovenproof kettle and add the lemon juice, 2 tablespoons of butter, salt, water, and sugar. Cover and bring to the boil on top of the stove.

3. Place the kettle in the oven and bake 30 to 40 minutes. Drain well. Squeeze between the hands to extract any excess liquid.

4. Melt remaining 2 tablespoons of butter in a skillet large enough

to hold the drained, squeezed endive in one layer. Add endive and brown on one side. Turn and brown on the other side. Serve hot.

YIELD: 8 servings.

Deep-fried Mushrooms

32 fresh, white mushrooms
Flour for dredging
Salt and freshly ground pepper
2 eggs
1 teaspoon water
1 teaspoon peanut oil
1 ½ cups fresh bread crumbs
Oil for deep frying
Tartar sauce (see recipe, page 352)

1. Trim off tips of mushroom stems, but leave the stems on. Rinse mushrooms under cold running water. Drain but do not dry.

2. Dredge mushrooms in flour seasoned with salt and pepper.

3. Beat the eggs with water and oil and place in a pie plate.

4. Toss or turn the mushrooms in the egg mixture until completely coated, then coat with bread crumbs. Let stand until ready to cook.

5. Heat the oil in a large skillet to 375 degrees. If a deep-fat thermometer is not available, drop a 1-inch cube of white bread into the fat. If the bread browns in 45 seconds, the temperature is correct. Deep fry the mushrooms until golden brown. Drain on absorbent paper toweling and serve hot with tartar sauce.

YIELD: 4 servings.

Le Cirque's Spaghetti Primavera

1 bunch broccoli
2 small zucchini
4 asparagus spears, each about 5 inches long
1 ½ cups trimmed, cut-up (1-inch lengths) green beans
Salt
½ cup fresh or frozen green peas
¾ cup fresh or frozen pea pods, optional

1 tablespoon peanut, vegetable, or corn oil
2 cups thinly sliced mushrooms
Freshly ground black pepper
1 teaspoon finely chopped fresh hot red or green chilies, or about ½ teaspoon dried
  hot red pepper flakes
¼ cup finely chopped parsley
6 tablespoons olive oil
1 teaspoon finely chopped garlic
3 cups cut-up (1-inch cubes) ripe red tomatoes
6 fresh basil leaves, chopped (about ¼ cup), or 1 teaspoon dried basil
1 pound spaghetti or spaghettini
4 tablespoons butter
2 tablespoons fresh or canned chicken broth
½ to ¾ cup heavy cream
⅔ cup grated Parmesan cheese
⅓ cup toasted pine nuts

1. Trim the broccoli and break it into bite-size flowerets. Set aside.

2. Trim off and discard the ends of the zucchini but do not peel it. Cut the zucchini into quarters. Cut each quarter into 1-inch or slightly longer lengths. There should be about 1½ cups, no more. Set aside.

3. Cut each asparagus spear into thirds. Set aside.

4. Cook each of the vegetables as specified separately in boiling salted water to cover. Cook each so that it remains crisp but tender. The broccoli, zucchini, asparagus, and green beans should take about 5 minutes. Drain well, then run under cold water to chill, and drain again thoroughly. Combine the vegetables as they are cooked in a mixing bowl.

5. Cook the peas and pea pods; about 1 minute if fresh, 30 seconds if frozen. Drain, chill with cold water, and drain again. Combine with the rest of the vegetables.

6. Heat the peanut oil in a skillet and add the mushrooms. Add salt and pepper to taste and cook, shaking the skillet and stirring, about 2 minutes. Add the mushrooms to the vegetables. Add the chopped chilies and parsley.

7. Heat 3 tablespoons of olive oil in a saucepan and add half the garlic, the 3 cups of tomatoes, salt and pepper to taste. Cook about 4 minutes, stirring gently so as not to break up the tomatoes any more than necessary. Add the basil, stir and set aside.

8. Add the remaining 3 tablespoons of olive oil to a large skillet. Add the remaining garlic and the vegetable mixture and cook, stirring gently, just long enough to heat through.

9. Drop the spaghetti into 3 or 4 quarts boiling salted water. Cook until almost but not quite tender. That is to say, al dente. The spaghetti,

when ready, must retain just a slight resilience in the center. Drain well. Return the spaghetti to the hot kettle to keep it warm.

10. Select a utensil large enough to hold the drained spaghetti and all the vegetables. To this, add the butter. When it melts, add the chicken broth, cream, and cheese, stirring constantly. Cook gently on and off the heat until smooth. Add the spaghetti and toss quickly to blend. Add half the vegetables and pour in the liquid from the tomatoes, tossing and stirring over very low heat.

11. Add the remaining vegetables. If the sauce seems too dry, add about ¼ cup more cream. The sauce should not be soupy. Add the pine nuts and give the mixture one final tossing.

12. Serve equal portions of the spaghetti mixture in four to eight hot soup bowls. Spoon equal amounts of the tomatoes over each serving. Serve immediately.

YIELD: 4 to 8 servings as a main course; 6 to 8 as an appetizer.

Fettuccine alla Romana

½ pound fettuccine
Salt
4 tablespoons butter, at room temperature, cut into 8 pieces
½ cup freshly grated Parmesan cheese
¼ cup hot heavy cream
½ cup freshly cooked peas, preferably freshly shelled
⅓ cup finely shredded, imported or domestic prosciutto
Freshly ground pepper

1. The important thing about this recipe is to have all the ingredients ready. The fettuccine must be tossed and served with the other ingredients within seconds after it is cooked. Heat a serving dish and plates for the fettuccine and place a colander in the sink.

2. Place the fettuccine into boiling salted water to cover and cook to the desired degree of doneness. This should not require more than 8 or 9 minutes for *al dente,* as preferred by Italians.

3. Test the fettuccine for doneness a strand at a time. Remove the strand with a fork, let cool briefly, then bite into it. When nearly done, add the butter to the hot serving dish.

4. When cooked, pour the fettuccine into the colander. Drain quickly and not too thoroughly. Pour the moist pasta into the serving dish and toss quickly. Add the cheese, cream, peas, and prosciutto and

continue tossing. Serve quickly on hot plates. Let the guests season the
fettuccine themselves with a pepper mill.

YIELD: 2 large or 4 small servings.

Curried Sweetbreads with Fettuccine

1 pair (about 1 ½ pounds) sweetbreads
Salt to taste
1 carrot, scraped and thinly sliced
1 small onion, thinly sliced
1 clove garlic, finely chopped
6 sprigs fresh parsley
2 sprigs fresh thyme, or ½ teaspoon dried
1 bay leaf
2 ½ cups chicken broth
10 tablespoons butter, at room temperature
½ pound mushrooms, thinly sliced
1 tablespoon curry powder
1 cup heavy cream
1 ½ pounds fettuccine or linguine
¾ cup grated Parmesan cheese

1. Place the sweetbreads in a basin of cold water and refrigerate
several hours. Drain and put the sweetbreads in a saucepan and add
cold water to cover. Add salt to taste and bring to the boil. Simmer 5
minutes. Drain and immediately run under cold running water.

2. Weight the sweetbreads, which improves their texture. To do
this, place the sweetbreads in a deep plate and cover with a saucepan.
Add weights to the saucepan. Refrigerate for at least 2 hours, or
overnight.

3. Place the sweetbreads in another saucepan and add the carrot,
onion, garlic, parsley, thyme, bay leaf, and chicken broth. Bring to the
boil and simmer 5 minutes. Drain, but reserve ½ cup of the cooking
liquid.

4. When the sweetbreads are cool enough to handle, pare off and
remove the unsightly tissues and membranes that surround them. Cut
the sweetbreads into ½-inch cubes and set aside.

5. Heat 2 tablespoons of the butter in a saucepan and add the
mushrooms. Toss them in the butter until they are wilted and start to
brown. Sprinkle with the curry powder and add the reserved ½ cup of

liquid. Simmer about 3 minutes and add the cubed sweetbreads. Add the cream and bring to the boil. Set aside.

6. Cook the fettuccine in boiling salted water to the desired degree of doneness. Drain and empty it into a large, hot bowl for mixing.

7. Immediately add the remaining butter and the hot sweetbreads mixture and toss. Sprinkle with cheese, toss quickly, and serve piping hot.

YIELD: 6 to 8 servings.

Pesto with Pistachios

6 cups (exactly ¼ pound) loosely packed, unrinsed basil leaves (see note)
½ cup shelled pistachios, preferably unsalted
⅓ cup loosely packed fresh parsley
1 cup grated Parmesan cheese
Salt to taste (some Italian chefs say you should not add salt until you are ready
  to use the pesto sauce; it preserves better without it)
Freshly ground pepper to taste
3 or 4 tablespoons finely chopped garlic
¾ to 1 cup olive oil

1. Rinse the measured basil carefully and pat or spin dry. Set aside.

2. If the pistachios have not been blanched, bring enough water to the boil to cover the pistachios when they are added. Add the pistachios and simmer about 2 minutes, or until the outer coating can be removed easily with fingers. Drain and remove the outer coating. Set aside.

3. Put the basil into the container of a food processor and add the pistachios and parsley. Add the cheese, salt, pepper, and garlic.

4. Start processing and gradually add the oil in a fine stream. Process until almost but not quite totally smooth in texture. Remember that when you use this sauce, in whatever quantity (it can be used a little at a time and the remainder will keep well in the refrigerator), it should be thinned with a little of the water in which your pasta is cooked. This sauce also freezes admirably.

YIELD: About 2½ cups.

NOTE: It is best if the basil is measured by weight (¼ pound) rather than by volume (6 cups loosely packed). The weight is more precise. The basil should be measured and weighed when unrinsed.

My Mother's Chicken Spaghetti

1 (3 ½-pound) chicken with giblets
Fresh or canned chicken broth to cover
Salt
3 cups imported Italian peeled tomatoes
7 tablespoons butter
3 tablespoons flour
½ cup heavy cream
⅛ teaspoon grated nutmeg
Freshly ground pepper
½ pound fresh mushrooms
2 cups finely chopped onion
1 ½ cups finely chopped celery
1 ½ cups chopped seeded green pepper
1 tablespoon or more finely minced garlic
¼ pound ground beef
¼ pound ground pork
1 bay leaf
½ teaspoon hot red pepper flakes, optional
1 pound spaghetti or spaghettini
½ pound Cheddar cheese, grated (about 2 to 2 ½ cups)
Freshly grated Parmesan cheese

1. Place the chicken with neck, gizzard, heart, and liver in a kettle and add chicken broth to cover and salt to taste. Partially cover. Bring to the boil and simmer until the chicken is tender without being dry, 35 to 45 minutes. Let cool.

2. Remove the chicken and take the meat from the bones. Shred the meat, cover, and set aside. Return the skin and bones to the kettle and cook the stock down for 30 minutes or longer. There should be 4 to 6 cups of broth. Strain and reserve the broth. Discard the skin and bones.

3. Meanwhile, put the tomatoes in a saucepan and cook down to half the original volume, stirring.

4. Melt 3 tablespoons butter in a saucepan and add the flour, stirring to blend with a wire whisk. When blended and smooth, add 1 cup of the reserved hot broth and the cream, stirring rapidly with the whisk. When thickened and smooth, add the nutmeg, salt, and pepper to taste. Continue cooking, stirring occasionally, for about 10 minutes. Set aside.

5. If the mushrooms are very small, leave them whole. Otherwise, cut them in half or quarter them. Heat 1 tablespoon of butter in a small

skillet and add the mushrooms. Cook, shaking the skillet occasionally and stirring, until the mushrooms are golden brown. Set aside.

6. Heat 3 tablespoons of butter in a deep skillet and add the onion. Cook, stirring, until wilted. Add the celery and green pepper and cook, stirring, for about 5 minutes. Do not overcook. The vegetables should remain crisp-tender.

7. Add the garlic, beef, and pork and cook, stirring and chopping down with the edge of a large metal spoon to break up the meat. Cook just until the meat loses its red color. Add the bay leaf and red pepper flakes, if desired. Add the tomatoes and the white sauce made with the chicken broth. Add the mushrooms.

8. Cook the spaghetti in 3 or 4 quarts of boiling salted water until it is just tender. Do not overcook. Remember that it will cook again when blended with the chicken and meat sauce. Drain the spaghetti and run under cold running water.

9. Spoon enough of the meat sauce over the bottom of a 5- or 6-quart casserole to cover it lightly. Add about one third of the spaghetti. Add about one third of the shredded chicken, a layer of meat sauce, and a layer of grated Cheddar cheese. Continue making layers, ending with a layer of spaghetti topped with a thin layer of meat sauce and grated Cheddar cheese.

10. Pour in up to 2 cups of the reserved chicken broth or enough to almost but not quite cover the top layer of spaghetti. At this point the dish may be left to stand, covered, for up to an hour. If the liquid is absorbed as the dish stands, add a little more chicken broth. Remember that when this dish is baked and served, the sauce will be just a bit soupy rather than thick and clinging.

11. When ready to bake, preheat the oven to 350 degrees.

12. Place the spaghetti casserole on top of the stove and bring it just to the boil. Cover and place it in the oven. Bake for 15 minutes and uncover. Bake for 15 minutes longer, or until the casserole is hot and bubbling throughout and starting to brown on top. Serve immediately with grated Parmesan cheese on the side.

YIELD: 12 or more servings.

Crème brûlée

3 cups heavy cream
6 tablespoons sugar
6 egg yolks
2 teaspoons vanilla extract
½ cup light brown sugar

1. Preheat oven to slow (300 degrees).
2. Heat the cream over boiling water and stir in the sugar.
3. Beat the egg yolks until light and pour the hot cream over them gradually, stirring vigorously. Stir in the vanilla and strain the mixture into a 5-cup baking dish.
4. Place the dish in a pan containing 1 inch of hot water and bake thirty-five minutes, or until a silver knife inserted in the center comes out clean. Do not overbake; the custard will continue to cook from retained heat when it is removed from the oven. Chill thoroughly.
5. Before serving, cover the surface with the brown sugar. Set the dish on a bed of cracked ice and put the crème under the broiler until the sugar is brown and melted. Serve immediately or chill again and serve cold.
   YIELD: 6 to 8 servings.

Lemon Lotus Ice Cream

4 lemons
2 cups sugar
4 cups (2 pints) medium cream
2 cups milk

1. Trim off and discard the ends of one of the lemons. Cut the lemon into thin slices. Remove the seeds from the slices and cut the slices in half to resemble half-moons.
2. Squeeze the remaining 3 lemons and combine the juice with the sugar in a mixing bowl. Add the lemon slices and refrigerate 2 hours or, preferably, overnight. Stir until all the sugar is dissolved.
3. Combine the cream and milk in the churn of an ice cream freezer. Chill thoroughly, preferably in an electric freezer, 10 to 15 minutes. Do not allow the mixture to freeze.

4. Add the lemon-and-sugar mixture to the cream mixture and install the churn in the ice cream freezer. Freeze according to the manufacturer's instructions and keep frozen until ready to serve.

YIELD: 6 servings.

Grapefruit Sherbet

2 cups sugar
4 cups water
2 cups freshly squeezed grapefruit juice
Crème de cassis, optional
Vodka, optional

1. Combine the sugar and water in a saucepan and bring to the boil. Add the grapefruit juice and cool. Chill thoroughly.

2. Pour the mixture into the container of an electric or hand-cranked ice cream freezer and freeze according to the manufacturer's instructions. Serve individual portions, if desired, with crème de cassis and a touch of cold vodka poured over.

YIELD: 2 quarts, or 12 to 14 servings.

Granité de fruits au cassis
Fruit Ice with Cassis

4 cups fresh strawberries or raspberries
2 cups water
1 ¼ cups sugar
2 tablespoons lemon juice
1 ½ cups sirop de cassis (cassis syrup), available in wine and spirit shops

1. Pick over the berries and remove stems. Rinse the berries in cold water and drain. Put the berries in the container of a food processor or electric blender and blend, stirring down as necessary. There should be about 2 cups of purée.

---

2. Combine the water and sugar in a saucepan and bring to the boil. Simmer 5 minutes. Cool, then chill thoroughly. Add the fruit purée, lemon juice, and cassis.

3. Pour the mixture into the container of an electric or hand-cranked ice cream freezer and freeze according to the manufacturer's instructions. Serve with more cassis poured over, if desired.

YIELD: 2 quarts, or 12 to 14 servings.

Granité au citron
Lemon Ice

2 cups sugar
4 cups water
Grated rind of 2 lemons
2 cups lemon juice

1. Combine the sugar and water in a saucepan and boil for 5 minutes. Add the rind and lemon juice and cool. Chill thoroughly.

2. Pour the mixture into the container of an electric or hand-cranked ice cream freezer and freeze according to the manufacturer's instructions. Serve, if desired, with cold vodka poured over.

YIELD: 2 quarts, or 12 to 14 servings.

Ann Seranne's Pumpkin Cream Pie

2 cups strained, cooked pumpkin (fresh or canned)
2 teaspoons cinnamon
⅔ cup brown sugar
½ teaspoon ground ginger
½ teaspoon salt
1 ½ cups milk
2 eggs, well beaten
½ cup heavy cream
Unbaked pastry for a 9-inch, 1-crust pie

1. Preheat the oven to 325 degrees.

2. Combine the pumpkin, 2 teaspoons cinnamon, sugar, ginger, and salt. Gradually add the milk and beat with a rotary beater or blend thoroughly in an electric blender. Stir in the eggs and the cream.

3. Line a 9-inch pie plate with the pastry and pour in the pumpkin mixture. Bake 50 minutes, or until a knife inserted near the center comes out clean. Serve warm with whipped cream, if desired.

YIELD: 6 to 8 servings.

Soufflé au gingembre
Ginger Soufflé

10 tablespoons butter
1 cup flour
2 ¼ cups milk
1 tablespoon grated fresh ginger, or 1 teaspoon ground ginger
8 eggs, separated
4 tablespoons chopped candied ginger
1 cup sugar

1. Preheat the oven to 375 degrees.

2. Rub the bottom and sides of a 10-cup soufflé dish with 1 tablespoon butter. Place the dish in the refrigerator and let chill.

3. Add the remaining butter to a mixing bowl and add the flour. Work the mixture with the fingers until smooth and thoroughly blended. This is called a beurre manié. Set aside.

4. Pour the milk into a saucepan and add the grated ginger. Stir and bring to the boil. Add the beurre manié gradually to the milk mixture, about 1 tablespoon at a time, stirring rapidly and constantly with a wire whisk. Continue until all the beurre manié is added and the sauce is quite thick and smooth. Cook, stirring often, about 5 minutes. Remove from the heat and add the yolks, stirring rapidly with the whisk. Return to the heat and cook, stirring, just until the sauce returns to the boil.

5. Spoon the sauce into a mixing bowl. Fold in the candied ginger.

6. Beat the whites until stiff and gradually add ¾ cup of sugar, beating constantly. Add about half the whites to the sauce, stirring and blending well. Fold in the remaining whites.

7. Remove soufflé dish from the refrigerator. Add remaining ¼ cup sugar and swirl the dish this way and that to coat the bottom and sides. Shake out excess sugar.

8. Spoon and scrape the soufflé mixture into the prepared dish. This mixture will more than fill the dish. That is all right. Smooth it over.

9. Place the soufflé in the oven and bake 20 minutes. Reduce the heat to 350 degrees and continue baking 10 to 15 minutes longer. When served, the soufflé will be quite moist in the center. For a firmer soufflé, continue baking another 10 minutes. Serve immediately.

YIELD: 6 to 10 servings.

Minetry's Miracle

1 pound unsalted butter
2 cups sugar
12 eggs, separated
48 amaretti (Italian macaroons)
1 cup bourbon whiskey
¼ pound (4 squares) unsweetened chocolate, melted
1 teaspoon pure vanilla extract
1 cup coarsely chopped pecans
24 double ladyfingers, separated
1½ cups heavy cream, whipped and sweetened to taste

1. Cream together the butter and sugar until light and fluffy. Beat egg yolks until light and beat them into the creamed mixture.

2. Soak the macaroons in bourbon.

3. Beat the melted chocolate into the creamed mixture. Add vanilla and pecans.

4. Beat egg whites until stiff and fold them into the chocolate mixture.

5. Line a 10-inch springform pan with ladyfingers. Align them neatly and close together over the bottom and around the sides of the pan. Alternate layers of the chocolate mixture and the soaked macaroons. Refrigerate overnight.

6. Unmold the sides of the dessert and, using a pastry bag outfitted with a star tube, decorate the top of the cake with whipped cream.

YIELD: 16 or more servings.

Charlotte Russe with Kirsch

8 egg yolks
1 cup sugar
2 cups milk
1 (1-inch) length of vanilla bean, optional
2 envelopes unflavored gelatin
¼ cup cold water
¼ cup kirsch
2 cups heavy cream
12 ladyfingers, split

1. Combine the egg yolks and sugar and work the mixture with a wooden spoon until smooth. Bring the milk to a boil with the vanilla bean. Add it gradually to the yolk mixture, stirring rapidly with a wire whisk. Cook over boiling water until thick.

2. Soften the gelatin in the cold water and add it to the custard, stirring until the gelatin dissolves. Remove the vanilla bean. Cool the custard but do not let it set. Add the kirsch.

3. Whip the cream until it stands in moist peaks and fold it into the custard.

4. Line the bottom of a 1½-quart charlotte mold with ladyfingers arranged in a daisy-petal pattern. Stand the remaining ladyfingers close together around the sides of the mold.

5. Pour the custard mixture into the mold, cover with waxed paper, and chill until set, about 2 hours. Unmold the charlotte russe and serve.

YIELD: 8 to 10 servings.

NOTE: If there is any custard mixture remaining after the charlotte mold is filled, it may be poured into individual custard cups and chilled until set. Serve with a fruit sauce.

Hazelnut Cheesecake

1 ½ cups (approximately 1 pound) shelled, toasted, hulled hazelnuts or blanched,
 toasted almonds
Butter
⅓ cup (approximately) graham-cracker crumbs
2 pounds cream cheese, at room temperature
½ cup heavy cream
4 eggs
1 ¾ cups sugar
1 teaspoon vanilla extract

1. Because of the importance of oven temperature, the nuts must be toasted well in advance of proceeding with the recipe. If they are not already toasted, preheat the oven to 400 degrees. Place the nuts on a baking sheet or in a skillet and bake them, stirring them often so that they brown evenly. When nicely browned, remove them and let them cool.

2. When ready to make the cheesecake, preheat the oven to 300 degrees.

3. Place the nuts in the container of an electric blender or food processor and blend. If you want a crunchy texture, blend them until coarse fine. If you want a smooth texture, blend them until they are almost pastelike.

4. Butter the inside of a metal cake pan 8 inches wide and 3 inches deep. Do not use a springform pan.

5. Sprinkle the inside with graham-cracker crumbs and shake the crumbs around the bottom and sides until coated. Shake out the excess crumbs and set aside.

6. Place the cream cheese, cream, eggs, sugar, and vanilla into the bowl of an electric mixer. Start beating at low speed and, as the ingredients blend, increase the speed to high. Continue beating until thoroughly blended and smooth. Add the nuts and continue beating until thoroughly blended.

7. Pour and scrape the batter into the prepared pan and shake gently to level the mixture.

8. Set the pan inside a slightly wider pan and pour boiling water into the larger pan to a depth of about ½ inch. Do not let the edge of the cheesecake pan touch the other larger pan. Set the pans thus arranged inside the oven and bake 2 hours. At the end of that time, turn off the oven heat and let the cake sit in the oven 1 hour longer.

9. Lift the cake out of its water bath and place it on a rack. Let the cake stand at least 2 hours.

---

10. Place a round cake plate over the cake and carefully turn both upside down to unmold the cake. Serve lukewarm or at room temperature.

YIELD: 12 or more servings.

French Bread-and-butter Pudding

½ cup mixed candied fruit
¼ cup kirsch
½ cup dried raisins
Butter
10 small thin slices French bread
1 quart milk
1 cup cream
1 cup granulated sugar
5 eggs
4 egg yolks
1 teaspoon vanilla extract
Confectioners' sugar, optional

1. Combine the candied fruit and kirsch in a small mixing bowl and set aside.
2. Place the raisins in another small bowl and add boiling water to cover. Let stand 5 minutes, then drain.
3. Generously butter one side of the bread and set aside.
4. Preheat the oven to 375 degrees.
5. Combine the milk and cream and bring just to a boil, then remove from the heat. Add the sugar and stir until dissolved. Combine the eggs and egg yolks, beat lightly, and add to the liquid. Stir in the vanilla extract.
6. Butter a 2-quart oval baking dish. Drain the candied fruits and sprinkle over the bottom of the baking dish. Sprinkle with raisins.
7. Arrange the bread slices, buttered side up, over the fruit. Strain the custard over the bread and fruit. Place the baking dish in a larger dish and pour boiling water around it. Set in the oven and bake about 40 minutes, or just until set. If desired, sprinkle with confectioners' sugar and run briefly under the broiler to glaze.

YIELD: 6 to 8 servings.

Crème renversée au caramel

1 cup sugar
½ cup water
4 whole eggs
4 egg yolks
⅛ teaspoon salt
1 cup heavy cream
2 ½ cups milk
1 teaspoon vanilla

1. Cook ⅔ cup of the sugar over low heat, stirring, until caramelized. Add the water and stir until smooth. Pour the mixture, which should be as thick as corn syrup, into a 1-quart ring mold; rotate to coat bottom and lower sides.

2. Beat together until blended, not foamy, the eggs, yolks, remaining ⅓ cup sugar, and salt.

3. Meanwhile, scald the heavy cream and the milk. Add this to the egg mixture and flavor with the vanilla.

4. The mixture may be strained, if desired. Pour the mixture into the prepared ring mold. Set the mold into a pan of boiling water and bake in a preheated 325-degree oven until set, about 45 minutes.

5. Immediately set the mold in cold water to cool quickly. Chill. To unmold, run the tip of a knife around inner rim of mold. Place serving plate over custard, then invert, holding mold and plate together. Shake gently; lift off the mold. Serve filled with whipped cream, if desired.

YIELD: 6 servings.

Bavarois à la vanille
Vanilla-flavored Bavarian Cream

4 cups milk
1 vanilla bean, split, or use 1 ½ teaspoons pure vanilla extract
8 egg yolks
1 cup sugar
3 envelopes unflavored gelatin
⅓ cup water
¼ cup mirabelle, kirsch, or other liqueur, optional
2 cups heavy cream

English custard (see following recipe)
Whipped cream, optional

1. Bring the milk to the boil with the split vanilla bean. Do not boil further. If the bean is not to be used, add the vanilla extract later. Remove the vanilla bean, if used, rinse it off, dry it, and reserve for later uses.

2. Place the yolks in a saucepan and add the sugar. Beat with a wire whisk until thick and lemon-colored.

3. Gradually add the milk to the yolk mixture, beating constantly. Use a wooden spoon and stir constantly, this way and that, making certain the spoon touches all over the bottom of the saucepan. Cook until the mixture has a custardlike consistency and coats the sides of the spoon. Do not let the sauce boil or it will curdle. Add the vanilla extract if used.

4. Soften the gelatin in the water and add it to the sauce, stirring to dissolve. Add the liqueur and strain into a bowl. Let cool.

5. Whip the 2 cups heavy cream until stiff and fold it into the sauce.

6. Rinse out a 10- to 12-cup ring mold without drying. Sprinkle the insides with sugar and shake out excess. Add the custard mixture and place in the refrigerator. Chill several hours or overnight until the custard is set.

7. When ready to serve, dip the mold into hot water and remove immediately. Wipe off and unmold. A damp, hot cloth could also be used on the mold to help loosen the Bavarian cream. Serve with English custard, and, if desired, whipped cream.

YIELD: 12 or more servings.

English Custard

5 egg yolks
⅔ cup sugar
2 cups milk
⅛ teaspoon salt
1 tablespoon liqueur, optional

1. Place the yolks in a saucepan and add the sugar. Beat with a wire whisk until thick and lemon-colored.

2. Meanwhile, bring the milk almost, but not quite, to the boil.

3. Gradually add the milk to the yolk mixture, beating constantly. Use a wooden spoon and stir constantly, this way and that, making certain that the spoon touches all over the bottom of the saucepan. Cook, stirring, and add the salt. Cook until the mixture has a custard-like consistency and coats the sides of the spoon. Do not let the sauce boil or it will curdle.

4. Immediately remove the sauce from the stove, but continue stirring. Set the saucepan in a basin of cold water to reduce the temperature. Let the sauce cool to room temperature. If desired, add a tablespoon of the liqueur used in the bavarois à la vanille (see preceding recipe). Chill for 1 hour or longer.

YIELD: 12 servings.

Oeufs à la neige
Meringues in a Custard Sauce

4 cups milk
1 ¼ cups sugar
1 vanilla bean, or 1 teaspoon pure vanilla extract
6 eggs, separated
½ teaspoon cornstarch
Pinch of salt
Kirsch or rum
¼ cup water

1. Bring the milk to the boil in a skillet. Add 6 tablespoons of the sugar and the vanilla bean or the vanilla extract. Stir to dissolve the sugar. Reduce heat and continue to simmer the milk.

2. Beat the egg whites until stiff. While beating, gradually add 6 more tablespoons sugar, the cornstarch, and the salt.

3. When the meringue is stiff, outfit a pastry bag with a star tube, No. 4. Fill it with the meringue and pipe it out in a 2-inch circle onto a baking sheet. Pipe out the meringue to make layer upon layer on the bottom circle. This will produce a small roundish beehive pattern or, if you prefer, a kind of rosette about 2 inches high. Continue making 16 to 18 rosettes, or until all the meringue is used.

4. Using a metal spatula, transfer the rosettes, as many as the skillet will hold, into the simmering milk.

5. Simmer about 30 seconds on one side, then, using a slotted spoon, gently turn the meringues over. Poach the other side 30 seconds.

6. Drain the meringues, which should be quite firm now, on paper toweling. Let cool while preparing the remainder of the recipe.

7. Strain the milk in which the meringues cooked. If a vanilla bean was used, remove it, rinse and wipe dry, then store in sugar for another use.

8. Beat the egg yolks until light and lemon-colored. Gradually pour into the strained milk. Stir over low heat just until the custard coats the spoon.

9. Flavor the custard with kirsch or rum. Then strain the custard into a wide, shallow serving dish and cover with the meringues. Chill.

10. Combine the remaining sugar with the ¼ cup water in a saucepan. Cook until the caramel is dark amber in color, but do not let it burn.

11. Before the caramel has a chance to set, pour it in a thin thread all over the tops of the meringues.

YIELD: 8 to 10 servings.

Mousse au chocolat

½ pound sweet chocolate
6 large eggs, separated
3 tablespoons water
¼ cup sweet liqueur, such as chartreuse, amaretto, mandarine, or Grand Marnier
2 cups heavy cream
6 tablespoons sugar
Whipped cream for garnish
Grated chocolate for garnish

1. Cut the chocolate into ½-inch pieces and place in a saucepan. Set the saucepan in hot, almost boiling water and cover. Let melt over low heat.

2. Put the yolks in a heavy saucepan and add the water. Place the saucepan over very low heat while beating vigorously and constantly with a wire whisk. Experienced cooks may do this over direct heat. It may be preferable, however, to use a flame-control device. When the

yolks start to thicken, add the liqueur, beating constantly. Cook until the sauce achieves the consistency of a hollandaise or a sabayon, which it is. Remove from the heat.

3. Add the melted chocolate to the sauce and fold it in. Scrape the sauce into a mixing bowl.

4. Whip the cream until stiff, adding 2 tablespoons of the sugar toward the end of the beating. Fold this into the chocolate mixture.

5. Beat the whites until soft peaks start to form. Beat in the remaining sugar and continue beating until stiff. Fold this into the mousse.

6. Spoon the mousse into a crystal bowl and chill until ready to serve. When ready to serve, garnish with whipped cream and grated chocolate.

YIELD: 12 or more servings.

Viennese Crescents

¼ vanilla bean
2 cups sifted confectioners' sugar
2 ½ cups flour
1 cup plus 1 tablespoon butter
1 cup granulated sugar
1 cup finely chopped almonds

1. Chop the vanilla bean and pound it in a mortar or pulverize it in an electric blender. Mix it with the sifted sugar and cover. Let stand overnight.

2. Preheat the oven to 350 degrees.

3. With a wooden spoon or fingers mix flour and butter. Add the granulated sugar and chopped almonds. Shape dough, a teaspoon at a time, into small crescents.

4. Bake on an ungreased cookie sheet for 15 to 20 minutes. Sift the vanilla sugar over the warm cookies.

YIELD: 3 dozen.

Lora Brody's Chocolate Cherry Torte

12 tablespoons butter plus butter for greasing pan
3 tablespoons fine, fresh bread crumbs
1 (24-ounce) jar pitted sour or morello cherries
6 ounces sweet chocolate, preferably Maillard brand
⅔ cup granulated sugar
3 large eggs
1 teaspoon pure vanilla extract
½ teaspoon almond extract or bitter-almond extract
½ cup ground almonds
⅔ cup flour
2 tablespoons confectioners' sugar
1 (8-ounce) can almond paste
Chocolate glaze (see following recipe)
Candied flowers for decoration

1. Preheat oven to 350 degrees. Place a baking rack in the center of the oven.

2. Butter the inside of a 9- or 10-inch springform pan. Add the bread crumbs and shake to coat the inside. Shake out excess. Set the pan aside.

3. Drain the cherries well and set them aside.

4. Put the chocolate in a small saucepan and set over simmering water until chocolate melts.

5. Put the 12 tablespoons butter and the granulated sugar into the container of a food processor or an electric mixer. Blend until light and creamy. Add 2 of the eggs, one at a time, and beat well after each addition. Beat in the vanilla extract and almond extract.

6. Stir in the chocolate and mix gently. If the food processor is used, turn it on and off to blend the ingredients.

7. Mix in the almonds and flour.

8. Beat in the remaining egg.

9. Pour and scrape the batter into the prepared pan. Smooth the top with a spatula.

10. Arrange the cherries, close together, in concentric circles from the outside to the center. The entire surface should be covered with cherries. As you add the cherries, press them gently into the batter so that only a small portion of the top of each cherry shows. If the surface of the cake is uneven, smooth it out with a wet rubber spatula. There may be a few cherries left over which may be put to another use.

11. Place the cake in the oven and bake 50 minutes to 1 hour. Take care not to overbake. The cake will look dry on top but should be quite moist inside. Remove from the pan. Let cool, right side up.

12. Put a length of wax paper on a flat surface. Sprinkle with confectioners' sugar. Work the almond paste with the hands to make a flat round cake. Place this on the wax paper and turn it in the sugar. Cover with another sheet of wax paper. Roll out the almond paste into a circle the same diameter as the top of the cake and about 1/16 of an inch thick. Peel off the top layer of wax paper. If the round of almond paste tears, you may patch it. Scraps of almond paste can be recycled or may be used to fashion decorations for the top of the cake.

13. Cut the almond paste into a round to fit the top of the cake exactly. Cover the cake with the almond paste round. Place the cake on a rack and place this on a sheet of wax paper to catch the drippings.

14. Pour the chocolate glaze over the cake, spreading it smooth with a spatula. The glaze should cover the top and sides of the cake. Chill the cake briefly and add a second coating of glaze.

15. Decorate the top with candied flowers such as roses or violets or with almond paste cut into decorative shapes. This cake will keep for two days in a cool, unrefrigerated place. It may be refrigerated, but this will dull the cake's gloss.

YIELD: 8 to 12 servings.

Chocolate Glaze

½ cup heavy cream
2 teaspoons pulverized, instant espresso coffee
8 ounces sweet chocolate, preferably Maillard brand

1. Put the cream in a saucepan and add the coffee. Bring to a slow boil.

2. Add the chocolate and stir gently until chocolate is melted and smooth. If there are any lumps, put the sauce through a fine strainer. Let the glaze cool briefly until it is spreadable.

YIELD: About 1½ cups.

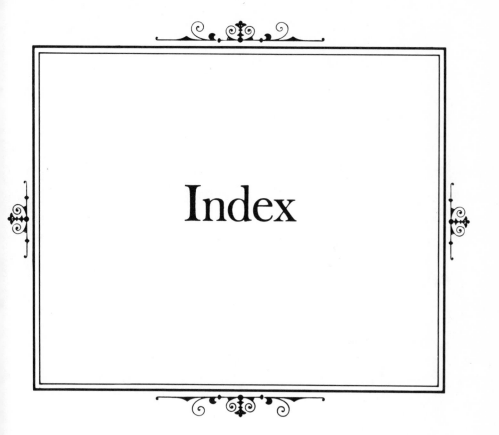

Index

"Berçeuse" (Gounod), 77
Bernstein, Leonard, 128, 134, 136
Bertholle, Louisette, 242
"Best Cook in Town, The" (magazine article), 34–35
Better Homes and Gardens cook books, 133
Better Than Store-Bought (Witty and Schneider), 237
Beulah, 10
Bible, the, 5, 18, 43, 44, 45, 93, 148
Biscuits, beaten, 34
Black Angus, 138
Black eye peas, 32
Blacks
    Claiborne (Mary Kathleen Craig) and, 25–28
    southern cooking and, 31–32
Blanche (servant), 29–30
"Blithe Spirits" (Claiborne), 114
Blue Fox, 137
Board of Trade Building (Chicago), 61
Bobby Van's, 214
Bo-Bo's, 208
Bocuse, Paul, 168, 170, 191, 192, 193, 195, 196, 200, 221, 224
Bohème, La (Puccini), 76
Bolitho, Hector, 263
Bond, Carrie Jacobs, 42
Bonheur, Rosa, 5
Boni, Ada, 248
Book of Household Management (Beeton), 261
Bossu, Le, 78, 85
Boston Cooking-School Cook Book, The (Farmer), 31, 238
Bouillabaisse, 87
Bouquet de France (Chamberlain), 260

Bourrel, Vincent, 256–57
Bovbjerg, Dana, 255
Brady, Diamond Jim, 139
Brailowsky, Alexander, 76
Brasserie Lipp, 78, 85
Brazil, 187
"Breakfast Club" (radio show), 75
Brevoort Hotel, 138
Bridgehampton, 162, 214
Brillat-Savarin, Jean A., 262
Brower, Charles Dewitt, 183
Brower, Thomas Paneahtak, 183
Brower Café, 183
Brown, Helen Evans, 131, 239
Browning, Robert, 104
Brunswick stew, 33
Brussels, 139
Buchwald, Art, 170
Buckett, James, 54
Buckley's, 171
Bugialli, Giuliano, 247–48
Bullock, Helen Duprey, 239
Bündnerfleisch, 99
Burger, Nash, 11
Burns, Robert, 5, 72
"By the Waters of Minnetonka," 41

Café Chambord, 139
Café de Paris, 158
Caipirinha, 188
Callvert, Isabel E., 236
"Camera Three" (television show), 179
Candide (Bernstein), 128, 136
Canfield, Cass, Sr., 132
Cape Cod Room (Drake Hotel), 138
Capote, Truman, 214
"Caprice Viennois" (Kreisler), 47
Caramels, 34

preparation of a clambake, 181

preparation of a veal cookbook, 215–16

reason for Claiborne's resignation from *The New York Times*, 209–10, 212

shared language of cuisine, 142

summer picnics, 162–64

in Switzerland, 195–96

visits of European, Chinese, and American chefs, 196

Gardiners Island picnic (1965), 174–79

genealogy of, 52–56

finnan haddie, 54–56

Giobbi and, 202

Gourmet and, 109, 112, 114, 118, 119–20

Hazan and, 202

hypertension problem of, 230

idea of God, 130

ill-fated courtship of, 134–37

importance of New Year's Eve and New Year's Day festivities to, 173–74

income from cookbook royalties, 174

jailed in East Hampton for drunken driving, 215

Kaye and, 202–3

Kennedy and, 200–2

the Korean conflict and, 88–94

assistant port director on Kwajalein, 93–94

on the U.S.S. *Alfred Naifeh*, 88–92

list of books by, 235

Lyon, Jr., and, 38–40, 60

mother and, 13–16, 57, 59, 60, 62, 92

effects of her suffocating love, 103–4, 108–9

final estrangement, 104–6

pneumonia attack in Switzerland, 103

recollections of her southern cooking, 30–35

musical favorites of, 43, 149

The New York Times Cook Book and, 131–34, 235, 236

first six-month royalty check, 164

success of, 133, 134

Nickerson and, 122–29

on *la nouvelle cuisine*, 195–96

one hundred favorite recipes of, 265–384

palm reader's predictions for, 130

Le Pavillon and

first visit, 139–40

Soulé and, 141–45

Philippe and, 109–12, 161

psychotherapy treatment of, 20, 107–9

public relations and, 120–29

attitude toward, 122–23, 174

recommended cookbook library, 233–64

recurring dreams of, 129–30

salt addiction of, 230

Sanders and, 38, 43–45, 58, 149

Seranne and, 112–15, 118, 120, 125

sexual problems of, 72, 107, 134–37

sister and, 22, 24–25, 73–74

sodium-restricted diet of, 229, 230–31

Soulé and, 153, 154

gold watch gift, 156–57

as a student in Paris, 76–86

Collard greens, 32
Collart, Yanou, 224
Colony restaurant, 121–22, 138, 139, 176, 177
Colorado, University of, 25
Colotta, Mr., 33
Columbia Broadcasting System (CBS), 179, 182
Comden, Betty, 170
Comédie, La, 65
Comme Chez Soi, 191, 224
Complete Asian Cookbook, The (Solomon), 236–37
Complete Book of Breads, The (Clayton), 253, 254
Complete Book of Pasta, The (Scott), 248
Complete Book of Pastry, Sweet and Savory, The (Clayton), 253–54
Complete Middle East Cookbook, The (Mallos), 250
Composition of Foods, Agricultural Handbook No. 8 (Watt and Merrill), 261
Connaught Hotel, 54
Continental Hotel, 157
Cooking and Baking the Greek Way (Theoharous), 243
Cooking for One Is Fun (Creel), 169, 245–46
Cooking of Provincial France, The, 245
Cooking of the Maharajas (Rao and Holkar), 244
Cooking On Your Own (Creel), 245–46
Cooking Techniques (Cox and Whitman), 258
Cooking with Herbs and Spices (Claiborne), 235
Cooper, Alfred Duff, 165
Cordon Bleu, 92
Corn breads, 23

Côte Basque, La, 155, 157, 158, 170
Cottage cheese, 8
Cotton Country Collection, The, 240
Country Cousin, The (Tarkington and Street), 263
Country sausages, 33–34
Couscous, 65, 72, 78
Couscous and Other Good Food from Morocco (Wolfert), 250
Coward, Noel, 43
Cox, Beverly, 258
Cox, Lillian, 15
Crab, deviled, 33
Crab gumbo, 33
Cracknell, H. L., 261–62
Craig, Augustus, 13
Craig, Claiborne, 13
Craig, James, 55
Craig, origin of name, 72
Craig, Raymond, 13
Craig and Claiborne (business partnership), 15
Craig Claiborne Journal, The, 212–14
Craig Claiborne's Favorites (Claiborne), 235
Craig Claiborne's Favorites (Claiborne—Volume 2), 235
Craig Claiborne's Favorites (Claiborne—Volume 3), 235
Craig Claiborne's Favorites (Claiborne—Volume 4), 235
Craig Claiborne's Gourmet Diet (Claiborne and Franey), 230, 235
Craig Claiborne's Kitchen Primer (Claiborne), 235
Creel, Henry Lewis, 126, 129, 169, 171, 172, 245
Crèmaillère, La, 246
"Crèmes de Carême, Les" (Claiborne), 119
Creole cooking, 33

Ethiopia, 212
Etude, 42
Eugénie-les-Bains (spa), 196

Fadiman, Clifton, 256, 263
Fannie Farmer Cook Book, The
(Farmer), 15, 238
Fannie Farmer Cookbook, The (re-
vised by Cunningham
and Laber), 238–39
Farmer, Fannie Merritt, 238
Faulkner, William, 214
Feijoada, 187–88
Ferber, Edna, 45
Fessaguet, Roger, 155, 170,
173, 176, 177, 178
Fevers, Floods and Faith (Hem-
phill), 18
Field, Eugene, 58
Fifty Years Below the Arctic
(Brower), 183
Filetti di tacchino, 82
Fine Art of Italian Cooking, The
(Bugialli), 247–48
Finnan haddie, 54–56
Fisher, M. F. K., 249, 262–63,
264
Fitzgerald, Ella, 40
FitzGibbon, Theodora, 259–
60
Flagg, Corrie, 41
*Flavors of the Caribbean & Latin
America, The* (Hawkes),
240–41
Florence, 83–84
Florence Lin's Regional Cookbook
(Lin), 241
Fluffo (shortening), 120–21
Foie gras, fresh, 192
Fonda del Sol, La, 210
Food (Root), 259
Food in History (Tannahill), 264
Food of France, The (Root), 151,
258–59

Food of the Western World, The
(FitzGibbon), 259–60
Foods and Wines of Spain, The
(Casas), 251
Foods of the World Series, 151,
244–45
Forum of the Twelve Caesars,
The, 210
"Four Indian Love Lyrics"
(Woodforde-Finden and
Hope), 42
Four Seasons, The, 150, 155,
199
*Four Seasons, 250 Original Recipes
from One of the World's
Great Restaurants, The*
(Margittan and Kovi),
245
France, 188–93
France, Roger, 155
Franey, Betty, 145
Franey, Claudia, 220
Franey, Jacques, 217, 218
Franey, Pierre, 50, 220, 235,
246, 267
Claiborne and
the Case of the Severed
Head, 215–19
collaboration in prepara-
tion of menus for publica-
tion, 165–72
cookbook royalties, 145
The Craig Claiborne Journal,
212–14
*Craig Claiborne's Gourmet
Diet,* 230, 235
the $4,000 dinner at Chez
Denis, 221, 222, 225
the Franey-Soulé dispute,
142–45
the Gardiners Island picnic
(1965), 175, 176, 177
preparation of a clambake,
181

International Chili Society Official Cook Book, The (Neely and Neely), 239–40
Invitation to Indian Cooking, An (Jaffrey), 244
Italian Family Cooking (Giobbi), 248
Italian Food (David), 248–49
Italian Regional Cooking (Boni), 248
Italy, 196

Jacques Restaurant, 74, 137
Jaffrey, Madhur, 244, 252
James, Ryan, 138
James Beard Cookbook, The (Beard), 236
James Beard's American Cookery (Beard), 238
Japan, 184–85
Japanese Cooking: A Simple Art (Tsuji), 249
Jeffers, Robinson, 44
Jimmy's Greek-American restaurant, 138
Jocelyn (Gounod), 77
Jockey restaurant, 246
Joe (servant), 28
Joe's custard pie, 28
Johnson, Howard, 162
Johnson, Robert B., 88
Johnson, Samuel, 119
Jones, Evan, 239
Jones, Gloria, 171
Joy of Cheese Cake, The (Bovbjerg and Iggers), 255
Joy of Cooking, The (Rombauer and Becker), 73, 74, 133, 235–36
Joys of Wine, The (Fadiman and Aaron), 256
Judson College, 13, 40
Junior League of Baton Rouge, Louisiana, 240

Junior League of Charleston, South Carolina, 240
Junior League of Memphis, Inc., The, 240
Junior League of Monroe, Louisiana, 240

Kafka, Barbara, 245
Karney, Beulah, 34
Kashmiri Song ("Four Indian Love Lyrics," Woodforde-Finden and Hope), 42
Kaufmann, R. J., 261–62
Kaye, Danny, 202–3
Keith, Ida Mack, 58–59
Kennedy, Diana, 200–2, 249–50
Kennedy, Eunice, 87
Kennedy, Jacqueline, 151, 176
Kennedy, Joe, 87
Kennedy, John F., 87, 88, 89
Kennedy, Paul, 250
Kennedy family, 87
Kenya, 211, 212
Kern, Jerome, 43, 149
Kidd, Captain, 174, 178
Kipling, Rudyard, 5
Knopf, Alfred, 51, 170
Knowles, John, 214
Koo, Dr. Wellington, 205, 207
Koo, Mrs. Wellington, 205
Korean conflict, 146
  Claiborne and, 88–94
  assistant port director on Kwajalein, 93–94
  on the U.S.S. *Alfred Naifeh*, 88–92
Kovi, Paul, 245
Kreisler, Fritz, 47
Ku Klux Klan, 46
Kutas, Rytek, 247
Kwajalein Island, 93–94

Claiborne as food editor of, 131–34
aboard the S.S. *France,* 193–95
in Africa, 212
in Alaska, 183
in Athens, 186–87
author of *The New York Times Cook Book,* 131–32
in China, 208
in France, 188–93
income from cookbook royalties, 174
in India, 186
interviewed for position, 124–29
in Japan, 184–85
national dish of Brazil, 187–88
offered "gift" from German restaurant, 153–54
resignation from (1972), 204–5, 208–12
restaurant criticism, 137–38, 150, 210–11
return to (1974), 214
in Switzerland, 195–96
in Taipei, 186
traveling assignments, 183–96
in Vietnam, 184
writes attack on New York City restaurants, 141–42
the $4,000 dinner at Chez Denis, 211, 225
Franey joins staff of, 165
union strike against (1962), 164
Whitman's account of Claiborne-Franey meal and its preparation, 168–72
New York Times Book of Wine, The (Robards), 256

New York Times Book Review, The, 11
New York Times Cook Book, The (Claiborne), 131–34, 235, 236
Claiborne's first six-month royalty check from, 164
success of, 133, 134
New York Times International Cook Book, The (Claiborne), 235
New York Times Magazine, The, 39
New York Times Menu Cook Book, The (Claiborne), 235
New York Times Studio, 33
Nge Kar Ang School, 50
Ngo, Bach, 252
Nickerson, Jane, 122–29
"Night and Day," 39, 43
Nixon, Richard, 146
Notre Dame, University of, 40, 69–70
Nouvelle cuisine, la, 195–96

Ochs, Adolph, 132
Oeufs à la neige, 140, 157
Oeufs brouillés l'estragon, 78, 85
"Oh, Promise Me" (De Koven and Scott), 42
Okinawa, 70–71
Okra gumbo, 33
"On the Road to Mandalay," 42
Operakällaren restaurant, 221, 225
Operation Torch (Allied invasion of North Africa), 62
Oran, 66–67
Ossorio, Alfonso, 170
Oxford English Dictionary, The, 72
Oyster gumbo, 33

Pace Hotel, La, 200
Paddleford, Clementine, 140–41
Palace Hotel, 98, 138
Papagallo restaurant, 82
Pappas, Lou, 243
"Pariah Pigs and Hallowed Hams" (Claiborne), 119
Paris, 76–80, 191
Parker House rolls, 23
Pastas, 202
Paula Peck's Art of Good Cooking (Peck), 237
Pavillon, Le, 112, 155, 156, 160, 162
  Claiborne and
    first visit, 139–40
    Soulé and, 141–45
  new management and decline of, 161
  Soulé and, 141–45, 158
  treatment of working staff, 143–44
Pavillon Henry IV, 78
Payne Whitney Psychiatric Center, 107
Peabody Hotel, 21, 92
Pearl Harbor, Hawaii, 60
Peas, black eye, 32
Pecan pie, 34
Peck, Paula, 237, 253
Pellaprat, Henri-Paul, 92
Pennsylvania, University of, 59
Pépin, Jacques, 170, 176, 177, 243, 257, 258
"A Perfect Day" (Bond), 42
Perry, Eleanor, 170
Petite Maison, La, 138
Philippe, Claude, 109–12, 161
Physiology of Taste, The (Brillat-Savarin), 262
Pierre Franey's More 60-Minute Gourmet (Franey), 235

Pierre Franey's 60-Minute Gourmet (Franey), 235
Pierre Hotel, 111
Pi Kappa Alpha, 57
Pipps, Jon, 53
Plaza Hotel, 112
Pleasures of Chinese Cooking (Chu), 241
Pleasures of Preserving and Pickling, The (Lesem), 254
Point, Fernand, 192–93
Point, Mado, 192–93
Polushkin, Maria, 246
Porgy and Bess (Gershwin), 172
Porter, Cole, 43, 149
"Pot likker," 32
Price, Mary, 246
Price, Vincent, 246
Prohibition, 139
Proust, Marcel, 33
Prudhomme, Paul, 30
Puccini, Giacomo, 93, 123
Puerto Rico, 187
Pyle, Ernie, 23
Pyramide restaurant, 192, 246

Quail *beauséjour,* 145
Quenelles de brochet, 159
Quiet American, The (Greene), 184
Quo Vadis, 139

Rabaudy, Nicholas de, 225
Raclette, 99
Rao, Shivaji, 244
Rattray, Helen, 218
Rattray, Jeannette, 170, 218
Rechtschaffen, Dr. Joseph, 230
Red snappers, 33, 48
Reinhard family, 101, 102
Reinhard Hotel, 99–101
Renaldo, Tony, 47
Renggli, Josef, 199, 245

CRAIG CLAIBORNE

Whitman, Alden, 168
New York Times account of
Claiborne-Franey meal
and its preparation,
168–72
Whitman, Joan, 168, 170, 258
Wilde, Oscar, 119
Windsor, Duchess of, 110
Wise, David B., 258
Wise Encyclopedia of Cookery, The
(Wise), 258
Witty, Helen, 237
Wodehouse, P. G., 149
Wolf, Anita, 47
Wolf, Sadie, 47
Wolfe, Thomas, 43, 44
Wolfert, Paula, 250
Wood, Helen, 55–56
Wood, Peter, 23
Woodforde-Finden, Amy, 42
WOR (radio station), 164
Worcestershire sauce, 31
World-of-the-East Vegetarian Cook-
ing (Jaffrey), 252
World's Fair (New York City—
1939), 155, 158
World War II, 23, 40, 146
Claiborne's naval career in,
60–72

in Casablanca, 64–66, 72
introduction to French
cooking, 65–66, 72
North African invasion,
62–64
officers' training school at
Notre Dame, 69–70
in Oran, 66–67
in the Pacific, 70–72
Claiborne (Lewis Edmond,
Jr.) and, 23–24, 66
Pearl Harbor, 60
Wrigley Building (Chicago),
75
"Wynken, Blynken, and Nod,"
58

Yale University, 32, 33
Yanagihara School of Classical
Japanese Cooking, 249
"You," 43
"You and the Night and the
Music," 43
Yueh, Jean, 241

Zane, Eva, 243
Zimmerman, Gloria, 252
Zuccotto alla Michelangelo, 200

CRAIG CLAIBORNE

RECIPES

Américaine lobster sauce for striped bass tout Paris, 338–39

Anchovies, shrimp with oranges and, 285–86

Ann Seranne's pumpkin cream pie, 372–73

Ann Seranne's rib roast of beef, 299

Artichokes, Mrs. Reardy's shrimp casserole with, 354

Asparagus, breaded calves' brains with, 323–24

Bagel and smoked fish brunch, 348–49

Bass, striped, tout Paris, 337–40

Batter
beer, for fried shrimp, 353
fritter, for fish or seafood Orly, 336

Batter-fried shrimp, 352–54

Bavarian cream, vanilla-flavored, 378–79

Bavarois à la vanille, 378–79

Beef
boiled, for summer salads, 281–82
chili con carne
with cubed meat, 303–4
with ground meat, 304–5
corned, home-cured, 305–6
grilled, and romaine salad Thai-style, 282–83
hamburgers, 301–2
pastrami, home-cured, 306
rib roast of, Ann Seranne's, 299

salad with herb mayonnaise, 281–82

steak
Mexican flank, 302–3
au poivre, 300–1

Beer batter for fried shrimp, 353

Berquist, Jane, timbales au Roquefort, 270–71

Beurre blanc for sole mousse in leek leaves, 317

Beurre de homard, 323

Billi Bi, 290

Black pepper veal loaf, 296–97

Blini, clams with, 273–74

Blue cheese dressing for Janice Okun's Buffalo chicken wings, 307–8

Boeuf bouilli, 281–82

Bouillabaisse, Long Island, 289

Brains, breaded, with asparagus, 323–24

Brandade de morue, 271–72

Bread
-and-butter pudding, French, 377
corn, 303

Brioche dough for coulibiac of salmon, 346

Brody, Lora, chocolate cherry torte, 383–84

Broth, fish, 339

Brown sauce
for poultry, 332
for steak au poivre, 300–1

Brunch, smoked fish and bagels for, 348–49

Buffalo chicken wings, Janice Okun's, 307–8

Butter
lobster, 323
white sauce for sole mousse in
leek leaves, 317

Cabbage, stuffed, 312–14
Calves' brains, breaded, with as-
paragus, 323–24
Caramel, crème renversée au, 378
Casseroles
grits and Cheddar cheese,
276
Mrs. Reardy's shrimp and arti-
choke, 354
Cassis, fruit ice with, 371–72
Cervelles de veau maréchale,
323–24
Charcoal-grilled duck, French
style, 329–30
Charlotte Russe with kirsch, 375
Cheddar cheese, grits casserole
with, 276
Cheese
blue, dressing for Janice
Okun's Buffalo chicken
wings, 307–8
Cheddar, grits casserole with,
276
feta, shrimp baked with, 355
Roquefort, Jane Berquist's
timbales au, 270–71
Cheesecake, hazelnut, 376–77
Cheese sauce, eggs and ham on
toast with, 279
Cherry chocolate torte, Lora
Brody's, 383–84
Chicken
creamed, eggs in ramekins
with, 278
cutlets Pojarski, 326–27
lemon, 327–28
with noodles Parisienne,
324–26
spaghetti, 368–69

wings, Buffalo, Janice Okun's,
307–8
Chicken livers, baked mousse of,
321–22
Chiffonade of lobster Chez
Denis, 284–85
Chili con carne
with cubed meat, 303–4
with ground meat, 304–5
Chinese fire pot, 359–62
Chocolate
cherry torte, Lora Brody's,
383–84
mousse, 381–82
Chou vert farci, 312–14
Cirque, Le, spaghetti primavera,
363–65
Clams with blini, 273–74
Cod, salt, mousse of, 271–72
Coquilles Saint-Jacques, 356
Corn bread, 303
Corned beef, home-cured,
305–6
Côtes de veau belles des bois, 292–93
Coulibiac of salmon, 343–48
Court bouillon, homard au, 322–23
Couscous, 310–11
Crème brûlée, 370
Crème fraîche, 271
Crème renversée au caramel, 378
Crêpes
for coulibiac of salmon, 347
with fines herbes, 357–58
seafood, Jean Vergnes',
357–59
Cucumber and dill mayonnaise,
341–42
Curried sweetbreads with fet-
tuccine, 366–67
Curry sauce for Jean Vergnes'
seafood crêpes, 358
Custard, English, 379–80
Custard sauce, meringues in,
380–81

CRAIG CLAIBORNE

tomato
    for black pepper veal loaf,
        297
    for chicken with noodles
        Parisienne, 325–26
velouté
    salmon and mushrooms
        with, 344–45
    for striped bass tout Paris,
        339–40
    vinaigrette with rosemary, for
        shrimp, oranges, and an-
        chovies, 286
    white butter, for sole mousse
        in leek leaves, 317
    white wine, for salmon baked
        in foil, 341
Sauce diable for pigs' feet Sainte-
    Menhould, 319
Sauerkraut balls, ham and,
    315–16
Saumon à l'oseille, 342–43
Scallops
    coquilles Saint-Jacques, 356
    Seviche, 269–70
Scotch eggs, 280
Seafood
    crêpes, Jean Vergnes', 357–59
    Orly, 335–37
    See also names of seafood
Seranne, Ann
    pumpkin cream pie, 372–73
    rib roast of beef, 299
Seviche, scallop, 269–70
Shad stuffed with roe, 332–33
Sherbet, grapefruit, 371
Shrimp
    baked with feta cheese, 355
    balls for Chinese fire pot,
        360–61
    Baratin, 270
    batter-fried, 352–54
    Mrs. Reardy's artichoke casse-
        role with, 354

with oranges and anchovies,
    285–86
Smoked fish and bagel brunch,
    348–49
Sole mousse in leek leaves,
    316–17
Sorrel sauce, salmon with,
    342–43
Soufflé, ginger, 373–74
Soufflé au gingembre, 373–74
Soup
    Billi Bi, 290
    cream of pumpkin, 287
    Long Island bouillabaisse,
        289
    Philadelphia pepper pot, 288
    tomato, 290–91
    turkey, 286–87
Spaghetti
    chicken, 368–69
    primavera, Le Cirque's,
        363–65
Squabs, stuffed, Derby, 330–
    31
Steak
    Mexican flank, 302–3
    au poivre, 300–1
Striped bass tout Paris, 337–
    40
Sweetbreads, curried, with fet-
    tuccine, 366–67

Tartar sauce for deep-fried mus-
    sels, 352
Thai-style grilled beef and ro-
    maine salad, 282–83
Timbales au Roquefort, Jane
    Berquist's, 270–71
Tomato
    sauce
        for black pepper veal loaf,
            297
        for chicken with noodles
            Parisienne, 325–26

with cream, for fish mousse, 334–35
soup, 290–91
Torte, chocolate cherry, Lora Brody's, 383–84
Tripe
Philadelphia pepper pot, 288
sautéed with onions, 320–21
Tripes lyonnaise, 320–21
Turkey soup, 286–87

Vanilla-flavored Bavarian cream, 378–79
Veal
black pepper loaf, 296–97
breaded calves' brains with asparagus, 323–24
chops
beauséjour, 293–94
with morels, 292–93
kidneys in mustard sauce, 319–20
ossobuco Milanese, 295–96

paillard of, 298
scallops, breaded, 297–98
stuffed breast of, 294–95
Velouté sauce
salmon and mushrooms with, 344–45
for striped bass tout Paris, 339–40
Vergnes, Jean, seafood crêpes, 357–59
Vésiga for coulibiac salmon, 348
Viennese crescents, 382
Vinaigrette sauce with rosemary, for shrimp, oranges, and anchovies, 286

White butter sauce for sole mousse in leek leaves, 317
White wine sauce for salmon baked in foil, 341

CRAIG CLAIBORNE